PRAISE FOR *RADICAL CONVERSION*

"Though Duncan draws on a rich array of disciplines and buttresses his assertions with sources both erudite and colloquial, his central thesis is entirely political and of immense value to all readers regardless of belief. Deeply incisive, searing, and prophetic, Duncan does something impossible and necessary: he calls the reader into a vision of social responsibility that is both primordial and progressive, both recondite and radical, both a repeal and a revolution."

—KATHLEEN GLENISTER ROBERTS, professor, Duquesne University

"Political theorist Christopher Duncan makes a compelling case for the future of democracy that depends on foundational themes found in the Judeo-Christian tradition, especially twentieth-century Catholic social teaching. Instead of continuing on the path of a materialistic and individualistic neoliberalism, he argues for a polity that defends the dignity of every person, the care for the marginalized, and a commitment to the common good built upon a non-theocratic but religiously open government that welcomes people both secular and religious. His thesis, bold and provocative, calls for a radical conversion in American society."

—JAMES L. HEFT, SM, founder and president emeritus of the Institute for Advanced Catholic Studies

"The radical conversion called for by Christopher Duncan requires unmasking the limits of individualism and uplifting personalism. As an advocate of Christian citizenship in the public sphere, Duncan challenges 'a liberal-capitalistic-possessive individualistic discourse' that excludes a politics of love. Duncan highlights Catholicism's oppositional stance toward an increasing embrace of neoliberalism that underscores individual rights, ignoring our communal commitments to one another. This work is a must-read for those in religious communication."

—RONALD C. ARNETT, author of *Communication Ethics and Tenacious Hope*

"Christopher Duncan explores and enriches the languages we use in the civil and political life of our American democratic polity. He constructs a narrative of the American liberal tradition that enables the reader to appreciate both the ways this tradition often enhances human well-being and at the same time how 'possessive individualism' is now reforming this narrative so it is no longer inclusive of the well-being of all. Duncan introduces a second narrative, a narrative of 'agape' of radical inclusive love, as it is embodied in Catholic social tradition. Bringing these two narratives into critical dialogue, Duncan challenges people of faith, Catholics in particular, to a radical conversion in which they are called to be catalysts and partners in tending and nurturing a language of public discourse that enables public conversations to move toward the common good of all."

—RAYMOND FITZ, SM, president emeritus and professor, University of Dayton

Radical Conversion

Radical Conversion

*Theorizing Catholic Citizenship
in the American Liberal Tradition*

CHRISTOPHER M. DUNCAN

CASCADE *Books* · Eugene, Oregon

RADICAL CONVERSION
Theorizing Catholic Citizenship in the American Liberal Tradition

Copyright © 2021 Christopher M. Duncan. All rights reserved. Except for brief quotations in critical publications or reviews, no part of this book may be reproduced in any manner without prior written permission from the publisher. Write: Permissions, Wipf and Stock Publishers, 199 W. 8th Ave., Suite 3, Eugene, OR 97401.

Cascade Books
An Imprint of Wipf and Stock Publishers
199 W. 8th Ave., Suite 3
Eugene, OR 97401

www.wipfandstock.com

PAPERBACK ISBN: 978-1-7252-8390-9
HARDCOVER ISBN: 978-1-7252-8389-3
EBOOK ISBN: 978-1-7252-8391-6

Cataloguing-in-Publication data:

Names: Duncan, Christopher M., author.

Title: Radical conversion: theorizing Catholic citizenship in the American liberal tradition / Christopher M. Duncan.

Description: Eugene, OR : Cascade Books, 2021 | Includes bibliographical references and index.

Identifiers: ISBN 978-1-7252-8390-9 (paperback) | ISBN 978-1-7252-8389-3 (hardcover) | ISBN 978-1-7252-8391-6 (ebook)

Subjects: LCSH: Catholic Church—Doctrines. | Christianity and politics—Catholic Church. | Christian sociology—Catholic Church. | Democracy—Religious aspects—Catholic Church.

Classification: JA71 .D85 2021 (paperback) | JA71 .D85 (ebook)

07/12/21

For Molly, my person
Loving you is easy cause you're beautiful . . .

Contents

Acknowledgments		xi
Introduction		1
1	*Christian* Citizenship	24
2	Euthyphro, Christianity, and Liberalism	63
3	Christianity and Alienation	96
4	Orestes Brownson and the Hartz Thesis	130
5	The Catholic Social Tradition and AMERICA	172
6	Inventing a Catholic American Political Tradition	205
7	Tending to Catholicism *and* America in the Modern World	251
8	Radical Conversion: A Conclusion	289
Bibliography		307
Index		319

Acknowledgments

After working on this project for the better part of a decade during service at four different universities, the list of people to thank or acknowledge is almost endless. I began this book while working at the University of Dayton and I credit my colleagues, students, and the Marianists for helping form me in my own Catholic-Christian faith and for imprinting their charism and ideals on my psyche and my soul during the years I was there. I carry them in my heart wherever I go. My two chief mentors from the Order were Father James Heft, SM, and Brother Raymond Fitz, SM. It is impossible to recount all that they taught me and to thank them with the necessary depth and humility required for their friendship, patience, and tutelage for almost twenty years. Jim Heft's infectious and passionate devotion to the questions and arguments that comprise the Catholic Intellectual Tradition and his never-failing commitment to Catholic higher education and our collective call to mission were transformative and inspired me year after year. The only thing I enjoyed more than our conversations was listening to his homilies every Sunday morning at the 10 a.m. mass. Brother Ray Fitz served UD as president for twenty-three years and then returned full time to the classroom and to serving the university and the city of Dayton, which he continues on in till this day. His Christian witness and love, and his modeling of servant leadership, stand as a never-ending source of inspiration for me and as the standard I aspire to despite my perpetual shortcomings. I had the distinct honor and privilege of teaching two courses with him every fall semester: Christianity, Citizenship, and Society; and with my great friends Dick Ferguson and Don Vermillion, Leadership in Building Community. Many of the ideas in this book were formed and tested in those classes. In all fairness to Dayton and Brother Ray, I should have been made to pay tuition for all that he taught me during those seven years on our walks together to and from class. There are very few ideas in this book that Brother Ray has not heard me try out, and I believe that his presence in my life is one of the greatest gifts I have ever received. There are literally dozens of other brothers, sisters, and priests from the Society of Mary, as well as a large body of lay Marianists and fellow travelers and faith-filled students whom I count as companions, friends, and teachers. I thank them all for the grace they have bestowed on me. I will not try to list them all, out of fear of missing anyone.

Because we are social creatures, it is our nature to seek out the company of others. Those of us who are truly fortunate find an intimate circle of people with whom you can share just about anything and know that you will still be loved and cared for and from whom you can always expect support and humor as well as an occasional challenge and gentle correction. I found such a group at UD, and I am thankful for the many nights we laughed together, prayed together, cried together, argued with one another, and shared story after story on the decks and porches of our homes, as well as an adult beverage or two. That group whom I will call the SFs included my great friend Dick Ferguson and brothers Regis Lekan, Bill Hunt, Rob Durkle, Fr. Pat Tonry, SM, Fr. Gene Contadino, SM, Fr. Tom Schroer, SM, Rich Munn, Steve Mueller, the mayor, Bruce Duke, the dearly departed Steve Yuhas, and the "godfather," Myron Achbach.

The members of my department at Dayton were also constant sources of inspiration and spirited conversation about all things political and religious. I especially want to thank Peggy Karns, Mark Ensalaco, Nancy Martrano, John Putka, Jeff Ingram, Jaro Bilocerkowycz, Natalie Hudson, Michelle Pautz, Grant Neeley, Peter Nelson, Rick Ghere, and Jason Pierce for their friendship and conversations over the years. I was also supported by wonderful deans in Paul Morman, Mary Morton, and Paul Benson during my time as chair and thank them for their support. While there were many others with whom I worked closely on important initiatives, I owe special thanks to Una Cadegan, Joe Saliba, Pat Palermo, Tom Eggemeier, Sandra Yocum, Donna Cox, Fran Pestello, Don Vermillion, Deb Bickford, Jean Poindexter, Terry Tilley, and Dan Miller. Finally, I especially want to thank David Darrow and Maura Donahue for their constant friendship and love for now almost twenty years.

At Duquesne University, I learned a great deal from the Spiritans and their charism, particularly the late David Smith, CSP, and I found wonderful conversation partners in Evan Stoddard, Ron Arnett, Janie Harden-Fritz, Kathleen Glenister-Roberts, George Worgul, and Jim Swindall. During my time at Wittenberg University, I befriended Jeff Ankrom and his wife, Sue. Not only are they wonderful friends, but Jeff is among the most thoughtful, faithful, and careful critics I know. He remains a constant source of insight, and I have loved every conversation and argument about the things in the world that matter and look forward to many more years of the same. I also want to thank the faculty from the history department, Molly Wood, Amy Livingstone, Dar Brooks Headstrom, and Tom Taylor, for their support and inspiration, as well as Nancy McHugh, Don Reed, Michael Ames, Heather Wright, Dave Wishart, Ed Hasecke, Rob Baker, Bob White, Warren Copeland, Brian Yontz, Adam Parker, Jim Welch, Maureen Massaro, Darrell Kitchen, and Mark Sullivan.

For the past five years, I have worked at Saint Louis University and finally had the chance to immerse myself in all things Jesuit. Since much of my time was spent as the Dean of Arts and Sciences, most of my closest relationships were with other administrators and department chairs. In my office, a talented and integrity-rich group of colleagues, Gary Barker, Jan Barber, Donna LaVoie, Carol Murphy, Delia King, Cathy Zimmer, and Jeremy Nagel, helped keep me sane and provided constant support, professionalism, and good humor that made it possible to retain some sort of life outside of that role. Other deans and VPs, including my good friend Mark Higgins, as well as Mardell Wilson, Dave Cassens, Brother Bill Rehg, SJ, Teri Murray, Bill Johnson, Tom Burroughs, Jonathan Smith, David Heimburger, and Jay Goff, served as comrades in arms during some very difficult years. The good work of chairs like Laura Franklin, Scott Martin, Toby Benis, Hal Parker, Peter Martens, Scott Ragland, Fr. Ted Vitali, CP, April Trees, Karla Scott, Jeff Gfeller, and Ellen Carnaghan, just to name a few, served as excellent examples of engaged academic leaders and as men and women for others, as we say in the tradition. Among the Jesuits at SLU, I was befriended by and learned a great deal from Fr. Chris Collins, SJ, Fr. David Meconi, SJ, Fr. Michael Barber, SJ, Fr. Ronnie O'Dwyer, SJ, Fr. David Suwalsky, SJ, and Fr. Steve Schoenig, SJ, and I am exceptionally grateful to them all. While there are dozens of faculty members I could thank, the following took the time to actively engage me as a scholar and not simply as an administrator I am thankful for that gift. Here I count Eleonore Stump, Jeff Bishop, Tobias Winwright, and Fr. Bill McCormick, SJ. Having now returned to the faculty full time after twenty years in some form of academic administration, I have been welcomed with open arms by the faculty in the Department of Political Science and have clearly found a supportive environment to pursue my scholarship and teaching. I look forward to spending this next phase of my career with J. D. Bowen, Sarah Kate, Morgan Hazelton, Ruth Groff, Matt Nanes, Ali Finusoglu, Ken Warren, Jim Gilsinan, Wynne Moskop, Steve Rogers, Nori Katagiri, Emanuel Uwalaka, and Bob Cropf.

As John Lennon teaches us, life is what happens while you are busy making other plans. Five years ago, I was married for the second time, to an amazing woman whom I had befriended years earlier, whose name at the time was Molly Schaller—and now Molly Armstrong Duncan. A devoted and faithful cradle-Catholic, a strong feminist, a loving mother, and a nationally known scholar in the area of student development with a particular reputation around the issues confronting college sophomores, an outstanding teacher and servant leader who has served in numerous capacities for twenty-eight years at the University of Dayton before moving to SLU as a professor and the Interim Dean of Education, she identifies herself first and foremost as "number six of eight" and as a graduate of Ohio State University. (For a Michigan graduate, that last item is particularly troubling.) To marry Molly is to marry into a large, close, and loving family, led since her father Jerry's passing in 2008 by her mother, Ann Armstrong, a daily Mass goer, voracious reader, and acute social critic in her own right. Joining Ann's children (Chris, Mike, Tom, Annie, Bob, Ed, and Danny), their spouses, children, grandchildren, and now great-grandchildren as part of their family has been one of the most surprising and unexpected graces I have received in my life. Their love, kindness, and generous spirits know no bounds, and I am blessed and honored by their willingness to welcome me in fully and completely as a member of the family this late in life.

Without Molly's abiding love, friendship, support, patience, keen intellect, and strong moral compass to help guide and sustain me, I would be substantially less of a person and much of what I am able to accomplish is due to her friendship and love. Most of my happiness these days I owe to her sacramental presence in my life. There is no way to adequately convey in words what she means to me, and dedicating this book to her is just one small nod in that direction. My previous wife, Laura Duncan, and I were blessed with three amazing children, Amelia Lawrie, Zoë Ann, and Holden David. They each owe a great debt to her as do I for the wonderful adults they have each turned out to be. There was no mother who cared for and loved her kids more than Laura did. This mattered a lot since, truth be told, I worked many more hours than was healthy. As this book was being completed, all three adult children were living close by in St. Louis and our regular Sunday dinners have been the highlight of my week.

When I started this book, they were all still children. By the time of publication, they will all be college graduates. Amelia worked on the construction of the bibliography for me just after graduation and so part of this book belongs to her. She is now a mom in her own right and, along with Kalan Potter, they have changed all our lives for the better by bringing my grandson, Arthur Christopher Potter, into the world. To hold him in your arms is to know what it is like to hold joy and is yet more evidence that God is not only great, but that God is good. Zoë (my dove) is an exceptional young and socially engaged artist, and her sharp wit and passionate heart remind me all the time why I love college students. Holden is the "left brain" of the family and is just beginning his career as a computer scientist in Dayton, Ohio. He is decent and kind and is one of the best men I know. As I grow older, I keep reminding myself to be more like him. Soon we will welcome Michaela Strunk into our family officially when she and Holden are married in the very near future. She is like another daughter to Molly and me already. My union with Molly also produced yet another unforeseen pair of gifts as I became a stepfather to Maggie and Johnny Schaller. Like their mom, they are both people who are strong in their faith, smart, loving, and filled with a sense of righteousness and a thirst for justice. Having them in my life to debate with, enjoy, love, and watch grow into the people they are called to be is a privilege for which I am immensely thankful. Maggie graduated from Dayton with a degree in human rights studies, and Johnny is a philosophy major at UD who will also graduate just as this book sees the light of day. I owe them a debt for their kindness and generosity to my family and me, and I look forward to many years in their good company.

Last year, I lost the single most important mentor I have ever had. Philip Abbott was my major professor at Wayne State University. He was a prolific political theorist with some thirteen books and edited volumes to his name along with numerous articles and book chapters. He was an expert in the field of American political thought and spent the later part of his career exploring the history and nature of the American presidency. His gentle nature, great sense of humor, and dedication to his craft, his students, and, especially, to me, were life changing. Through his courses and the writing of my dissertation, he provided guidance without control, correction with care, and made it his mission to help me become what I wanted to be rather than having a preconceived idea of what I should become. It has now been thirty years since I first met him and one year since he left this world behind for the next, but I will forever be his student and I will miss him each day going forward until I see him again. Some debts can only be forgiven because they are impossible to repay. Such is what I owe to my teacher and my friend, Phil Abbott.

My own family is a complicated matter with many moving parts over the years, but two of the constants are my brothers, Craig and Jeff. Strong-willed and loving men (tough but not hard, as my dad would say), they are both gifted and talented artists and athletes and among the hardest-working people I know. Folks who know me sometimes think that I am a little intense. I tell them that between my brothers and my father, David Lawrie Duncan, I am number four on that scale. The best compliment I can pay them is to say what everyone who knows them would say: if you could only pick three people to take into battle with you, they would be the three. I love them and their children with all my heart and thank them for all their cheerleading and encouragement over the years. My two brothers and a sister from other mothers, David Rodriguez, Mike Curry, and Joan Curry, have been in my life and my heart for over forty years now, and their love and friendship remains an ever-present sign to me of a gracious loving God. My dad is the biggest constant in my life. A Detroit man in the way Elmore Leonard might write about, my father's presence, love, and level of support has been thick and strong since the moment I was born. He was at my dissertation defense years ago and truth be told he looked more pained than anyone else in the room. As the questioning went on, I worried just a little that he might punch someone. A printer and a salesman by trade, he has closely read and proofread each of my books, including this one, with a keen eye for detail. His wife of almost fifty years, Judy Duncan, and her children—my brothers Rudy, Cindy, and Scott, along with their extensive families—have been sources of great love, happiness, and fun over the course of my life, and Judy's presence as a second mom was again one of those things in life that you did not know you needed until you realized how much would have been missing without it. For loving my dad and us for all these years, thank you, Judy.

My own mother left this life two years ago. When she passed, her name was Mary Kay Franks and she was the loving wife of Gerry Franks, a wonderful grandfather to my kids and a kind friend to me. But my mom came into this world as the only child of Earl and Edna and was known to them as Mary Kay Thorsby. A force to be reckoned with who marched to her own beat in life, my mother and I raised each other in many ways. Her pride in and love for her family—whoever was in at any particular time—were paramount for her, and her leaving me before this book was done is a source of sadness. She was not a patient person; she lived her life moving ever forward and without much hesitation or fear. Her spirit is part of me and my brothers, and I mourn her passing every day.

Finally, I need to thank Nicole Young, a graduate assistant at Saint Louis University, who read the rough draft of this manuscript with a sharp eye and a critical fearlessness that only the young have. Her suggested changes in style, sentence structure, and the important questions about clarity and meaning she raised greatly improved this book. I did not always listen to her advice and that is probably a mistake. For every sentence that is still too long, know that in all likelihood Nicole said to cut it down and I demurred. Rachel Martens worked the text into its final technical format with speed and care that I can only marvel at! Anyone in need of an editor should remember her name. As I finished my term as dean and decided to return to the faculty, my provost, Chet Gillis, and my president, Fred Pestello, generously provided a year-long sabbatical, without which I would not have been able to complete this book. I am grateful for that priceless gift of time. That time, along with the support of the College of Arts and Sciences and Dean Mike Lewis, came at just the right critical moment in my career and I am deeply thankful for it. As is always the case, any mistakes or errors of judgment are fully my own.

With gratitude,
Chris

Introduction

For a man's words flow out of what fills his heart. A good man draws good things from his store of goodness; a bad man draws bad things from his store of badness. So, I tell you this, that for every unfounded word men utter they will answer on Judgment day, since it is by your words you will be acquitted, and by your words condemned.

—Matthew 12:36–37

SPEAKING AMERICAN

Philip Abbott writes that "new vocabularies, however modestly they appear to contribute to social change, are a prerequisite to the formation of new political institutions."[1] That insight serves as the methodological inspiration for the work ahead. At its most basic, what it tells us is that the words and languages people use to describe and negotiate the social and political worlds they inhabit serve to authorize, legitimate, and, indeed, foster and sustain the sociopolitical spheres in which they live. They are not separate from the "reality" or "reflective" of it, but instead integral and inseparable from reality. One of the chief architects of "linguistic contextualism," J. G. A. Pocock, articulates this as well as anyone, writing,

> The technique, however, does not necessarily involve starting with language and working outwards, to show what meanings it can be said to have borne; it does not involve starting with the assumption that language "reflects" social reality, selecting in obedience to conventional wisdom some aspect of social structure as predictably "reflected," and endeavoring to

1. Abbott, *Shotgun Behind the Door*, 187.

demonstrate parallels, correlations or connections between the two. It should be thought of as an inquiry into the process of "reflection," rather than as based on a simple mirror-object assumption concerning its nature; we are interested in what elements of social experience are articulated in political speech, in how the process of articulation goes on, in how the articulations come to be organized in paradigmatic languages and elaborated in theoretical, philosophical, historical and other intellectually autonomous structures.[2]

Human beings cannot "be" or believe what they cannot call by name(s); language is part and parcel of *how* we think; and, in the process of such "linguistic" thought, the objects and concepts that are thought about are themselves momentarily fixed, subsequently transformed, made meaningful, and used to dictate the way in which the shared world will be viewed and lived. Obviously, this is not a new idea. Its bluntest formulation can perhaps be found in a fragment from the sophist Gorgias over twenty centuries ago when he argued: "Nothing exists and if it did we could not know it and even if we did our language is insufficient to allow us to talk about it." This assertion, on my reading, implies that "reflective" capacity of language is either nonsensical or so radically incomplete as to be of no real utility. Building on that implication, and the fact of his own occupation as a teacher of rhetoric, I take Gorgias to be saying that in effect language "controls" reality rather than the other way around. If true, then the one who dictates what words are used and what they mean wields enormous power. "Linguistic" philosophers like Richard Rorty take this lesson to heart and articulate an approach to political philosophy based on the art of description or, more importantly, "re-description." He explains the process in the following manner:

> The method is to re-describe lots and lots of things in new ways, until you have created a pattern of linguistic behavior which will tempt the rising generation to adopt it, thereby causing them to look for appropriate new forms of nonlinguistic behavior.[3]

As a self-described utopian thinker, Rorty's emphasis was clearly on transformation and change. Yet unlike many more traditional thinkers, Rorty declined to engage existing or historically antecedent "descriptions" argumentatively. Instead, he set as his goal "to make the vocabulary [he] favor(s) look attractive."[4] Because he was not a historian like Pocock, Rorty

---

2. Pocock, *Politics, Language, and Time*, 36.
3. Rorty, *Contingency, Irony, and Solidarity*, 9.
4. Rorty, *Contingency, Irony, and Solidarity*, 9.

was ostensibly uninterested in knowing what others mean, or meant, by the language they used. The languages of others was only of interest to him insofar as it corresponded to his task of "achieving our country," as he described it.[5] Abbott (and your author) share with Rorty his belief that change—at least nonviolent change—depends on at least a significant shift in the mode of political discourse and the content of the language therein. However, knowing that language matters still leaves a number of questions unanswered that are at least equally important, like how to construct and present one's new language so that others will adopt it and begin to behave accordingly and, perhaps most importantly of all, exactly which "language" and mode of discourse *ought* one to promote and why.

It is on these latter two questions where I part company with Rorty and have argued elsewhere that as a result of his "answers," he effectually undermines his own professed political project.[6] Others have made the larger philosophic arguments against Rorty's approach and his positions, and still others have demonstrated quite effectively that even on his own terms there were severe and pertinent limits that he either fails to recognize or ignores. My own approach takes its bearings from Rorty's failure to recognize appropriately the historical-political context in which he is operating as well as the linguistic resources and limitations of the same.[7] As to the second question concerning what particular language ought to be nurtured and promoted, my own ultimate foundationalism and his outright rejection of it makes fruitful argumentation very difficult.[8] Leaving that disagreement aside for now, it is the first question that is of concern at this early stage.

Using the concept of language metaphorically, a simple way of getting at the practical or procedural questions surrounding transformation and institutional change would be to ask how best one might teach a new language to someone. Without getting into any sort of pedagogical analogy, common sense would dictate that to be effective the "teacher" must be bilingual, i.e.,

---

5. Rorty, *Achieving Our Country*.

6. Duncan, "Question for Richard Rorty," 382–413.

7. Jean Elshtain does a particularly insightful job of calling attention to the real difficulty in Rorty's project on p. 328 of her essay "Don't Be Cruel" in her *Real Politics*, when she asks him to "re-describe" a story of a Greek mother of three boys who is forced by a German soldier to decide which son is to be spared while the others are killed in a way that would render it anything other than horrifying.

8. Although my own politics are very close to Rorty's, I come to them through foundational arguments that he would either attempt to "josh me out of" or compel me and other fellow travelers to keep private. As an intellectual and a person of faith, both approaches are equally divisive and offensive. Ironically, then, in so marginalizing what for many are the very reasons they share his political goals, Rorty potentially betrays his own ends in a very unpragmatic fashion.

must know both the language of the student and the one he or she proposes to teach to the student. The process itself is then one of "translation" and juxtaposition as much as it is exposition. Now in the case of someone like Rorty, who was ultimately interested in supplanting the original language of the "student" altogether, the ultimate goal is to wholly transpose the subject's consciousness to the point that he or she now "thinks" in the new language rather than translating it from the old. But before such a thing could take place the initial translation and juxtaposition must be accomplished. So, the first question our revolutionary re-describer must ask is obviously what political language does the student/citizen currently "speak"? In the case at hand, that question is simply answered at the macro-level with the answer that the student/citizen is "speaking American."

The political language of Americans is a complicated issue because of the nature of American politics and culture itself. Writing of democratic peoples in general and Americans in particular, Tocqueville argued that "the continual restlessness of a democracy leads to endless change of language as of all else."[9] While Tocqueville was writing about Americans' use of the English language itself, his observations are just as pertinent in the domain of political life. Although I will discuss the notion of American exceptionalism in more detail later, one need only think briefly about the difficulties of trying to explain American politics and political categories even to West Europeans, let alone Asians or Africans. Simply think about the strange odyssey over the last fifty years of the term "liberal" in American political life to get a sense of the rapidity and fluidity of change, including the challenge of making meaningful sense of the labels we employ to represent various views and ideas. In a democratic nation like this, there is no central or controlling authority charged with rendering authoritative pronouncements on language. Tocqueville seems on point when he claims that "among such peoples the majority lays down the law about language as about all else."[10] Outside of the academy, which now speaks almost wholly to itself, language is employed with an eye toward utility and an almost abject parsimony (think here of the need to express positions on complicated political ideas in fifteen- or thirty-second sound bites, or, on a different note, watch two teenagers text each other for a while). Since it is controlled by that majority, language comes to reflect their interests, which Tocqueville says are more in the area of "business than study, in trade and politics than in philosophic speculation or fine writing."[11] He continues this line of thought claiming:

9. Tocqueville, *Democracy in America*, 478.
10. Tocqueville, *Democracy in America*, 478.
11. Tocqueville, *Democracy in America*, 478–79.

> Most of the words coined or adopted for its use will bear the marks of these habits; they will chiefly serve to express the needs of industry, the passions of politics, or the details of public administration. Language will spread out endlessly in that direction, but metaphysics and theology will slowly lose ground.[12]

As the practical needs of the majority come to shape the language of the nation at the same time as numerous terms and linguistic changes are proliferating, an odd paradox emerges which again Tocqueville captures quite well, writing:

> This abundance of abstract terms in the language of democracy, used the whole time without reference to any particular facts, both widens the scope of thought and clouds it. They make expressions quicker but conceptions less clear. However, in matters of language democracies prefer obscurity to hard work.[13]

Hence, we have more and more ways of actually saying less and less. As the topics themselves narrow so too does the "marketplace of ideas" itself constrict and leave us in the linguistic equivalent of Henry Ford's original car showroom where you could have any color you want so long as it's black. In other words, as long as we talk about the permitted things we can use whatever words we like. So it is that synonyms, euphemisms, and colloquialisms multiply endlessly and swiftly while the depth and nuance of our conversations grow more shallow and blunt all the time. Particularly in politics, we label quickly so that we can either accept, dismiss, or discard with intellectual ease. The price we pay for this, however, is that no one need treat anything we say with any more gravity or thought than we do what they have to say.

So, what is it that causes this state of affairs? What inclines democracies in general and the US democracy in particular to behave this way, linguistically speaking? The broad answer to those questions is found just pages into the second volume of *Democracy in America* in Tocqueville's discussion of equality and individualism in democracies. In the chapter on language, he speaks to the linguistic leveling that takes place in a society that does not have rigid classes where both "learned" and "vulgar" systems of language develop alongside each other and does not have an "accepted judge" or "permanent court" "to decide the meaning of a word," as resulting in everyone using "the same words ... without discrimination."[14] That leveling

---

12. Tocqueville, *Democracy in America*, 479.
13. Tocqueville, *Democracy in America*, 482.
14. Tocqueville, *Democracy in America*, 479–80.

and general conflation of the "learned" and the "vulgar" is the by-product of the devotion democratic people have to social and political equality. Such a devotion renders distinctions between the "learned" and the "vulgar" politically reprobate and subverts the very idea of any kind of authority. In his famous passage, Tocqueville exclaims of democratic peoples:

> But their passion for equality is ardent, insatiable, eternal, and invincible. They want equality in freedom, and if they cannot have that, they still want equality in slavery. They will put up with poverty, servitude, and barbarism, but they will not endure aristocracy.[15]

In the area of language, one can see this at work quite readily by observing the lengths to which presidential candidates and other political figures who were educated in some of the finest and oldest schools in the nation will go in order to appear "common" in their speech and mannerisms. Before Donald Trump came along, this phenomenon was perhaps best displayed during the 2000 presidential campaign when a middle-aged man in a public television focus group claimed after watching the debates that he was for George W. Bush because "he doesn't make me feel stupid." (Notice that he did not say that President Bush did not condescend or talk down to him, but rather implied that he and the soon-to-be president were roughly equal in their mental capacities.)

Because of *equality's* particular status, political languages that embrace certain forms of hierarchy or seek to differentiate between people based on certain characteristics for the purpose of weighing their worth or value higher than another's are out of bounds. Of course, this does not mean that hierarchy does not exist in the United States any more than it means that there are not social classes, but rather that whatever hierarchies or classes do exist must do so *because* of equality rather than in spite of it.[16] Here the operative term is "equality of opportunity." That term, as now popularly understood, requires that no one is either arbitrarily helped or harmed in their "race" for the happiness that they have a right to pursue as Americans.

---

15. Tocqueville, *Democracy in America*, 506.

16. On this point please see the critically important arguments of Patrick J. Deneen in his book *Why Liberalism Failed*. While this book was quite far along before Deneen's was published, I would argue that his immanent and penetrating critique of liberalism represents the consequences of the world first described by Louis Hartz sixty years ago. This book shares with Deneen's a sensibility concerning the decay and consequent inversion of the formative principles of liberalism that lead ultimately not to liberation, but to centralization and uniformity and finally to a post-liberal world that is frightening and dangerous to human flourishing and dignity.

It is in the pursuit of happiness that equality and the second rail of American political culture meet: that rail is individualism. The primacy of equality places the focus squarely on the singular person and their capacity and right to choose freely within only the most nominal *de jure* limits on their personal way of life and path to happiness. Because of the primacy of *equality*, no one's choices are considered fundamentally any better or worse than anyone else's. The representative colloquial expression that captures this best is the prevalent phrase "as long as you're happy—that's what matters." In Tocqueville's more eloquent exposition, he claims:

> Individualism is a calm and considered feeling which disposes each citizen to isolate himself from the mass of his fellows and withdraw into the circle of family and friends; with this little society formed to his taste, he gladly leaves the greater society to look after itself.[17]

This privatization of the person and subsequent withdrawal from much of public life that American society allows for (if not encourages) ultimately means that political languages that create and attempt to enforce "positive" social and political obligations on "private citizens" are considered highly suspect and even "un-American." The result of this prohibition is the propensity Tocqueville ends his chapter with:

> Thus, not only does democracy make men forget their ancestors, but also clouds their view of their descendants and isolates them from their contemporaries. Each man is forever thrown back on himself alone, and there is danger that he may be shut up in the solitude of his own heart.[18]

Now, while Tocqueville himself went on to argue that American's tendency to join all kinds of associations and participate in a robust civic life through them served to "combat the effects of individualism," and prevent the merger into the more perverse "egoism," contemporary evidence suggests that such forms of "social capital" are in decline.[19] Indeed, as Mary Ann Glendon has suggested, the dominant talk in America is "rights talk,"[20] with its corresponding emphasis on insulating and fortifying the distance between the government, community, and other citizens from the solitary individual. The result is a continuing affirmation and reification of what

17. Tocqueville, *Democracy in America*, 506.
18. Tocqueville, *Democracy in America*, 508.
19. See Tocqueville, *Democracy in America*, vol. 2, chs. 4–7. On the decline of social capital see Putnam, "Bowling Alone," 3–9, and Bellah et al., *Habits of the Heart*.
20. See Glendon, *Rights Talk*.

C. B. Macpherson described as "possessive individualism," and which he defined after an intricate and lengthy historical argument using the following seven propositions that are quoted here in their entirety:

1. What makes a man human is freedom from dependence on the wills of others.

2. Freedom from dependence on others means freedom from any relations with others except those relations which the individual enters voluntarily with a view to his own interest.

3. The individual is essentially the proprietor of his own person and capacities, for which he owes nothing to society.

4. Although the individual cannot alienate the whole of his property in his own person, he may alienate his capacity to labor.

5. Human society consists of a series of market relations.

6. Since freedom from the wills of others is what makes a man human, each individual's freedom can rightfully be limited only by such obligations and rules as are necessary to secure the same freedom for others.

7. Political society is a human contrivance for the protection of the individual's property in his person and goods, and (therefore) for the maintenance of orderly relations of exchange between individuals regarded as proprietors of themselves.[21]

For my purposes, these propositions serve as a shorthand for the boundaries of American political discourse—what some will call our "first language."[22] Along with other aspects that I will flesh out in a later chapter, they will comprise the essence of the dominant form of American liberalism and so, unless specified, any references to "liberalism" will be relying on these propositions as referents. In terms of the question raised above regarding the process for political language and change, it is necessary to be cognizant of one's starting point and to know the linguistic filter through which any new political language must ultimately pass before any new vocabulary can come on line. Yet, as we can infer from the reductionist nature of the argument so far, change will be exceedingly difficult because the liberal paradigm that emerged in democratic America revolving around *equality* and *individualism*, and the corresponding mode of discourse is so seemingly impenetrable given the almost solipsistic and tautological manner in which the language itself comes to function. No one managed to understand this problem more acutely and insightfully than Louis Hartz.

21. Macpherson, *Political Theory of Possessive Individualism*, 263–64.
22. See Bellah et al., *Habits of the Heart*; Abbott, *Political Thought in America*.

THE GROUNDHOG DAY PROBLEM

In his book *Human Scale*, Kirkpatrick Sale tells a story about a man who stops another on the street and asks him for directions to the train station. After pausing to think on it for a while, the man looks his questioner in the eye and says with a straight face that if he were going to the train station, he would not start from here.[23] That, in a nutshell, is exactly the problem that any theorist or actor in the context of American political culture must face. It is what we might want to call the *Groundhog Day* problem. For those who do not remember the Bill Murray 1993 comedy, he is a weatherman out on location for Groundhog Day who, through some time distortion, keeps waking up to relive the same day over and over again. The catch, however, is that he is the only one who retains a memory of the days he is reliving. Everyone else in the film is also reliving the same day, but for them it is new again and again—they do not know that they are stuck in this loop. After numerous iterations of the day, Murray eventually commits suicide and learns that even this will not stop the process, as he wakes up yet again. Once persuaded the day will literally never end, he sets out on a path of relentless self-improvement in his quest to woo the love interest of the movie played by Andie MacDowell. He embarks on a plan to have "first date" after "first date" and learn what her passions are, what makes her tick, and what sort of behavior she is repulsed and offended by. After a vast succession of such dates, Murray comes consistently closer to that one perfect "first" date (perfection for him being defined as her having such a great date that she falls into his bed at the date's end). After what must be months and months if not years of such dates (he learns to play the piano, recite poetry, and speak French!), he finally comes as absolutely close to his goal as is humanly possible and still she pulls back at the last possible moment. There is no more room for improvement, no words, acts, gestures, talents, and so on that he can master. It simply is not going to happen. As the focal point of the film, we are supposed to see through the premise how Murray is eventually transformed when the day finally ends; however, I want to suggest that we focus on MacDowell's character instead. Why, we must ask, does she not finally succumb, given Murray's final "perfection"?

The answer I would give to the question is as simple as it might be profound, namely that she simply was not the kind of woman who slept with a man on the first date—any man. Despite the growing intensity of her temptation, it was not in her nature to take that final step (the irony for Murray, of course, is that he was a shoe-in on the "second" date that never could come).

---

23. Sale, *Human Scale*, 512.

Murray simply could not get where he wanted to go from where he started. It may well be the case that this is exactly the "problem" with American political culture—that despite all historical, political, philosophical, theoretical, and practical temptations and reasons for change, it cannot finally be other than what it is. Unlike the virtue my reading imparts to MacDowell's character, those who have relived the same "day" again and again in the context of American political life and thought tend to be the frustrated Bill Murrays of our cultural dramedy. Day after day, year after year, movement after movement, crisis after crisis, the center or root language of American political discourse shifts and shakes, but ultimately holds. And, to conclude the metaphor, each successive entity bent on change and transformation must start the political "day" over again with at least the strong suspicion that their work will be in vain.

To read (even after all this time) Louis Hartz's famous work, *The Liberal Tradition in America*, is to see the Groundhog Day problem in action over time. Using John Locke as a historical exemplar, and even more as the metaphoric representative of the American liberal mind, Hartz paints a sharp picture of an American political mind that is impregnably built on its own particular understanding of and, indeed, faith in the bourgeois-liberalism of the great contract theorist's *Second Treatise of Government*. Important and careful work has been done on the question of whether the Locke starring in Hartz's drama is the true *historical* Locke. Still other work has insightfully questioned whether Americans' deeds matched their words, i.e., whether we "walked" the liberalism we "talked." However, such accounts, though valuable in their own right, miss the larger point and significance of this still powerful and relevant argument.[24] Profitable too are the myriad works that have argued for a less monolithic understanding of the American political experience through their foci on the details and nuances of particular events, ideas, and thinkers that have real and powerful anomalistic value.[25] But, these accounts—often by intention rather than inattention—fail to grasp the fuller sweep of American ideological history, thereby providing

---

24. On the historical Locke, see the fine work of Richard Ashcraft in his *Revolutionary Politics and Locke's Two Treatises of Government*. On the question of America's fidelity to liberalism, see the work of Rogers Smith in "Beyond Tocqueville, Myrdal and Hartz" and his magisterial *Civic Ideals*.

25. Among Republican scholars, see Bailyn, *Ideological Origins of the American Revolution*; Banning, *Jeffersonian Persuasion*; Pocock, *Machiavellian Moment*; and Wood, *Creation of the American Republic, 1776-1787*. See also Diggins, *Lost Soul of American Politics*; Kramnick, "Republican Revisionism Revisited"; and Pangle, *Spirit of Modern Republicanism*. Two of the best works on the role of religious ideas in early American discourse are Sandoz, *Government of Laws*, and Shain, *Myth of American Individualism*.

texts and even subtexts but, ultimately, an insufficient context. Finally, there are accounts—intellectually stimulating and polemically inspired though they are—which seem to have far too much interest in the political battles and efficacy of their own day to worry much about the historical-intellectual accuracy of their projects.[26] Despite all of this rich and varied literature (and the fact that this work too falls into the "anomalistic" and, even partly, into the last category), I still hold that Hartz's larger argument is both highly significant (in the scientific and colloquial sense of the term) and even prophetic.[27] Failure to grasp the explanatory power of Hartz's model is to fail both in trying to understand the American political mind and to court disaster for any innovative or fledgling political-theoretical project aimed at shifting and changing the nature of our political discourse. *Pace* the Groundhog Day problem, it may be the case that such projects are ultimately doomed anyway, but knowledge of where one is starting from remains necessary despite its insufficiency (and perhaps even the impossibility of real movement).

Hartz's argument is premised on the idea that America is a society whose political *ethos* and conceptual core "begins with Locke and thus transforms him, stays with Locke, by virtue of an absolute and irrational attachment it develops for him."[28] Ideologically, this leads to an American political mind that "has within it, as it were, a kind of self-completing mechanism, which insures the universality of the liberal idea."[29] That "mechanism," as the argument goes, is the by-product of a political landscape which lacked the "thesis" of feudalism or the existence of the *ancien régime* that European liberalism came about as a revolutionary response to. In America, Locke is both a revolutionary figure *and* our conservative exemplar at the same time. Conceptually, the result of this odd sort of ideological schizophrenia is a self so perfectly divided against itself that stasis and the appearance of a constant normalcy is the political result. Hartz calls this "a remarkable force: this fixed, dogmatic liberalism of a liberal way of life."[30] For some, this lack of real ideological or linguistic dissonance has been a cause for celebration and a reason for our relative political stability (especially given the fact that we were a revolutionary country).[31] For Hartz and others of his ilk (your

26. The classic example of work in this genre is Beard, *Economic Interpretation of the Constitution of the United States*.

27. For an important defense of the value of "consensus theory," see Fowler, *Enduring Liberalism*.

28. Hartz, *Liberal Tradition in America*, 6.

29. Hartz, *Liberal Tradition in America*, 6.

30. Hartz, *Liberal Tradition in America*, 9.

31. See Boorstin, *Genius of American Politics*; Boorstin, "Our Unspoken National Faith," 327–37.

author included), however, it is deeply frustrating and even disturbing. In the first place, it offends the sensibilities of any intellectual to the extent that Hartz's pithy assessment that in America "law has flourished on the corpse of philosophy" is on target.[32] Second, for any humanist who sees diversity and the ideal of an authentic pluralism as necessary for true human flourishing and creativity, the tendency to transform "eccentricity into sin" ultimately stands as a denial of a fundamental aspect of the human condition—namely difference.[33] Finally, and laden with irony, "the basic ethical problem of a liberal society [as it exists in America]," which Hartz describes thusly: "not the danger of the majority which has been its conscious fear, but the danger of unanimity, which has slumbered unconsciously behind it: 'the tyranny of opinion' that Tocqueville saw" is ultimately itself anti-liberal![34] Aside from these concerns, there are still other important arguments to be made from the perspectives of philosophy and truth-seeking, social justice, and political realism (the *ought* question from above).

READING AND RIGHTING AMERICA

Although the tone struck above is a decidedly discordant one, it is important to note first that this line of attack is itself part of a long-standing tradition of American political theorizing that is critical of certain variations of American exceptionalism. Second, note that as a brand of that sort of criticism, it too stands a very strong chance of reifying and strengthening that which it seeks to deconstruct and confront.[35] Indeed, as is often the case with work within the genre, my true goal is not to eclipse "individualism" or "equality," but rather to redefine and reorient those ideas such that they embody what might be thought of as the "spirit" of the concepts rather than the mere "letter," as it were.[36] Furthermore, while in tension with the

---

32. Hartz, *Liberal Tradition in America*, 10.

33. Hartz, *Liberal Tradition in America*, 12.

34. As Robert Booth Fowler puts it, "It was Hartz's judgment that consensus liberalism was in its very consensus a denial of the liberal principles of freedom and individualism and was unsuited for a diverse world." Fowler, *Enduring Liberalism*, 29.

35. For an excellent and thought-provoking discussion of both the concept and of American exceptionalism and the phenomenon that is in all likelihood at work here, see Abbott, *Exceptional America*, especially chs. 1–2.

36. Larry Siedentop's magisterial history *Inventing the Individual* provides an excellent account of the development of these ideals beginning with the teachings of St. Paul and working up till the dawn of the sixteenth century. In that book, Siedentop demonstrates that the roots of liberalism's most important contributions to political thought, like the moral equality of all human beings, were the by-product of Christian

boundaries of American exceptionalism as they currently exist, this work is also of a piece with it insofar as its own emphasis on "newness" and quasi-utopian possibility is part and parcel of that concept. As Philip Abbott put it while fleshing out exactly this line of demarcation as it concerned American political thought and exceptionalism, "Nothing is possible in the way of political experimentation except individual initiative, and on the other, everything is possible."[37] This, as I have said, remains a hopeful work; it is also an *American* work.

As a work both in the domain of and about American political thought, it is my intention to work within the broader reaches of American political discourse. Using the approach of Robert Bellah and his coauthors in *Habits of the Heart* and mirrored in Philip Abbott's *Political Thought in America*, I will contend that while the language of "liberalism," as understood through the work of people like Tocqueville and Hartz and defined with some general precision in Macpherson, represents America's first or primary mode of political discourse. There are indeed "second languages" that have been utilized with some success and which provide at least some political/cultural resources for those interested in shifting the terms of the debate to some effect. In earlier work, I have focused on "republican" discourse and ideology as an important alternative to American liberalism and tried to note how that language was made manifest in the political thought and *praxis* of groups like the Anti-Federalists and the Southern Agrarians.[38] Here, I will attempt to bring into focus important elements and ideas drawn from what has been called American's "biblical language."

The religious roots of American political thought are well known and begin with people like John Winthrop and his Massachusetts Bay Puritans. In Winthrop's oft-quoted sermon, *A Modell of Christian Charity* (1630), he lays out the framework for communal (and by inference political) success in explicitly Judeo-Christian *covenantal* terms.[39] Although in contemporary political discourse notions of "covenant," "compact," and "contract" are used interchangeably (with the former two falling into increasing disuse altogether), the tradition that the Puritans drew from understood those terms in profoundly different ways. I will make this argument in greater detail,

---

thought and the interplay between the ideals of the Gospels and the working out over centuries of the relationship between the faith and the political order through the work of the Catholic Church and its intellectuals and leaders as they confronted the secular authorities in the West.

37. Abbott, *Exceptional America*, 1.

38. See Duncan, *Anti-Federalists*; Duncan, *Fugitive Theory*.

39. Ismail Kurun provides an excellent account of covenantal thinking and the religious contributions to the rise of liberalism in *Theological Origins of Liberalism*.

but for now, borrowing a simple set of definitions from James B. Torrance, "a covenant is a promise binding two people or two parties to love one another unconditionally" and "a contract . . . is a legal relationship in which two people or two parties bind themselves together on mutual condition to affect some future result."[40] Hence, Winthrop's idiom and intention are not incidental or for dramatic effect when he claims,

> Now the only way to avoid this shipwreck and to provide for our posterity is to follow the counsel of Micah, to do justly, to love mercy, to walk humbly with our God, for this end we must be knit together in this work as one man, we must entertain each other in brotherly affection, we must be willing to abridge ourselves of our superfluities, for the supply of other's necessities, we must uphold a familiar commerce together in all meekness, gentleness, patience and liberality, we must delight in each other, make our conditions our own, rejoice together, mourn together, labor, and suffer together, always having before our eyes our commission and community in the work, our community as members of the same body, so shall we keep the unity of spirit in the bond of peace, the Lord will be our God and delight to dwell among us.[41]

The soon-to-be twelve-term Governor concludes this early sermon with his allusion to the ideal of a "city on the hill." While there is certainly a heavy emphasis on the duties and obligations of individual citizens in this quasi-utopian vision, it is absolutely essential to understand that success is premised on the existence of God's grace (his self-giving love) as both the model—his covenant with his people—and guarantor. While contract oriented or legalistic readers are inclined to read the whole of the sermon as a kind of theological *quid pro quo* (i.e., obey the rules and God will reward you, disobey and you will be punished), this is poor theology for thoughtful Christians. If the notion that "God is love" is taken seriously, then it is literally impossible for God to ever "punish" in the causal manner implied in such a scenario. God's love is constant—he keeps the covenant and loves unconditionally. Through "sin" (the willful turning away from God), men and women can, however, break the covenant, thereby suffering as a result of their own actions and not as a result of God's. Leaving the propensity to sin aside for now, the tough questions in the "biblical" tradition subsequently become how to manifest those virtues and practice the requirements as listed, the greatest of which is *agape* (spiritual love), toward each other within the context of daily life and

---

40. Torrance, "Covenant Concept in Scottish Theology and Politics," 146.
41. Quoted in Levy, *Political Thought in America*, 12.

social/political interaction. Such practical and prudential questions must, by their very nature, be worked out with a particular historical context and by admittedly fallible human beings. What is essential to remember is that the "goal" itself remains unchanging and transcendent—extra-human in the sense that we cannot alter it no matter how strong, knowledgeable, willful, and so on, we become. This, then, is the hallmark of this "second" language of American political discourse: the initial questions must be (1) what is it that God asks of us, and (2) how do we do it in a way where the means do not pervert or distort the ends? This is obviously a very different premise than a mode of discourse whose first questions have to do with maximizing human/individual liberty and independence from others in both the determination and pursuit of appropriate ends. It also leads to very different outcomes than those that might flow from questions concerned with maximizing wealth, power, or other such worldly values—and, even those of equality or democracy themselves. This is not to say that these values might not be essential once all is said and done, but only that they alone, or in combination, can never be sufficient. All the values in the tradition I will argue for in the coming work must ultimately be measured against their propensity and likelihood for helping us fulfill our duties and obligations under the covenantal rubric of unconditional love.

To accomplish this task, and hopefully provide at least a rationale for change, I propose in the following chapters to "read" back into the American narrative a religious language and mode of discourse. That narrative ought to resonate with Americans on an intellectual level if not a "linguistic" one by drawing out the implications and understandings that are both embedded in and authorized by that submerged way of talking and, hence, at least potentially, being. Far from teaching Americans a new language, my plan is to reintroduce them to a way of talking and a vocabulary that *should* be appealing and at least vaguely familiar to large numbers of American citizens. It is, admittedly, also quite problematic and potentially controversial at this late date. At its most basic, the argument contends that while the Christian gospel was not itself "political," its logic carries with it from the beginning the seeds of human liberation, equality, and—derivatively at least—a basic framework for social justice that the initial justification for, and promise of, liberalism eventually sprouted and grew strong from.[42] This set of claims is laid out and made operational through the arguments of the first three chapters.

Chapter 1, "*Christian* Citizenship," provides a brief overview of Christian political history in the West and is intended to point out that while there

---

42. Again, see the work of Siedentop in *Inventing the Individual* for a much deeper and historically sophisticated account of this phenomenon.

is no direct political teaching, there are certainly implications for a *praxis* of the permissible and the impermissible. In other words, just because there is no explicit political argument does not mean that there are no boundaries of consistency that can be derived from the text. The chapter traces the current status of religion and politics in the context of American constitutional and ideological development.

In chapter 2, "Euthyphro, Christianity, and Liberalism," I provide an argument regarding liberalism and the development of secularism as a political ideology. This will call serious attention to the fundamental inconsistencies and cleavages that have emerged ever more starkly in the American liberal regime to the detriment of the idea of Christian citizenship developed in chapter 1. The chapter concludes by making the case that liberalism was originally and logically inseparable from the theological *ethos* it was embedded in and sustained by. It does this by noting the rupture and distance that now separates contemporary liberalism from its points of origin and which renders it unmoored and theoretically incoherent outside of a postmodern paradigm.

In chapter 3, "Christianity and Alienation," I attempt to carve out what might best be called a Christian theory of individualism. Using the work of thinkers as diverse as Thomas Aquinas, Karl Marx, Richard Weaver, Wendell Berry, Glenn Tinder, and Charles Taylor, my goal is to stake out a soft teleological position with regard to human flourishing. That argument takes its bearings from a social and dialogical conception of individual formation and development that stands in stark contrast to the notion of "possessive individualism" that I contend has come to dominate contemporary liberal theory and politics.

In chapter 4, "Orestes Brownson and the Hartz Thesis," the book resituates itself in the domain of American political thought and begins its attempted recovery of the "biblical" language of what I will come to call a post-liberal (or in a more unwieldy manner, a pre-postmodern) America.[43] In this chapter, Hartz is some ways hoisted on his own petard as I demonstrate that he himself succumbs to exactly the sort of "irrational Lockianism" that he wants everyone else to transcend by failing to see the resources within a properly understood "liberalism" that Brownson forcefully taps into.

---

43. See Duncan, "Liberalism and the Challenge of *Fight Club*," 119–44. In that essay, I define "post-liberal" as a personality form that embraces the foundationalist notion of inalienable rights while simultaneously rejecting the teleological view of the world that such a set of claims was traditionally linked to. In other words, the sort of person who believes that "God" gave human beings certain rights but does not expect anything from us in return.

In chapter 5, "The Catholic Social Tradition and AMERICA," I look at the changing relationship between the Catholic Church and American liberalism in the wake of heavy Catholic immigration and the rise of the industrial state and modern capitalism. Here I argue that once the Church gave up on the idea of a confessional state, it cleared the way for it to take a far more confrontational and prophetic stance regarding the material and ideological conditions of the times in the name of social justice and equality. I conclude the chapter with a critique of the dominant constitutionalism of the day which prized "substantive due process" and "liberty of contract" in the name of "neutrality" as it pertained to so-called class legislation. The Church's then nascent doctrine regarding social questions rejects neutrality as always unjustly favoring the interests of the strong and the powerful over the weak and the marginalized, and thus takes the side of the least among us as it begins to offer a competing vision of the good society.

In chapter 6, "Inventing a Catholic American Political Tradition," I build out from the initial attempts of the Church to secure prophetic space in the liberal order in the name of the gospel message to a more robust and intentionally deconstructed counter-theorization designed to recall liberalism to its better angels. Starting with a broad discussion on the nature and function of the idea of "tradition" itself, I try to demonstrate the latent or embedded catholicity that can be discerned in the American liberal tradition itself as encapsulated in theologian John Courtney Murray's contention that the American founders "built better than they knew."[44] Using Murray's natural law-inspired claim that "what is not true will somehow fail to work,"[45] I unpack his attempt to make American liberalism safe for Catholicism as well as intellectually and political sustainable itself.

In chapter 7, "Tending to Catholicism *and* America in the Modern World," we move from the theoretical bridge-building and corrective work of John Courtney Murray to the more robustly affirmative work of Jacques Maritain, the eventual launch of the Church's own systematic engagement with the modern world through the Second Vatican Council and documents on Catholic teaching like *Gaudium et Spes*. In Maritain, we see perhaps the most important Catholic philosopher of the twentieth century provide an unapologetic, full-throated, and theologically grounded defense of democracy properly understood. A leading thinker at the forefront of the movement toward universal human rights, Maritain argues forcefully against the idea of secular sovereignty of both state and self, and instead places everything in service to the concrete human person created in the image and likeness of

---

44. Murray, *We Hold These Truths*, 46.
45. Murray, *We Hold These Truths*, 100.

God. Guided by the claim echoed in the work of John Paul II that the human person was of infinite value and should never be treated as a means but only as a beloved end, Maritain asserts, *pace* Thomas Aquinas, that "the good of one person is worth more than the whole universe of nature."[46] As such, the political order must be placed in service to the common good understood now as the good of all in their particularity, not as some collectivized version of the general will. It is there where the Church's social teaching becomes definitive as it attempts to drive political institutions and citizens alike to in effect love what they ought to love: each other.

And finally, in chapter 8, "Radical Conversion: A Conclusion," I attempt to bring home the larger general themes and theorizations through attentiveness to an instance of the particular in the form and the work of the political activist and philosopher Michael Harrington, as I argue for an approach of visionary gradualism. At its core, the book concludes with a call for conversion and redirection in the name of securing and enlarging what remains the greatest and most profound political endeavor to date for those who remain committed to the ideal of the equal dignity and worth of each and every human being.

CONCLUSION

While much of the work that follows is analytic and quasi-dialectical, perhaps even agonistic, in form, it is meant to be dialogic in terms of its ethical commitments. What I mean by this is that while the work is in many ways deeply critical and confrontational at times, my goal is not simply to deconstruct and *redescribe* the world in a manner that I find superior or simply more pleasing. My intention is not to win an argument, but rather to both say something true about important matters and to be true to the tradition from which I am working in *conversation* with the tradition I am confronting. I realize that the provocative nature of the title, *Radical Conversion*, itself suggests that the work to follow might simply be another totalizing narrative that marginalizes alternative voices in a bid for an alternative hegemony, but that is the exact opposite of my intention. In attempting to provide a counter-hegemonic narrative to the American liberalism I contend has dominated our national political discourse, I hope to open up the necessary space for a liberal-democratic order that is both more sustainable as well as intellectually and morally defensible.

In their work on dialogic ethics, Arnett, Fritz, and Bell claim that the central question of their line of thinking can be put as such: "To what do

---

46. Maritain, *Person and the Common Good*, 20.

I want to belong and why?"⁴⁷ In many ways, *that* is the question I am trying to answer for myself and also for others in the form of describing what I believe is worthy of devotion. They frame the chapter from which that sentence is taken with the following quote from Paulo Freire:

> Dialogue is the encounter between men, mediated by the world, in order to name the world. Hence, dialogue cannot occur between those who want to name the world and those who do not wish this naming—between those who deny others the right to speak their word and those whose right to speak had been denied them. Those who have been denied their primordial right to speak their word must first reclaim this right and prevent the continuation of this dehumanizing aggression.⁴⁸

Though my project here is not nearly profound enough to merit association with the sort of forces of oppression that Freire was confronting in his work, it is in its own way a project of *reclamation* insofar as the liberalism and the neoliberalism it challenges in the name of Christian love ultimately eclipses and elides authentic alternative voices and ways of being that are central to many human beings' identities and lives. In doing so, it also progressively denies the resources of this important alternative "language" and its corresponding way of being in the world to others for whom it might be life-giving as well as, quite literally, a *saving* choice. In terms that a proper liberalism should resonate with, Arnett, Fritz, and Bell go on to state what should be obvious, namely that

> the persons, groups, and institutions with which we associate shape us and the narrative ground on which we stand. Our reflective consideration of the goods protected and promoted by those we seek to join opens our awareness of the implications of belonging to a given set of friends, a particular group, or an admired institution.⁴⁹

The catch here, however, is that the social order in which a given human being or group of people is ensconced must be designed and maintained in such a way that actual choice is truly possible and that they have the necessary freedom and reflective capacity to answer the "why" question as well. In the larger argument that follows in this book, I attempt to help clear the theoretical, philosophical, political, and theological space needed for this to happen. Additionally, I then attempt to demonstrate the "what" and the

---

47. Arnett et al., *Communication Ethics*, 82.
48. Cited in Arnett et al., *Communication Ethics*, 82.
49. Arnett et al., *Communication Ethics*, 82–83.

"why" of a particular set of choice-worthy goods, friends, and institutions that flow out of a picture of Christianity and the Catholic social tradition and thought that I believe represents at least one of the best hopes for a socially constructed community[50] that is committed to retaining the dialogic ethic as opposed to reifying the existing hegemonic order of American liberalism.

This work of "conversion" is guided by the conviction that the Christian story, particularly in its Catholic form, presents us with a narrative that is grounded in the fundamental truth derived from the Incarnation that each and every human person is equally sacred, loved, and cared for in a ubiquitous and unconditional way.[51] Furthermore, this fact means that every person is obligated to see, love, and care for other persons in the same way. In place of the abstract commitment to "individualism," I will argue that it is a thoroughgoing "personalism"[52] that represents the true calling of the liberal-democratic regime properly understood for reasons that are moral as well as practical and prudential.

Although Kathleen Glenister Roberts's work was not directed at my particular subject matter, I do believe that there are strong analogues that I can draw that will let me conclude this section on the right note. In her book *The Limits of Cosmopolis: Ethics and Provinciality in the Dialogue of Cultures*, Roberts's target is the ideal of the cosmopolitan identity as a morally superior mode of being to that of the so-called provincial or place-bound person who exists in a particular culture and is entrapped in the limited and pejoratively "traditional" *ethos* and worldview of his or her particular home. Her reasons for targeting for critique the transnational and transcultural citizens of the world are overtly moral and ethical. When she claims,

---

50. Two older books remain important contributions for thinking about how societies change and how they *ought* to change: See Berger and Luckmann, *Social Construction of Reality*; Berger, *Pyramids of Sacrifice*.

51. One of the more powerful statements of this idea comes from the work of Pedro Morandé, who writes in "Relevance of the Message of Vatican Council, *Gaudium et Spes*" on p. 149, "By his incarnation the Son of God has united himself in some fashion with every man. He worked with human hands, he thought with a human mind, acted by human choice, and loved with a human heart. . . . [This] allusion to the Incarnation is not merely a pious proclamation of the dignity of each person; it is the affirmation that each human being, in his openness to the gift of God, is capable of experiencing a freedom that does not come from the social order, that proceeds any juridical recognition, and that establishes a criterion not subject to the dialectical consensus of historical circumstances."

52. While I will rely heavily later in the book on Jacques Maritain's account of "personalism," there are a number of important works in this area that I have consulted. Beginning with the foundational work of Mounier, *Personalism*, the readers should also see Spaemann, *Persons*; Walsh, *Politics of the Person*; and the wonderful introductory text by Burgos, *Introduction to Personalism*.

"The cosmopolitan identity claim allows individuals to relieve themselves of undesirable or unpopular cultural identities; it also relieves them of responsibility for real persons," we see the root of her own ethical commitments, namely responsibility for others.[53] Her concerns are encapsulated just a little later in her claim that "to imagine the abstract instead of loving the particular is to put ethics at risk."[54] For my purposes, Roberts's *cosmopolitan* is in essence equivalent to an idea developed in chapter 2 that undergirds much of my critical apparatus, namely, that "liberalism" fraudulently presents itself as a comprehensive philosophy of life when it is really only a philosophy of government. Put differently, "liberalism" presents itself as something neutral and unencumbered by history or certain kinds of substantive commitments when in reality it strives for comprehensiveness and seeks to drive any other comprehensive or heavily encumbered modes of life out of the public sphere altogether. Roberts's cosmopolitan seeks such standing at the individual level in his or her attempt to stand above "cultural particularism" while "aspiring to the universalist power that speaks for humanity"; a privilege she argues that is "invented by a totalizing Western liberalism."[55]

That attempt to "speak for humanity," in turn, bespeaks an interesting irony that has critical moral implications; namely that the cosmopolitan, rather than creating space for authentic individualism, both implicitly and explicitly asserts the superiority of their own self-professed mode of existence. Roberts puts it like this:

> Yet paradoxically, the new cosmopolitanism is not acceptance of multiple perspectives and lived experiences, but an imposition of totality and homogenization. It is a return to Western cultural bias that glorifies individuality, progress, science, and capital.[56]

She adds to this critique a little later with her claim that "cosmopolitanism announces that all humans stand on the same ground; it homogenizes space and defaces uniqueness. In short, it uproots us."[57] In this way, we glimpse briefly the difference between what "equality" becomes under the possessive American liberal regime and what "equality" means in a Christian sense. The latter, I argue, calls upon us to embrace one another in all our particularity as beings created in the image and likeness of God. It affirms our distinctiveness while celebrating our commonness. When viewed through

---

53. Roberts, *Limits of Cosmopolis*, 30.
54. Roberts, *Limits of Cosmopolis*, 33.
55. Roberts, *Limits of Cosmopolis*, 61.
56. Roberts, *Limits of Cosmopolis*, 71.
57. Roberts, *Limits of Cosmopolis*, 86.

this kind of conceptual lens, it is a very easy move to the critical claim that "human beings deserve *more* than 'tolerance.' Tolerance is no substitute for love of the person and ethical action is the universal community."[58] Building out from the work of Emmanuel Levinas, Roberts's position drives us to a thick commitment to *solidarity* as the moral imperative. While a liberal regime of "rights" may be absolutely necessary for the common good to emerge, it proves to be, for the Christian, radically insufficient. Sufficiency for the Christian would entail a view that holds, in Levinas's words,

> the equal dignity of each and every soul, which is independent of the material or social conditions of people, does not flow from a theory that affirms, beneath individual differences, an analogy based on "psychological constitution." It is due to the power given to the soul to free itself from *what has been*, from everything that linked it to something or engaged it with something. . . . In place of liberation through grace there is autonomy, but the Judeo-Christian leitmotif of freedom pervades this autonomy.[59]

For Roberts, the ideal of Christian freedom "comes because of the Cross and is constantly renewed through the Eucharist," and she goes on to contend that "while the Incarnation, Passion, and Resurrection are 'historical events' in terms of human perception, the sacrament of the Eucharist is timeless. Therefore freedom is constantly renewed."[60] In this way, I propose we see, at least for the Christian, that the true grounding of the equality and rights which the Declaration of Independence holds, by virtue of a creator, we all possess, flow not from nature or, most certainly not, from a contractual arrangement, but rather from an intentional and deeply personal act of sacrifice by an all-loving God maintained and renewed though daily communion and the reception of the transubstantiated body and blood of Jesus. That *political* death was not so that sin in general could be eradicated, but rather so that the specific and embodied sins of each and every actual person could be washed clean. It is that liberation from spiritual bondage that becomes the perquisite for the true liberation of human beings that is the bedrock of the liberal-democratic spirit and the commitments to the free and equal community of persons such a regime rightfully demands.[61]

To know and understand this is to ground our political commitments in something beyond the will, preferences, and any given political culture and

---

58. Roberts, *Limits of Cosmopolis*, 126.
59. Quoted in Roberts, *Limits of Cosmopolis*, 154.
60. Roberts, *Limits of Cosmopolis*, 154.
61. Patrick Deneen's book *Why Liberalism Failed* is essential for understanding this basic argument in much greater detail than I am able to do in this book.

to ensure that we continue to hold sacred our right to "name the world" and speak in the language of truth. And that truth is we must love one another as real human beings in all our variety and difference with our whole hearts or die. Radical conversion is what are called to, not what we are compelled to.[62]

---

62. For a powerful and unapologetic account of the demands on the Catholic faithful to enter the public sphere explicitly as people of faith, see Chaput, *Render Unto Caesar*.

1

Christian Citizenship

For the sake of the Lord, accept the authority of every social institution: the emperor as the supreme authority, and the governors as commissioned by him to punish criminals and praise good citizenship. God wants you to be good citizens, so as to silence what fools are saying in their ignorance. You are slaves of no one except God, so behave like free men, and never use your freedom as an excuse for wickedness. Have respect for everyone and love for our community; fear God and honor the emperor.

—1 Peter 2:13–17

Do not conform any longer to the pattern of the world, but be transformed by the renewing of your mind.

—Romans 12:2

INTRODUCTION

In a 1938 issue, the *New Republic* kicked off a series on the Catholic Church in politics with an introductory essay provocatively titled "Is There a Catholic Problem?"[1] That a highly influential journal of *liberal* political thought in the United States of America was willing to couch their forthcoming discussion in language that imbibed of the same bitter wine as work on the so-called "Jewish question" in some European circles is, by the present standards, quite unsettling. And, indeed, the text itself recognizes its own proximity to the edge of respectability by noting the reluctance the editors had in opening up the topic, "In view of the real dangers of bigotry and prejudice, sometimes directed against religious groups in this country and even now being suffered by Jews, Catholics and Protestants in Germany."[2] Yet open it they did.

Although the short piece was hardly a polemic or anti-Catholic diatribe, it did manage to simultaneously reveal two important prejudices and lob a not-too-veiled threat at Catholic citizens. The first bias comes in the form of a devotion to what Michael Perry has recently labeled an "exclusionist"[3] view of the relationship between church and state as evidenced by the simple sentence: "It is *true* that State and Church in this country are and should remain completely separate."[4] The second prejudice is entwined with the first and is best characterized as a devotion to a kind of "progressive vanguardism" that viewed religion as something to be neither "seen nor heard" in the modern political world lest the wheels of progress and secular perfection be brought to a halt.[5] Such a view is betrayed by phrases like: "When Catholic action begins to threaten the fundamentals of democracy itself and to stand in the path of social progress . . ." or "Intelligent American Catholics ought therefore to be particularly zealous to hold open the doors of political democracy and civil freedom so that Catholics themselves may have an opportunity to keep step with the changes in human affairs."[6] While certainly praiseworthy and unobjectionable in and of themselves, the primacy given to "democracy," "civil freedom," "social progress," and "keeping in step" is, of course, to miss the point for Catholics and other religiously minded citizens, i.e., fidelity and faithfulness to God, his revelation, and call to his disciples. Finally, the "threat" comes in the form of a portended

1. "Is There a Catholic Problem?," 32–33.
2. "Is There a Catholic Problem?," 32.
3. See Perry, *Under God?*
4. "Is There a Catholic Problem?," 32. Emphasis mine.
5. This is not a well-crafted term, but I wanted something that would help me get beyond the confines of the term "progressives" and at something akin to the description Christopher Lasch gives of an American Left whose members' "confidence in being on the winning side of history made progressive people unbearably smug and superior." See Lasch, *True and Only Heaven*, 36.
6. "Is There a Catholic Problem?," 33.

backlash against any so-called "Catholic pressure group" by "victims" whom one cannot "expect to remain forever silent and inactive under such pressure," and toward whom Catholics who "fear" arousing "religious prejudice" ought to exercise "self-control."[7]

Behind the assertions and "advice" was certainly a familiar strain of American trepidation regarding the Catholic Church, but there was an even more familiar subtext that has only grown larger and more pronounced since its publication, which has called for the deracination of religion from the public sphere altogether. Take the following passage from the piece, for example, and substitute the term "Christian," "Protestant," "Muslim," "Jewish," or "Evangelical" for the term "Catholic." Then, ask whether or not it would have been equally valid for the editors and, more importantly, if it would not be as relevant today in the minds many American political commentators.

> Just as Catholics have a political and religious freedom with which others should not interfere, so the citizens in general have rights with which Catholics should not interfere. Catholic authority has a perfect legal right to tell Catholics that they should not read certain books or see certain plays, or speak on behalf of certain causes or seek divorce in the courts or practice birth control. But when, through political or economic pressure, they bring about the denial of freedom of the press or of speech or of worship to others, or force the expression in restrictive legislation of moral standards which the majority of our non-Catholic citizens do not acknowledge, they are interfering with the liberty of Americans who do not give allegiance to the authority of the Church.[8]

Just who or what, one must wonder, is a "citizen in general"? Everyone I know is a citizen of a particular kind and ultimately irreducible to simply a part of some amorphous sum. Be that as it may, it is my sense that there were certain authoritative acts performed, laws passed, or policies adopted by said "citizens in general" for non-religious reasons that would not have been discounted and declared out of order on their face nearly as broadly as implied above. I would suggest that the editors here are using the term "citizen in general" as a euphemistic and undefended term for their own vision of the "ideal citizen" in America. Said citizen, then, must be understood to be one who sheds his or her particularity—especially his or her religious particularity—at the city gates or the door of the polling place.

7. "Is There a Catholic Problem?," 32.
8. "Is There a Catholic Problem?," 32.

Hence, despite their frequent self-supposed nods to political tolerance and pluralism like the assertion that "it is superfluous to say that most of the millions of Catholic communicants in this country are good citizens and good neighbors,"[9] the reality is that they can only truly be the latter (good citizens) by distancing themselves from their religious communion and identity. If they were to accept those terms, however, they would no longer be truly *Catholic* communicants, at least that will be one of the central contentions of this work. A companion contention to that theological one will be a political one, namely that if such a religious negation is demanded, then the participants would no longer be truly American *communicants* either. I will explore the tension between *American* citizenship and religious identity in the following pages in an attempt to both flesh out a theory of *Christian* citizenship and *American* citizenship in the United States. To answer to the *New Republic*'s question about whether there is a Catholic *problem*—either then or now—my answer will be that if there is not a problem, then there should be; and it would be both right and good.

APOCALYPTIC CITIZENSHIP: A BRIEF HISTORY OF CHRISTIAN-POLITICAL TIME

Classical political thought, understood through the lens of Aristotle, placed citizenship and political participation in the polis at the apex of human activity for the majority of human beings who were incapable of living the contemplative or philosophic life. In the public sphere, human beings could realize their *telos* by leaving behind the realm of necessity and production and entering the world of freedom and action. The "happiness" achieved therein is called "public happiness" by Hannah Arendt and consists of "the citizen's right of access to the public realm, in his share in public power—to be 'participator in the government of affairs' in Jefferson's telling phrase."[10]

Given its emphasis on the restoration of the Kingdom of David on earth, Judaism cannot be viewed as wholly antagonistic to that classical vision. Jewish citizenship—at least under the right historical-religious circumstances—made perfect sense. Sadly, the lack of those circumstances, i.e., the existence of a Jewish state (until recently), let alone a Jewish world order, helps us explain the tragic political history of a people. But what of a faith whose principal figure declares fervently that his kingdom is not of this earth? What of a faith populated at its earliest stages by the poor,

9. "Is There a Catholic Problem?," 32.
10. Arendt, *Human Condition*, 127.

dispossessed, and marginalized who were denied citizenship and the possibility of participation?

Upon his return from the desert and the start of his public ministry, Jesus proclaimed that "the kingdom of heaven is close at hand" (Matt 4:17). He preached the message of the apocalypse and held that the day of reckoning was soon to come. Whereas the Greek and Roman political theorists like Plato, Aristotle, and Polybius had sought to theorize the lasting political order that would hopefully defeat the destructive nature of time itself,[11] Christians were taught to pray for its destruction: "your kingdom come, your will be done" (Matt 6:10). In his words, followers are told: "Do not suppose that I have come to bring peace to the earth: it is not peace I have come to bring, but a sword" (Matt 10:34). Only with the end of life as we know it can the true beginning be made. The Gospels are, of course, filled with the most radical of all social and political inversions ranging from the displacement of wealth and power to the love of one's enemies to the elevation of the lowly to the outright rejection of the most basic values of the world, like life itself. Rather than self-aggrandizement, the Christian is pushed to die to the self and turn away from the things of this world: "Anyone who prefers father or mother to me is not worthy of me. Anyone who does not take his cross and follow in my footsteps is not worthy of me. Anyone who finds his life will lose it; anyone who loses his life for my sake will find it" (Matt 10:37–39). For the early Christians, the end was thought to be near, and good riddance; what was the value of this meager and pitiful existence when compared to the glory of eternity? The initial answer was none.

As radical as this psychological reorientation might have been on some level, the sociological and political implications were initially quite small. People already excluded politically and marginalized socially turning their figurative backs on the society and political order that had rejected them first has an air of making a virtue of necessity about it. When that turning away from the world as construed is juxtaposed to the assertion to "give back to Caesar what belongs to Caesar—and to God what belongs to God" (Matt 22:21), one can discern an indifference to politics and perhaps even an affirmative obligation to apoliticalism on one hand, and on the other, a stifling injunction toward conformity and political obedience. While the political implications as filtered through the Gospels might have had a starkly "conservative" quality to them, the seeds of a more radical social vision were being planted in fertile soil awaiting future sowers. Embedded in Jesus' rejection of the Pharisees, and through assertions like that found in Matthew 7:24 ("Therefore, everyone who listens to these words of mine and acts on

---

11. See Pocock, *Machiavellian Moment*.

them will be like a sensible man who built his house on rock"), there is a crucial social leveling and universalism that becomes increasingly visible. In a staunchly hierarchical society, the gospel of Jesus Christ suggests rather forcefully that his teaching is available and applicable to all people in all places whatever their social, religious, or political strata. In his words, "Anyone who does the will of my Father in heaven, he is my brother and sister and mother" (Matt 12:50). While not intended to be a call to arms, at least on my reading of the text and the context, widespread dissemination and embrace of such a message could not help but beget a new sense of possibility and foster at least the nascent stirrings of social criticism.

The paradox, though oversimplified, of the early Christian confrontation with the political order of the day that can be derived from this reading of the gospel and the times is one whereby Jesus provided his followers with a radical theory of equality without a theory of political action. While not articulated as plainly as Martin Luther's doctrine of the "inner" and the "outer-man" would be some fifteen hundred years later, the psycho-politico bifurcation was on some level already manifested at least implicitly at the beginning with Jesus himself. In a world that was about to end soon, whatever social or political tension was generated by said paradox was mostly inconsequential (especially once the relative social position of the Christian was factored in). However, in a world where the apocalyptic vision wanes in the face of both time and distance from its herald, it is only natural that the sociopolitical contradictions become more vivid and prominent in the minds of earthbound mortals who are becoming increasingly conscious of their status as actors within an existing history rather than members of some sort of pre-historical vanguard.

Christ's "silence" or refusal to resolve the paradox or explain the mystery explicitly is both a blessing and a curse for his human followers and disciples. Without accepting its larger import, there is a parallel that can be drawn between the silence that I am speaking of here and the silence of the Christ figure in Dostoevsky's story of the Grand Inquisitor in *The Brothers Karamazov*. There, the inquisitor-priest berates the returned Christ for both delivering human beings to freedom when he came the first time while simultaneously attempting to cow him with accusations of hypocrisy were he (Christ) to reinsert himself into human history in any sort of authoritative manner. In other words, the "political silence" of the Gospels, as construed so far, is intentional and purposeful while at the same time resisting the temptation to be authoritarian or dictatorial. This theme is captured in the description of the third temptation of Christ in the desert as described in Matthew 4:8–10:

> Next taking him to a very high mountain, the devil showed him all the kingdoms of the world and their splendor. "I will give you all these," he said, "if you fall at my feet and worship me." Then Jesus replied, "Be off Satan! For Scripture says: *You must worship the Lord your God, and serve him alone.*"

In that refusal lies both human political liberation and yet another affirmation of our free will—for better and worse.

I am not in a position to render an authoritative theological judgment on the ultimate meaning of that refusal—though many others have tried, or at least claim to have tried. Two broad responses to that silence seem to be logically possible, namely that the absence of a positive political program calls the Christian to patience, endurance, and political abstinence—our time in the desert, if you will. The second possible meaning is that political participation is allowed, if not required, and represents at least one important sphere in which human beings are meant to work out both their individual and collective historical destinies. While early Christians themselves had little real choice in the matter, as they were relegated to the former reading whether they agreed with it or not, there are of course reputable individuals and denominations who have asserted the authority of the first reading of the silence even after the political space and historical opportunities were carved out for their participation. The latter reading of the silence, however, has by far been the more prominent and widespread of the two.[12]

A generation or so after the crucifixion of Christ, in a context where the coming apocalypse began to seem less imminent, the task of propagating and, indeed, clarifying the faith in the service of the nascent church fell to the Apostle Paul. It is his epistle to the Romans that contains the earliest, and for about seventeen hundred years, most authoritative treatment of the Christian-political question. In the famous passage found in Romans 13:1–6 we read,

> You must obey the governing authorities. Since all government comes from God, the civil authorities were appointed by God, and so anyone who resists authority is rebelling against God's decision, and such an act is bound to be punished. Good

---

12. Luke Bretherton has written a magisterial account of contemporary Christian political theology, *Christ and the Common Life*. That important volume appeared long after most of this book was finished, but his introduction to the thought of mainstream Christian denominations and how their approaches play out in the political arena around substantive questions concerning the economy, foreign relations, and other crucial areas of human political concern, as well as his account of the positive case for a Christian-inspired democratic regime, are inspired by his close and critical readings of Scripture and the Christian tradition broadly understood.

behavior is not afraid of magistrates; only criminals have anything to fear. If you want to live without being afraid of authority, you must live honestly and authority may even honor you. The state is there to serve God for your benefit. If you break the law, however, you may well have fear: the bearing of the sword has its significance. The authorities are there to serve God: they carry out God's revenge by punishing wrongdoers. You must obey, therefore, not only because you are afraid of being punished, but also for conscience's sake. This is the reason why you must pay taxes, since all government officials are God's officers. They serve God by collecting taxes.

Much as with Socrates's assertion in the *Apology* that a philosopher should lead a private rather than a public life, there is a sad irony in Paul's own martyrdom at the hands of the governing authorities. Of course, no coherent reading of that text can excuse the Christian of his or her ultimate responsibility to God and the primacy of obedience to God and his law. The first commandment, "You shall have no other Gods except me" (Exod 20:3), when coupled with Christ's injunction to not only render unto Caesar that which was his, but to God that which was God's, clearly anticipates that there will be incommensurable choices in the Christian's future. In such instances, the import of Paul's teaching, as evidenced by his own choice, is noncompliance without resistance, rebellion, or martyrdom.

History, however, would soon conspire against the oppositional opportunities afforded those early Christian witnesses and disciples through a confluence of events beginning with Constantine's Edict of Milan in AD 313 (the act that ended the official persecution of Christians and called for toleration of Christianity) and ending with the Edict of Thessalonica in AD 380, whereby Christianity was made the religion of the realm. By AD 392, when paganism was declared "treasonous," the persecution of other religions and sects by Christians operating through the apparatus of the state was in full swing. Obviously, the image of the Christian as political outsider could no longer be sustained, despite its theoretical potential for continuation. Now thoroughly entangled with the state and the questions of earthly power, Christians were forced to work out the boundaries of their new sociopolitical positions from within a dramatically transfigured historical context. The impact on the faith and the faithful, as well as the course of Western political history, was, to say the least, enormous and everlasting.

The theoretical task of working out that new relationship fell in large measure to St. Augustine. Unfortunately for him, however, that task was dramatically reoriented and transformed by the fall of Rome in AD 410. The impact on his thought and the subsequent relationship between Christianity,

Christians, and the state is much too vast to recount here in even the most modestly detailed manner. Suffice it to say that the next thousand years of Western history could be characterized as the working out of an incredibly tense, violent, and complicated relationship between the realms of the sacred and the secular. In the course of that process, the boundaries between Church and state shifted and re-shifted, contorted, amalgamated, and transposed to such a degree that discrete conversations in the domains of faith and theology and politics and power could no longer be meaningfully sustained. All important societal questions were both religious and political at the same time, and the tactics by all parties fused into one large struggle for power and superiority. Along the way compromises were made and remade culminating in a full-blown theory of Papal Monarchy by the thirteenth century. Nothing could be more symbolically emblematic of the eventual conflation of the two realms than the fact that among the models for Machiavelli's late thirteenth-century masterpiece of political realism, *The Prince*, was Pope Alexander VI!

In the course of that long history of struggle, the political place and status of the average Christian was lowly, muted, and mostly stagnant. As emblematic as Machiavelli's "hero" was of the developments in one layer of social strata, the reality laid bare by the Catholic Church's leading classical revivalist, Thomas Aquinas—that there was no functional equivalent in Latin for the Greek term *politeuesthai* (meaning "to act like a citizen")—was perhaps even more telling in its own right. The political plight of the average Christian was subjugation and serfdom rather than anything approximating a meaningful notion of citizenship. Relegated to Arendt's realm of production and necessity, the typical subject was neither seen nor heard as both their faith and their civic personalities stagnated and perished in the rote rituals and vice-like sociopolitical constrictions of the epoch. Although he was not a democratic theorist in any meaningful sense of the term, Aquinas's reconceptualization of natural law in such a way as to distinguish legitimate from illegitimate rulers and to provide an extra-human standard against which to judge positive law certainly provided an essential tool in the political tool chest for the republican/liberal theorists who followed in his wake a couple of centuries later. The articulation of a political sphere in the service of virtue and in opposition to sin reinvigorated political discourse and rescued political life—at least theoretically—from the domain of the wanton and/or the simply powerful. This recovery of a positive civic personality called to sit in public judgment would seem to reject the initial interpretation—the call to *apoliticalism*—of Christ's "silence" into serious question as the only legitimate interpretation. In other words, while it may still be the case that a turning away from the political sphere is a legitimate Christian response to the political world, so too, *pace* Aquinas, is active participation and citizenship when carried out with the appropriate intention and regard for Christian teaching and the lessons of the faith.

The gap, however, between the permissible, the possible, and the preferred, regarding the level and nature of Christian political participation would still need to be worked out politically and historically despite the heavy theological underbrush removal that had taken place. Among the more vivid and telling historical examples that can be used to exemplify the very real conflicts and dangers associated with such a working out, none is perhaps more apropos then that of the German Peasants' Revolt and the response to them of the great reformer himself, Martin Luther.

Among the most fundamental of Luther's theological contributions was his notion of the "priesthood of the believer." In many ways, this central idea was the foundation for the entire Reformation. It also contained, in somewhat chrysalistic form, the essence of modern liberalism with its foundational notions of liberty of conscience, equality, and individualism. While Luther himself explicitly rejected the notion of liberal-politicization of his theological contribution, there were others in his immediate world who grasped the possibilities right away. Between 1524 and 1526, the German peasants revolted against the German nobility and issued a treatise called the Twelve Articles, in which they asked for a series of rights that included positive rights to hunt, fish, and cut wood, and negative rights to be free from the excessive service and rents that were being demanded by the lords. In a very "Lutheran" idiom, they argued in Article 3:

> It has been the custom hitherto for men to hold us as their own property which is pitiable enough considering that Christ has redeemed and purchased us without exception, by the shedding of His precious blood, the lowly as well as the great. Accordingly, it is consistent with scripture that we would be free and we wish to be so.[13]

Luther's own response, when confronted with this attempted conflation, was summed up a little less polemically than his not-so-subtly-titled letter: "Against Robbing, Murdering, Hordes of Peasants" in his "Admonition to Peace," where he argued against the logic of the Articles directly writing:

> If your enterprise were right, then any man might become judge of another. Then authority, government, law, and order would disappear from the world; there would be nothing but murder and bloodshed.... This article would make all men equal, and

---

13. *Twelve Articles*, 160.

> turn the spiritual kingdom of Christ into a worldly kingdom; and that is impossible. A worldly kingdom cannot exist without an inequality of persons, some being free, some imprisoned, some lords, some subjects, etc.[14]

Despite Luther's call to arms and the vicious suppression of the radicalized peasants, the notion of Christianity as a conceptual resource and living force for political liberation was quickly being made present. In the next two centuries, such arguments moved at a furious *pace* from the radical fringe to the political mainstream as the age of revolution gave birth to the first modern republics in the West. Perhaps the most prominent and representative text of that era is John Locke's *Second Treatise*. Like many such texts, though, it is important to read that one as both giving form to a pre-existing "lived" reality as well as with an eye toward its foundational potential. In other words, while Locke's seminal work certainly functioned as a sort of intellectual independent variable for events that followed in the wake of its publication and the thinking of the historical actors who authored and inspired those events, it was also a dependent variable as well. Donald Lutz describes one of the most salient features of Lockean theory as being "the theory of consent articulated by John Locke can be found in many of its particulars a half century before the publication of the *Second Treatise*."[15]

In that well-known text, however, Locke does bring the relationship between politics and religion to rational existence quite vividly and succinctly. Rejecting both traditional divine-right theory and Luther's reconfigured state-centric version, Locke famously places natural law reasoning into service on behalf of individual rights and liberties, and, subsequently, on behalf of political self-determination and constitutionalism. Attributing being itself to the "workmanship of one omnipotent and infinitely wise Maker," Locke argues that the law of nature "teaches all mankind who will but consult it," that we are all "equal and independent," and that "no one ought to harm another in his life, health, liberty, or possessions."[16] Building on that foundation, Locke asserts later in the *Treatise* that the only legitimate exercise of power by one person over another must be the by-product of mutual consent. In his words, "Men being, as has been said, by nature free, equal, and independent, no one can be put out of his estate and subjected to the political power of another without his own consent."[17] Yet, even this consent is itself limited as a result of our condition as created beings.

14. Luther, "Admonition to Peace," 171, 181.
15. Lutz, "Liberty and Equality," 227.
16. Locke, *Second Treatise of Government*, 5.
17. Locke, *Second Treatise*, 54.

As Locke puts it in an earlier section of the text, "no man can by agreement pass over to another that which he has not in himself—a power over his own life."[18] That power is reserved for the Maker. Such it is that Christian liberty is not to be confused with license or an idolatrous or prideful individualism. Such a mindset harkens back to the neglected clause of Article 3, where the revolting peasants went on to delimit their own claims to liberty arguing: "Not that we want to be absolutely free and under no authority. God does not teach us that we should lead a disorderly life according to the lusts of the flesh, but that we should live by the commandments . . ."[19]

So it is that theorists and political actors operating from Christian foundations sought to make manifest the ontological status and proper interrelationship of individualism, liberty, equality, consensual and limited government, obedience, and order. Both tyranny and atomistic-libertarianism must be understood as antithetical to this emergent sociopolitical ontology. However, getting the theological argument "right" is, of course, not the same thing as saying much about the world as it is; as the saying goes—even the Devil believes in God. Conforming the world to the Word, if you will, ultimately involves action and questions of power and its uses. In multifaceted ways the political history in the West during the seventeenth and eighteenth centuries provides a number of different windows through which to view various attempts to work out in real time the answers to the political and social questions that emerged from this theological point of departure. Broadly speaking, the most important forces at work are two of the perennial political constants, "construction" and "destruction." Christian citizens engaged wholeheartedly in both.

As alluded to above, it was certainly the case that Locke's *Treatise* gave form and intellectual coherence to what was an already extant political "substance." The centrality of consent and the notion of the "contracted" community should be seen as the defining characteristics of that "substance." These ideas, in turn, cannot be understood fully without serious consideration of the Christian ontology from which the most ardent adherents and prominent political thinkers and actors derived their respective rationales and justifications. This is not to say that some sort of "class" analysis is out of place, but rather that no correct mode of analysis can be wholly detached from this crucial theological nexus without begetting a serious misunderstanding of the period. While the larger history of Locke's political form is at least as old as the book of Exodus, it is best exemplified in its "modern"

---

18. Locke, *Second Treatise*, 16.
19. *Twelve Articles*, 160.

iteration by the American Puritans.[20] The term that best acknowledges its lineage while maintaining its contemporary relevance and descriptive value is the idea of the *covenanted community*. Though there is an expanding literature on this subject, I rely here on the work of Donald Lutz for developing my conceptual framework.[21]

While the idea of a "social contract" may be appropriate for comprehending the general *ethos* of the early liberal political world, it is too imprecise to apply to Locke's work and the reality of the American Puritans. Lutz distinguishes among three terms that have been used frequently to refer to the collective agreements entered into by individuals and groups of individuals, namely: contracts, compacts, and covenants.[22] Acknowledging that they are often used interchangeably, Lutz argues that each denotes a different form of agreement. In his words:

> A contract usually implied an agreement with mutual responsibilities on a specific matter. A contract carried with it a restricted commitment such as a business matter or a marriage, and involved relatively small groups of people. The contract could be enforced by law, but did not itself have the force of law.
>
> A compact, on the other hand was a mutual agreement or understanding that was more in the nature of a standing rule. ... The word had the root meaning of "knitting together" or "bringing the component particles closely and firmly into the whole." A compact, therefore, was an agreement creating something that we would recognize as a community.
>
> A covenant ... was any agreement established or secured by God ... had God as the witness and securer of the agreement. A religious covenant thus was essentially an oath, and if it established a political community, political obligation was secured by the oath, rather than merely resting upon the fact of consent having been given.[23]

Among the early American Puritans, the notion of compacting together in covenanted communities was the formative rule.[24] Those acts of political "construction" initially predated Locke's work by fifty or sixty years, but they represented an attempt to give full meaning to the idea of Christian

---

20. See Elazar and Kincaid, *Covenant Connection*.
21. Lutz, "Liberty and Equality."
22. Lutz, "Liberty and Equality," 227.
23. Lutz, "Liberty and Equality," 227–28.
24. See Lutz, *Popular Consent and Popular Control*.

citizenship as it had been developing since the time of Aquinas. Those civil compacts, in Lutz's words,

> were often viewed as instruments for enhancing the keeping of the religious covenant, and in colonial documents and early state constitutions, we find statements outlining the Calvinist virtues of frugality, moderation, hard work, etc., and the dedication of civil society to the creation of a Christian way of life.[25]

These attempts to build a series of "cities on the hill," so to speak, represent the ultimate attempt to make the world conform to the Word as it had come to be understood by mid-seventeenth-century Protestantism. Back home (England), however, such acts of "construction" were fundamentally impeded by a recalcitrant and entrenched older order. There, political "destruction" became the order of the day.

The Puritan Revolution of the 1640s represented the flip side of the political coin to the American cities on the hill. Denied the quasi-blank slate of the American "state of nature," the Puritans of the English middle class were forced to engage the forces of George I on the battlefield in order to secure political rights and power. Fighting under the mantra "no bishop, no king," they cut off the head of divine-right both literally and figuratively and created the first piece of political space for liberal-republican political constructs in the kingdom. While that first attempt was both deeply flawed and short lived, it did open the door to the eventual consolidation and gains that would take place during Locke's day thirty years later in the Glorious Revolution. There is little doubt that numerous non-religious forces played large roles in the destructive and constructive events of the period. There is also little doubt that from Aquinas's work on the question of tyrannicide to the Huguenot tract *Vindiciae contra Tyrannos* (*A Defense of Liberty Against Tyrants*) to the closing sections of Locke's work, where he lays out a natural law justification for political revolution that the legitimacy of taking up arms against unjust rulers was couched in a religious language of sin, judgment, purification, and redemption. Whatever the particulars, the larger import of this movement was the sense that obedience to God and his will as discerned was to be unconditional and obedience to men and rulers was always conditional and tentative based on their keeping the faith.[26]

It is, of course, exactly the tension between religion and politics or church and state embodied in such a construction that continues to fuel contemporary debates in American politics over the proper relationship

25. Lutz, "Liberty and Equality," 230.
26. See Duncan, *Anti-Federalists*, ch. 1.

between the spheres. Despite the nation's overtly religious beginnings and persistently high levels of religiosity, there has been a strong and decisive shift toward strict separation and exclusionism driven, ironically, by the very claims of individual rights and liberties that were first secured for citizens in the West in the name of religion itself. Such a situation is no doubt the by-product of the movement from founding small independent communities and even relatively homogenous states to founding a pluralistic nation-state. Whatever its validity in the general scheme of American politics, James Madison's initial solution to the question of factions in Federalist Paper 10 has worked out almost seamlessly in the area of religion in American politics. Faiths, denominations, and sects have multiplied endlessly with each iteration and variation ultimately succumbing to the countervailing force of provisional majorities, the state, or their own desire to preserve theological autonomy and integrity in their relegation to, or acceptance of, "privatization." In other words, the price that most religious groups have paid for being mostly left alone by other citizens and the state is their reciprocal agreement to leave others alone as well. The questions I want to raise in the next sections have to do with whether this "check your religion at the door" approach to American citizenship is theologically sound, legally/constitutionally required, politically desirable, and actually feasible. By way of prelude, my answers will be no, no, no, and no.

FAITHFUL CITIZENSHIP

The faithful who would be true disciples can find numerous scriptural calls to act from and by their faith. While James's dictum that "faith is like that: if good works do not go with it, it is quite dead" (2:17) is perhaps the most widely cited passage, there are many such exhortations to act on the teachings of Christ. For example, in Luke 6:46–49, we read,

> Why do you call me, "Lord, Lord," and not do what I say? Everyone who comes to me and listens to my words and acts on them—I will show you what he is like. He is like the man who when he built his house dug, and dug deep, and laid the foundations on rock; when the river was in flood it bore down up on that house but could not shake it, it was so well built. But the one who listens and does nothing is like the man who built his house on soil, with no foundations: as soon as the river bore down on it, it collapsed; and what a ruin that house became!

Without piling on a series of proof texts, there are other ways to make the same theological case for the requirement of publicness among Christians beginning with the single most important moment of Christian history—the Incarnation itself. As the *Catechism of the Catholic Church* puts it, "Belief in the true Incarnation of the Son of God is the distinctive sign of the Christian faith."[27] Without digging too deeply into the theological history surrounding the understanding of the Incarnation, the belief that in Jesus Christ, God became man while remaining God, and that, in doing so, God became like man in all things except sin, has profound historical/social implications for believers. By entering into human history concretely, Christ validates and ennobles the "city of man" and, in turn, the lives of human beings dwelling within it. As Michael Himes claims of the Incarnation,

> Catholics try to hold this belief radically and so insist that in Christ God does not merely seem to be human or act in a human way, but has become human. In the words of an ancient hymn quoted in Philippians 2:6–11, he has become human as all human beings are human, that he is like us in all things except sin. The Catholic tradition has recognized that, if this radical claim of the Incarnation is true, then you and I and God share humanity in common and so, to become like God, we should be as fully human as we can. Thus, whatever enriches and deepens our humanity, whatever makes us braver, wiser, more intelligent, more responsible, freer, more loving, makes us holy, i.e., like God.[28]

Taking Aristotle's assertion at face value for now, when he argues that "the science that studies the supreme good for man is politics,"[29] and combining it with the logic of the Incarnation, it is a fairly straightforward move to claim that properly discerning what is "good for man" provides a critical path toward becoming more "fully human" and, hence, more "like God." Since what is meant by "politics" is by definition public (of the polity, or *polis*) rather than private (of the household, or *oikos*), the relationship between a Christian faith grounded in a radical understanding of the Incarnation and publicness becomes logically self-evident. To echo Barth, such a faith cannot, by definition, be private without committing a serious theological error and distortion of a properly understood faith.[30] Aristotle's understanding of the political is, of course, significantly broader and more encompassing than the limited and pejorative views of politics in

---

27. *Catechism of the Catholic Church*, 463.
28. Himes, "Finding God in All Things," 101–2.
29. Aristotle, *Ethics*, 64.
30. For the best compact account of this line of thought, see Himes and Himes, *Fullness of Faith*; Marty, *Public Church*.

contemporary discourse where common conceptions of what is truly political tend to be linked inextricably to various forms of state action and the work of the political class itself. Hence, to argue that Christianity—especially in its Catholic variety—is *public* and therefore *political* by nature is not the same thing as claiming that the state and its functions and various appendages and apparatuses are beholden to the church or the faith in its normal course of operation. Instead, it is meant to suggest that the state does not rightfully possess a monopoly over public space.

Although this notion of a "shared" public space flies in the face of much of modern thought from Machiavelli and Hobbes to Rousseau and, of course, Marx, who depicted the state's autonomy and dominance in the public sphere, for better and worse, as unrivaled as it is, it may be more reasonable and accurate to embrace the former understanding if our intent is to understand the human experience as it is actually lived. In particular, one who is simultaneously a Christian and a citizen cannot neatly compartmentalize their psyches and commitments such that they can be one and not the other on demand. To be both a Christian and a citizen is to be both always and everywhere at the same time.[31] While the roles might be intellectually distinctive like that of a father and a husband, the person as a person is not divisible. Hence, I would read many state-centric accounts of public space as normative arguments rather than descriptive accounts of the political world, i.e., what should "trump" what, rather than an empirical account or factual depiction. However, critical questions remain unanswered: namely, *how* that public space should be shared and *how* the nature of the relationship between faith and politics ultimately will be structured in any given place and at any given time.

THE AMERICAN PUBLIC SQUARE

In their year 2000 letter to the faithful, titled "Faithful Citizenship: Civic Responsibility for a New Millennium," the National Conference of Catholic Bishops conclude with the following call:

> We urge all citizens to register, vote and stay involved in public life, seeking the common good and renewing our democracy.
> The call to faithful citizenship raises a fundamental question. What does it mean to be a believer and a citizen in the year 2000 and beyond? As *Catholics*, we can celebrate the Great Jubilee by recommitting ourselves to carry the values of the Gospel and church teaching into the public square. As *citizens*, we can and

31. Neuhaus, *Naked Public Square*.

must participate in the debates and choices over the values, vision, and leaders that will take our nation into the next century. This dual calling of faith and citizenship is at the heart of what it means to be Catholic in the United States.[32]

As argued throughout this chapter, such a call should not be seen as inconsistent with Christianity, and, indeed, should be seen as a legitimate requirement of the faith in its publicness. Christians, as the standard metaphor goes, are called to be the "leaven" in their society for the common good.[33] However, what is authorized and required by the faith of Christian citizens is no guarantee of what is constitutionally or legally permitted by the particular place and time in which they find themselves. Despite the propensity of Americans to be both believers in God (92 percent) and Christians (86 percent) of some ilk, there is a strong bias in favor of the general notion of the separation of church and state that makes a phrase like "carry the values of the gospel and church teaching into the public square" problematic and discomforting for many Americans, including many who believe in the gospel and the teachings of the Catholic Church. Why that is the case, given the high degree of religiosity and the large proportion of faithful in the nation, is an important question that needs to be addressed.

The three broad possible answers given here are speculative rather than empirical, and do not need to be mutually exclusive. First, despite their own faithfulness, large segments of the American public have internalized and embraced the idea of a privatized religion, whose public effects and political consequences are to be kept indirect in the name of minority rights, toleration, or some sort of devotion to "neutral discourse."[34] Second, their religion is viewed as something strictly personal and otherworldly in its concerns and objects, and is therefore considered unrelated to either the public sphere or to politics proper. Or third, despite their desire to bring their faith to bear on the political world, they are legally restrained from doing so by the state and its representatives. However, none of these speak to the motives or desires of those who are not religious and do not have faith. Regarding to the first point, it strikes me that such a position simply

32. United States Conference of Catholic Bishops, *Forming Consciences for Faithful Citizenship*, 11.

33. "The kingdom of heaven is like the yeast a woman took and mixed in with three measures of flour till it was leavened all through" (Matt 13:33).

34. For the most comprehensive treatment of this idea, see Rawls, *Political Liberalism*. See also Ackerman, *Social Justice in the Liberal State*. I would also argue that aside from internalizing on some level these academic arguments, the typical citizen's lack of confidence and ability to articulate the tenets of their faith leads to a certain kind of embarrassment and reticence to engage others with whom they do not share a tradition.

cannot bear the weight of even simple observation. Outside of academic circles, most people simply do not think with that level of sophistication (and often do not trust those who do). The second point is probably more valid in America given the basic contours of what Harold Bloom called the "American Religion."[35] However, this is as more of a cultural artifact than it is a theologically valid position. It also is much more pronounced among certain Protestant denominations and sects than it is among Catholics. Though to the extent that the position is held by certain believers, it is not politically relevant from a *praxis* perspective insofar as those who hold such positions are themselves not seeking any share of public space, only protection from it. Hence, it is the third point that really brings the question to a head. Americans are uncomfortable bringing their faith and its commitments (or having others do so) into the public sphere because they believe that they are in some manner trespassing against the formal or common law of the land. The question then becomes whether such a belief is warranted, and, if so, whether the "law" they are responding to is properly grounded, legitimate, and just within the context of the American regime.

Regarding the sagacity of the belief itself, I believe that there is little room for argument that the American public square is legally inhospitable to most forms of faith-based public policy, let alone attempts to "sanctify" the public sphere. One need only consult the determination on the part of courts to banish even the most banal and trite expressions of "faith" or religious belief from the public square. Stories abound of grade school children sent home from school for passing out prayers, praying at the lunch table, and so on. Traditional blessings at high school graduations or before football games are the subjects of state intervention as if one moment the people of small town USA will be praying that God blesses their children as they go forth in the world and the next some latter-day Charlemagne will be receiving the presidential oath of office from an American Pope. Now while

---

35. See Bloom, *American Religion*. Briefly, Bloom's argument then was that American religion in most of its varieties and denominations had succumbed to a certain kind of Gnosticism which placed the individual's relationship with God at the center of their "faith" and intellectualized their understandings such that shared understandings and authoritative understandings were severely diminished. Now three decades later, I believe that the significant growth in American's who describe themselves as "spiritual" but not "religious" is the next iteration of Bloom's thesis come to the fore. Here, I would also point to Neuhaus, who notes with concern the thesis that "truly 'indigenous' American religion is incorrigibly individualistic, experiential, subjective, and therefore only 'emotivist' in its public assertions." As evidence of underlying symptoms of the public sphere's "nakedness," he cites a little later Jerry Falwell's famous (infamous?) claim in the face of the civil rights movement's call on people of faith for support, "Preachers are not called to be politicians but to be soul winners." Neuhaus, *Naked Public Square*, xii, 10.

admittedly a touch polemical, I do not mean to diminish the real pain some people may have experienced by either feeling excluded by the actions of majorities or from a sense of compulsion to assent in some manner to something antithetical to their own consciences. However, the notion that any of these actions and a host of others actually rise to the level of an "establishment of religion" on par with something like the Church of England should strike even the most strident as more than a little silly. If that assertion rings at all true, then the reasonable person must assume that there is something more going on than a farfetched fear of theocracy.

I would argue that the subtext of the virulent and even reactionary attempts to banish religion from the public square is not ultimately based on a heartfelt fear of a theocratic state emerging in the United States, but rather on a less substantially articulated *positive* political program of secularization and an ideology of secularism. Himes and Himes provide an important and useful set of definitions and offer a crucial distinction between these two concepts that is important for this line of argument:

> Secularization designates the fact of the removal of many areas of social life—the arts, education, law, government, economic institutions—from the control of religious bodies. Secularism is an ideological denial of the reality of transcendence.[36]

Like the authors, I would argue that secularization has been by and large beneficial for both the specific institutions and disciplines that are now free to pursue the logic of their respective subject areas without the confusion often wrought by certain kinds of inappropriate categorical juxtapositions. An easy example of this would be something like the removal of astronomy from the confines of a nonscientific, theologically anchored vision that required geocentrism as its starting point. The benefits, however, of discreet shifts toward secularization do not also apply to a secular worldview that would, by its own logic, leave no public space for religion or theology.

At its simplest, the secular is aligned with the temporal and the worldly and is best described as something "living for an age or ages." This renders any claims of transcendence moot. In turn, all truth claims are historically particularized in that they become true for now, but not simply true. Everything becomes alienable just as everything may become permitted. However, just like exclusionists often overemphasize the true threat of theocracy, those who fear secularism tend to radically overstate the likelihood of nihilism. Neither are real and immediate threats in America. Nihilism, though, is not the real issue as even values unmoored from the

---

36. Himes and Himes, *Fullness of Faith*, 3.

transcendent are still values—tradition is still a powerful and respectable force. What *is* at issue is whether values that *are* grounded in something transcendent will be allowed to have import and a public hearing under a secular regime and age. Like all ideologies, secularism seeks hegemony. At its most benign, it will privatize religion and bar it from the public square. At its most insidious, it will seek to eradicate it from all aspects of human existence—including even the consciences of individuals. Liberal-secular regimes, like France, engage wholeheartedly in the attempt to privatize religion. Non-liberal secular regimes, like the former Soviet Union, engaged ruthlessly in the latter (as the character Winston Smith came to understand in *1984*, 2 + 2 really could equal 5).

The positive side of secularism is the fundamental human liberation it offers us—in a secular regime we are limited only by the laws of nature (not to be confused with natural law), tradition, and our own wills and imaginations. That, of course, is also the dark side of secularism, as much of the twentieth century bears witness to. Not all brands of human "creativity" are worthy of respect. Unfortunately, what secularism cannot ultimately do is justify the choice between a liberal-secular regime and a non-liberal-secular regime. As such, all past, present, and future political arrangements become equally valid even if we do not find them equally preferable or desirable. The trouble for Christians who are citizens in such regimes is that they cannot accept secularism without rejecting their Christianity. Such a truth is exceptionally odd when we consider the fact that Christians have lived as Christians under virtually every other political ideology, regime type, and economic system that has existed and ascended to hegemonic status in the last two thousand years. A brief list of such entities would include all of Aristotle's regime types: monarchy, tyranny, aristocracy, oligarchy, constitutional democracy, and even anarchy, as well as capitalist regimes, socialist regimes, fascist regimes, and so on. There are Christian Democrats and Christian Republicans, there are Christian liberals and Christian conservatives, there are Christian feminists and Christian environmentalists, and on and on the list could go. What there cannot be, however, are Christian secularists (though there can certainly be Christians who favor various forms of secularization itself). From my vantage point, other than those political orders that are explicitly and repressively non-Christian theocracies or totalitarian, the only system or ideological order that the Christian cannot find some sort of "home" in is one predicated on an all-encompassing secularism. At issue here, then, is whether the United States of America is, by intention and design or by default and political fiat, the kind of place, ultimately, that cannot or will not shelter people of faith. Simply put, can you be both a citizen and a Christian in America?

Two broad questions emerge from that last query which need to be addressed, the first is historical and the second is normative. The first question can be framed like this: Was the United States founded, and hence intended, to be a secular nation? This is a *constitutional* question. The second, and much less manageable question, is whether, regardless of the answer to the former, *should* the United States be a secular nation? This is a distinctively *political* question. Taking my own cue from Hartz, I would argue that his dictum that "law has flourished on the corpse of philosophy in America" could just as readily be changed to "law has flourished on the corpse of *politics* in America." For Hartz, the Supreme Court (as he saw it prior to what many would think of as the judicial activism of the 1960s) was best characterized as a set of "Talmudic judges examining a single text."[37] As such, the Court and its members took control of numerous issues that only in America would have been thought of as ripe for constitutional adjudication rather than something to be decided at the ballot box or in the legislative branches of the regime. In other words, in many instances the United States Supreme Court has conflated *political* questions and *constitutional* ones, such that the distinction is not even relevant for most of the American citizenry any longer. As such, the American courts in general, and the Supreme Court in particular, have become the forums in which we settle the most pressing and divisive questions concerning how we will live together and what the public square will look like.

Although it is now unchallenged in the understanding of the Court that it is a policy-making body rather than strictly an interpretive one, even the Court operates within a historical context. While the policy making role certainly enhances the stature of the Court and its sheer political power, it also has the effect of rendering the men and women who serve on it more pedestrian and ordinary.[38] In turn, they are more readily seen as enfolded, encumbered, and bounded by their time and place than may be desirable for people whose roles are often depicted as being above the political fray. Related to the logic of "linguistic contextualism" (the idea that you could not think what you could not say) described in the introduction, my own approach to the question of the judiciary, religion, and the public square draws

---

37. Hartz, *Liberal Tradition in America*, 10.

38. While most of us are probably suspect at this late day of Hamilton's nod toward the idea of a "natural aristocracy" in Federalist Paper 78, where he claims: "Hence it is that there can be but few men in the society who will have sufficient skill in the laws to qualify them for the stations of judges. And making the proper deductions for the ordinary depravity of human nature, the number must be still smaller of those who unite the requisite integrity with the requisite knowledge if the members of the judiciary are, indeed, just like the rest of us, then the claims for their unique powers become highly questionable to say the least." Quoted in Madison et al., *Federalist Papers*, 442.

heavily on the logic outlined by Steven D. Smith, who in turn relied on a framework suggested by William James. In his densely researched article "Separation and the 'Secular': Reconstructing the Disestablishment Decision," Smith rejects—as do I—the viability of a strategy of "originalism" that would entail "psychoanalyzing the dead" founders as overly complicated, unwieldy, and too prone to error to yield verifiable and recognizably significant—let alone replicable—results. Too many framers, too many texts, too many variables to control for—indeed, too much subjectivity and selectivity required of the would-be investigator, whether judge or scholar.[39] In place of that approach, Smith suggests relying on a historical strategy that revolves around the notion of a "public understanding" and the Jamesian idea of a "genuine option." This is described in the following manner:

> According to James, a genuine option represents a choice between *live* alternatives—ones that are real and possible and that a person may seriously contemplate adopting. A genuine option is also a choice between alternatives that are *momentous*, not merely trivial. The differences between genuine and nongenuine options, James pointed out, inhere not in the options themselves but in the perspective of the chooser.[40]

As Smith points out, James was concerned with personal decisions, but the idea has great usefulness for understanding collective choice as well. The assumptions of such a move would mean that in order for the public to choose something, they would actually have to believe that it was a realistically possible alternative and that it was worth doing, i.e., nontrivial. In the context of this argument, any question about the Supreme Court's role in the area of religion and politics would have to have involved choices from among political/constitutional arrangements that the public could relate to as real choices from within the historical horizon in which they lived and chose. An easy way to get at this would be to ask why there were no Marxists in the republic? The answer, of course, is because such a thing would not actually be possible for another sixty years—it was not a real choice. In light of this discussion, the question then becomes what sort of role was *possible* for the Supreme Court and its members under the circumstances of the eighteenth-century political mind as it existed in America, and, in the context of what was then chosen, what sort of jurisprudence concerning the relationship between religion and politics was possible for they themselves to choose as

---

39. For a sweeping overview of the complexity of the founder's views on religion, see Huston, *Founders on Religion*.

40. Smith, "Separation and the 'Secular,'" 4.

a "genuine" model. Simply put, was a fully and completely secular public square really a genuine choice at the time?

The answer Smith gives and that I concur with is that secularism was *not* a genuine choice. I will explain why in a moment, but to make the point clear here, if the founders themselves could not conceive *politically* of a naked public square with regard to the relationship between religion and politics, it is logically impossible that they could have *intended* to give the Supreme Court or any other entity a mandate to secularize it (the public square) *constitutionally*. Now while it may well be the case that their construction was either imprecise or malleable enough to allow such a thing to come to pass, it simply could not have been part of the intended design. The *Oxford English Dictionary* defines secularism as "the doctrine that morality should be based solely on regard to the well-being of mankind in the present life, to the exclusion of all considerations drawn from belief in God or in any future state."[41] Remembering that even the first great liberal—John Locke—did not apply his doctrine of toleration to atheists, and in keeping with the current framework, the simple question becomes whether such a doctrine was in fact a genuine *historical* alternative that we could imagine any serious American political thinker/actor choosing in the late eighteenth century? Common sense about the nature of the times suggests the answer is a simple no. Beyond that, however, the historical context in which the nation itself emerged provides significant evidence in support of the antisecularism thesis, as Smith so aptly demonstrates.

Calling secular government and politics "the option that wasn't," Smith makes a crucial distinction between the notion of "church" and the idea of "religion," the former being an institution and the latter being the foundation for a person's worldview and identity.[42] As Smith puts it:

> Religious premises, assumptions, and values provided the general framework within which most Americans thought about and discussed important philosophical, moral, and political issues. For that reason, Americans of the time could not seriously contemplate a thoroughly secular political culture from which religious beliefs, motives, purposes, rhetoric, and practices would be filtered out.[43]

Americans could entertain the notion of a separation between a particular or established church and the state—which of course they did as per the First Amendment's establishment clause. They too could have chosen what

41. See Glenn and Stack, "Is American Democracy Safe for Catholicism?," 5–48.
42. Smith, "Separation and the 'Secular,'" 7.
43. Smith, "Separation and the 'Secular,'" 7.

Smith calls "institutional relations" whereby the association of church and state "meant active and direct intervention by each institution in the internal decisions, functions, and affairs of the other";[44] that was clearly the most prevalent model since the fall of Rome. This, however, the founders of the national government—though not those of a number of American states—rejected. A public sphere that was bereft of religion and religious discourse, however, was not part of their option set. That possibility would need to be fostered and historically constructed at a later date.

To illustrate practically how this distinction between "church" and "religion" might be played out at the conceptual level, I would point to Locke's own formulation in *A Letter Concerning Toleration*, where he argues:

> It may indeed be alleged that the magistrate may make use of arguments, and thereby draw the heterodox into the way of truth, and procure their salvation. I grant it; but this is common to him with other men. In teaching, instructing, and redressing the erroneous by reason, he may certainly do what becomes any good man to do. *Magistracy does not oblige him to put off either humanity or Christianity.* But it is one thing to persuade, another to command; one thing to press with arguments, another with penalties.[45]

On my reading, the ability to compel with penalties would be the by-product of a conflated and "institutionally related" view of the relationship between church and state. Locke's formulation allows for a person's religion to be brought to bear in a very forceful, visible, and, indeed, influential manner even by the state's representatives, let alone the average citizen. This is a much more historically and theoretically plausible and genuine "choice" than the sort of bifurcated a-historical fabricated citizen-type proffered by theorists of "neutrality." If, then, secularism could not have been realistically chosen and church-state integration was rejected, what were the original and rudimentary constitutional contours and boundaries of the relationship and how did they evolve such that one option—integration—was rendered an anachronism and another that was hitherto unthinkable—secularism—became viable?

---

44. Smith, "Separation and the 'Secular,'" 5.
45. Locke, *Letter Concerning Toleration*, 20. Emphasis added.

JEFFERSON'S "WALL" AND RELIGION IN THE AMERICAN PUBLIC SQUARE

In 1802, President Thomas Jefferson responded to a letter from the Danbury Baptist Association that had inquired about his resistance to proclaiming national days of fasting and thanksgiving in the manner or his two predecessors, Washington and Adams. His careful and measured response[46] to their question has become the dominant metaphor undergirding much of modern constitutional jurisprudence regarding the establishment and free exercise clauses of the First Amendment. Jefferson writes,

> Believing with you that religion is a matter which lies solely between man & his god, that he owes account to none other for his faith and worship, that the powers of government reach actions only, and not opinions, I contemplate with sovereign reverence that the act of the whole American people which declared that their legislature should make no law respecting an establishment of religion, or prohibiting the free exercise thereof, thus building a wall of separation between church and state.[47]

Jefferson's metaphor delivered "religion" to the private realm and, thus, secularism made its way into the world of "genuine choice." This occurred despite the degree to which so much of Jefferson's own normative political theory and philosophy rested on the belief in at least a deity and the moral wisdom of Jesus Christ. Since the American public square could not have been a wholly secular one, the question remains: What did the First Amendment's clauses concerning establishment and free exercise actually mean, and how have they come to mean what they do today?

---

46. Despite numerous scholarly attempts to downplay or recast Jefferson's letter as either an insignificant "courtesy" note or actually a rebuff to "separationism," there is a good case to be made that Jefferson meant more or less what he said. In a brief editorial titled "Separation, Integration, and Accommodation," Derek Davis argues persuasively that Jefferson chose his words carefully and with firm intention. In a note to his attorney general, Levi Lincoln (whom Jefferson asked to carefully review the letter before sending it), Jefferson wrote, "Averse to receive addresses (letters), yet unable to prevent them, I have generally endeavored to . . . [make] them occasion, by way of answer, of sowing useful truths and principles among the people, which might germinate and become rooted among their political tenets. . . . The Baptist address . . . furnished an occasion, too, which I have long wished to find, of saying why I'd not proclaim fastings and thanksgivings, as my predecessors did." Davis, "Separation, Integration, and Accommodation," 8. It is important, however, to note that Jefferson's particularity and care extends to the use of the term "church" as compared to "religion." It is equally important as well to remember that this utterance itself had no constitutional standing despite its contemporary "common law" status among many Americans.

47. See "Jefferson's Wall of Separation Letter," 1.

On the first question, I take my lead from Michael Perry and the work of Glenn and Stack. Working out from the simple question, "What does the non-establishment norm forbid government to do?" Perry claims *pace* Justice Black in the *Everson* case,

> Government may not take any action that favors a church in relation to another church, or in relation to no church at all, on the basis of the view that the favored church is, as a church—as a community of faith—better along one or another dimension of value (truer, for example, or more efficacious spiritually, or more authentically American). The non-establishment norm deprives government of jurisdiction to make judgments about which church (or churches), if any, is as such better than another church or than no church. The norm requires government to be agnostic about which church—which community of faith— is better; government must act without regard to whether any church is in fact better.[48]

Neutrality between denominations, sects, religions, theology, and even faith itself is what the establishment clause demands—government cannot take a side on what are ultimately questions of conscience and belief. The clause itself, as interpreted, says nothing about individual citizens and what they may or may not do on the basis of their faith. It also says nothing about what elected representatives may do on the basis of faith. Instead, what it says is that you cannot tell other people what to believe or even to believe at all—one's faith makes its demands upon the individual ascribing to it, not those whom the person of faith acts upon. *Why* something is done is not supposed to be constitutionally significant, but rather *what* is actually done. Much like my unwillingness to try and psychoanalyze the dead to discern their true intentions, I am quite uncomfortable with attempts to know what is in a person's heart being viewed as a political question. In other words, while as a human being, philosopher, or a voter I am quite concerned with the reasons a person does a particular thing, as a person whom a law or piece of policy acts upon, I am only concerned with its effects. Hence, regarding the establishment clause itself, the only pertinent question is whether the government's action itself violates the principle of neutrality or agnosticism by compelling me to believe something that I do not believe or by treating another faith or faith itself as superior to mine or non-faith itself.

Now it may well be the case that certain actions taken by the government make it easier for certain people to practice their particular faith. Take, for example, things like school vouchers or tax write-offs for

---

48. Perry, *Under God?*, 6–7.

charitable donations: these neither compel nor favor faith, but rather allow it to proceed. To make a particularly banal analogy, the government builds a lot of roads and bridges but it does not, as far as I know, have a position on whether driving is itself "good" or "bad." Hence, the government's role is not one best compared to an arbitrator, but rather a referee, which is how Glenn and Stack more or less describe the original meaning of the establishment clause in their provocative essay, "Is American Democracy Safe for Catholicism?"

Using a distinction between "civil liberty" and "civil liberties" as their conceptual framework, Glenn and Stack argue that "'civil liberty' is the language of Blackstone, common law and *The Federalist*" (and I would add of John Winthrop and the New England Puritans as well).[49] It is defined as "no other than natural liberty, so far restrained by human laws and no further, as is necessary and expedient for the general advantage of the public."[50] Expounding on this theme, the authors quote a former Supreme Court Justice who was himself quoting Blackstone's editor and claimed that "civil liberty" consisted of "that state in which each individual has the power to pursue his own happiness according to his own best interest, and the dictates of his conscience, unrestrained, except by equal, just and impartial laws."[51] Noting that the laws need only be "equal, just, and impartial," the authors correctly suggest that the true emphasis is at least as much on restraining individuals as it is on liberating them. This "civil liberty regime" is contrasted to the contemporary notion of "civil liberties" that the authors argue is modern and steeped in the idea that "rights are trump."[52] In other words, in place of the significant emphasis the former regime placed on "restraint," the newer regime type gives much more weight to liberating the individual from various social or political restraints or prohibitions beyond those necessary for minimal order. Under such a regime, notions of the good give way to notions of the right, and individual choice and preference maximization becomes the dominant political position. In common parlance, this regime is best denoted by the claim: "I know what's best for me, and as long as I don't hurt anyone else, what I do is nobody's business but mine." To the extent that this mood comes to dominate, the number of laws regulating human behavior should consistently decrease and personal choices should continuously increase.

---

49. Glenn and Stack, "Is American Democracy Safe for Catholicism?," 11.
50. Glenn and Stack, "Is American Democracy Safe for Catholicism?," 11.
51. Glenn and Stack, "Is American Democracy Safe for Catholicism?," 11.
52. Glenn and Stack, "Is American Democracy Safe for Catholicism?," 12.

Since the primary source for determining what sorts of actions should be "restrained" in the name of the good was religion and its moral traditions, the "civil liberties regime" must, by implication, consciously and persistently drive religion and its mode of discourse out of the public square. However, this was not, historically speaking, a "genuine choice" for the American founders, citizens, or regimes in the late eighteenth century. As such, it could not have been intended by the Constitution itself. What was intended, Glenn and Stack's work persuasively suggests, was a much more *political* model of "public religious pluralism" that "permitted legislatures to work out pragmatically the relation between religious belief, churches, and government without conforming to a constitutional theory of what the outcome should be."[53] Quoting Madison in Federalist Paper 51, the authors claim that "the Madisonian regime publicly assumed that 'religious rights' included influencing public policy through truck and bargaining among the multiple sects." In Madison's words:

> In a free government, the security for civil rights must be the same as for religious rights. It consists in the one case in the multiplicity of interests and in the other, in the multiplicity of sects. The degree of security in both cases will depend on the interests and sects; and this may be presumed to depend on the extent of the country and number of people comprehended under the same government.[54]

This position is tantamount to what later on is called by liberals, like John Stuart Mill, a strong practical case for the notion of an unregulated "marketplace of ideas" argument. If the religious arguments for particular positions are indeed poor ones, or the policies promoted for religious reasons are wrongheaded, then why not air them in public and let the proverbial chips fall where they may so long as no one is forced to adopt those reasons or rationale against his or her will. The sheer act of voting itself always implies that someone will be compelled to live by a particular rule or under the electoral direction of someone they did not will, unless unanimity is achieved. Like Glenn and Stack, I believe that a fundamental shift has taken place in the American regime as a result of a critical change in the way in which the establishment clause was interpreted. That change was radically out of step with our political history and traditions.

---

53. Glenn and Stack, "Is American Democracy Safe for Catholicism?," 12.

54. Glenn and Stack, "Is American Democracy Safe for Catholicism?," 12. Also note that I have made this same general case in Duncan, "Liberalism and the Challenge of *Fight Club*."

While I will have more to say in a later chapter on the political-historical and theoretical underpinnings of this change in regime type, I would like to point to two rather ironic "sources" of the jurisprudence that emerged in the mid-twentieth century. First, it is ironic that a presently confused establishment clause jurisprudence represents the very notion of toleration itself. In the name of not infringing on anyone's right to a free conscience, the Supreme Court and much of American culture have decided that we ought not even be burdened by religiously inspired ideas or justifications in the public/political sphere. Take for example the case of a moment of silence for prayer and reflection which the court has struck down while suggesting that something called a moment for silent reflection might be constitutional. What real difference is there in the policy's outcome by inserting or removing the word prayer from the law? As long as no one is required to pray or reflect under penalty of expulsion, jail, or fine, what real difference is there? It may be the case that the policy itself is rather silly and it may even be the case that it cheapens prayer and religion (my own belief), but neither of those is a good constitutional reason for striking it down. The government has not taken a side because, as is always the case, when a government bothers to take a side on something, certain behaviors are rewarded and certain behaviors are punished—otherwise there is little reason for government action in the first place (certain symbolic acts excluded for now). What really makes privatization of religion or secularism in the name of tolerance ironic is the fact that tolerance and respect for religious diversity were themselves the by-product of serious religious thinking in the first place.[55] Theologically first and politically second, the early liberals like Locke and then later Jefferson and Madison understood that the only true faith was voluntary faith! In other words, to truly believe meant allowing others to choose for themselves. While there are certainly good practical political reasons for taking the same position (i.e., avoiding conflict), they are not principled or transcendent positions insofar as the goal is not freedom of conscience but peace. If the utility of an established church proved better at ensuring less conflict, then that is what pragmatism would require. It was religious thinkers who understood that there were things more important than peace.

The second quasi-ironic source of the shift in establishment clause jurisprudence is detailed in the work of Philip Hamburger, who makes a persuasive argument for the role of religious prejudice itself in helping foster the movement toward a secularist reading of the establishment clause.[56] In his lengthy history of the idea of separation of church and state in the

---

55. Smith, "Separation and the 'Secular,'" 9.
56. Hamburger, *Separation of Church and State*.

United States, Hamburger argues that among the political precursors to the secularist reading were late nineteenth- and early twentieth-century nativist and anti-Catholic/anti-Semitic movements like those associated with the Know-Nothings and the Ku Klux Klan. Disturbed by the advances of Catholics in American life and their attempts to share in public financing for their sectarian schools, secularists and certain groups of Protestants began using the arguments for the separation of church and state as a tool to deny them such benefits through what are now called Blaine Amendments. The political logic was quite simple, since Catholics—especially in the South—were in the distinct minority. Keeping the proliferation of separate schools from occurring and thus forcing Catholic children to attend majority Protestant public schools would simultaneously ensure that tax dollars were not divided and diverted more than need be, and that Catholics could be either "Americanized" or at least contained. The goal of such groups was never to secularize the public schools and remove religion from the classroom, but rather to convert or marginalize those whose religious beliefs they disagreed with. The double irony here is that their religious bigotry worked too well from their perspective while also turning the religiously inspired argument for religious toleration on its head.

Now none of the above is meant to suggest that by the time the Court made its earliest decisive moves in the direction of a secularized public square such arguments were driving their thinking on the matter. Nor does it mean that the arguments for separation might not stand once detached from their religious moorings or bigoted political context. Bad people can have good ideas and good conclusions can emerge from faulty premises. However, it does demonstrate the need on the part of those who would transform the public square to introduce alternative justifications for their decisions. Put another way, it makes precious little sense for someone to claim something to the effect of, "I have reasoned from religious premises as a political actor that religious premises are not to be admitted to the public square." Neither does it seem that any self-respecting Court by the mid-twentieth century in America could, with any public credibility, link its thinking to a convoluted political strategy designed to actually sustain a particular religion while suppressing or marginalizing others. Hence, intellectually at least, the Court deciding to begin the process of secularization has significant problems to overcome in that they could not use the original religious arguments for toleration without an odd duplicity. Neither could they rely on the bigoted strategy of their separationist predecessors with any legitimacy. Finally, the Constitution itself could not have meant historically what they were now beginning to say that it meant regarding the establishment clause. Thus, the move to the wall metaphor.

While a significant number of American citizens, including a number who ought to know better—journalists, judges, academics, and lawyers—regularly speak as if the phrase "separation of church and state" appeared somewhere in the Constitution, history and the document itself demur. Though the Supreme Court is clearly the most visible and powerful institution regarding the structure of the relationships between church and state and religion and politics, it too is obviously embedded in the larger political culture and therefore responds to the changing political climate as much (if not more) as it affects the nature and structure of the conversation and debate therein. In turn, the Court tends to be much less doctrinaire than many legal and academic scholars on questions of secularization and the establishment clause, but, therefore, they are also much less consistent. Where deductive logic readily dictates certain kinds of absolutist positions in the realm of thought and theory, politics proper muddles through routinely on the basis of certain kinds of cognitive dissonance and logical inconsistency. This is not necessarily a criticism, but rather a warning that there are real difficulties in attributing to the Court too much coherence in the area of establishment clause jurisprudence. However, if we do not demand precision so much as accuracy regarding the way the thought and law is trending, it is, I believe, possible to speak of an increasing tendency in the constitutional arena toward secularism and the privatization of religion. What is significantly less clear, however, is that there is a good *legal* or *constitutional* reason for the departure from the competitive pluralist model articulated by Glenn and Stack and asserted by Madison himself.

In 1947, without much in the way of justification, Jefferson's sentiments from his letter of 1802 made their first appearance in a Supreme Court decision and the once viable option of an established church in any political jurisdiction came officially to an end as the United States Supreme Court summarily began applying the non-establishment norm to the states as well as the national government. In turn, the other "genuine option" of "institutional relations," as Smith called it, met, for the first official time, the emergent option of a secularized public sphere. Fortunately, perhaps, constitutional questions are not conducted on the basis of dichotomous choices—secularization or institutional relations. The larger struggle is waged in the arena of seemingly small and deceptively inconsequential questions like whether families can be reimbursed for transportation to parochial schools, or whether states can loan textbooks to private school children, or whether children should be released from public schools to attend religious education classes, or whether tax deductions for tuition expenses at private schools are permissible, and so on. There are, of course, larger cases having to do with school prayer, voucher programs, school curriculum, and facilities usage to name a few. At each juncture, the Court and its changing membership is forced to configure and reconfigure the political sphere and the space afforded to religion within it, and citizens of faith have had to decide how to respond.

Since the 1940s, the resulting jurisprudence has not been particularly pretty or coherent, and confusion, discord, and vast public uncertainty concerning the relationship between religion and politics has been the result.[57] This already lengthy chapter is not the place to try and map out the various doctrinal rivers, streams, and tributaries that make up the uneven flow of establishment clause cases and "precedents." Instead, I would simply like to spend a little time "deconstructing" what, despite noted flaws over the last thirty or so years, is still considered *the* pivotal case in contemporary establishment clause jurisprudence, *Lemon v. Kurtzman*.[58] I do this to unearth the elements of the secularization shift itself and to demonstrate the very real viability of a naked public square as a now "genuine choice" and political-cultural signifier or mode of discourse.

---

57. Just by way of idiomatic comparison regarding the blatantly oppositional tone rather than outcome in two important and historically proximate establishment clause cases look at the following two passages, the first from the majority opinion in *Everson v. Board of Education*, 330 U.S. 1, 67 S. Ct. 504 (1947), and the second from the majority opinion in *Zorach v. Clauson*, 343 U.S. 306, 72 S. Ct. 679 (1952). Justice Black for the Court: "The 'establishment of religion' clause of the First Amendment means at least this: Neither a state nor the Federal Government can set up a church. Neither can pass laws which aid one religion, aid all religions, or prefer one religion over another. Neither can force nor influence a person to go to or to remain away from church against his will or force him to profess a belief or disbelief in any religion. No person can be punished for entertaining or professing religious beliefs or disbeliefs, for church attendance or non-attendance. No tax in any amount, large or small, can be levied to support any religious activities or institutions, whatever they may be called, or whatever form they may adopt to teach or practice religion. Neither a state nor the Federal Government can, openly or secretly, participate in the affairs of any religious organizations or groups and *vice versa*. In the words of Jefferson, the clause against establishment of religion by law was intended to erect 'a wall of separation between church and state.'" Justin Douglas for the Court: "We are a religious people whose institutions presuppose a Supreme Being. We guarantee the freedom to worship as one chooses. We sponsor an attitude on the part of government that shows no partiality to any one group and that lest each flourish according to the zeal of its adherents and the appeal of its dogma. When the state encourages religious instruction or cooperates with religious authorities by adjusting the schedule of public events to sectarian needs, it follows the best of our traditions. For it then respects the religious nature of our people and accommodates the public service to their spiritual needs. To hold that it may not would be to find in the Constitution a requirement that the government show callous indifference to religious groups. That would be preferring those who believe in no religion over those who do believe."

58. *Lemon v. Kurtzman*, 403 U.S. 602, 91 S. Ct. 2105, 29 L. Ed. 2d 745.

The *Lemon* case, decided in 1971, was actually three cases consolidated into one. At issue was a set of programs in Rhode Island and Pennsylvania that provided aid to church-affiliated elementary and secondary schools. The support included subsidizing teacher's salaries and purchasing textbooks and instructional materials for the teaching of secular subjects. The Court found that both programs violated the establishment clause of the US Constitution. Chief Justice Burger wrote the majority opinion and created what is now known as the Lemon Test. That test contains the following elements that a piece of legislation needs to meet if it is going to pass constitutional muster: "First, the statute must have a secular legislative purpose; second, its principal or primary effect must be one that neither advances nor inhibits religion; finally, the statute must not foster excessive government entanglement with religion."[59] Despite an early admission by Burger that "candor compels acknowledgement, moreover, that we can only dimly perceive the lines of demarcation in this extraordinarily sensitive area of constitutional law," and noting that "the language of the Religion Clauses of the First Amendment is at best opaque," he feels comfortable asserting that "its authors did not simply prohibit the establishment of a state church or a state religion. . . . Instead they commanded that there should be 'no law *respecting* an establishment of religion.'"[60]

The emphasis on the term "respecting" is Burger's, and much of the edifice erected in *Lemon* stands on the meaning given to it. This is the word which allows the Court to read into the framers' motives their own contemporary construction of the clause without seeming to violate the integrity of the text. It does so by allowing the Court to pursue probabilistic thinking. As Burger puts it: "A given law might not *establish* a state religion but nevertheless be one 'respecting' that end in the sense of being a step that could lead to such an establishment and hence offend the First Amendment."[61] Even if we leave aside the historical truth that at least regarding the states no such thing could have been intended given the existence of established churches and religious tests for office, etc., that existed before, during, and after the writing and ratification of the Constitution, and even if we grant the legitimacy of the application of those provisions to the states via incorporation, the apparent ease with which the Court moves from a construction whose focus is on the verb (establish) to one that gives equal weight to the preposition (respecting) should strike us as problematic. Furthermore, to then read the term "respecting" (i.e., regarding, concerning) as an invitation to look

---

59. *Lemon v. Kurtzman*, cited in *Constitutional Interpretation*, 1409.
60. *Lemon v. Kurtzman*, cited in *Constitutional Interpretation*, 1409.
61. *Lemon v. Kurtzman*, cited in *Constitutional Interpretation*, 1409.

as carefully or carelessly as one might like, as indicated by the phrase "*in the sense of being a step that could lead to such an establishment,*" would seem to create a kind of judicial "elastic clause" regarding the relationship between religion and politics that empowers the Court to substitute *its* preferences and will for that of the legislature and the people who elected them. Harkening back to Perry, we might ask why the Court does not simply ask whether the laws in question demonstrate a preference for religion over nonreligion or for the authority/truthfulness of one faith over another, or attempt to take a side in questions of conscience and belief? Those questions would seem to shift the burden away from what may or may not happen in the future, to what is immediate and present. At its simplest, the question becomes: In the context of a Bill of Rights designed to protect individuals, who is harmed, imposed upon, or coerced by a particular policy, and does that harm, imposition, or act of coercion rise to the level of a constitutionally impermissible action on the part of the government?

Certainly, the laws in question make it easier for private schools to operate and for parents to choose to send their children there, but who is actually harmed in a constitutionally meaningful way with regard to faith, belief, or conscience? If the "harm" is not particularized but instead general, potential, or abstract, it is unclear that it would meet the test of an actual case or controversy in need of constitutional adjudication. By focusing on who may be "helped" by a particular policy rather than who is actually harmed, the Court would seem to be erecting a rather odd standard that equates facilitating someone's preferences with fostering or generating them. Put another way, even if the establishment clause means that some government policy cannot act to promote a particular belief or system of religious beliefs any more than it could to prevent or deny them, it is most improbable that money filtered to religious schools would really cause someone to adopt a belief or religion just for the benefit of some indirect tax dollars. Though the argument no doubt can be made that such spending may reduce the allocation to public schools or other programs, there is nothing that compels a given legislature to appropriate money at any specified level to those schools or other programs that would make the zero-sum approach anything more than a chimera. Now the fact that a given legislature or legislator may lack the political will to offset any loss to the public schools or other programs through the raising of additional monies in the form of increased taxes or fees is an important consideration for a voter but not a judge to consider. A public that believes that its elected representatives are misspending public funds has recourse available to solve its own problem without need of the Court or the Constitution.

The fact that the Court did not choose to see the case as a question best left to citizens and legislators when it was clearly possible for them to have done so begs the question as to what the Court's own constructional intent was. In other words, if their opinion did not prevent some demonstrable harm from taking place, it is only reasonable to assume that they were sustaining something on the basis of either principle itself or were intending to promote some perceived good. Bereft of preventing harm or promoting some "good," there is precious little reason for law in the first place. Since there is no demonstrable harm being suffered by an individual or group so much as there is a legitimate disagreement over a piece of public policy (or a mistake on the part of the Court in its jurisprudential reasoning), we must ask what principle or good the Court itself hopes to achieve by its decision. Without any irony intended, it is my contention that the "good" that the Court intends is the separation of religion and politics. While the language they use will suggest that some harm is being avoided, it is in fact a "potential" or "future" harm that they ultimately are attempting to secure the American public square and its constituent elements from, rather than an existing or even immediate threat.

After noting that the policies in question easily satisfy the first two prongs of the test—there is a "secular purpose" and the "primary effect neither advances nor inhibits religion"—the Court hones in on the issue of "excessive entanglement" as its focal point. In the words of the opinion, "We conclude that the cumulative impact of the entire relationship arising under the statues in each State involves excessive entanglement between government and religion."[62] This, however, is in reality a projection and extrapolation of the Court's rather than a legal finding or fact. While the Court is no doubt correct when it notes the difficulty that "inheres in the situation" when a teacher is asked to differentiate the "religious from the purely secular aspects of pre-college education," it is unclear why the degree of difficulty in doing something ought to be a *legal* mark against it. Many things that government has attempted to do are fanciful, difficult, and impracticable—they are prudent or imprudent, not constitutional or unconstitutional based on such assessments. While the Court is subsequently quick to point out that "a dedicated religious person, teaching in a school affiliated with his or her faith and operated to inculcate its tenets, will inevitably experience great difficulty in remaining religiously neutral," they say nothing to justify why *neutrality* is the standard that ought to be adhered to. Furthermore, they say nothing here that is not or should not be true for any person of faith teaching in any context. For example, if a Christian teacher has decided to move into

---

62. *Lemon v. Kurtzman*, cited in *Constitutional Interpretation*, 1409.

the inner city of Detroit or Los Angeles to teach poor and disadvantaged students in the public schools *because* of his faith, should he be disallowed from explaining why he is there if asked? If the state cannot discriminate on the basis of religion when hiring (over 75 percent of Americans claim Christianity as their faith), it only follows that public schools will be hiring Christians as well to teach and will need to police them for their neutrality. If it makes sense to assume that those Christian teachers can resist the desire to proselytize or that the state can ensure that they do not, why, then, should we not be able to assume the same thing about parochial schoolteachers until proven otherwise?

Likewise, when the Court argues in the name of protecting religious institutions from the state that the policies create "a relationship pregnant with dangers of excessive government direction of church schools and hence of churches," one must wonder whether, if the school has the option of entering into the relationship with the state or not, that potential fear is one that is rightfully justiciable. Indeed, the Court's constant references to what *could* happen as opposed to what has happened, suggest that the position they come to enshrine is one where our collective lives, politically speaking, would be made better if we sever religion and politics as completely as possible. While that may in fact be true, it is in no way clear that ease and lack of conflict are the true goals of human beings properly understood, or even healthy for a democratic society. The Court itself, however, strikes out on its own here and assumes that their task is to protect us and society from risk by authoring what it implies it has discovered in our written documents, traditions, and logic. Take the following passage as an example of the most sort of *a priori* leaps of reasoning the Court is willing to take in its attempt to demonstrate that if the establishment clause does not mean what they say it means, then it *ought* to:

> A broader base of entanglement of yet a different character is presented by the divisive political potential of these state programs. In a community where such a large number of pupils are served by church-related schools, it can be assumed that state assistance will entail considerable political activity. Partisans of parochial schools, understandably concerned with rising costs and sincerely dedicated to both the religious and secular educational missions of their schools, will inevitably champion this cause and promote political action to achieve their goals. Those who oppose state aid, whether for constitutional, religious, or fiscal reasons, will inevitably respond and employ all of the usual political campaign techniques to prevail. Candidates will be forced to declare and voters to choose.... Ordinarily political

debate and division, however vigorous or even partisan, are normal and healthy manifestations of our democratic system of government, but political division along religious lines was one of the principal evils against which the First Amendment was intended to protect. The potential divisiveness of such conflict is a threat to the normal political process.[63]

Without meaning to be too facetious, can it truly be the case that somehow democracy itself can be endangered by *candidates being forced to declare and voters to choose*? That for many is, of course, the essence of a democratic system of governance. Why, one must wonder, would people be any more likely to come to blows over this issue than, say, abortion or war or a host of other highly controversial questions? While the Court's desire for an orderly and reasoned public discourse should be shared by all reasonable people, it cannot legitimately come at the price of limiting what can and what cannot be talked about without creating an evil as great as it seeks to avoid and without itself seeming to violate a different portion of the same constitutional amendment. In its final attempt to legitimize its own position, the Court concludes the case with the following a-textual, a-historical, and wholly normative assertion:

> Under our system the choice has been made that government is to be entirely excluded from the arena of religious instruction and churches excluded from the affairs of government. The Constitution decrees that religion must be a private matter for the individual, the family, and the institutions of private choice.[64]

For those whose faith—because of its public nature—will not and cannot let this be the final word without in effect denying their God the quandary is obvious. Whether the policy itself is a good one or a poor one is, under the logic of this chapter, ultimately not really the Court's to make. And, finally, even if it would lead to a greater peace, if we stopped talking about divisive things, most people probably believe that there are things more important than peace. Perhaps if Christians had invented the articles and demands of their faith rather than receiving them they would have chosen differently, but such was not the case. Christianity is, by definition, a problem for a state devoted to secularism and privatization as much as it was a problem for a state devoted to paganism. Given that, the current *status quo* is not realistic, and the notion of a religion-free public square will in all likelihood

---

63. *Lemon v. Kurtzman*, cited in *Constitutional Interpretation*, 1412.
64. *Lemon v. Kurtzman*, cited in *Constitutional Interpretation*, 1413.

not be realized without serious and sustained efforts at suppression and re-education for which, thankfully, there is not much political will. In other words, the question over how the public sphere will be arranged remains an open one despite the continuing presence and cultural affirmation of Jefferson's misunderstood metaphor.

CONCLUSION

In this chapter, I have attempted to do a number of things at once. First, I have tried to demonstrate that there are good historical as well as theological arguments for something I have called *Christian* citizenship. Second, I have tried to describe what I see as the increasing political, legal, and cultural barriers in America for the continued cultivation and refinement of that ideal, and I point toward the historical, philosophical, and constitutional bases for their existence. I have argued that despite their prevalence, such arguments are both antithetical to the persistence of the Christian faith and not required by reason, tradition, or a fair reading of the Constitution itself. In the chapter that follows, I will try to complete the argument begun here and claim that even if the logic of the American regime did seem to require the privatization of faith, that such a requirement would be not only politically and philosophically unfeasible, but also politically undesirable for reasons only hinted at and implied in this chapter.

2

Euthyphro, Christianity, and Liberalism

Do not suppose that I have come to bring peace to the earth: it is not peace I have come to bring, but a sword. For I have come to set a man against his father, a daughter against her mother, a daughter-in-law against her mother-in-law. A man's enemies will be those of his own household.

—Matthew 10:34–35

"Simon, Simon! Satan, you must know, has got his wish to sift you all like wheat; but I have prayed for you, Simon, that your faith may not fail, and once you have recovered, you in your turn must strengthen your brothers." "Lord," he answered, "I would be ready to go to prison with you, and to death." Jesus replied, "I tell you, Peter, by the time the cock crows today you will have denied three times that you know me."

—Luke 22:31–34

INTRODUCTION

Plato's dialogue *Euthyphro* is both an instructive and cautionary piece of political theater from which to continue and extend the arguments of the previous chapter. At the level of metaphor, the dialogue calls upon us to think seriously about the relationship between the young and the old or the traditional and the progressive with a degree of circumspection and intellectual humility that is often absent in revolutionary nations. At the level of political philosophy, it raises fundamental questions about the relationship between politics and religion, and ultimately about the relationship between positive law and the good. This, then, forces upon the reflective reader a real awareness of the difficulty of compartmentalizing and *disentangling* the two spheres at the level of practical reason, politics, and policy.

The setting for the dialogue finds the reader at the king-archon's court in Athens circa 399 BC, where Socrates has appeared to face the charges that will ultimately lead to his execution—namely that he brought false gods into the city, corrupted the young, and made the worse argument the stronger. Upon arrival, he encounters a young man named Euthyphro who has come to court to prosecute his own father for the murder of a man who himself had committed murder. It is not incidental that the aged Socrates is himself to be prosecuted by a "young and unknown" man named Meletus (2b).[1] In any case, after listening to Socrates's assessment of his situation, Euthyphro worries that in prosecuting Socrates, Meletus will "start out by harming the very heart of the city" (3a). Euthyphro then explains to Socrates that he is there to prosecute his own father despite the fact that most people believe such a prosecution is impious. As Socrates furtively puts it, "Euthyphro, most men would not know how they could do this and be right. It is not the part of anyone to do this, but one who is far advanced in wisdom" (4b). Taking the Socratic bait, Euthyphro accepts the mantle "wise" and explains that the fact that his own father is the accused makes no difference since the only question is whether he acted justly or not. In his words: "For they say, it is impious for a son to prosecute his father for murder. But their ideas of the divine attitude to piety and impiety are wrong, Socrates" (4e). With that claim, the Socratic interrogation about the nature of piety begins full bore. That exchange, however, is not the primary focal point for my purposes.

To grasp the metaphoric import of the dialogue, it is important to understand the severe patriarchal and familial culture from which the polis itself emerged.[2] The prosecution of a father by a son symbolized a seismic

---

1. Plato, *Trial and Death of Socrates*. All quotations and citations are by line number.
2. See Fustel de Coulanges, *Ancient City*. Fustel de Coulanges traces in great detail

historical transition from an older form of piety and justice rooted in the sanctified family to a newer form of justice steeped in the emergent civic religion. The fact that contemporary readers understand and feel drawn to both the sort of Kantian appeal to principle made by Euthyphro and the unease felt by his critics in undertaking the prosecution suggests that some significant tension between our duties to family and polity has survived the last twenty-three centuries of Western political development. Indeed, our inability to actually resolve this tension to anyone's true satisfaction has led us to try and "paper over" it through the notion of recusal. By asking public officials not to participate in actions that place them in the kind of situation Euthyphro sought out to avoid both impropriety and the appearance of impropriety, we acknowledge and finesse this basic aspect of the human condition. That sort of reasonable accommodation, however, is as far as we in the West are willing to go. At the end of the day, we side with Euthyphro's broader assertion that "one should only watch whether the killer acted justly or not; if he acted justly, let him go, but if not, one should prosecute, even if the killer shares your hearth and table"(4c). Such a definitive position, regardless of either past practice and tradition or emotion itself, is the price thought necessary to maintain the ordered liberty and social stability associated with the rule of law rather than the rule of men. We must be willing, metaphorically speaking, to prosecute and condemn the past in order to vindicate and sustain the new and distinctive present. Below I will suggest that this sort of ideological "patricide" in the name of order and stability comes to characterize American liberal political theory and, though less consistently, constitutional jurisprudence with regard to the secularization of the public sphere and the relegation of religion to the private and individual consciences.

Beyond the metaphoric value of the dialogue, there are also more substantive issues raised by Plato that are pertinent and even philosophically analogous to the question of how the public space itself will actually be configured with regard to religion and politics. In his questioning of Euthyphro to discover the true nature of the "pious" and the "impious," Socrates draws Euthyphro into a seeming dilemma when he admits that different gods find different things pious and impious. That position is the product of Euthyphro's assertion that "what is dear to the gods is pious, what is not is impious" (7a). In turn, Socrates suggests that those disagreements (about

---

the emergence of the city-state from an ancient world where each family was its own religious and political unit with the father serving as the chief priest and "theologian" of a system of worship revolving around the family's deceased male ancestors and the hearth.

the ultimate good or truth) lead to conflict among both the gods and, in turn, men themselves. As Socrates puts it,

> What subject of difference would make us angry and hostile to each other if we were unable to come to a decision? Perhaps you do not have an answer ready, but examine as I tell you whether these subjects are the just and the unjust, the beautiful and the ugly, the good and the bad. Are these not the subjects of difference about which when we are unable to come to a satisfactory decision, you and I and other men become hostile to each other whenever we do? (7d)

Euthyphro agrees that those subjects about ultimate values or goods are in fact the ones that lead to the greatest conflict. Socrates then prods him to the position that in such a world something might in fact be both pious and impious, depending on who is being asked. That, of course, does not suffice for Socrates, since he is seeking that which is not subject to the will and whim of the god or person in question, but rather the "form" or eternal definition of piety, i.e., knowledge instead of opinion. In his words, "It is loved because it is pious, but it is not pious because it is loved" (10d). After a few more iterations of the same kind of conversation, Euthyphro relents and excuses himself and Socrates goes to answer the charges against him.

Most relevant for the current discussion is the charge that Socrates brought new gods into the city. In the context of this argument, I would like to replace the term "new gods" with God or religion. In other words, Socrates has violated the civil religion of the polis by calling it into question on the basis of a competing religion. He has threatened the order and stability of the city by unsettling the consensus on the questions concerning the just and the unjust, the beautiful and the ugly, and the good and the bad through his constant and public questioning of prominent Athenians and their children. He does this, as most readers know, because the gods have told him to. As Socrates explains to his own jury in the *Apology* itself: "You have heard me give the reason for this in many places. I have a divine sign from the god which Meletus has ridiculed in his deposition" (31c). If we recast the sentence to say that Socrates brings his gods into the city (read: challenges the civic religion) because that "faith" demands it, is it not the case that Socrates is imprisoned and executed because he wanted to be both a citizen and a faithful servant of the divine at the same time, and the city's need for hegemony could not allow it?

One of the great ironies of the *Apology* is Plato's imputation to Socrates of the statement, "A man who really fights for justice must lead a private, not a public, life if he is to survive for even a short time" (32a). The irony here is at least twofold. First, Socrates did not ultimately lead a private life (i.e., he did not practice his faith in private). Second, it is almost farcical to imagine that what has been *the* central political question—what is justice?—should be excluded from the public/political sphere (i.e., privatized) as well. Yet, this is precisely the correct assessment given the nature of the charges and the ultimate outcome of the trial. While such may indeed be the price of peace, it is a "peace" achieved at the expense of other important values—important *liberal* values (that the Greeks of the fourth and fifth centuries BC did not need to be concerned with) like freedom of conscience and religion. In this chapter, I will attempt to extrapolate from this line of thought and apply the logic and questions raised in the context of the American liberal state. It will be my argument that despite a great historical and theoretical debt to Christian theology and political activism, contemporary liberal thought and legalism is now attempting to unmoor itself from those foundations with little thought to the "piety" or negative practical implications of such a move. Furthermore, as part of that unmooring, liberalism as a political ideology must undertake decisive actions regarding the place of faith and citizens of faith in the public square that are themselves inconsistent and incompatible with liberalism itself. Those inconsistencies, in turn, beget very real contradictions that will ultimately be resolved either at the expense of liberalism's primary normative commitments or by a return to first principles and a more robust and, yes, disorderly public square.

A SECULAR PURPOSE?

The constitutional theorist Mark Tushnet claims that "the jurisprudence of the religion clauses is a mess not because we do understand the Constitution, but because we do not understand religion."[3] There are at least two important senses in which that assertion is correct. The first has to do with the way religion functions psychologically within a particular person. The second has to do with the *secular* nature of religion and theology—Christianity in particular—and its relationship to society itself. In this chapter, I want to avoid the deeper philosophic questions about identity and focus on the more readily accessible elements of the phenomena to make Tushnet's *prima facie* case about the lack of judicial understanding of religion itself. Here again I continue with Socrates as my exemplar. Later in chapter 3, "Christianity and Alienation," I will argue that there is an irreducible tension at the level of first principles between the liberal conception of the self and the Christian-Catholic conception of the self which can be integrated

3. Tushnet, "Reflections on the Role of Purpose," 1008–9.

into a more robust and pluralistic social matrix, but never resolved or settled definitively.

During his defense in the *Apology*, Socrates exclaims that "throughout my life, in any public activity I may have engaged in, I am the same man as I am in private life" (33a). As noted above, this is precisely what he believes has led to his downfall; had he remained a "private" person rather than a public figure he may have been spared the trial. Likewise, if he had modified his public persona and conformed to the expected norms of the civil religion by not raising such pointed and destabilizing questions the way he did, then he may have been spared as well. However, as Socrates puts it a little later in his defense, these options were not feasible:

> If I say that it is impossible for me to keep quiet because that means disobeying the god, you will not believe me and will think I am being ironical. On the other hand, if I say that it is the greatest good for a man to discuss virtue every day and those other things about which you hear me conversing and testing myself and others, for the unexamined life is not worth living for man, you will believe me even less. (38a)

Socrates can be fruitfully read as arguing that he is either incapable or unwilling to repress or hide the religious sources of his personal mode of civic engagement. Taking him at his word, we must assume it is something that he could not do and remain true to himself. If, indeed, Socrates's religion is both an inseparable and irrepressible part of his psychological makeup, such that he cannot enter the public sphere on any other grounds, then he must either be allowed to enter as he is, excluded from public life, or, if possible, "converted." We know what the Athenian option was, i.e., they executed him, and we know that for most liberals that option would be rejected. However, I would argue that their rejection of the Athenian course of action flows out of their tendency to view his actions *politically* through the lens of "free speech." What, we can ask, would many of those same liberals (here now speaking of the "exclusionists") think if the case of Socrates is viewed through the lens of religious fidelity and faithful citizenship? In other words, what if Socrates presented himself in the public sphere in order to bear witness religiously speaking rather than as a philosophic interlocutor? What if his intention to prod the city "like a gadfly" toward a fuller realization of and adherence to the good as he understood it was a matter of faith? Under the rubric of what is perhaps the most pronounced branch of liberal theory and the reasoning of a significant number of Supreme Court Justices and judicial precedents in contemporary America, that sort of lens would make his case dramatically more problematic. While he would certainly not be put to death or even imprisoned, the person of faith (the "Socrates") would be asked to either (1) alter his comprehensive doctrine or (2) dissemble ("... when an individual either advances a political justification as definitive when in fact her intentions derive from a comprehensive doctrine, or advocates as definitive a justification she either does not believe or believes only marginally").[4] Refusing both courses of action, then, places the proverbial ball back into the hands of the representatives and theorists of the liberal state.

As a state that was democratic but not liberal, Athens had options available that are mostly unthinkable for a country like the United States, where democratic decision-making must function within the context of a regime that is liberal and rights-based first and foremost. Unable to kill, exile, or engage in forced conversion of those who persist in bringing religion into the public square, the liberal state in its emergent American form must rely on persuasion, exclusion, or hypocrisy (dissembling) if it is to keep the faithful at bay. Constitutionally, this is accomplished by the logic of the other two prongs of the Lemon Test, namely that the legislation or policy enacted "must have a secular legislative purpose" and that "its principal or primary effect must be one that neither advances nor inhibits religion."[5] By examining the "purposes" and "effects" of public actions, the Court can try to discern and even form the intentions and, hence, consciences of those who have given a particular piece of legislation or policy civic life. Taking for granted that neither the Court nor liberal theorists are in favor of hypocrisy, the functional outcome of requiring that religion neither intentionally guides nor is unintentionally fostered in the case of a given piece of public policy is either exclusion or conversion. Hearkening back to the notion of political languages, the "secular requirement" (both at the point of input and output) constrains the choices available for conducting public business, thereby either silencing those who "speak" religiously (exclusion) or coercing them to speak "secular" (conversion). Whether this is justifiable within the confines of liberalism itself is questionable. However, before that question can even be addressed, the terms of debate need to be seriously rethought and the false dichotomy upon which it is predicated must be rejected. By juxtaposing the "secular" to the "religious," the Court demonstrates, in yet another manner, its serious misunderstanding of religion in general and Christianity in particular.

At its simplest, I would argue, the Court misunderstands what is really possible for a state to do regarding religious belief. While it may allow or

4. Murphy, "Rawls and Liberty of Conscience," 254–57.
5. *Lemon v. Kurtzman*, quoted in *Constitutional Interpretation*, 1409.

disallow certain practices, no state has nor could come to have the ability to create religious belief. Whether one believes that said belief is the gift of the Holy Spirit or the by-product of reason strictly speaking, it is not ultimately within the dominion of any state to either give belief or take belief away from one who has it. Certainly, a given state could officially endorse or sanction belief just as certainly as it could renounce or repress it, but it ultimately cannot, by definition, create or destroy it. Now this should not be taken to mean that particular churches, practices, or individuals cannot be helped or harmed by the state based on their ascribed beliefs, behaviors, or lack thereof, but only that in so helping or harming the state in reality does nothing to help or harm *faith* itself. States can and, of course, have mandated certain practices and actions regarding the practice or physical manifestations of this religion or that's institutionalized creed or belief. Likewise, states have outlawed and punished many such practices as well. Ecclesiastical or liturgical control, however, goes only to the *form* of worship, not the substance. Faith, like gravity, exists or doesn't exist regardless of the human will. However, a critic might claim that my argument is purely semantic and that even if "faith" itself is out of the state's reach, no one should be compelled to behave in accord with the tenets of someone else's faith or be denied the ability to behave in accord with their own. Exceptions to this would be when the boundaries of public safety and the requirement that the same rights are reserved to others to the same degree come into play. While I will make the case momentarily that the hidden premise of their own position is itself ironically based on a religious argument, I will let it go for now and turn to a far less semantic point regarding the attempt to dichotomize the sacred and the secular.

As I argued in the previous chapter, for Christians, the Incarnation itself explicitly problematizes any attempt to separate the temporal from the eternal for Christians. Here, I would like to extend that argument still further and give it a particularly Catholic slant. When asked what differentiates the Catholic theological tradition from prominent Protestant traditions, Michael Himes argues that it is the *sacramental principle*.[6] In his provisional definition of that principle, Himes claims,

> The *sacramental principle* means that what is always and everywhere the case must be noticed, accepted, and celebrated somewhere sometime. What is always and everywhere true must be brought to our attention and be embraced (or rejected) in some concrete experience at some particular time and place.[7]

---

6. Himes, "Finding God in All Things," 91.
7. Himes, "Finding God in All Things," 91.

By concentrating on the "concrete" and the "particular," Himes focuses our attention on the world around us, on what is present and accessible to human beings in a mediate sense. For Catholicism, the relationship between God and humanity is indirect due to the nature of God rather than the ignorance of man—whatever else is true, Catholicism is not a Gnostic faith.[8] In Himes's words, "'God' is the theological shorthand that we use to designate the Mystery which grounds and undergirds all that exists . . . we are speaking about that which is itself not grounded on anything else."[9] At the root of that mystery as far as human beings are concerned is the central question: Why are we here? Why, to borrow from Heidegger, "does anything exist rather than nothing"?[10] The answer that Himes gives is because of God's inscrutable grace; because of God's self-giving love. For Christians, "the reason anything exists is that it is the object of love. All things that are, are loved into being."[11] It is in the unpacking of that idea that the real meaning and import of the sacramental principle can itself be made manifest.

Building out from the second commandment—"You shall not take the name of the Lord your God in vain"—Himes cautions against talking about God with too much specificity, "it is a warning against overconfident theology and too-simple preaching."[12] It is the flip side of the first commandment against idolatry insofar as both commandments are about confusing God with what is not God by in effect limiting and circumscribing that which is boundless. Proceeding with caution, Himes argues that "there is some way of talking about God that is less hopelessly inadequate than other ways," namely, that "God is love."[13] Calling the notion of *agape* (unconditional love, or as Himes says, "the gift of the self to the other asking nothing in response") "what the Christian tradition claims is the least wrong metaphor for God,"[14] Himes argues that "everything that is, to the extent that it is, is loved."[15] The opposite of that love (God's love) is not "damnation," it is "non-being."[16] Hence, according to the logic so far, "everything we encounter

---

8. This point will become very important when we look at the "American Religion," as Harold Bloom calls it. See Bloom, *American Religion*.
9. Himes, "Finding God in All Things," 91.
10. Himes, "Finding God in All Things," 97.
11. Himes, "Finding God in All Things," 97.
12. Himes, "Finding God in All Things," 93.
13. Himes, "Finding God in All Things," 95–96. See also 1 John 4:8, 16.
14. Himes, "Finding God in All Things," 96.
15. Himes, "Finding God in All Things," 98.
16. Himes, "Finding God in All Things," 98.

is rooted in grace."[17] Subsequently, the sacramental principle should be seen as a call to the faithful to quite literally pay attention, to notice and acknowledge the gift of God's love in the created world. Moving away from the more pedestrian and narrow understanding of the traditional seven sacraments, Himes can say without hesitation:

> By a *sacrament* I mean any person, place, thing, or event, any sound, taste, touch, or smell, that causes us to notice the love which supports all that exists, that undergirds your being and mine and the being of everything about us.[18]

In turn, "there is nothing that cannot become a sacrament for someone, absolutely nothing."[19] Returning finally, to the core conversation concerning the so-called secular requirements as put forth in *Lemon*, the notion of the sacramental principle generates a logic—for believers—whereby we can claim that everything that is "secular" is in fact sacred. The reverse cannot, of course, be true; namely, that everything sacred is secular, because that would imply that the boundless and creative grace (*agape*) that *is* God has somehow been exhausted or used up. The only proviso to the first assertion—that everything secular is in fact potentially sacred—is that someone must notice, accept, or celebrate it somewhere at some concrete and particular time in some historical place. While not meaning to purposefully confuse the subject too much more, it needs to be made clear, à la the Socratic implication from the *Euthyphro*, that the secular—what surrounds us every day in every imaginable way—does not become sacred *because* we notice it and acknowledge it, but rather that it cannot be recognized as sacred until someone responds to it as such. Once it is responded to in such a way, i.e., recognizing it at as a visible sign of God's grace, its embedded sacramental or sacred nature is not created, but made manifest or visible whereas before the response was simply latent. Hence, "secularity" is not simply the singular nature of any thing, but instead a thing's nature is ultimately the by-product of our response to it. For the Christian, God is in all things; the choice they have is whether to "see" it or ignore it.

As if the water was not murky enough, I want to make one final point along these lines: it is entirely consistent with the argument so far to say that everything that is sacred and is available to human beings sacramentally *can* have a secular purpose. Indeed, it would be difficult to imagine that something meaningful to someone would not in some manner, however

---

17. Himes, "Finding God in All Things," 98.
18. Himes, "Finding God in All Things," 99.
19. Himes, "Finding God in All Things," 99.

potentially obscure, also be useful in their daily life. Though many things may indeed be vain or be done in vain (as measured by the outcome), it is nonsensical and irrational to imagine that something is done, created, made, tried, etc., *because* it was vain or futile. Additionally, it is also then the case that anything which is done may, whether intended or not, have the principal effect of advancing (or perhaps inhibiting) religion as no one has the power to know what may or may not make the latent sacramentality of a given thing visible and thereby call someone, somewhere, to "notice" God and God's grace. At the risk of impropriety, let me provide an extreme example of this kind of phenomenon. Taking Hitler's "Final Solution" as an example of a wholly "secular" piece of public policy (evil and genocidal, yes, but a policy nonetheless), could we not say that for many of those upon whom the policy was carried out, the direct effect was to decrease their faith in God? For yet another group of those same human beings, is it not possible to imagine that the direct effect was to actually strengthen their belief in God? Indeed, it is impossible for me to imagine that a policy of such horrendous magnitude did not ultimately compel a *religious* response—either turning toward or away from God—in all who were subjected to its force. Consequences can be both primary and unintended at the same time without logical contradiction. It is simply the case that the oft-used cliché that "God works in mysterious ways" is far truer than we would like to imagine.

Returning now to the issue of misunderstanding that began this section, it simply cannot be the case that for Christians in general and Catholic-Christians in particular that the sort of conceptual box built by the Supreme Court and certain brands of liberal theory can retain their structural integrity without resorting to an a-phenomenological and wholly shallow caricature of both religious believers and religion itself. Those who would do so need to take the words of Himes and Himes to heart and then rethink the options outlined at the start:

> Religion cannot advance claims regarding ultimate values and simultaneously admit that it has nothing to say about the world in which men and women are educated, choose professions, make money, educate their children, decide issues of peace and war, make budgets, pass laws, and carry on the vast majority of their waking hours. Any religion which does is simply incredible.[20]

---

20. Himes and Himes, *Fullness of Faith*, 17.

"LIBERALISM'S RELIGION PROBLEM"

It has been said that the bumper sticker for "postmodernism" would probably read: "Be tolerant or die!"[21] On a less ironic level, the same general sensibility inheres in certain brands of contemporary liberal theory. It has also, *pace* the argument in chapter 1, seeped into much of contemporary American jurisprudence—especially in the area of the First Amendment's religion clauses. Conceptually, "toleration" as an ideal propagated out of both an emergent theory of respect for each individual, and his or her right to freedom of conscience, becomes conflated constitutionally with the notion of "neutrality." Like parents who love all of their different children equally, the American legal system demonstrates its fidelity to all citizens by restraining both itself and the other varied branches and levels of government from taking any authoritative position—positive or negative—on any particular religious belief system, or on the general idea of religion itself. It does this, in theory at least, while simultaneously preserving the rights of most citizens to freely embrace and practice, or refrain from doing so, whatever particular religious system to which they ascribe. Coincidentally and not unintentionally, this demonstration of fair-mindedness not only serves to exhibit a profound respect for each individual citizen, it also helps the American polity enormously in achieving the relative peace and stability most states so avidly desire. By neither playing favorites nor denigrating anyone's particular religious choices, the political hope is that the fervent religious wars and battles of much of human history can be successfully avoided. This is hardly a minor goal or ignoble project, and, a few skirmishes aside, it has for the most part worked pretty well in practice. However, the overall consensus on which that success rests has become increasingly uneasy because the would-be *praxis* has itself become significantly more difficult to sustain for a variety of reasons, not the least of which are the internal contradictions that are made more manifest with each new iteration of theoretical self-awareness.

Simply put, liberalism's attempt to position itself as the referee or rules keeper who sends various religious participants and the state to politically neutral corners in the name of toleration, fairness, and the assumed mutual desire for non-interference, is slowly but unavoidably being exposed as a theoretically incoherent and practically unsustainable fiction. While posited by many as the place where history, *pace* Hegel, might find itself at least at the beginning of its "end," the American liberal regime increasingly finds itself mired in the gooey muck of a persistent dialectical process that can

---

21. Jamieson, "Poverty of Postmodernist Theory," 456.

only possibly be thwarted by relinquishing its privileged position above the fray and joining the struggle as another worthy contender. In other words, liberalism's future as a worldview and stable political system depends on the willingness of its supporters and theorists to provide an affirmative and coherent defense of it as at least *a* vision, if not *the* vision, of the "good life." This means that liberalism must be cast as itself a choice rather than the context in which other choices are made. What it can no longer maintain with any intellectual credibility is that it should be relieved of the need to defend itself and compete by virtue of its own self-referential and tautological assertion that its role is procedural and not substantive. This means that it will have to get involved with the messy business of truth claims and value judgments in ways that it has successfully avoided in its more recent historical iterations.

Such a call is itself nothing particularly new. As Sir Robert Filmer put it in his seventeenth-century critique of an emergent liberalism,

> If such as Maintain the Natural Liberty of mankind, take offence at the Liberty I take to Examine it, they must take heed that they do not deny by Retail, that Liberty which they affirm by wholesale: For, if the Thesis be true, the Hypothesis will follow, that all men may Examine their own Charters, Deeds, or Evidences by which they claim and hold the Inheritance or Free-hold of their liberties.[22]

What has changed, however, in the course of Western political history in general and in American political thought in particular is the hegemonic and paradigmatic status of the liberal ideal in its modern form. This is due to the fact that it is now a self-evident proposition of a sort without need of justification but rather refinement, explication and application. As such, it is all other worldviews that are subsequently forced to play defense as they accommodate themselves to overarching liberal parameters and ideological bench marks by either refraining from public disputation or demonstrating that their public activity is consistent with the requirements of neutrality and tolerance. By way of a simplistic example, it is seen as wholly reasonable and understandable that John Rawls would address the question of "toleration for the intolerant" in his magisterial work on justice, but inconceivable that a serious American political thinker would even think about tackling the question of say "intolerance for the tolerant" with a straight face. Of course, we are "intolerant" of those who tolerate the wrong things, that is illiberal things, but we would not cast it that way. We would rather think of ourselves in good Rousseauean fashion as simply forcing the wayward to be free, i.e., to live up to the demands of the liberal ideal they had at least tacitly

22. Filmer, *Patriarcha*.

agreed to. But, this begs the questions first of the "right" and subsequently of the "good," whether liberalism likes it or not.

Rawls's *Theory of Justice* is widely considered the most important work in political philosophy in the second half of the twentieth century by fellow travelers and critics alike. While I will not rehash or attempt to confront this very complex and much discussed and debated work here in any detail, I do want to suggest that its approach is highly emblematic of, and compatible with, the kind of ahistorical or "transcendent" brand of liberalism being sketched so far. Like the early contract theorists, Rawls's systemic conclusions are derived rather handily once the initial premises are accepted. While not being so bold as to practice anthropology without a license like Locke or Hobbes, Rawls does posit his own conceptual version of the "state of nature" in the form of his "original position," and its counterpart, "the veil of ignorance." Looking for an objective point of departure for conversations about distributive justice, Rawls places his readers into a pre-political, pre-social situation in which they have no knowledge of who they are, what the world they will inhabit will look like, or how it will be structured. A given "individual" will not know if they will be born male or female, rich or poor, black or white, healthy or sickly, gay or straight, intelligent or mentally challenged; they will not know their nationality or ethnicity, nor even their likes and dislikes. All a person will know is that he or she will enter a world with scarce resources with which any given individual will want to maximize his or her share in order to pursue whatever their particular version of the good life might turn out to be. These individuals are then asked to construct the broad distributive and political principles (a social contract) that will govern this soon-to-be-inhabited world based purely on their now thoroughly objective "self-interest(s)." (Since we could literally be anyone, the way to think about this is along the lines of what any "self" would minimally want/need to pursue their life's project).

The implications for a theory of justice can be made evident quickly. First, we would all want equal shares of the primary goods of the world unless an unequal distribution would generate more goods overall for each of us, i.e., through economic growth. Second, we would all want to share in decision-making. Third, we would all want the maximum liberty consistent and compatible with the same liberty for others to pursue their own life projects. In academic philosophy, this view is one that prioritizes the "right" over the "good"; it is fundamentally concerned with process rather than ends and goes by the term "justice as fairness." In such a world, the "good" is plural and assumed to be whatever results from the free actions and exchanges of individual citizens pursuing their individual ideas of happiness. In turn, any comprehensive or transcendent conception of what used to be called "the good life" (like one that might be derived from religious belief and devotion) is relegated to the private realm of individual conscience. As Ackerman argued in a similar vein, the language of public/political discourse must be "neutral" with regard to such ideas since they ultimately end up involving "a privileged insight into the moral universe which is denied the rest of us."[23]

In Rawls's own subsequent work, *Political Liberalism* (1993), he extends both Ackerman's argument and his own formulation of justice in a direction designed to reflect the structural and essential diversity and pluralism of liberal-democracies by turning his attention away from the more abstract notions of *A Theory of Justice* to the idea of "over-lapping consensus." Simply put, this approach takes the "reasonable" and shared ("over-lapping") points of agreement between various "comprehensive doctrines" and contends that they represent the basis for social unity and sound constitutionalism. The central concept that emerges from this argument is the idea of "public reason." This idea is on par with Ackerman's notion of "neutral" dialogue, with the exception being that certain long-standing beliefs that may have once involved "privileged insights" might now be admissible because they are sufficiently widespread and agreed upon that no one tradition or group "owns" them. In this manner, the less "consensus," the less legitimacy.

Now, of course, there is something both inherently appealing in this idea for those who are in favor of limiting the amount of coercion and potential oppression and violence in a given society as a practical matter, as well as for those who take the principle of toleration as an ethical idea seriously. When one begins to think through the actual content of the current "consensus," there is also a large comfort factor, i.e., it does not ask for much in the way of positive duties or changes in the way the majority of people in advanced liberal-democracies live, and it severely limits the amount of intrusion permitted into our personal choices and affairs by other individuals and groups. However, a number of questions are in fact begged by both the original version of the argument as well as the "political" version. This includes whether the "original position" can have any real currency if the construction of the human person is so remote from reality and, perhaps, even the truth that its ultimate usefulness or analogic import is rendered superfluous. Or, what if the actual ability to sustain a particular "consensus" itself somehow depends on a given comprehensive doctrine whose initial entrance into the public realm or discourse did in fact violate the principle of neutrality? Holding off on those questions for now (this is part of the subject matter of chapter 3), there is a less philosophic question that is of particular importance for a nation like ours; namely, what do we do with

---

23. Ackerman, *Social Justice in the Liberal State*, 10.

people who hold comprehensive ideals that carry within them an injunction against privatization, i.e., ideals that explicitly reject neutrality?

Although sometimes caricatured as "intolerant" by their opponents and detractors, most of the religiously devout Americans are not members of the standard groups to whom that title is typically applied. Neither, however, are they merely another interest group vying for their piece of the proverbial political pie. Christians who reject privatization and refuse to dissemble, are, or at least ought to be, different. Unlike ascriptive characteristics such as race, gender, IQ, and social class, one's faith is ultimately a free choice. In choosing it, one does not merely accumulate interests, but, much more significantly, obligations and duties. Particularly problematic is that those duties and obligations are not of the traditional negative variety associated with traditional liberalism, i.e., do no harm, but instead they are positive duties to actually do good and prod others to do so as well through witness, evangelization, and political action and public policy. While the American liberal state has been very tolerant of the first of these activities (witness), it has been increasingly cautious regarding the second (evangelization), and for the most part denied the validity of the last (political action) as a breach of the public "faith" and a violation of the rules of "neutral" discourse. Yet, Christians persist. In doing so, they create an ongoing problem for the liberal state.

In his essay "Liberalism's Religion Problem," Stephen Carter deftly and succinctly captures the essence of the dilemma an activist Christianity creates for the liberal state. Carter sets the stage by recounting a story about the civil rights activist and a founder of the Mississippi Freedom Democratic Party (MFDP), Fannie Lou Hamer, and her encounter with the Johnson Administration and Hubert Humphrey in the summer of 1964. The MFDP had challenged the credentials of the all-white Mississippi Delegation to the Democratic National Convention in an attempt to have members of their own integrated slate seated in their stead. Worried that this would taint his nomination and celebration, Johnson sent Humphrey as his soon-to-be vice president to "buy her off."[24] Carter describes that meeting in the following way:

> Humphrey, believing that he was undertaking a political negotiation, asked Fannie Lou Hamer what she wanted. Mrs. Hamer, a devout evangelical Christian, responded: "The beginning of a New Kingdom right here on earth." Humphrey, evidently stunned, explained that his political future was on the line if he could not close a deal with her to end the credentials challenge.

24. Carter, *Culture of Disbelief*, 21.

He apparently wanted her to understand that his nomination would create a strong voice for racial equality at the highest levels of the White House, reason enough to compromise. Fannie Lou Hamer, who had survived beating and torture in a Mississippi jail for insisting on her constitutional rights, was unimpressed. This was her reply: "Senator Humphrey, I know lots of people in Mississippi who have lost their jobs for trying to register to vote. I had to leave the plantation where I worked in Sunflower County. Now if you lose this job of Vice President because you do what is right, because you help MFDP, everything will be all right. God will take care of you. . . . But if you take the vice presidential nomination this way, why, you will never be able to do any good for civil rights, for poor people, for peace or any of those things you talk about. Senator Humphrey, I'm going to pray to Jesus for you."[25]

That ended the negotiation. I relay the story that Carter got from David Marsh's book *God's Long Summer*, for the same sorts of reasons that Carter himself uses it: "because it has much to teach us about what happens when strong religious commitment runs up against the world of secular politics."[26] It is especially pertinent for the politics of a liberal regime.

Fannie Lou Hamer certainly had what could be called a "secular" interest in achieving her political goals. But, on even a jaded reading, it would be difficult to comprehend her response to Humphrey and Johnson as either self-interested or partisan under any politically relevant meaning of those terms. This reality, despite the fact that Humphrey was a decent man who really was committed to the movement's political and social causes, rendered her and those like her virtually incomprehensible to him. With all they ostensibly agreed on, they had nothing left to talk about. Even in 1964, when religion played a significantly more public role—prayer in school was widespread, "under God" had only recently been added to the Pledge of Allegiance, and so on—one could only imagine the voracious outcry that would have been heard had Hubert Humphrey accepted Hamer's logic and announced in some speech that the MFDP ought to have its delegates seated in order to further the achievement of the New Kingdom on earth. Fortunately for Humphrey and others, his agreement with Hamer's point of departure was not a prerequisite for their larger shared political vision. There were excellent "liberal" reasons for supporting and furthering the cause of African American civil rights. Indeed, Carter is quick to note that there is often real consistency between the liberalism of the Enlightenment

25. Carter, *Culture of Disbelief*, 21.
26. Carter, *Culture of Disbelief*, 21.

and democracy in particular. In his words, "The process-based liberalism that formed the heart of legal theory for a large part of the second half of the twentieth century is entirely consistent with a Christian view of the world."[27] However, while that similarity is not coincidental, it cannot be taken for granted.

As Carter so aptly puts it regarding this last point and the issue of compatibility: "From the Christian point of view, however, these commitments [liberal commitments], while important, are insufficient. The first and highest duty of the individual Christian believer is to Christ."[28] To reiterate my previous point, Christianity not only requires more of its believers than liberalism asks, it may be the case that it requires more than liberalism can allow. As Carter himself puts it: "The liberal state is uncomfortable with deep religious devotion.... Religious belief is reduced to precise parity with all other forms of belief, an act of leveling that is already threatening to religion itself."[29] According to Carter, and I concur, this is because

> liberalism as a theory cannot help but take on a triumphal character, for the ideals of liberalism have largely triumphed in the political world; the state nowadays is a liberal state. The trouble is that the state and the religions are in a competition to explain the meaning of the world. When the meanings provided by the one differ from the meanings provided by the other, it is natural that the one on the losing end will do what it can to become a winner.[30]

This competitive depiction is certainly apt, as far as it goes. However, it actually gives liberalism more credit than would care to accept and positions it in a philosophical house that it is simply not large enough to inhabit. In turn, the juxtaposition of religion in general, and Christianity in particular, to the liberal state makes the faith much smaller than it is intended to be. Here I take my lead from Michael McConnell, who makes the following argument: "It cannot be stressed too strongly that liberalism is not a coherent comprehensive philosophy of life. It is a prescription for government. As a comprehensive philosophy, it quickly collapses into self-contradiction."[31] It does so insofar as it is perceived to be "a continual pushing away of orthodoxies," as some would claim of it, because, of course, it "would end up pushing itself away, for its strictures against orthodoxy would apply with as

27. Carter, *Culture of Disbelief*, 23.
28. Carter, *Culture of Disbelief*, 22.
29. Carter, *Culture of Disbelief*, 22.
30. Carter, *Culture of Disbelief*, 23.
31. McConnell, "Getting Along."

much force to itself as any other belief system.... It is a demonstration that, on its own terms, liberalism understood as a comprehensive worldview is self-contradictory."[32] This is by now a fairly standard mode of criticism and owes much of its initial force to the early work of people like Leo Strauss.[33] It is also why liberals like Richard Rorty have ultimately accepted both the burdens and the liberation provided by anti-foundationalism.[34] Yet, it still bears reiteration because there are those who remain confused on this point and believe that liberalism can deliver something more in the way of substance. But, to believe this is to confuse the relationship between means and ends as I will argue briefly below and in greater detail later. (This is not lost on Carter as he makes clear later in his essay, but it could be made much sharper.)[35]

To the extent that McConnell's point has been dissonantly ignored, any number of ill-fated attempts to give substance to form have been embarked on with both greater and lesser self-consciousness about the logical difficulty entailed in the project. Pushed too hard logically in one direction, liberalism as a philosophy of life gives us Nietzsche's man-god who is "beyond god and evil"; pushed too hard in the other direction, and we get C. S. Lewis's "men without chests,"[36] who are so paralyzed by the strictures of "neutrality" that they can no longer act at all. Socially speaking we end up living in either Kierkegaard's *Present Age*, where "virtuosity and good sense consists in trying to reach a judgment and decision without ever going so far as action,"[37] or in the "anti-necessitarian" world of Roberto Unger, where "the real question becomes whether you can fully acknowledge the contingency of social worlds and complete the unfinished break with the spirit of classical social doctrine while nevertheless continuing to make normative claims."[38] From my perspective, I am glad that most people do not push too hard in either direction for the most part. T. S. Eliot said explicitly what the vast majority of Americans seem to know and embody implicitly, namely,

---

32. McConnell, "Getting Along," 2.

33. See Strauss, *Natural Right and History*; Strauss, *Liberalism Ancient and Modern*. For my own interpretation and argument regarding Struss and his school of thought, please see Duncan, "Democratic Posturing and Peculiar Liberalism," 281–311.

34. Rorty, *Contingency, Irony, and Solidarity*.

35. Carter, *Culture of Disbelief*, 24. Carter writes just a page later that "a theory developed in order to explain the organization of the state ... becomes a theory about the organization of everything."

36. Lewis, *Abolition of Man*, ch. 2.

37. Kierkegaard, *Present Age*, 33.

38. Unger, *Social Theory*, 39.

that Liberalism may be a tendency towards something very different from itself, is a possibility in its nature. For it is something that tends to release energy rather than accumulate it, to relax rather than fortify. It is a movement not so much defined by its end, as by its starting point; away from, rather than towards, something definite.[39]

In other words, liberalism creates the preconditions that makes a vast array of individual life choices possible, but in and of itself cannot serve as anyone's calling. There are, of course, people who have a liberal temperament or disposition as contained in the cliché of "living and letting live," but that only tells us something about how they respond to the choices, decisions, pursuits, and callings of others; it tells us nothing about what it is they themselves are called to or prefer. Simply put, the value of "liberal" autonomy can only be realized by "spending" it. Sticking with the metaphor, the liberal state polices the fairly amorphous boundaries of the marketplace of life and to an extent determines what a given individual or group may "purchase" with their autonomy funds. If, however, "autonomy" is itself reified and considered possible of accumulating value through its preservation or saving rather than through its spending or use, an unfortunate paradox is created from which there is no real theoretical escape. Every choice or use of one's autonomy decreases the available autonomy absolutely, thereby decreasing the amount of personal "wealth" that a given individual has. In a world where autonomy itself has been reified and ranks among the highest of social values—if not the highest—this means, in turn, that the "social worth" of a person is decreased in proportion to their loss of autonomy. It is like the parable of King Midas in reverse, i.e., autonomy represents social gold and every time a person uses it, it becomes something other than gold, or less extrinsically valuable. Now since, just as with Midas, "gold," no matter what its extrinsic value is, is not enough to sustain human life—let alone human flourishing—everyone must "spend" part of their store of autonomy just to live at all.[40] But, the question is how much?

A liberalism posited as a philosophy of life rather than of government calls the individual to be increasingly miserly with his or her autonomy—to preserve it and keep it safe. As this phenomenon increases and the culture itself reinforces and enshrines such behavior as "normal," those who persist in making long-term commitments and subject themselves to various modes of authority are progressively viewed with a combination of pity, suspicion, and disdain. Meanwhile, those who embrace this ideal of at least

39. Eliot, *Christianity and Culture*, 12.
40. See Taylor, *Ethics of Authenticity*.

the relatively autonomous life must persistently hold their commitments lightly and lead what can be characterized as "provisional lives." No one has captured this ideal with greater insight and sympathy than the conservative critic David Brooks in his book *On Paradise Drive*. After a wickedly funny and poignant romp through the American suburban and exurban culture, Brooks does point out the immense personal costs that result from the expansion and reinforcement of this basic mindset. In his words,

> Under the influence of pragmatism, truth does not inhere absolutely in an idea; truth happens to an idea. An idea is held to be true when it turns out to be useful and good, when it serves its purpose in making life better at that moment for that individual. . . . Individual betterment is the center around which the entire universe resolves. This is a brutal form of narcissism. The weight of the universe is placed on the shoulders of the individual. Accordingly, in modern American culture, the self becomes semidivinized. People feel free to pick and choose their own religious beliefs, because whatever serves the self-journey toward happiness must be godly and true. . . . It means that the central question of life is not "what does God command and love?" but rather "what is my destiny and fulfillment."[41]

Because the metric against which one measures his or her particular "progress" in life is itself "self" determined, nothing can be sustained with the sort of conviction that may require suffering or prolonged anxiety. Such beliefs would simply not be sufficiently useful under any common-sense understanding of the term. This does not mean that various ideals and forms of life may not be strenuous—indeed, Brooks understands like Nietzsche that living in such a way requires its own brand of discipline—but rather that the admiration and respect for one's convictions is inversely related to the depth and tenacity with which they are held. The weak person is now the one who does not know when to quit rather than the other way around. In Brooks's words, "There are few rules, this mentality holds, that apply in all situations. What may be true for you may not be true for me. What may be true for me now may not be true for me later."[42] In this way, we are encouraged on the one hand to "spend" our autonomy—indeed even to fully exhaust it—but to do so with the proviso that we can always have it back if we are willing to endure the messiness involved with such an enterprise. What used to be a sign of immaturity, the desire to have one's cake and eat it too, as the adage once went, becomes a sign of one's

---

41. Brooks, *On Paradise Drive*, 276.
42. Brooks, *On Paradise Drive*, 277.

growth and development into a fully cognizant human being. This is why liberalism—caricatured though it is here—has such great difficulty with strong religious beliefs, especially strong Christian beliefs. And it is among the reasons that Carter claims that Christianity in America today has two basic choices, either to surrender to the larger culture or to become what he calls a "resisting faith."[43]

To be a "resisting faith" in this context is a strange idea for some insofar as there is no established church that one must struggle against for public space, recognition, or even viability. Certainly in a nation where 86 percent of the citizenry claim to be some brand of Christian, Christianity in general has no obvious fear of suppression or repression along at least any of the familiar historical political lines. Fighting against "nothing," however, is increasingly proving more difficult than fighting against some particular establishment or "thing" has ever proved to be. The liberal state as a *state* tends to suffocate with indifference rather than oppress with malice and violence. Its strategy is to refuse to engage in the marketplace of ideas and to prevent entrance into the public arena for those who are unwilling to accept the basic rules of "neutral" engagement. Domestication and conformity is then the price that strong belief must pay for entrance into the public realm while, ironically, strong "interest" is respected and encouraged by the political process. When those with such beliefs refuse both conformity *and* indifference, as Christians are effectively called to do, religion becomes a problem that the liberal state cannot ignore as it is currently constituted. The state as a *state* pushes back, and suddenly to those on the other end of the push, the force feels much like the force of any other state in many ways. This is not meant to equate the American liberal state with those that have engaged in heavy-handed acts of suppression like the Chinese, Saudis, or other authoritarian regimes. Because of its own commitment to the rule of law and individual rights, the liberal state has been highly—though imperfectly—restrained in its use of overt power against dissenters (especially when there are potentially so many of them). Without this standard political tool at its disposal, the liberal state is forced to push back by offering a *positive* vision of its own sense of the good. In other words, it must engage in an argument that explains why being a *liberal* citizen is better or preferable to being a *Christian* citizen. The first task, then, for a liberal state embarking on such a course is to recognize what to many was already obvious; namely, that there can be no such thing as a "neutral" defense of "neutrality." Accustomed to serving as the "house" and dealing the cards, the liberal state must take a seat at the table with everyone else; in other words, liberals must

---

43. Carter, *Culture of Disbelief*, 25.

become at least theoretical partisans. But, in doing so, they are of course putting themselves at risk, because they may not win the argument.

GETTING ALONG IN AMERICA

According to Bob Dylan, "sometimes Satan comes as a man of peace." Although his political agenda at the time was different than the one guiding this work, the point is an important one: not "fighting" battles that may be morally required can be its own kind of sin, and perhaps equally worthy of Dante's seventh level of hell—the one reserved for traitors. "Peace" can be even more seductive than "war" because it asks so little of its adherents. While fascism beckons its people to war, liberalism, when wrongly understood, can become a siren of peace. For Christians who remain impervious to its sweet song, liberalism must do something many of its defenders and critics alike believe it is ill-equipped in its present theoretical iteration to do: namely, take a side. Though Christians are called to both peace and civility, they are only means to the ends of serving God and doing God's will. Glenn Tinder has captured the tenuous nature of the Christian's civic personality as well as anyone, writing,

> [Christians] have always infuriated politically serious people. Christians are traditionally, in their relations with governments, obedient yet disrespectful. Thus, they violate the *ethos* of both secular radicals (disobedience grounded in disrespect) and of conservatives (obedience grounded in respect). Eschewing absolute principles, they are unreliable allies of either right or left.[44]

This "disrespectful obedience" is grounded not in a response to a particular state or political order, but rather in the belief that all states by virtue of their very existence as "states" are part of the necessary but wholly insufficient secular order. Called as they are to agapic or selfless love as an ideal, Christians know that no society or regime, whether fully theocratic or expansively liberal, can adequately promote or accommodate the fullness of the Christian vision because of both their a-transcendent nature and the omnipresence of human sin and what are now called "structures of sin." This should not be taken as an indication of some wholesale leveling or indiscriminate rejection of differentiation among various regimes and regime types, but instead as an acknowledgment of the imperfectability of human

---

44. Tinder, *Political Meaning of Christianity*, 210. When Tinder uses the phrase absolute principles in this context, it is hopefully obvious that he is referring to absolute "ideological" principles and not religious ones.

institutions period. Clearly, certain states are preferable and more defensible than others, while some are all but indefensible by definition. However, unlike the popular American claim that holds that the United States is the greatest nation on earth because we are the freest nation on earth, the appropriate metric for a Christian would have to do more with the degree to which conditions in a particular state are conducive to the full expression of the Christian faith by its adherents. That expression, though, is not simply a code word for power—indeed, I would make the argument that theocracies themselves are among the worst states in which to realize an appropriate Christian life. Instead, a state conducive to Christianity would be one that removes as many obstacles and barriers to the assertion of agapic love as possible and which allows for the most expansive flowering of that love in the form of public policy and orientation to its citizenry. The important caveat for all Christians as *Christians* is that what is done for reasons of faith does not cross the line and attempt to utilize state power to require faith or professions from others. What the liberal theorist may require out of a desire for peace and stability—no establishment of religion—the Christian requires *because* they understand that faith not chosen freely is not really faith.

In turn, this does not mean that the nonbeliever or different believer has a right to be shielded politically or legally from a reasonably delivered message lest their ears be offended, nor does it mean that the Christian has a right to be protected from alternative or even atheistic messages and policies. As someone might say, let all the flowers bloom. As long as entry into the democratic process remains relatively open, procedural norms retain their integrity, and faith itself is not legislated in either form or substance, then one's intention, motivation, and the substantive nature of what passes procedural muster should not be impeded by some unsustainable commitment to neutrality by the legal system. In those cases where one's conscience or particular confession is pushed by a set of outcomes beyond its limit, one retains the option of conscientious objection, civil disobedience, or, perhaps under certain circumstances, outright resistance or revolution. The truth is that most citizens are probably opposed to and even offended by at least some of the policies and laws currently on the books for reasons as innumerable as those that led to their adoption in the first place. While religion may add a little extra spice (and even gravitas) to a given debate, its suppression does not appreciably change the basic facticity of a given situation. I sincerely doubt that those who are on the losing end of a particular policy debate would comfort or console themselves with a phrase like the following: "Well, at least we didn't lose to the Christians." Indeed, it may be that exactly the opposite is true, namely that one might take comfort in losing a particular political battle to those who sought their victory in the name of love rather than some more parochial or self-serving interest.

Now of course there are going to be a number of areas where the line separating what is done *from* faith and what is done *to* faith will not be easily drawn—public school curricula come immediately to mind. It is also true that many Christians themselves will not act in good faith, to which I would respond, without meaning to be flip, politics is messy. There will be times when the democratic process itself is going to have to be the arbitrator of "right" and "wrong." There are also going to be times when a regime devoted to minority rights is going to have to rely on either extra-democratic or non-democratic (used here in a non-pejorative sense) institutions and processes, e.g., the Supreme Court or supermajorities to make certain decisions about the close calls. However, in those cases, assuming that my own argument is at all valid so far, the object of inquiry will not be the intentions or motives, but the results and effects measured and quantified as objectively as possible. Under this scheme, the Lemon Test could not survive and something much more respectful of the rough and tumble interplay between worldviews would have to be substituted. Whatever this might be, it would need to reject the idea that being "offended" and being "harmed" were only different in degrees.

This is, I believe, partially in keeping with the provocative but only half-right argument of Stanley Fish a decade or so ago. In an article and subsequent exchange with Father Richard John Neuhaus and others, Fish argues bluntly,

> If you persuade liberalism that its dismissive marginalizing of religious discourse is a violation of its own chief principle, all you will gain is the right to sit down at liberalism's table where before you were denied an invitation; but it will still be *liberalism's* table that you are sitting at, and the etiquette of the conversation will still be hers. That is, someone will now turn and ask, "Well, what does religion have to say about this question?" And when, as so often will be the case, religion's answer is doctrinaire (what else could it be?), the moderator (a title deeply revealing) will nod politely and turn to someone who is presumed to be more reasonable. To put the matter baldly, a person of religious conviction should not want to enter the market place of ideas but to shut it down, at least insofar as it presumes to determine matters that he believes have been determined by God and faith. The religious person should not seek an accommodation with

liberalism; he should seek to rout it from the field, to extirpate it, root and branch.[45]

The half-right part of the argument that surrounds this claim is that those who take their religion seriously and want it to play a more expansive public role must understand that in doing so they are now significantly more at risk for a number of potential outcomes that they might not find wholly desirable. The outcome alluded to by Fish is co-option. If Christianity is allowed to "sit at the liberal table," such that it is willing to be treated as simply one voice among many others while simultaneously respecting the parity and rights of other voices also present, it faces the prospect of becoming just another interest group vying for public resources and power. In turn, this may mean that a kind of inverse Lemon Test might ensue within the religious community; namely, the fear of entanglement of the state and religion. In other words, there is the risk that continuous participation in the political process on such grounds might dilute and reorient the fundamental identity of the church and its members.

The second potentially problematic outcome that Fish points to is marginalization, i.e., religion might lose or be ignored. While this may be the case at the national level due to what might be called Madisonian considerations related to size and diversity, it certainly would not be the case in many local or even some state jurisdictions. However, the point itself is well taken and can be viewed from two related angles. The first, as stated, is that by entering the political battlefield as a serious competitor, religion and its political program face the prospect of calling serious attention to themselves and creating a context whereby those who oppose them now feel compelled to organize and bring resources to bear against them in ways that they have been mostly free from up until now. For example, things like tax-exempt status might suddenly be placed at risk or the ability to send children to parochial schools or to homeschool might be made much more difficult. The other side of this coin is that those motivated by religious ideals who do manage to carry the day must be willing to risk serious resentment and anger on the part of those whom they will now be wielding power over. Ironically speaking, this might mean that those who took political action in the name of "love" might find themselves reviled and resented by those very folks they were reaching out to by joining the process in the first place. Subsequently, they may end up creating a world that is more damaged and wounded than the one they originally entered. This final point itself carries the seeds of yet another unintended and injurious consequence for the faith in that as the amount of negative attention increases in depth and breadth

45. Fish, "Why We Can't All Just Get Along."

some number of the faithful will themselves become disaffected and uncomfortable in their new socially scorned positions and walk away from public activity or even the faith itself.

In response to all these possibilities, as well as to the very real temptations of power itself, it is entirely possible that religious citizens might indeed come to embrace the combustible position Fish offers them in the last part of the paragraph: "*The religious person should not seek an accommodation with liberalism; he should seek to rout it from the field, to extirpate it, root and branch.*" In doing so, they would be following out the logic dictated by the metaphoric language of "competition" used by Carter and Fish alike, but they would at the same time fall victim to the same serious misunderstanding that plagues Fish's argument, namely (and ironically) his "foundational secularism." In broad terms, Fish starts from the concrete and the finite limits of the world as it is. As a result of this, everything appears to be a scarce resource and all contests gravitate toward zero-sum conclusions. In that world, what Christianity gains, liberalism loses and vice-versa. But, what if it is the contest itself that matters rather than the outcome? For the Christian, earthly or secular "victory" is simply not possible. Wounded by sin and with few exceptions drawn to it on a regular basis, the honest Christian knows that the final "victory" is determined by God's grace and human "effort." The Christian does not "win" the game because he or she triumphs in the political arena on any given day; the Christian wins the moment he or she enters the arena *as* a Christian with the intentions, means, and ends of a Christian always before him or her. The following prayer, often attributed to the late Archbishop Oscar Romero, captures this point as poignantly as anything I could write:

> It helps, now and then, to step back and take a long view. The kingdom is not only beyond our efforts, it is even beyond our vision. We accomplish in our lifetime only a fraction of the magnificent enterprise that is God's work. Nothing we do is complete, which is a way of saying that the Kingdom always lies beyond us. No statement says all that could be said. No prayer fully expresses our faith. No confession brings perfection. No pastoral visit brings wholeness. No program accomplishes the Church's mission. No set of goals and objectives includes everything. This is what we are about. We plant seeds that one day will grow. We water the seeds already planted, knowing that they hold future promise. We lay foundations that will need further development. We provide yeast that produces far beyond our capabilities. We cannot do everything, and there is a sense of liberation in realizing that. This enables us to do something, and

to do it very well. It may be incomplete, but it is a beginning, a step along the way, an opportunity for the Lord's grace to enter and do the rest. We may never see the end results, but that is the difference between the master builder and the worker. We are workers, not master builders; ministers, not messiahs. We are prophets of a future not our own.[46]

While there is a sliver of truth to Fish's rather harsh critique of the work of people like Stephen Carter, Michael McConnell, and George Marsden, when he claims that: "What they desire is the full enfranchisement of religious conviction. What they fear is the full enfranchisement of religious conviction," and that they "set out to restore the priority of the good over the right but find the protocols of the right—of liberal proceduralism—written in the fleshy tables of their hearts,"[47] it is the truth of a newly "enlightened" college freshman. There is no room for nuance in Fish's world and every nod toward conciliation is treated as capitulation or hypocrisy; failure to take one's position to its starkest and most dogmatic conclusion is used as evidence of one's lack of conviction, and any hint of inconsistency is considered some sort of intellectual death knell for one's whole argument. Under the guise of making arguments like theirs more forceful and compelling, Fish pushes them to be more extreme and accept what he believes to be the logical conclusions of their arguments. One suspects, however, that this is at least disingenuous, if not intellectually dishonest, on his part. My guess is that Stanley Fish's real target is not religion at all, but liberalism itself. By pushing these authors to positions that he knows will be considered extreme, Fish would, if successful, finally have the theocrats, so often rumored but rarely seen, among the ranks of American Christians. In turn, I believe that Fish hopes that American "liberals" would regain the courage of their own convictions and build even stronger and higher additions to the existing "wall of separation."[48] As the saying goes, "With friends like these . . ."

Regardless of Fish's intentions, there would be significant backlash from many sectors of the American political and intellectual community if

---

46. The prayer was part of a homily written by Fr. Ken Untener, titled "Prophets of a Future Not Our Own," and delivered originally in 1979 by Cardinal Dearden.

47. Fish, "Why We Can't All Just Get Along," 12.

48. Certainly, any depiction of Fish as a *liberal* is highly problematic given his long-standing and voluminous criticism of liberalism itself (see his book *There Is No Such Thing as Free Speech*, for example). However, for all his calls for committed action, he rarely makes clear what he is committed to. For Fish to be Fish, he requires the liberal state to exist and to attempt to enforce the very "neutrality" he derides. For a strong critique of Fish in this vein, see Owen, "Church and State in Stanley Fish's Antiliberalism," 911–24.

these writers and others like them took his "advice" to heart. This in and of itself is, of course, not a good reason for refraining from such an approach. In the larger scheme of Christian history, enduring said backlash would be among the smaller acts of "suffering" one could expect a believer to endure on behalf of the faith. It is clearly part of my argument so far that Christians need to be bolder and more visible in their practice of the faith even at the price of peace at times. However, there are more profound and strategic reasons for refusing to take Fish's bait that Neuhaus and others make clear in their various responses. Strategically, the sheer power and magnitude of the current culture of liberalism in the United States makes this approach untenable and ill-conceived—one must begin from where one is rather than where one wishes they were. Additionally, there are substantial areas of agreement on a number of norms and values that make wholesale departure from the current consensus rather silly as well as difficult. A properly restrained and understood liberalism is perfectly consistent with a stronger Christian presence, as argued in the previous chapter. Finally, the most important reason for rejecting Fish is, of course, that the path he suggests is itself un-Christian.

At its most basic level, Christianity seeks the conversion of hearts and the transformation of human behavior in a manner reflecting that conversion with an eye toward eternal salvation and resurrection after bodily death. While it should be clear that I believe there are serious political implications that can be derived from the logic of the faith, it is also true that Christianity is not a theory of governance. While the faith can be *practiced* in virtually any particular state or under any sort of regime (almost), it is certainly true that some states and regimes are more hospitable than others. Any state as a *state*, however, is not equipped to facilitate conversion or salvation due to its limited array of tools and objectives. All states as *states* tend toward monism and uniformity, including, ironically, the liberal state. Fish's notion of "routing" the opposition suggests that it is the natural order of any group of believers—religious or not—to seek uniformity and dominance over those who oppose them, and, subsequently, to turn the power of the state once gained toward this purpose. In his response to Fish, Neuhaus explains why this logic is inappropriately applied to Christianity:

> Christianity does propose a unified conception of life, but that unified conception of life comprehends and makes possible the pluralistic character of life as we experience it. A unified conception of life does not require monism. John Courtney Murray said that pluralism is written into the script of history, and I would add that it seems God did the writing. By pluralism,

> I mean a world in which people live by significantly different accounts of reality, including moral and religious reality, and must learn to live together. Given the variousness built into creation—and especially into people and cultures—ours would be a pluralistic world even if everybody on earth became Christian, for there are obviously and necessarily different ways of being Christian.[49]

"Unity in diversity" is the way most Christians put this idea. Although there are limits to what the Christian can tolerate, the most expansive category is the list of things that the Christian must not only tolerate, but come to appreciate and even love *because* they are different manifestations of God's creation. It is not for the sake of peace or as a result of some political program that the Christian embraces diversity, but rather because that is what God wills for us. Difference is a fact of creation, and as creation is itself good, so too is difference. As Neuhaus puts it,

> In the Christian view, tolerance is not a compromise of truth but obedience to truth. . . . We do not kill one another over our disagreements about the will of God because it is the will of God that we do not kill one another over our disagreements about the will of God.[50]

He goes on to explain that this approach is made necessary by two factors, namely "cognitive humility and love for neighbor." While never relieved of the need to choose and to act by virtue of being human, the Christian must always recognize that because their knowledge is imperfect and their motives always tainted by the potential for sin they must be cautious of certainty and, therefore, be predisposed to suffer harm rather than doing it. While it took the faithful a long time to recognize this explicitly, and while the temptations to coerce remain strong in many human hearts and minds, the fundamental truth of this proposition is contained in the very core of the faith and made real by Christ's sacrifice itself. As suggested in chapter 1 and stated bluntly by Neuhaus, "Religious freedom is mainly an achievement of religion."[51] It is not done in the name of peace or order, but in the name of love.

---

49. Neuhaus, "Why We Can Get Along," 7.
50. Neuhaus, "Why We Can Get Along," 7.
51. Neuhaus, "Why We Can Get Along," 9.

AFTER THE FALL

After his conviction and sentencing by democratic Athens, the Socrates of Plato's *Crito* is given the opportunity to escape and famously refuses based on theory that in doing so, he would further weaken the city of his birth and betray both the implicit or tacit deal he struck with them, as well as his own integrity. Recall this earlier quote from David Brooks: "An idea is held to be true when it turns out to be useful and good, when it serves its purpose in making life better at that moment for that individual."[52] If Brooks's depiction of the American moral mind is at all on target, the figure of Socrates must be a complete and utter enigma to it. The paradoxical implications of this in a nation ostensibly filled with Christians and other religious citizens who believe in God (96 percent) is almost unfathomable on its face. While we reject postmodernism in principle, we enact its larger possibilities in fact. In such a place, work like Richard Rorty's *Contingency, Irony and Solidarity* is no longer radical or audacious philosophy so much as it is a kind of dense journalism. He is scratching a phantom limb, as it were, of an age now past. As such, he and others of his ilk are awaiting a confession rather than a conversion from the American people. While there are those who would like to place the blame for this on institutions like the Supreme Court,[53] the reality is that this state of affairs could not have occurred without fairly massive public assent, if not indeed actual consent. Simply put, many of those American citizens who are also Christians have lost their way. They have forgotten where they came from and, like Euthyphro, prosecuted their "past" on the basis of a principle that they cannot defend without it. Hence, while it remains clear that Christianity can in fact survive without liberalism, it is less clear that liberalism can survive without Christianity *and*, more importantly, Christians in the long run.

Embedded in this chapter is an argument that will be made more explicitly and grounded theologically in the following chapter. Essentially, liberalism in its original historical formulation is itself the by-product of a religiously grounded "comprehensive doctrine" that requires the continuing assent—tacit and often inexplicit as it may be—of large swaths of the American citizenry to certain core religious (Christian) assumptions and ideals concerning the anthropology of the human person for its continuing philosophic and in all likelihood political sustainability. To the extent that such assumptions and ideals are either discarded, undermined, or relegated to the private sphere or individual conscience, and denied both their public

---

52. Brooks, *On Paradise Drive*, 276.
53. See Muncy and Neuhaus, *End of Democracy*.

character and a meaningful public hearing by the very regime they helped give life and legitimacy to in the first place, said regime puts itself at great risk for both theoretical and historical implosion. Finally, a theory of liberalism that encourages and promotes such a process is internally inconsistent and at odds with itself. As such, it will require increasing levels of anomalyic reconstruction and shoring up to remain coherent that will, in turn, continue to undermine its overall hold on the collective minds and consciences of a significant numbers of American citizens over time.

These sorts of claims are not particularly new insofar as they go to the issues of foundationalism and justification that used to haunt Enlightenment thinkers. However, they are no longer in vogue among most contemporary philosophers or theorists. What, though, we must wonder will be the result if the answer to Roberto Unger's question of "whether [we] can fully acknowledge the contingency of social worlds and complete the unfinished break with the spirit of classical social doctrine while nevertheless continuing to make normative claims" is no? In other words, what if for psychological, philosophical, or theological reasons significant numbers of Americans cannot accept the easygoing stance of a self-professed "freeloading atheist" like Richard Rorty and embrace liberalism out of either emotivism or pure reason itself?[54] What if a majority needs a reason to believe? What if Robert Kraynak is correct when he claims that he will show that

> liberal democracy is unable to vindicate these lofty claims about human dignity, either on the practical level of daily living in a modern mass society or on the theoretical level in the arguments of the liberal philosophers. Hence, [concluding] liberal democracy cannot stand on its own and needs support from the biblical claim that human beings are made in the image and likeness of God[?][55]

If liberal democracy itself is desirable as a political order, but is also historically, philosophically, and morally contingent on having citizens who consent to it and believe that it is correct, who, in turn, will not do so without some transcendent justification, what should a good liberal do? In chapter 3, I will flesh all these details out, and I will argue that there is no compelling justification for liberalism that has emerged which is superior to or as reliable as the Christian case for achieving widespread agreement among free citizens, especially citizens of faith, on the fundamental ideals and assumptions of the liberal state. Furthermore, I will contend that no substitute justification that is not itself "illiberal" has been found for forming people

54. See Duncan, "Question for Richard Rorty," 385–413.
55. Kraynak, *Christian Faith and Modern Democracy*, 11.

into good "liberals." People, in other words, who respect the equal dignity and worth of all and embrace the pluralism and diversity of the world. People who are dedicated to protecting a wide array of individual rights and liberties such that an expansive notion of personal autonomy properly understood can be ensured. Simply put, the explanatory or persuasive power of religion itself is required. In other words, I will try to demonstrate that it is not the truth that sets us free, but rather it is the truth that makes many of us care about and defend freedom for others in the first place.

3

Christianity and Alienation

The men left there and went to Sodom while Abraham remained standing before Yahweh. Approaching him he said, "Are you really going to destroy the just man with the sinner? Perhaps there are fifty just men in the town. Will you really overwhelm them, will you not spare the place for the fifty just men in it?" . . . Yahweh replied, "If at Sodom I find fifty just men in the town, I will spare the whole place because of them." . . . He said, "I trust my Lord will not be angry if I speak once more: perhaps there will only be ten." "I will not destroy it," he replied, "for the sake of the ten."

—Genesis 18:22–33

I tell you solemnly once again, if two on earth agree to ask anything at all, it will be granted to you by my Father in heaven. For where two or three meet in my name, I shall be there with them.

—Matthew 18:19–20

Then to all he said, "If anyone wants to be a follower of mine, let him renounce himself and take up his cross every day and follow me. For anyone who wants to save his life will lose it; but anyone who loses his life for my sake, that man will save it."

—Luke 9:23–25

FAITH HAS CONSEQUENCES

There are two mistaken readings of the concluding argument from chapter 2 that need to be quashed before they take intellectual root. While both misreadings have considerable historical lineage, both are now all but discredited among intellectually serious thinkers even while retaining some residual semantic currency in the culture at large. These are best thought of as the utilitarian arguments for religious belief and they both rest on the same basic assumption that people need to believe that there is some good and truthful reason for obeying certain moral imperatives. In its standard formulation, the argument goes something like this: If there is no God, then right and wrong are simply subjective ideas and people would feel released from the need to obey rules and strictures with which they disagreed without guilt or hesitation beyond the fear of getting caught or some other reprisal. In this case, religion becomes a useful fiction that serves the ends of social control by giving people significant extra-human incentives for controlling themselves and obeying the moral rules of society. The second version of this line of thinking is simply the flip side of the first, insofar as it goes to the question of institutional legitimacy rather than individual behavior. Here, religion becomes the final refuge for those charged with issuing authoritative edicts and commands to others, who are either skeptical or simply require some seemingly definitive brand of justification as the price for their acquiescence. This set of questions is at least as old as Plato who, according to J. Peter Euben, grounded his own project in the following sort of question twenty-three hundred years ago: "How is it possible for men to stop short of regarding anything as possible once they regard all arrangements as conventional if not arbitrary?"[1]

While the questions themselves remain valid, especially in an age where deep skepticism is something of a categorical imperative for the intellectually serious person, the argument that I was asserting, and would now like to make in greater detail, is quite different and ironically reverses the utility argument in an unexpected and an uncomfortable way. At its simplest, the argument places careful and thoughtful Christians in the positions or roles of *aliberal* vanguards of *liberalism*. Metaphorically, the Christian is like the great-great-grandparent to the liberal "child." While the latter may never have known nor even be in a position to recognize the former, and might even be unwilling to recognize the progenitor as progenitor for whatever reason, the truth of the relationship remains and is temporally and logically ordered. Whatever the particular attributes and characteristics that

---

1. Euben, "Battle of Salamis," 359–90.

the younger offspring might have acquired, and however broad or deep the subsequent differentiation of the child is from the elder relative, the genetic code itself retains its integrity even as it morphs from generation to generation. Over time, later generations will become so distant and bloodlines and histories so tangled and diffused that it will induce a sort of prideful forgetfulness that deludes the offspring into the false belief that they were somehow self-begotten. This is the residual effect of a Cartesian mindset of emptying out the self that still holds sway even over many so-called postmodern men and women as they attempt to claim a self-sufficiency that they know to be false even while acting, thinking, and speaking as if it was true. This extended metaphor is not intended to suggest in any way that the Christian progenitor to the liberal progeny was complete, whole, or fully revealed such that all subsequent generations were mere patinas on the original; indeed, much of the time it has been the case that each new generation has further enhanced and expanded the revelation first glimpsed in the elders. But in its pride, the "youth" also forgets and denies as well. When that happens, the revelation is made smaller, less full, and harder to know in its entirety. At its simplest, the argument that follows rests on the idea that Christianity is intellectually *necessary* for liberalism even when historically it has been *insufficient* for its flourishing.[2]

Having now pushed this line of thinking about as far as it will go, I will acknowledge what is no doubt an important immediate objection that can be raised here, namely "gratitude" or "acknowledgment" aside, so what? To answer that question, I want to first borrow a story whose import might at first seem impolite, but whose deeper meaning I think is apropos for responding to the objection. The story is one told by Kirkpatrick Sale in the acknowledgments of his book *Human Scale* and goes something like this: Long ago there was a tribe whose predominate food supply was based on corn. One year, they discovered that the entire crop was infected in such a way that anyone who ate from the tainted food supply would go insane. Faced with the choice between starvation and insanity, the tribe decided to eat the corn and live. However, before they did so, certain members of the

---

2. It is important to note here that I am not arguing that the liberal political order is the only one compatible with Christianity, i.e., only liberal-democratic states are justifiable under Christian theology, or even that the liberal state is the most consistent with Christian social teaching. Rather, I am arguing that to the extent that the liberal state is a coherent idea at all it is so because of what it owes to Christian thinking and logic. To return momentarily to the metaphoric imagery of this section, nothing, if we bracket off some sort of determinism, about the great-great grandparent's own genetic makeup is wholly determinative of the genetic makeup of the later great-grandchild, but, whatever that particular child's makeup is, could not have been were it not for the makeup of the progenitor's.

tribe were singled out and given only the corn stored from the previous year's crop that had been reserved for the gods. That way, the tribe reasoned, there would at least be some members of the tribe who would remember that the others were insane. Without unpacking this idea to too great a degree, I would hope that the readers could readily see that there are obvious reasons why it might be beneficial for the perpetuation of the "sane" ranging from the simply practical—someone needed to plant the corn for the following season and care for those who were not well—to the less ephemeral reasons, like the need that the tribe had to maintain its historical integrity, dignity, and cultural longevity. In other words, even if we assume—in good liberal fashion—that there is no legitimate moral grounds for preferring the "sane" to the "insane," there are still very real and pragmatic reasons for preserving the distinction between them; namely, that by underscoring their differences, both groups are preserved and made better off. Such is the case I want to suggest for Christians and liberals regardless of whether someone is either one or the other or both.

Hopefully, the reader will excuse the rhetorical flight of fancy above and recognize that it is not my claim that those who do not accept the Christian-centric framework being developed are "insane." However, I do want to suggest that those who arrive at the larger principles of liberalism from some sort of Kantian-inspired "original position" rather than through a theological—faith seeking understanding—or revelatory framework, are different in ways that matter. This is hardly a radical statement, and I am certain both sides in general would readily stipulate to the crux of the observation. What neither side could stipulate to in good faith would be which of them had eaten the "good" corn. In other words, who is the standard-bearer of "normalcy" and, therefore, the rightful claimant or philosophic proprietor of our public narrative and its civic discourse? Harkening back to the introduction of this book, what will the dominate political "language" of the American public square ultimately be and why?

For a person who—*pace* Aquinas—believes that grace completes reason, the answer to the query above is both/and. And, as I tried to demonstrate in the first chapter, for much of American history the constitutional public square also was broad enough to hold both groups with only minimal discomfort and occasional conflicts as well. However, over the course of the last fifty years or so, as the "exclusionist" view has come to dominate constitutional thinking on the question of religion. Ironically, it has done so by claiming to be more inclusive and by insisting that with regard to religious discourse that no particular "narrative" be privileged or even accorded public acknowledgment. The result has been to require and enforce a sort of sterile uniformity in the name of diversity and respect for difference.

Everyone, it seems, must either eat the same "corn" or at least never let on to the others publicly that they ate from a different crop lest someone be offended or marginalized in some way. But, to return to the question at hand more directly, what if it is actually the case that the privileging of some is indeed the prerequisite for the survival of all?

T. S. Eliot's suggestion that it is entirely likely that liberalism—especially, I would contend, in its most contemporary form—*may be a tendency towards something very different from itself* has certainly been borne out with the advent of certain strains of postmodernism. To the extent that such thinking has moved from philosophy and literature to the world of politics, it has remained fairly well ensconced in the liberal context if not its rationalism, i.e., the least radical and most accepted (tacitly though it often is) variant takes the priority of the "right" over the "good" and the derivative enshrinement of widespread toleration that quickly results as axiomatic. However, a largely unintended consequence of the postmodern iteration of so-called liberal neutrality has been its recent appropriation by a number of conservatives and even the devoutly religious for their own particular ends.

Once Enlightenment rationalism and materialism are themselves decentered from their privileged positions and rendered just one tradition or narrative among many, the level social field that results is suddenly much more hospitable to modes of thinking and belief that could not pass muster under the previous thought regime's intellectual dicta. A recent example of this in action would be to look at the demands of the religious fundamentalists seeking accommodation for biblical stories of creationism in contemporary science curricula based on the plea to "teach the controversy" rather than on their more ardent belief that they are right and the evolutionists are wrong. While the mainstream scientific community itself continues to rely on an empirical and experimental methodology at least as old as Copernicus to sustain its truth claims, the philosophers of the age have rendered their approach just one of many ways of knowing that can be no more privileged that the rest. While I believe that in the long run this represents a dangerous and self-destructive strategy for the faithful, its short-term utility is obvious.[3] Where none can claim superiority, truth claims become oppressive and must be recast in such a way that the viability of other's worldviews are not threatened. In the case of the fundamentalists, when you have been operating at a deficit for so long in terms of public respect and accommodation, parity is as good as victory. Unfortunately, it is also a recipe for impotence, indifference, and irrelevance in the long run—and not just for the religious.

3. See Duncan, "Christian Right's Postmodern Turn," 50–76.

While the distinction between the "objective" and the "subjective" may be difficult to maintain in the realm of values and faith in a pluralistic society, the distinction between "fiction" and "nonfiction" must be retained if any values are to be held with much seriousness. What I mean by this distinction is that while a robust liberalism might require its citizens to withhold judgment or condemnation of differing worldviews in the name of tolerance and fairness, it does not (and I will argue, should not) encourage citizens to hold their own hard-won and heartfelt beliefs and ideals lightly. A liberal society that wishes to preserve itself must cultivate citizens who are *confidently humble*. To treat one's own beliefs and values as fictional would mean to hold them without confidence. To treat one's own values as objectively true for all would be to lack the humility necessary for a functional pluralism. This humble yet confident stance marks the Christian at his or her best. In such a position, we can find the essence of the journey to the Cross: i.e., the confident Christian knows that salvation is at hand and is willing to undergo immense suffering if needed to achieve it, while at the same time, he or she is humble such that they ask no one to hang upon the Cross against their will. I would contend that contemporary liberalism in its "modern" form (e.g., Rawls) is confident but not humble, i.e., it believes that it is self-sufficient. In its "postmodern" form (e.g., Rorty), I would contend that it is humble but not confident, i.e., it believes that everything is ultimately fictional. Only those who accept and believe in a "hierarchy of ends" can ultimately be *confident* in their beliefs. And, only those for whom the highest end is the respect and agapic love of the Other can be truly *humble*. While this may apply to non-Christians as well (as I will argue below), it is at least the mark of a Christian. Without such people, the liberal order may indeed be able to sustain itself as a modern version of Plato's "city in speech"—an ideal, but it will not be able to sustain itself as a real city unless Christians or those like them are allowed to rule—that is, participate as *Christians* in the public realm. Christians, in turn, must get their own theology right and themselves right with their theology in order to fulfill their now privileged role—i.e., their spiritually required civic duties—correctly and faithfully.

Now, of course, I realize how outlandish this argument will sound to many, if not most, Americans. If Tocqueville got "us" right almost two hundred years ago when he said that we would endure barbarism and even slavery in equality to aristocracy if push came to shove, then the picture here of some sort of Christian-Platonic-Guardians preserving the "liberal city" will raise both hackles and probably the enmity of any "nonbelievers" who have made it this far. I am also certain that there are many "faithful" readers who are now bristling at the suggestion that the Christian faith may require them to defend a "liberal" political order that seeks their marginalization, capitulation, and even silence. I hope that by the end of this chapter both might be convinced that this is at least worth continued dialogue. By way of foreshadowing, I would remind my liberal readers that the life of the Guardians in Plato's *Republic* was not one that most people would find desirable. Hence, if it does reek of elitism or aristocracy, it is not of the variety that will induce envy or jealousy. For the Christian readers, I would only say that we should never forget that ours is a demanding faith whose exemplar—while certainly risen—first had to die a painful and quite lonely death.

INDIVIDUALISM AND EXALTATION

Glenn Tinder asks in his fine work *The Political Meaning of Christianity*, "To what extent are we now living on moral savings accumulated over many centuries but no longer being replenished? To what extent are those savings severely depleted?"[4] Tinder believes the extent to which that is happening is both significant and unsustainable. The "account" is dwindling quickly and the result is an ever-increasing specter of moral insecurity. For Machiavellian realists, who rely on the power of a Prince who is properly "feared" (though not hated), this is not ultimately a *political* problem. Nor is it a political problem on a literalist reading of Thomas Hobbes's *Leviathan* insofar as self-interested or possessive individualism drives both the formation and perpetuation of the political community through the body of the contractually constituted sovereign. It is, however, a very real problem for those liberal theorists and partisans who believe that the liberal state's claims to legitimacy rest first and foremost on an essentially moral or normative foundation like Locke, Kant, Rawls, or the vast majority of American citizens.

While a simple Marxist reading of the *Second Treatise* can easily depict it as an ideological stalking horse for the English middle class and their political interests, the larger message of the text and its ultimate force, authority, and longevity are clearly rooted in its straightforward and highly accessible normative logic. After thousands of years of relatively un-reflexive acquiescence on the part of the human race and a view of the "citizen" as subject, the rapacious and all-encompassing rejection of nonconsensual political authority that took place in the West in just a few short generations is nothing short of amazing. Although Hegel was no doubt premature when he declared history to be at an end in 1806, the fact that *the* philosopher of his age would even think to draw such a conclusion suggests that the liberal idea broadly construed had penetrated the political *ethos* in a manner that went well beyond what a rational calculation could have possibly yielded

---

4. Tinder, *Political Meaning of Christianity*, 51.

in such a short time span. Thinking emblematically, it is incredible that the time from the textual birth of one of the most radical and convention-shattering set of ideas in 1681 to the proclamation that such ideas were "self-evident" truths in 1776 is just ninety-five years! Simply put, Locke and his fellow travelers must have tapped into something in the human psyche that seems metaphysically *essential*. What, we must ask, made so many so open to a shift in thinking whereby the revolutionary became the common sense in the space of what is basically the span of a single life?

Since a number of readers would no doubt reject the Thomistic answer that such a thing was "imprinted" on the human heart, a historical candidate for the role of "least common denominator" must be found. Here the only reasonable contender for the part would seem to be Christianity and the larger Judeo-Christian tradition. Here, I concur with the argument of one of the leading thinkers of the twentieth century, Jürgen Habermas, who explains in an interview with Eduardo Mendieta,

> For the normative self-understanding of modernity, Christianity has functioned as more than just a precursor or a catalyst. Universalistic egalitarianism, from which sprang the ideals of freedom and a collective life in solidarity, the autonomous conduct of life and emancipation, the individual morality of conscience, human rights, and democracy, is the direct legacy of the Judaic ethic of justice and the Christian ethic of love.[5]

Now it is certainly true that just because the liberal tradition as a normative tradition rests on this particular historical foundation does not necessarily mean that it cannot be sustained and perpetuated independently and on its own terms. Indeed, this was ostensibly Hobbes's own political project[6] before Locke, and obviously the driving force behind Kant's moral philosophy and Rawls's neo-Kantian work as well. In fact, virtually the entire history of post-Lockean moral theory in the West represents the attempt to find a non-theological basis for the primary moral commitments entailed in liberal theory. The perceived inability to actually accomplish this feat for much of that history ultimately gives the world Nietzsche. In the postmodern era, a good deal of politico-moral theorizing can be subsequently characterized as an attempt to maintain and expand the central commitment of liberal morality in a foundationless or emotivist moral world. The fact that this project as well as its Enlightenment counterpart has so far failed, philosophically speaking, does not mean that all hope is lost, but neither should anyone be optimistic about the future prospects, given this difficult intellectual history.

5. Habermas, "Conversation about God and the World," 149.
6. See Owen, "Tolerant Leviathan," 130–48.

Bereft of some overarching and unifying theory to replace Christianity (assuming the historical argument above has any validity), the choice for liberal morality and its sustaining political order will remain the by-product of the general will, luck, and power. This "foundation," such as it is, seems entirely too precarious by itself to rest something valuable on, especially given that the primary political form tasked with sustaining the liberal regime is increasingly one marked by a secularist mass democracy and the rule of the bureaucratic state. Why? Because the primary moral commitment in liberal moral theory itself exists in a fundamental tension with the inevitable drift toward the conformity and uniformity that such a state seems destined to beget. Ironically, that primary moral commitment begins and ends with the ideal of the inviolable human person, or what we could earlier have called the sacred or exalted individual properly understood. Stripped to its core belief, liberalism's central philosophic and moral commitment is to the free and flourishing individual human being. All of the attendant political commitments associated with it as a political ideology, including its defense of natural rights, liberty, equality, democracy, limited government, and private property are ultimately in service to that end. However, despite the truth of this assertion on its face, a central question remains which cannot itself be answered from within the tradition as it is currently constituted and understood in philosophic circles: Why should an individual human being as an individual be the central preoccupation of moral philosophy and political theory instead of the state, the family, the class, the race, the gender, the ethnicity, the caste, and/or the religious identity? What makes the *individual* human being, regardless of all those other possible and often traditional and time-tested variables, worthy of its exceptional and privileged place in our moral and political discourse? In simplified form, why liberalism at all?

On that question, despite valiant attempts over the past four hundred years to give a credible explanation on its own terms, liberalism *qua* liberalism has nothing to say on this score that would persuade those who are not already convinced and committed to the central belief or value of the approach in the first place. It should not be forgotten that the proponents of divine-right monarchy changed their minds under the threat of the sword, the guillotine, and the gun—not on the basis of an argument. While most political change will occur in this manner, i.e., through violence or the threat of violence, it is particularly paradoxical for liberalism to rest ultimately on such a coercive foundation. This is exactly the kind of dilemma mapped out so well in Alasdair MacIntyre's early essay: "Notes form the Moral Wilderness." To demonstrate that its advent was corrective and radical rather than simply an instance of the bourgeoisie's successful will to power or proof that "might makes right," liberalism has to be placed into a larger historical context, narrative, and tradition. Failure to do so entails surrendering its moral legitimacy and theoretical warrants for reasoning men and women. Though MacIntyre was writing about those Marxists who wanted to reject the immoral excesses of Stalinism, the logic of the argument is the same. In MacIntyre's words,

> There are then some grounds for a suspicion that the moral critics of Stalinism may have done no more than exchange one dominant pattern of thought for another; but the new pattern gives them the illusion of moral independence. Yet the very nature of their new morality must make their answer to the question which I originally posed seem extraordinarily thin and unconvincing even to them. Why do the moral standards by which Stalinism is found wanting have authority over us? Simply because we choose that they should. The individual confronting the facts with his values condemns. But he can only condemn in the name of his own choice.[7]

Substitute divine-right monarchy for Stalinism and liberal individualism for its moral critics, and the problem is evident. So how is one to escape the moral wilderness in the case at hand? Elongate the historical view an iteration or two and see if the story can be made more sensible, consistent, and reasonable.

In taking this step, we quickly shift liberalism from the beginning of the story to the end or midpoint of some fuller tale. While there may be other worthy contenders that some may wish to argue on behalf of, for my money it is the Judeo-Christian story that holds out the most cogent and coherent promise for understanding the "truth" of a properly understood individualism and its political counterpart, the liberal state. I say this because the Christian story is both revolutionary and without easy precedent as both a moral and nonfictional narrative.[8] In simplified form, the Christian tale in particular can answer why we should privilege individualism without recourse to simply power, might, or personal preference. Liberalism, on its own, cannot.

---

7. Quoted in Knight, *The MacIntyre Reader*, 33–34.

8. I have used this distinction earlier but wanted to clarify it here. By stepping away from the object/subjective dichotomy and using the fiction/nonfiction distinction, no one has to commit to the ultimate truth of the proposition only to the fact that the storytellers and their followers believe it to be true and thereby think, judge, and act accordingly. Few people who read about unicorns actually make finding one their life's work, but many who believe in Jesus Christ do in fact seek to emulate him and ultimately to know him.

While the true beginning of the Christian story is the book of Genesis and God's claim that he has made man and woman in his own image (Gen 1:27), the most vivid warrant for human dignity provided by Christianity comes through the Incarnation and the subsequent crucifixion (the latter at least requires no transcendent commitments to believe). Glenn Tinder's reading of this pivotal event is that through the crucifixion, "God has established his solidarity with the human race and with all its members; in consequence, every person is exalted and glorified." He goes on to assert further that, as a result of that action of the Lord, "the dignity of the individual, often ineffective and trite as a human ideal, becomes the law of all being and history," and that it becomes ultimately "the source of all political obligations."[9] Among the keys to this assertion is the recognition that God's solidarity is with each human being individually rather than collectively. In other words, God does not love *humanity* in general. God loves and sacrificed his only Son for each human being as an individual person. God loves the particular person and calls upon each of us to do the same. Among the better biblical images on this score comes from Matthew 10:30–33, when he quotes Jesus as having said:

> And yet not one falls to the ground without your Father knowing. Why, every hair on your head has been counted. . . . So if anyone declares himself for me in the presence of men, I will declare myself for him in the presence on my Father in heaven.

What does it mean to declare for Christ? It means to obey the great commandment: "Love one another; just as I have loved you, you must love one another" (John 3:34). To accomplish this, the Christian must attempt to love each human being as an individual person in a manner that transcends the common-sense world of friends and lovers, and instead aim at self-less or agapic love—love without conditions, love without calculation of costs and benefits, and love even in the face of hate and threats to one's own person. For the Christian, each soul must be valued in its own right, with its own dignity, and with its own destiny. Each individual is a sacred part of the larger mystery of human existence and cannot be arbitrarily sacrificed or made the means for another's ends without violating the great commandment. Tinder again captures the *political* implications of this ideal:

> The concept of the exalted individual implies that governments, and all persons with power, must treat individuals with care. . . . However variously care may be defined, it always means that

---

9. Tinder, *Political Meaning of Christianity*, 7.

human beings are not to be treated like things we use, discard, or just leave lying about . . . no one is to be casually sacrificed.[10]

While such a position does not point explicitly to a particular political order, it does point toward a certain type of political *regime*.[11] Though the insurmountable barriers to creating a society on earth that perfectly reflects, or in all likelihood even tries to approximate, a world where every person was considered "exclusively as an end, not as a means" implies that there can never be such a thing as a Christian society or nation properly understood. It is impossible to imagine a regime that was at least using this ideal as its point of departure which did not guarantee certain rights to individuals and which did not specify certain duties or obligations for them as well.[12]

Now the American liberal state is closely and favorably associated with the securing of individual rights and liberties that demonstrate the privileged place of the individual in the political regime. However, the regime is rightfully faulted for paying significantly less and less attention to the concept of duties.[13] This diminished attention is the result of an increasing secularization of the regime and the concomitant forgetfulness or ignorance on the part of its citizenry of the deeper historical and philosophical moorings which can serve to legitimize their political claims in the first place. Many of us, it would seem, have eaten the tainted corn. In the short run, it may not matter much insofar as there are still funds in the nation's moral account. We "live" better than our increasingly thin theory suggests we should. But to what extent this is just the by-product of rote habit is an important question for those who believe for reasons, however selfish or duty-centered, that such a regime is worth preserving. To the extent that the moral-theoretical narrative of liberalism is increasingly viewed as fictional or made up, I would contend that it grows proportionally weaker and less sustainable—let alone intellectually defensible beyond our collective and possibly fickle preferences. To aid in the process of returning our collective story to the genre of nonfiction in a manner keeping with the Christian narrative, put forward above it is necessary to name and debunk a critical counter-narrative within the liberal story that has emerged and exists in competition with it around the question of human anthropology itself.

---

10. Tinder, *Political Meaning of Christianity*, 32.

11. On the idea of the "regime" as the political soul or *ethos* of a country as compared to the idea of the nation or the state in a physical or even a constitutional sense, see Strauss, *Natural Right and History*.

12. Tinder, *Political Meaning of Christianity*, 62.

13. See Glendon, *Rights Talk*.

THE MYTH OF NATURAL MAN

Anthropology can be defined as the science that deals with the origins, physical and cultural development, biological characteristics, and social customs and beliefs of humankind. Hence, on some level, everyone who attempts to say something meaningful and truthful about some aspect of human existence is engaged in some aspect of anthropology, broadly construed. I am sure that to the professional anthropologist this is often a source of real frustration and indignation. Political theorists, as much as anyone, can easily be accused of practicing anthropology without a license. To say something about how political communities *ought* to be put together typically involves addressing the objective condition of the variables or the parts of the political community—it is obviously difficult to get where you would like to go if you have no idea where it is you are starting from. Sometimes this is easy. No political theorist would think the bottom of the ocean is an appropriate place to found a political community. Even if our *social* customs or *beliefs* did not prevent this, our *biological characteristics* make this almost absolutely impossible. Despite the contrariness of the profession, I doubt that anyone would argue with this as an objective statement: political communities should not be founded under the ocean because human beings are biologically unsuited to live at the bottom of the ocean. Most questions are not this easy.

Among the more difficult and, yet, perennial anthropological questions that political theorists and moral philosophers struggle with is an amorphous variable called "human nature." Another is the even trickier question of human origins. However "evolutionary" one is in his or her thinking, most theorists believe that there is at least some relationship between the two questions, i.e., human origins and human nature. In addition, virtually all political theorists believe that there must be some relationship—even if it is an antagonistic one—between human nature and properly formulated political development. This nexus is certainly true for liberal political theorists and moral philosophers. Unfortunately, their story of human origins is often a fictional one. A very useful fiction, *politically* speaking, in its original time and place, but not as useful under the present circumstances as it used to be. In fact, many would argue that it has in fact become a destructive fiction under our present circumstances. For those of us who believe that the dominant liberal story of human origins is fictional, it follows that we find the various conceptions of human nature which flow out from that story are also unduly fictional. Finally, to the extent that both the conception of human origins and human nature cannot be sustained as nonfictional accounts, any political theorizing that rests upon those foundations is itself compromised and highly dubious.

Although their particular accounts of human nature differ in significant ways, the account of human origins relied on by the major liberal contract theorists, Hobbes, Locke, and Rousseau, are very similar at the general level. In each account of the state of nature, the human person is depicted as a radically a-social creature, an unencumbered individual. For Hobbes, this individual's a-sociality is a source of fear and violence and quickly produces in the typical human being a desire for the security of a strong and protective state. For Locke, the a-sociality of the human person is a source of radical inconvenience and makes ease and happiness difficult to come by so various social groups are sought to divide labor and rationalize material existence, i.e., the family, society, and the minimal state. For Rousseau, our a-sociality is actually *not* a source of distress at all. His individuals lack the self-consciousness to know what they are missing and are defined by their capacity for pity rather than their tendency to violence and domination. The discussions and debates around the thought of these three thinkers is vast and legion and I will not rehash it here except in the most cursory manner. The reason I call each of these accounts fictional, despite their relative differences, is simple—their asocial individuals are neither real nor possible. They are like unicorns—easily imagined, but never to be seen.

This does not mean that for *political* purposes these analogical constructs are without value—like Rawls's even more fictional "original position," the work of these thinkers helps stir the political imagination and provides resources for thinking through the important questions surrounding our collective life together as citizens, especially in their particular context and time. Taken out of those contexts and reified, however, the asocial conceptual frameworks can yield both unintended political consequences and incoherent philosophic thinking. Regarding early liberal thinking, Benjamin Barber's polemical question helps us raise the specter of the former when he writes,

> Yet in democratic times, when the initial emancipatory struggles are concluded, philosophies of resistance lose much of their political force. To posit and theorize the individual as an abstract solitary may be helpful on the way to loosening feudal bonds and demarcating a clear space for rebels attempting to individuate themselves from a hierarchical and oppressive order. But it may appear as an obstructive exercise in nostalgia in an era when the extent and quality of citizenship are in question and when the bonds that hold together free communities are growing slack.[14]

14. Barber, *Conquest of Politics*, 18–19.

It is not that the thinking involved can be depicted as some simplistic example of historical relativism and cast aside. Instead, it is a call to understand the truths contained within the theories, and the goals of the theorists themselves, as socially embodied and constituted within history rather than determined and strictly limited by their context as a more vulgar historicist reading might try to suggest. Understood in this manner, Rousseau's famous pronouncement that "man is born free and he is everywhere in chains"[15] is very useful for thinking through the need for political change and even pointing in a possible direction for said change to move. As a statement, it is true enough and speaks to both his time and to generations of readers to come who can relate to the sentiment expressed by the phrase and the very real and, hence, nonfictional feelings the phrase creates. However, none of the phrase is, nor needs to be, literally true for it to be useful—indeed it is probably more useful politically as written than it would be if it was written in a more literal manner. A more accurate, but less effective, opening line might read: Human beings were not made to be enslaved by other human beings or to obey laws promulgated without their consent; currently human beings in my country or part of the world are forced to obey other human beings and laws which have been put in place without their consent. This is truer—though obviously much less rhetorically powerful—for a number of reasons. First, while some people may actually have been in chains, most were only in metaphorical chains. Second, while it may be the case that human beings were not born subjects to particular men or women or set of laws it does not follow that they were in fact born subject to no one and nothing. At a minimum, nature imposed certain biological necessities on us like the need for air, food, water, and shelter. Additionally, while I cannot prove it definitively, it seems safe to say that all human beings who survived were born subject to at least a parent if not a family of some sort. Hence, while Rousseau's opening line remains true enough in its proper rhetorical and historical context, it is also the case that a statement like "man is not born free and few, if any, are anywhere in chains" is also true at the same time, despite the fact that the two are almost perfectly contradictory assertions.

Why belabor this in such a way? Because to only read Rousseau or Locke is to only read one chapter in a much longer story and believe that you have heard everything. What my more truthful and less interesting sentence does is raise the obvious question that Rousseau's formulation assumes and does not argue for: Why is being free *good* and why is being enslaved *bad* for human beings? Though it seems intuitively obvious to many

---

15. Rousseau, *Social Contract*, 1.

readers, especially contemporary readers, the fact is that when Rousseau uttered those memorable words, much of human political history and most of the powerful leaders of his day would not have had the same intuition. For most of them, human freedom had been a mistake for most human beings and therefore, the *chains* forged by society were both necessary and good. Ultimately, Rousseau's argument is more normative than it is historical or political, which begs the question: How do we choose between the two competing versions of morality and the political assertions that flow from them? In other words, we must ask: Why is it that human beings should not be enslaved by other human beings or forced to live under laws that they do not have the opportunity to consent to?

A Christian reformulation of Rousseau could help solve this problem and answer the question in a nonfictional manner. Such a reformulation might look like this: *Each human being has a particular destiny that he or she must discern in free communion with other human beings because we are each created in the image and likeness of God. Anything that prevents such a discernment by a particular person violates that individual's human dignity and is wrong.* Now this assertion says more or less what Rousseau says, but it does so in a way that leaves open the important questions that his phrasing either would not, could not, or felt that it did not need to answer, i.e., why freedom is good and slavery is bad. How? It adds to the nonfictional human story such that a fuller and more comprehensive tale can be told about the nature of the human person and why the individual is to be exalted. For this more proper Christian anthropology, I rely again on the important work of Kenneth and Michael Himes.

In their work, *Fullness of Faith: The Public Significance of Theology*, Himes and Himes demonstrate in a very thoughtful and authoritative manner how the Catholic Church's teachings on human rights as found in documents like *Pacem in Terris* can be "derived from its understanding of reality and the human person."[16] Beginning from John's assertion that God is agape or pure self-gift and thinking through the command to "Love one another; just as I have loved you, you must love one another" (John 3:34) and the injunction to "be perfect as your heavenly Father is perfect" (Matt 5:48), the authors develop a view of the Trinity that simultaneously requires that God be seen as the "giver and receiver and gift" such that they can claim that "God is the name of the relationship of an endless perfect mutual self-gift: In the traditional Catholic imagery, the Father gives himself totally to the Son, the Son gives himself totally to the Father, and the Spirit, proceeding from

---

16. Himes and Himes, *Fullness of Faith*, 55.

both, is the bond of that pure agapic love."[17] As the argument is extended, the authors come to the following conclusion: "Thus the doctrine of the Trinity is an essentially radical political statement: it maintains that not only is human existence social but that the grounds of all being is relationship."[18] Combining this understanding of the Triune God with the understanding of human beings as created in the image and likeness of God (*imago Dei*) and the call for perfection on our part leads the authors to assert that "to maintain that the human being is created in the image of God is to proclaim the human being capable of self-gift."[19] The logic of that claim allows them then to conclude that "the human person is the point at which creation is able to respond by giving oneself in return. The fundamental human right is the right to give oneself away to another and ultimately to the Other."[20] The process of discernment noted above entails determining what particular gifts an individual has to offer and how to go about offering them in a particular time, place, and among particular human beings.

This is about as distant from the American liberal's image of the independent individual as we can imagine and it, in turn, forces the faithful to think in very different ways about the nature and purpose of society and the notion of individual rights. Under this scheme of rights, the authors argue: "The most fundamental human right is the right to exercise the power of self-giving, the opportunity for entrance into relationship. . . . All other rights are derivative."[21] While such an argument is not at odds with the Lockean notion of "self-ownership," it does render such a claim woefully incomplete. Under the approach outlined here, we "own" ourselves in order that we might give ourselves away.[22] Simplistically, it is like my giving my children money to place in the collection basket in church—if they pocket the money they have misunderstood why I gave it to them in the first place. All other rights, in turn, are best thought of as enabling rights or derivative from the grounding right, i.e., the rights we create constitutionally or in the law must make it easier or more likely that we will be able to answer the call to community and agapic love.

The rest of the argument is now fairly straightforward if the position described is theologically sound. Whoever refuses to give themselves to the Other is choosing to distance themselves from God and God's call to

---

17. Himes and Himes, *Fullness of Faith*, 57.
18. Himes and Himes, *Fullness of Faith*, 59.
19. Himes and Himes, *Fullness of Faith*, 59.
20. Himes and Himes, *Fullness of Faith*, 59.
21. Himes and Himes, *Fullness of Faith*, 63.
22. See Hollenbach, "Communitarian Reconstruction of Human Rights."

perfection. Likewise, any structural elements created socially or politically that make it more difficult or less likely that others will be able to perform the act of self-gift, or those elements that we refuse to create that would make it more likely and less difficult for others to give themselves away in agapic relationship, are by definition sinful (wrong). Finally, this leads us to the conclusion that all public policy must ultimately confront the rather amorphous question of whether it is intended to and likely to make self-gift more likely and less cumbersome or not. To do this is not easy, and numerous consequences—both intended and unintended—must be considered before taking action. It is also not something that is simply a problem for the state or government. However, neither is it something that is only up to individuals and non-state institutions. All are responsible—individually and collectively—to the extent that they are able to do what they can so that others can do what they must.

With this argument in place, the liberal story now reads very differently. The individual is now a radically social person rather than an asocial person. As a result, individual rights are to be safeguarded so that individuals can discern and fulfill their individual call and the duties entailed in that call to others in a required but not determined act of free self-gift. Others are called to reciprocate. In turn, the political organization of a given group of individuals must be designed to make this easier and less cumbersome. In this way, many of the aspects of liberal theory can now be more adequately justified, i.e., why government must be limited, why equality is an essential value, why liberty is a good, and why some brand of democracy is probably called for. Hence, liberalism is rendered much less "emotive" when viewed within the larger Christian tradition. Current historical and political trends, however, suggest that it will become increasingly more difficult to tell this larger story and that those who hear it will be less and less capable of relating to it. To the extent that nothing more compelling is offered in its stead, there is a risk that the American regime will not be able to sustain itself philosophically at first and perhaps politically soon thereafter. This story of decline, however, is also part of the Christian narrative, and includes all states eventually.

ALIEN NATION

It is no doubt true that most American Christians, including most Catholics (and, hence, most Americans) do not really see themselves in the expanded story above. It has become, for most of us, a foreign way of thinking—if it ever was familiar. Indeed, it is probably so foreign that its own usefulness is highly dubious. Unfortunately, there are no real good alternatives as I see it. Christians are called to be prophetic and, in doing so, demonstrate their faithfulness. They are not required to be successful. To argue that we do not know ourselves, that we are foreign to ourselves, that we are in the most basic sense alienated from ourselves, estranged from ourselves, because we do not recognize our true nature is to reject one of the central assumptions of modern men and women. It is to reject the Cartesian foundation of the modern self and its corollary method for knowing that self. As a modern nation, it is to some extent to reject what it means to be an American. Descartes famously portrays the modern self's own method for coming to know itself in the following way:

> Now I will shut my eyes, I will stop up my ears, I will divert all my senses, I will even blot out from my thought all images of corporeal things—or at least, since the latter can hardly be done, I will regard these images as nothing, empty and false as indeed they are. And as I converse only with myself and look more deeply into myself, I will attempt to render myself gradually better known to myself.[23]

This is the prelude to the famous dictum, *cogito, ergo sum* ("I think, therefore I am"). Once again, it is not that this method is without important value, philosophically speaking. Who can argue that the reflective self portrayed above is without real value, especially in this day and age? Who too does not see the need for a healthy skepticism in the quest for knowledge and truth that the method prods us toward? But, taken in isolation, or privileged as *the* way of knowing the self, it is deeply at odds with certain obvious truths about the human person, especially their social nature described previously. In so being, it too is a source of alienation as much or more than it is a source of insight. Giving this method greater privilege than it merits serves to undermine its own project and thus leads eventually to increasing levels of cognitive dissonance on the part of the self in order to sustain its larger narrative. As that dissonance grows more acute, the "true" self actually becomes less and less well known to the person and the epistemological gap becomes a source of political turmoil as we increasingly construct political communities for individual human beings who in essence do not, ontologically speaking, exist. For example, think about the old canards about communist society—caricatured as it was—and human nature. The essential argument used to go that it was not so much that communism was a bad idea, but that it was impossibly utopian because human beings were not built by nature to live that way. Truth be told, liberalism in its austere and possessive form

---

23. Descartes, *Meditations of First Philosophy*, 23.

often won that argument by default, i.e., it never demonstrated that it was not similarly impossible or unsustainable, just that it was not *as* utopian as the alternative. Simply put, the argument here is that getting *Being* wrong will ultimately matter, politically speaking.

We can know with a high degree of confidence that the more austere liberal theorists—those who utilize or have been interpreted as utilizing the unencumbered self as an *ontological* rather than a *political* starting point—are mistaken because even those who reject the existence of God will ultimately agree that the story of the solitary individual knowing him- or herself by looking inward is a fictional one, however useful it might be. The following analogy should be instructive on this point.

Imagine a newly minted human being who is literally unencumbered except by his or her body and its own reflexive desire for survival, e.g., we gasp for breath without any prodding, we steer way from pain and suffering instinctively. Imagine this human being's body being thrown into the middle of the ocean on a pitch-black night. No stars, no moon, no horizon of any type, and, most of all, no other people. Instinctively, we can imagine that this being tries to "swim" in order to not simply drown. They have no reason to pick any particular direction over another. Indeed, they do not really have any reason to prefer life over drowning, but they seem to anyway. However, given human physiology and the fact that the individual will be either right side or left side dominant, the direction they pick will matter even less than it already did because they will ultimately swim in a circle as result of that same body. Analogically speaking, the person in the ocean who is attempting to "know" who they are, why they are here, where they should swim to, will never escape the solipsistic and self-defeating strategy of looking within the self to know it better. Nothing other than the needs of the body can be known in this situation, and those do not require reflection, only response on the part of a person. This is a person stuck figuratively in what Hannah Arendt calls the realm of necessity—ostensibly a subhuman state of being dominated by "labor," according to her and her Greek predecessors.[24] The only escape from this predicament—the only path to true human individualism—is through other people and our social, cultural, historical, linguistic, religious, and political encumbrances. This is what is best called the dialogical understanding of the self as compared to the Cartesian monological view, and is best viewed through the work of the philosopher Charles Taylor.

While Taylor's corpus of philosophic work is vast and highly complex, the argument that I am relying on here comes from two fairly sparse,

---

24. See Arendt, *Human Condition*.

accessible, and yet powerful texts, one called *The Ethics of Authenticity* and the other a printed version of a talk he gave at the University of Dayton titled "A Catholic Modernity?" In the former text, Taylor acknowledges the power of the modern individualistic ideal that he associates with the concept of autonomy or "self-determining freedom."[25] Herder, whom Taylor calls the ideal's "major early articulator rather than its originator,"[26] modern authenticity is described in the following way:

> Herder put forward the idea that each of us has an original way of being human. Each person has his or her own "measure" is his way of putting it. This idea has entered very deep into the modern consciousness. It is also new. Before the late eighteenth century no one thought that the differences between human beings had this kind of moral significance. There is a certain way of being human that is *my* way. I am called upon to live my life in this way, and not in imitation of anyone else's. But this gives a new importance to being true to myself. If I am not, I miss the point of my life, I miss what being human is for *me*.[27]

Taylor is clearly correct when he calls this a powerful moral ideal that

> accords a crucial moral importance to a kind of contract with myself, with my own inner nature, which it sees as in danger of being lost, partly through the pressures towards outward conformity, but also because in taking an instrumental stance toward myself, I may have lost the capacity to listen to this inner voice.[28]

To "hear" that inner voice requires the individual to "look" within the self to discover their own original voice and "way of being human," in a very Cartesian manner. As I said earlier, this is an idea of very real critical importance. At its best, it calls upon each individual to take personal responsibility for the choices and decisions he or she makes, and ultimately, for the condition of the world around them that those choices help produce. At its worst, however, it produces self-absorbed narcissistic human beings who are incapable of recognizing any authority as legitimate and hence are unable to pledge fidelity, give loyalty, or even to truly love another without equivocation and the preservation of their "exit options." Paradoxically, such a person at the deepest level of their Being is ultimately only capable of

---

25. Taylor, *Ethics of Authenticity*, 28.
26. Taylor, *Ethics of Authenticity*, 29.
27. Taylor, *Ethics of Authenticity*, 28–29.
28. Taylor, *Ethics of Authenticity*, 29.

treating other people as "means" rather than "ends." In other words, in their quest for an authentic life which demands that each person be treated, in good Kantian fashion, as an end rather than a means, the modern individual in a contemporary liberal political order can never be legitimately asked to give him- or herself completely over to the good of another person insofar as such a sacrifice either spiritually, intellectually, or physically represents an illegitimate form of bondage and the rendering of one's self as a means to the Other's project or calling. Indeed, when pushed to its logical conclusion, in the name of not allowing anyone to be treated as a means, individuals must even be prevented, or at least discouraged, from giving themselves fully to anything or anyone lest they participate in the violation of their own autonomy and destroy their own authentic selves!

In this way, what was supposed to liberate us from the will of others and provide refuge from conformity in fact renders us all frightfully similar sorts of beings. We become "individuals" in name only. The very choices and decisions that serve to most radically differentiate one person from another, namely what and who we completely give our full selves to with a kind of reckless abandon, we are now, at least theoretically, prevented from making and acting on. Not only are the Cross and the events of Calvary utterly incomprehensible in the context of such a world view, but it becomes virtually impossible to even explain why families and children are positive goods according to thinkers like Stanley Hauerwas.[29] Even many of those who have no interest in comprehending the former would seem to have an interest in being able to do the latter. But, given the reverence for authenticity and at least the rhetorical prominence of a tendency toward its narcissistic form, the question remains whether and how such an important idea can be saved from collapsing in on itself. To borrow an expression from a previous chapter, how can American liberalism recognize that the convent and the concentration camp are not just different in degree, but different in kind from each other? How can the individual in our ocean on the dark night be rescued without being rendered a slavish or dependent conformist rather than a fully authentic individual?

To make the citizens who refuse to hold their commitments lightly or to refrain from giving themselves fully to other people or ideas less alien in the liberal nation requires reframing rather than reforming the ideal of authenticity in a manner that brings it into closer alignment with the life and condition of the human person as lived rather than philosophically constructed for political ends. A simple analogy again might be useful. What if being an individual is like being a piece of a puzzle? Each piece is unique

---

29. Hauerwas, *Community of Character*.

and nonconforming to each other puzzle piece, whole unto itself while at the same time incomplete? Each piece is capable of being viewed in isolation without reference to any other piece, but also capable of being viewed wholly in reference to each piece it is fitted to connect with and to each piece, those pieces are connected to without doing any damage whatsoever to its own autonomous existence. In this way, each individual piece of the larger human puzzle retains its integrity and can be known independently from its fuller context. However, it cannot be known fully or completely in this manner. To have a meaningful existence, to even know that it is indeed a piece of a puzzle means that there have to be other puzzle pieces because to be absolutely novel would in essence be to not be knowable at all. Everything and everyone exists in relationship to something or someone else. That is the very nature of individual existence itself—to be in relationship but not to be the same.

For human beings, to be in relationship is to be in relationship first and foremost to other human beings. As Taylor puts it,

> The general feature of human life that I want to evoke is its fundamentally *dialogical* character. We become full human agents, capable of understanding ourselves, and hence of defining an identity, through our acquisition of rich human languages of expression. . . . No one acquires the languages needed for self-definition on their own. We are introduced to them through exchanges with others who matter to us. . . . The genesis of the human mind is in this sense not "monological," not something each accomplishes on his or her own, but dialogical.[30]

He goes on to explain that with important issues like our identity we are always in conversation with "significant others," such as parents and friends to historical figures and texts broadly construed. Sometimes we see ourselves as others do and there is continuity, but at other times we struggle against those views. In neither case are the views of other's determinative, but they are always the point of departure; other people define what is significant, they provide what Taylor calls the inescapable horizons for our lives. We can no more set or determine what is significant by ourselves than we could make a literal horizon from the middle of that dark ocean—horizons in any of their forms come from outside of us. We are free to choose our response, of course, but we cannot choose what we are responding to. The reification of choice itself and the soft nihilism it entails, i.e., the idea that the act of choosing is the *only* value rather than an assessment of what is chosen and why, is to deny not only the basis for morality itself, but also to deny any basis

---

30. Taylor, *Ethics of Authenticity*, 32–33.

for a coherent identity of any sort. The choosing being without any external or historical referent point whatsoever is a fully and wholly novel being, a being that is not knowable to others nor to whatever "self" there still is; it is to take up space but not to have any meaningful existence; it is to essentially not exist. The most simplistic example might help here: Take the word *sgtwplawsmlpppp*; it takes up space, it formally exists, but it is unknowable, not meaningful, and not useful in any manner to any reader. I can choose it, as I did here, but I cannot give it meaning without recourse to other words or concepts that I have not created. In this way, Taylor is exactly right to claim that "to shut out demands emanating beyond the self is precisely to suppress the conditions of significance, and hence court trivialization."[31] (I would go further and say to court non-being itself.) Furthermore, his conclusion then follows quite naturally from this when he asserts,

> Only if I exist in a world in which history, or the demands of nature, or the needs of my fellow human beings, or the duties of citizenship, or the call of God, or something else of this order *matters* crucially, can I define an identity for myself that is not trivial. Authenticity is not the enemy of demands that emanate from beyond the self; it supposes such demands.[32]

To conclude what has been perhaps a little belabored discussion, the reader might be tempted to ask why this rather dense philosophical discussion matters so much. What, in other words, are the real, if any, penalties or political consequences for getting this wrong? And, what, if any, are the benefits or political consequences for getting this rather esoteric philosophical question right? First, for whatever reason, the idea of authenticity and its counterpart liberal-individualism matter hugely to Americans and other like-minded citizens in the world, and so it behooves us to give as full and intentional account of it as we can as social theorists and political philosophers as part of our accepted role in the world. Less self-centeredly, the truth is that regardless of that task's own importance, the American regime and its consequent political order does and will continue to reflect the "monological" grounding in ways that will increasingly place individuals further and further at odds with their own nature. This will, à la Taylor's argument above, deprive them of the self-realization they seek and make them less and less capable of achieving the happiness they believe it is their right to pursue. For the Christian, this institutionalized alienation will not only deny them the general happiness that believers and nonbelievers alike wish, but it is actually sinful and detrimental to their eternal soul.

31. Taylor, *Ethics of Authenticity*, 40.
32. Taylor, *Ethics of Authenticity*, 40–41.

Whether done culturally, philosophically, politically, or some combination of all of these, the enticement or temptation to forgo the deep and even complete giving of the self to others in agapic love does great damage to the interior being of the Christian. They become, in a sense, walled off from themselves. Ultimately, a nation so committed to such a process either explicitly or implicitly will undermine and destroy the very things it claims to, and *ought* to, value. If such a process succeeds, whether by intention or default, human beings may well be free, but that is all they will be. And, despite the bumper-sticker value of such an idea in the contemporary liberal state, freedom is not an end, it is a means whose value can only be realized by spending it—there is complete freedom in the middle of the dark ocean, but such a place is nowhere for a human being to live.

A NATION OF ALIENS

So where *should* a human being live? More precisely, where should the human being of the Christian narrative—the radically social and yet individually exalted human being—live? The simple answer, of course, is not alone—neither physically nor psychologically.[33] Yet, the modern human condition is often described as one of loneliness or at least aloneness. Tocqueville saw the tendency in the democratic individuals of the first new nation almost two hundred years ago, and it is even more pronounced today. In his famous words,

> Such folk owe no man anything and hardly expect anything from anybody. They form the habit of thinking of themselves in isolation and imagine that their whole destiny is in their own hands.
>
> Thus, not only does democracy make men forget their ancestors, but also clouds their view of their descendants and isolates them from their contemporaries. Each man is forever thrown back upon himself alone, and there is danger that he may be shut up in the solitude of his own heart.[34]

Now while many have worried about the civic implications of this phenomenon, my concern here is less *republican* and more *liberal*, i.e., why this is a bad thing for the individual first and foremost. The Christian knows in multiple ways that it is not good for human beings to be alone because of their nature, but modern individualists here again have no such resources

---

33. See Wells, "Rethinking Service," 6–14.
34. Tocqueville, *Democracy in America*, 508.

to rely on. If they want to make this case, it will once again have to be a function of preference and not nature, i.e., there is no way to declare being alone or not alone more desirable beyond an individual's choice. But, we can now say that this is simply wrong, because even the capacity to rebel against our sociability is in fact a by-product of dialogic or other-derived identities. I can choose loneliness if I want to, but I must choose it against a horizon that tells me it is an unnatural and detrimental choice as it relates to my happiness and self-realization. However, this argument too is an artifact of its own kind. Knowing this to be the case does not mean that it is an apt description of the human condition as lived. Granting that there are no such things as self-created horizons of significance is not the same thing as recognizing that such horizons are transcendent. What begins as willful ignorance—acting purposefully against what we know to be true—over time becomes simply ignorance. That is to say, the first rebels were self-conscious about their rebellion and denied the social nature of the human person because it was useful *politically* to do so. The contemporary offspring of those original rebels though have reified the fruits of the rebellion themselves. In this way, Nietzsche becomes the brilliant but perfected modern rather than the first postmodern. He believes what others only knew was an important and even necessary chimera for their emancipation from oppression and bondage. Subsequently, those who follow in his wake—analytic philosophers, pragmatic political theorists, behavioral social scientists, certain natural scientists, and contemporary technocrats and bureaucrats prostrate themselves, and through their unintentional but pronounced intellectual obeisance grant the chimera foundational status in one of the more bizarre moments of irony in intellectual history.

Why ironic? Because in the first place the so-called rejection of all moral orders as arbitrary compels those who issue such pronouncements to admit that the rejection itself is also arbitrary. Second, because the very thing they were trying to raise up—the autonomous, authentic, and dignified individual—is actually debased and displaced as a result. Glenn Tinder puts it this Christian-centric way,

> In our pride, we persistently look for a morally pure vantage point that will make us independent of God and give us access to God's cosmic sovereignty. This search often is political. Thus, Plato claimed a morally pure vantage point for the philosopher-kings, and Marx tacitly did for the working class. But Christianity tells us that no such vantage point is available to human beings.... Sin is ironic. Its intention is self-exaltation; its result is self-debasement. In trying to ascend, we fall. The reason for

this is not hard to understand. We are exalted by God; in declaring our independence from God we cast ourselves down.[35]

Secularly speaking, this process is in essence what C. S. Lewis referred to as the abolition of man in his book by the same name. There is simply no way to do justice to this still profound and relevant text here, but the brief Lewis provides on behalf of "traditional man" and against the "natural man" (as discussed earlier) is of critical importance to help close out the current argument and for the case I will make in the next chapter. If indeed Nietzsche, or at least his chief character Zarathustra, is simply the most grandiose personification of the solitary, a-social individual of the contract theorist's state of nature, then their work is oddly of a piece with that of Plato's and Marx's. This is the case insofar as the individual in the state of nature, or even the original position, is also rightly seen as being positioned in that "morally pure vantage point" intended to make them "independent of God." While Locke's foray into metaphysics might be seen as differentiating him from the non-theism of Rousseau or Hobbes, his ultimate majoritarianism and his epistemological theory ultimately render his work of a piece with theirs on this score. Simply put, the "general will" is only a collectivized version of Nietzsche's *overman*. Both the people and the overman are in effect "beyond good and evil" because both entities see themselves as the authors of good and evil. Hobbes is perhaps the most explicit on this point, but it is easily unearthed in Locke once some of the natural law pretense is done away with. And this is where Lewis's little book becomes controlling.

Based on a series of lectures and collected under the title *The Abolition of Man* in 1947, Lewis builds his case against the emergent emotivism of his time from the educational ground up. Beginning with what many might have ignored, Lewis discovers that the roots of the prevailing culture have penetrated deep into the soil through his close reading of an elementary school textbook designed ostensibly to teach students English. In the pages of what he calls *The Green Book*, by authors he nicknames Gaius and Titius, Lewis discerns a critical philosophic subtext that has little to do with the stated purpose of teaching English, but which in its own innocence belies a destructive and dangerous moral tendency of the age. He sums up these two tendencies as the notion that all predicates of value are only statements about the emotional state of the speaker and that such statements are not important.[36] In turn, Lewis argues that the schoolboy who thought he was learning about literature will in fact learn "that all emotions aroused by local

---

35. Tinder, *Political Meaning of Christianity*, 39.
36. Lewis, *Abolition of Man*, 15.

association are in themselves contrary to reason and contemptible."[37] This movement which Lewis believes will serve to "cut out of his soul, long before he is old enough to choose, the possibility of having certain experiences which thinkers of more authority than they [Gaius and Titius] have held to be generous, fruitful and humane."[38] This process, Lewis rightfully notes, is quite new and contrary to much of human history and, I would add, basic common sense. In his words,

> Until quite modern times all teachers and even all men believed the universe to be such that certain emotional reactions on our part could be either congruous or incongruous to it—believed, in fact, that objects did not merely receive, but could *merit*, our approval or disapproval, our reverence or contempt.[39]

Furthermore, the so-called debunking that modern education engages in has significant unintended consequences—significant political consequences as well as spiritual ones—which Lewis constructively points out. On the political side of the ledger, he suggests that "by starving the sensibilities of our pupils we only make them easier prey to the propagandist when he comes. For famished nature will be avenged and a hard heart is no infallible protection against a soft head."[40] Simply put, the inculcation of certain sentiments that are *acknowledged* to be true are the prerequisites for rationality rather than the products of it. Take something like justice, for example. While what is just and unjust is open to vigorous debate and disagreement—and is perhaps even relative in some manner from age to age and culture to culture—the belief that *justice* is better than *injustice* cannot itself be relative without doing irreparable harm to our ability to communicate at all with each other. Take the case where someone called something that was diametrically opposite to our conception of justice—something we would identify as patently unjust—just. Though we may argue with them vehemently about the particular thing's status, they would not call their thing unjust, they would call it just. They would still believe that justice was the right thing and injustice the wrong thing even if the content was wildly different. All this means is that there is no way to discern that justice is better than injustice independently of the terms themselves. Only by accepting that hierarchy is the conversation about justice possible in the first place.

---

37. Lewis, *Abolition of Man*, 19.
38. Lewis, *Abolition of Man*, 20.
39. Lewis, *Abolition of Man*, 25.
40. Lewis, *Abolition of Man*, 24.

I am reminded here of a line from a movie called *Heist*, in which the character played by Danny DeVito yelled to one of his henchmen something to the effect of, "Everybody wants money—that's why they call it money!" To prefer justice to injustice is not itself a rational or an irrational choice, it is the context for choosing and deciding and, hence, is pre-rational or foundational. In Lewis's words, "No emotion is, in itself, a judgment: in that sense all emotions and sentiments are alogical. But they can be reasonable or unreasonable as they conform to reason or fail to conform."[41] Justice or loyalty or kindness or courage, and so on, are never susceptible to questions of truth or falsity, nor are their opposites; but they are crucial attributes for understanding, explaining, and living a human life among other human beings. Furthermore, as well as being inherently reasonable without being themselves reasoned, they are also strictly speaking objective in their orientation. When I believe someone to be loyal or disloyal it is for me a fact, not merely some hoped-for state of affairs lest I become paralyzed by self-doubt taken to its logical extreme. This set of givens Lewis calls the *Tao*—the way. And for Lewis, the *Tao* is passed on through a process of "initiation" rather than "conditioning"; it is "propagated," not a form of "propaganda."[42] Imagine trying to teach a young person about justice without starting from the assumption that justice was something good, noble, worthy. The former simply must be accepted before any training can take place. Yet, the former is itself a sort of training, an imprinting of what it means to be human by one generation onto the next, i.e., to be human is to think that justice is something good and worthy and that justice is important. If either the teacher or the student was to successfully negate those starting premises somehow, it would make no sense whatsoever to talk about justice because it would not matter enough to spend any time on. Its worth and value must be presumed. The effective negation on the part of the authors of *The Green Book* of exactly that presumption leads to the creation of what Lewis refers to as men without chests.[43]

Telling us in his next lecture that the practical result of a society of human beings strictly educated in this manner would be the eventual destruction of that society, Lewis goes on to argue that modern attempts to somehow supersede the *Tao* are in effect attempts to deny any purchase for "practical reason" whatsoever. These things that are simply the "givens" or the "horizons of significance" which are known to all but not created by

---

41. Lewis, *Abolition of Man*, 30.

42. Lewis, *Abolition of Man*, 32–33.

43. For Lewis, those "men without chests" were those who lacked any real spirit or courage in themselves and their convictions. They were unwilling to stand up for anything of consequence and to put themselves at risk for their ideals.

anyone represent exactly the things which the modern mind as represented by Gaius and Titius must reject in the name of pure reason. The quest is ultimately a futile one according to Lewis, and I would liken to the moral equivalent of Zeno's paradox concerning the arrow. The old paradox suggests that an arrow fired from a bow can never logically strike the target at which it was aimed. Why? Because the arrow must first travel half the distance to the target and then half that distance and so on and so forth. However infinitesimally small the distances become, the logic would seem to hold. Practically speaking, however, we know that the arrow will indeed hit the target under normal firing circumstances. Furthermore, we can bet safely that the most ardent rationalist we can find will not trust the pure logic to the point of standing between the arrow and its target. Yet, for some reason the same thinkers seem to have no trouble jumping in front of the "moral arrow" in the name of pure reason, or, more critically, placing an entire society in front of that arrow because they somehow are persuaded that it cannot hit the target either. One must question either the hubris, the insanity, or the intentions of such people who would place everyone at risk by denying what everyone knows with *almost* absolute certainty—the only kind available to human beings—to be true. While it may be good science to phrase assertions in the form of probabilities and degrees of confidence to preserve the necessary element of falsifiability, it is bad practice to let the 5 percent that one lacks in confidence preclude all action based on the 95 percent degree of confidence one has that the claim is true. In other words, if the arrow is systematically fired at the target one hundred times and ninety-five of those times it strikes the target and five times it fails to for various reasons, isn't it better to proceed as if the arrow will strike the target rather than as if it will not? Yet contemporary moral theorists like Lewis's authors seem to think it best not to proceed at all until the arrow strikes the target one hundred times out of every one hundred. Not only is this no way to think, it makes life—at least moral life—impossible.

Human beings living life in the one-hundred-out-of-one-hundred camp are indeed so far removed from life as it is lived as to be not in essence really human at all. To live in a society of such people would be to live in a nation of aliens for the human being. If I might be permitted an absurdity, or at least what *should be* an absurdity, for a moment and ask, "Why don't human beings eat their babies?" Not why practically, but why rationally? All around the world there are adults starving to death and a glut of children who will grow up in all likelihood to be either starving adults or who will die young from malnourishment. Why not simply solve both problems at once? For the person who is disgusted—hopefully the vast majority, if not every reader—why are you disgusted? Failing to be able to explain the root of your disgust as most of us probably will, try to give our strict rationalists their argument, i.e., if simple human revulsion or sentiment is not a good enough reason, then why shouldn't we eat our babies? On its face let me say that it is far easier to make the case that one *ought* to eat one's children than it is to make the case that one *ought not* to based simply on physical needs, though I will not do it here. Suffice it to say that proving in the hard one-hundred-out-of-one-hundred sense that human beings should not eat their children seems like a silly exercise to the extent that everyone (at least ninety-nine out of one hundred) already believes that they should not. It is difficult to know what evidence could be deduced that would persuade those remaining skeptics who favor child cuisine that they were wrong to do so such that they would stop based on our logic. Indeed, carried to its own logical conclusion, a society of child eaters would in fact be so far removed from the human *Tao* that no one who disfavored child eating would ever have the chance to grow up assuming a constant state of hunger among those who were. If magically some lone group of anti-child eaters did manage to make it to adulthood somehow in a society of child eaters, we can imagine that the child eaters who raised, or somehow allowed, the anti-child eaters to escape their logical fate would come to think *they* were insane and alien.

And this, then, leads me finally to Lewis's larger and still more disturbing argument concerning his authors and the trend they represent. Granted that the *Tao* is not a stagnant unchanging entity, Lewis avoids charges of a petrified traditionalism[44] by allowing that the *Tao* develops and becomes more fully realized at various times.[45] However, what cannot be granted is the idea that there are competing systems of value vying for dominance in the community of human beings. In Lewis's words:

> This thing which I have called for convenience the *Tao*, and which others may call Natural Law or Traditional Morality or the First Principles of Practical Reason or the First Platitudes, is not one among a series of possible systems of value. It is the source of all value judgments. If it is rejected, all value is rejected. If any value is retained, it is retained.[46]

---

44. The theologian Jaroslav Pelikan distinguished between the ideas of tradition and traditionalism in the following way: "Tradition is the living faith of the dead; traditionalism is the dead faith of the living. Tradition lives in conversation with the past, while remembering where we are and when we are and that it is we who have to decide. Traditionalism supposes that nothing should ever be done for the first time, so all that is needed to solve any problem is to arrive at the supposedly unanimous testimony of this homogenized tradition." Pelikan, "Christianity as an Enfolding Circle," 57.

45. Lewis, *Abolition of Man*, 58.

46. Lewis, *Abolition of Man*, 56.

To rebel against the *Tao* would be like

> a rebellion of the branches against the tree: if the rebels could succeed they would find that they had destroyed themselves. The human mind has no more power of inventing a new value, than of imagining a new primary colour.[47]

Rejection of the *Tao* is, then, the rejection of value altogether, or the embrace of nihilism. What Nietzsche understood and the causal critics like Gaius and Titius probably do not, is that the success of such an embrace would by definition mean the end of the human being as human being as evidenced by the creation of the *overman* and, in all likelihood, large numbers of *last men*.

This attempt to overcome what is ultimately the nature of the human being leaves the critics who are powerless to create value with a very narrow range of choices or degrees of freedom. Freed from *value*, the human being must rely on what is usually called "instinct." This, in turn, would have the effect of rendering the particular nature of the human being a ridiculous idea and instead would make us part of nature in general. There would be nothing unique or special about human beings and certainly no way to defend individual dignity or the value of any particular individual person. In practical terms, those *overmen* and *overwomen* who exist in the post-human world will have to decide what the *Tao* of the brave new world will look like, and they will on some admittedly distorted Cartesian level have to look within themselves and within themselves alone to decide and choose which horizons of significance to create and which to not create. They will have to become individuals who will need to "sacrifice their own share in traditional humanity in order to devote themselves to the task of deciding what 'Humanity' shall henceforth mean."[48] But here the irony is now quite thick, because in the escape from *human* nature as described above, the *overhumans* have fled into the hands of *nature* itself over which they have even less control because, to steal a phrase from Augustine, we are not the authors of the things we love. To the extent, then, that the new race of mortals succumbs to their own instincts and imposes their wants on others, nature has in fact won as complete a victory as possible insofar as human beings *qua* human beings have now effectively ceased to exist. As Lewis writes,

> However far they go back, or down, they can find no ground to stand on. Every motive they try to act on becomes at once a

---

47. Lewis, *Abolition of Man*, 56.
48. Lewis, *Abolition of Man*, 76.

petitio. It is not that they are bad men. They are not men at all. Stepping outside the *Tao*, they have stepped into the void. Nor are their subjects necessarily unhappy men. They are not men at all: they are artifacts. Man's final conquest has proved to be the abolition of Man.[49]

CONCLUSION

Aliens "shut up in the solitude of our own hearts" is what we become when we reject a "dogmatic belief in objective value."[50] However, that value is not to be found in the realm of pure reason, but in the realm of practical reason. Practical reason is only to be found in the company of others and in the process of living together. It is what makes that life together possible, meaningful, and human. To remain recognizable to ourselves and to assert our individual value and worth paradoxically requires the existence and persistence of the Other. But that Other cannot merely exist for my use, to be useful, he or she must exist as an end unto him- or herself. Selves that are both independent and in relationship at the same time is the requirement for remaining *human* beings and not simply beings in general. The price of our individual dignity and exaltation is the acknowledgment and conformity to the idea that we cannot confer those things on ourselves. Because we must live together to live as human beings, we must choose a way of living together that both acknowledges this condition and sustains it in the face of persistent challenges from both the malevolent and the indifferent. This requires a politics that is truly radical in the original sense of the term; a politics that understands what is fundamental and works to preserve it. Hence, now that we know that we must live together in order to be who we are meant to be, the central political question remains to be answered: *How are we going to live together in a fundamentally human way?*

At a minimum, such an endeavor will require the persistence of men and women who understand this and resist the temptations and ideologies of the age which call us toward nonhuman states of Being and to a politics that reflects that nonhuman state. The most prominent candidates for resistance, for reasons articulated and implied, are those Christians—and in particular, Catholics—who understand this and act on it in appropriate ways because they remain the least alienated from the *Tao*. What those ways of living together in the context of this country are is the subject matter of

---

49. Lewis, *Abolition of Man*, 77.
50. Lewis, *Abolition of Man*, 84.

the rest of this book. But at a minimum, the words of Glenn Tinder must be taken to heart when he asserts,

> Certainly the survival of individuals in their full humanity will often be determined by their capacity for standing out against the incivility of their times. Perhaps the survival of civilization will be decided by such individuals—a saving remnant who will take on the responsibilities implicit in the true political art.[51]

---

51. Tinder, "Against Fate," 51.

4

Orestes Brownson and the Hartz Thesis

Then to all he said, "If anyone wants to be a follower of mine, let him renounce himself and take up his cross every day and follow me. For anyone who wants to save his life will lose it; but anyone who loses his life for my sake, that man will save it."

—Luke 9:23–25

Do not be afraid of those who kill the body but cannot kill the soul; fear him rather who can destroy both body and soul in hell. Can you not buy two sparrows for a penny? And yet not one falls to the ground without your Father knowing.

—Matthew 10:28–29

Enter by the narrow gate, since the road that leads to perdition is wide and spacious, and many take it; but it is a narrow gate and a hard road that leads to life, and only a few find it.

—Matthew 7:13–14

DYING TO THE SELF

Among the central features of John Rawls's theory of distributive justice is his interesting defense of *inequality*. After leading his readers to see the logic of, and self-interested justification for, absolute equality in the economic realm, he draws out of them the necessary caveat that allows his own system to avoid the pitfalls of a vulgarized communism. At its simplest, that caveat allows for inequality—even an inequality that is potentially very extreme—so long as a certain condition is met. That condition holds that an inequality is just if by its existence the position of the least well off in society is improved. In other words, Rawls attempts to codify Adam Smith's dictum that "a rising tide lifts all ships" into a moral requirement, i.e., a rising tide *must* lift at least the ships of the poorest to be a just tide, so to speak. The power of Rawls's well-known argument is that this preference for the least among us does not depend on anything extra-human for its justification—it is what rational, self-interested individuals would themselves choose as a central principle of justice from the original position behind the veil of ignorance. In this way, the sacrifices of real selves who end up in places of privilege in a given society are in fact not sacrifices properly understood, but rather the simple results of the social contract they would have made had they not known their relative position in the world beforehand. Without probing this idea in any deeper way, I want to use it at face value to raise a simple rhetorical question: If those liberal thinkers who would follow Rawls's lead in this matter can accept *material* inequality under the proper conditions, why could they not accept a certain kind of *spiritual* inequality on the same grounds? In other words, what if privileging a certain comprehensive doctrine of the good does in fact create greater good for all and especially the least well off?

Individuals in the "original" position would rightly balk at the idea that they would enter a world in which there was a singular comprehensive doctrine or religious identity that they would have to conform to regardless of their own beliefs or desires. Isn't it possible that those same self-interested individuals would accept the priority of a certain kind of good over the right if in fact by doing so their right to pursue their own vision of the good was enhanced dramatically by doing so? For example, suppose that the only way to secure the ideal of the rights-bearing individual of liberal theory was to privilege an account of human origins that rendered the individual sacred. An account, if you will, that took that ideal as a conclusion from which to start theorizing rather than as a premise to be demonstrated and vindicated later. A "given" or "inescapable horizon" as per the argument of the previous chapter. Wouldn't the same rational actor agree to this premise as well regardless of his or her own particular comprehensive doctrine or lack thereof? Wouldn't this answer the criticism of elitism that would no doubt be leveled by many against the argument of the preceding chapter? Assuming that such a state is at least possible, we can move on to the question raised at the close of the previous chapter, namely *how* we can live together in a fundamentally human way?

The answer to this question is in essence the "true political art" that Tinder spoke of at the close of chapter 3. How, in his terms, do we construct and maintain a civilization and a political regime that allows for the survival and flourishing of individuals "in their full humanity"? What does it mean to produce and sustain individuals who have the capacity to "stand out against the incivility of their times?" The answer, which at first will be quite controversial, I draw from the work of T. S. Eliot, who writes unflinchingly, "However bigoted the announcement may sound, the Christian can be satisfied with nothing less than a Christian organization of society—which is not the same thing as a society consisting of exclusively devout Christians. It would be a society in which the natural end of man—virtue and well-being in community—is acknowledged for all, and the supernatural end—beatitude—for those who have the eyes to see it."[1]

Such a position is not music to the ears of most Americans, who have been well trained to recoil at any hint of the idea of the United States as a "Christian Nation." Hopefully, the previous chapters have conveyed to the reader that this is not possible even if someone thought it was desirable—states are by their very nature secular institutions concerned with temporal problems and questions. However, it is still possible that a nation of Christians, properly understood, and those whose beliefs and orientations are similar to those of the Christian, could be a highly desirable state of affairs despite that reality. On what grounds could reasonable men and women reject the ideal of "virtue and well-being in community" as appropriate ends and the possibility of "beatitude" for those so inclined? Are not virtue and well-being part of any scheme of practical wisdom, however they are ultimately defined? Even the most atheistic or Machiavellian ruler would ultimately stipulate to the goals of virtue and well-being for their regime; simply ask what the defense of a non-virtuous society aimed at willfully harming its inhabitants would look like? A ridiculous idea on its face. While what various rulers and people have thought constituted virtue or well-being for a given society and its inhabitants has varied in the extreme, no one that I am aware of has attempted to defend the "bad life" as preferable to the "good life." As argued previously, even liberalism must contend that its own

---

1. Eliot, *Christianity and Culture*, 27.

"neutrality" on the question of the "good" is in fact an attempt to affirm the *virtue* of neutrality and its contribution to the well-being of the community and the individuals within it. This point, again, is not merely semantic, but foundational, practically speaking. Accepting the goal of "well-being" is the price of participation in the conversation among human beings about how they will live together. Those who theoretically could be conceived of as proffering a doctrine of personal and communal detriment and destruction or annihilation—the functional embrace of nihilism or nothingness—would be unrecognizable and incomprehensible to other human beings; they would in fact not be human *beings* strictly speaking. To be human is to seek a state of "being" that is "well." Even in suicide, human beings talk about a future state of well-being in which their pain will be alleviated, the world will be a better place, and so on. That the person taking his or her own life is mistaken about the result of their actions is not relevant; the goal itself is. Once this line of practical reasoning is stipulated to, space opens up quickly for a deeper understanding of Eliot's larger argument concerning a Christian organization of society.

Eliot himself is quick to point out that he is not talking about theocracy or even a state religion, and neither am I. The term "organization" as it is being used should not be taken to connote an institutional and legal framework associated with certain brands of contemporary religious fundamentalism. As argued previously, a project like that ultimately misunderstands the nature of religion—especially Christianity—by confusing the sacred and the secular such that the former ceases to be viable as the immaterial is in effect rendered just another piece of material or the supernatural is redefined as the merely natural. Instead, by "organization" I am referring to what is best conceived of at this point as the structure of our social intentions rather than our social structures *per se*. That is, I am interested in what might at its simplest be called the *why* of our society, rather than the *what*, for now. Two examples should suffice as metaphors to get this conversation on track. The first story goes like this: A man walking down a mountain one day noticed another man pushing a wheelbarrow of stones up the mountain and yelled out to the man, "Where are you going?" Exasperated and impatient, the man pushing the wheelbarrow up the mountain yelled back, "I'm pushing these rocks up the mountain; what does it look like I'm doing?" The man walking down the mountain then continued on his way and came up to a second man pushing a load of stones up the same mountain and he called out to him, "What are you doing?" The second man smiled widely and responded in a heartfelt manner, "I am building a cathedral!"

The same tasks, the same effort, the same ultimate result, and, yet, the typical reader certainly sees the two actions in fundamentally different lights. In essence, the two identical acts are so qualitatively different that they become not merely differences in degree but truly differences in kind. For the first stone-pusher, the task is drudgery and work; it seems to lack any meaning or transcendence beyond the immediate act and moment. It is, strictly speaking, secular—something existing only for *a* time and *a* place—something that exists essentially in reference only to itself, something wholly *literal*. For the second stone-pusher, however, neither the stones nor the act of pushing them up the mountain were limited in such a way. Both the stones and the act of pushing them existed for the sake of something else, something other than themselves, something non-immediate and, hence, something transcendent or out of time itself. To gauge the action only in secular terms would require reducing the action of the second man to its natural or time-bound state. The intention and the imagination of a future time and state of the world—one where a cathedral actually existed where none was before—cannot be comprehended by the purely secular thinking that circumscribes the actions of the first man. Hence, when I move from Eliot's argument to my own version, the notion of a Christian organization of society begins with the organization of the social imagination and social intentions, i.e., *why* we are doing what we are doing as a society rather than merely *what* we are doing. In a Christian scheme, the latter should always be secondary to the former and subservient to it. In other words, no one should simply push bricks up a mountainside for the sake of pushing bricks up a mountainside. To answer the most immediate objection to this way of thinking, or what I would call the *why* question, I turn briefly to a second story; a cautionary tale, if you will.

The second story comes from the old book by H. G. Wells, *The Time Machine*. Set in the year AD 802,701 (or what appears to be the end of time, for all intents and purposes), Wells paints a picture of a society inhabited by two social groups, the Morlocks and the Eloi. The Morlocks are powerful and technologically advanced creatures (at least they have and know how to use if not build technology) who live below the Earth's surface. They use the technical power to create an idyllic and materially carefree world on the surface of the planet which the Eloi inhabit. The Eloi are true innocents living in what easily resembles a sort of futuristic garden of Eden. They want for nothing and appear to live with relatively little fear or anxiety about the future or even of death itself. This is perhaps a good thing because the dark secret of the utopian community is that the Eloi are so well taken care of and consequently made docile by their lack of physical or material want—temperature and climate are maintained perfectly, food and water are plentiful and easily procured—by the Morlocks, because they represent the Morlocks's chief source of food. While on one level, once the shock of cannibalism is overcome, the situation might be viewed—pragmatically and secularly—as optimal on some level for both the Morlocks and the Eloi. How?

While the Eloi may experience the pain and suffering of loss periodically, they do not appear to know death itself. Members of their species live comfortable and pain-free lives without knowledge of their own death or any sense of their own finiteness. When their time comes, they simply cease to be present anymore and this, one must imagine, simply seems natural. There might be wonder, but there is no fear or anxiety. The Morlocks on the other hand—though painted in dark colors by Wells—work hard and do know death and anxiety in their own way. There are obvious prices they pay for the survival of their species which may give them some legitimate claims of desert for their efforts. (One could picture the book—and subsequent movies—being reacted to quite differently if the surface dwellers looked like the Morlocks and *vice versa*, but that is another argument.) Despite that possibility, I can imagine few if any readers who would be content with the social arrangement of Wells's future world on its face. Why the Eloi live like they live would seem to matter to us. We believe, I would argue, that it would matter to the Eloi themselves. As content and happy as they are with the *status quo*, we would collectively believe that they should know *why* they live like they do; they would want to know the structure of the Morlocks's intentions as well as the fruits of their actions at a particular time. Furthermore, many of us no doubt believe that once the Eloi understood the *why* of their situation, they would probably reject it despite the hardship it may in fact cause—they would have to labor for themselves and would come to know and fear death.

Only a particular kind of religious orientation or organization of society—a transcendent, supernatural, non-secular organization—can ultimately pose and answer the *why* question rather than the *is* question without tautological reasoning or an endless reductionism. In other words, when asked why this sort of society rather than that, the only reason most people can give in isolation is either because they prefer it, or because that is the way it has always been. The latter is of course no answer at all, but rather a simple restatement of the fact that it is, and the former simply begs the question of why one prefers it *ad nauseam*. That is, unless one simply uses the pleasure and pain principle of the physical world to make the distinction. But, of course, that would result in appreciation for the lives of the Eloi and the rejection of difficult "cathedral building" altogether. While the secular world of the here and now and of the necessary tasks for living clearly matters for human beings, it can no more provide its own justification for a certain mode of existence by itself any more than the single human being can provide his or her own "horizons of significance" or direction in the dark ocean from the previous chapter. Simply put, a non-secular orientation is necessary to even ask the question why this rather than that social and political structure, and it is equally critical when the time comes to question or justify the current order. Unfortunately, that point is increasingly less clear, visible, or even understood in the contemporary American context.

Before explaining this phenomenon, it needs to be said that the secular matters—nothing I have said ought to be taken as disparaging or as somehow negating that—no one would want to have a cathedral builder who did not also understand the necessity of pushing stones up the hill. The point I am making is that the secular is itself incomplete if meaning and purpose matter. Much of what happens in contemporary liberal nations, I would argue, has become just so much brick pushing and, metaphorically speaking, the life of the Eloi has become the goal—blissful ignorance and ease without either a conscious history or future. The noted psychologist Robert Coles explains this phenomenon in his book *The Secular Mind*. Drawing his phrase from the theological work of Paul Tillich, Coles distinguishes the secular mind and the sacred mind in the following manner:

> The heart of it, I surmised, was the distinction he wanted to make between Man the thinking materialist and Man the anxiously aspiring creature who bows his head and prays, and who "looks outside himself to Another, to God," for explanations, understanding, guidance.[2]

To be fully secular is to be fully absorbed with the world as it is—either by choice (the first stone pusher) or by default (the Eloi and the Morlocks); it is to be preoccupied with the details of life and allow them to subsume all meaning, purpose, and intentionality on our part. For example, if the clichés we sometimes hear in jest, like, "I live to eat and I eat to live," or "I work to live and I live to work," betray any truth about a human life, they suggest an existence that is absurd or vacuous at best and a simple beast-like existence at worst—my dogs do not ask why this life rather than that life. Other than physical pleasure and the absence of pain (subjective and emotive ideas in many regards), such an existence provides little in the way of help for choosing this society rather than that. In an inversion of the argument made in chapter 2 concerning the "sacramental principle" (by which anything or anyone could be made sacred by seeing the hand or face of God in the thing or person in question), anything, including what is inherently sacred, can be rendered secular and ordinary by failing or refusing to see God's work in

---

2. Coles, *Secular Mind*, 4.

it. Take for example church attendance itself. For Coles (quoting Tillich), it becomes of a piece with the secular mind when it becomes merely "a weekly social rite, a boost to our morale."[3]

The American preoccupation with utility and the pragmatic approach to life has the tendency to render everything smaller than it need be and smaller than it is by limiting our questions of the thing or a person to what they are *for* rather than why they *are* or how they came to be such as they are. Everything and everyone that has been created has a story that at some point in time involved an intention and purpose, which is the context for learning and knowing its meaning and place among the other things in the world—its relatedness, if you will. By only focusing on the uses of the thing much of what it is remains hidden and obscured. The religious mind in general and the Christian mind in particular—especially the analogical, allegorical Catholic-Christian mind—reveals and draws out what is obscured by refusing to allow the secular the only word. This attention to the revelation of the extraordinariness of the ordinary when robustly pursued transforms the immediate everyday world into a glorious and sacred mystery waiting to be drawn out in all its fullness. When applied to the individual person we know that as long as there is life in their bodies he or she can never be fully revealed or known. The individual remains exalted and sacred more for *why* they exist than the fact that they do. In other words, the overwhelming potentiality or possibility that inheres is each and every human being to more fully and completely realize their call, reveal their own personal mystery to the world and others, and know their Creator through agapic (self-giving) love requires that each of us treat that person with all the care and tenderness of a newborn child. If we fail to do this, we distort or disfigure what he or she was capable of becoming by making him or her into a mere means to our own immediate and secular ends and desires—a process that I would call de-sanctification.

Agapic love is reckless and dangerous, and under the right circumstances can even mean a death sentence. From a secular or worldly perspective it is irrational because "it is a love given without manifest reason or justification . . . it precludes the calculation of consequences."[4] While a preoccupation with the secular does not preclude commonsense understandings of love, it does preclude selfless love that is unconcerned with the calculation of consequences because standard cause-and-effect equations are in many ways the essence of the secular mind at work. As a secular ideology, liberalism takes the rights-bearing, self-interested individual as

3. Coles, *Secular Mind*, 5.
4. Tinder, *Political Meaning of Christianity*, 24.

its point of departure. Such a being cannot be theoretically even asked to ignore calculations of such a kind without negating the prohibition against treating another—in this case, the self as Other—as a means. I will not dwell here on the paradox embedded in an ideology that simultaneously claims to liberate people to pursue their own independent vision of the good, but tells those whose visions are the most demanding, selfless, and, one might even say, noble and inspiring that they are in effect unjust. There is, I would argue, a huge difference in treating other people as ends rather than means and understanding ourselves only as ends. Christians (like parents to their child) must always try to see the self as a means, as a facilitator, as a mediator as a servant to the Other. We are called on to spend ourselves fully. Should such "recklessness" be prohibited or at least discouraged? Practically speaking, one must wonder the fate of such a world if it somehow could really exist. It would be a world ensconced in what I would call the reverse Midas problem.

Midas, as the story goes, was given the power to turn everything he touched into gold. So great was his love for wealth that it eventually undid him and caused the death of his daughter. As a parable or myth about the dangers of greed, the story remains instructive. But what if the value in a particular culture was not "gold" but personal autonomy? Suppose that the great sign of personal wealth in a given place was the lack of significant extra-personal attachments—the ability, if you will, to retain an almost infinite variety of possible choices by refusing to give oneself over to any particular choice that would thereby commit the self to a particular course of action, or a belief, or a way of life, or another person. Metaphorically speaking, each time that person "touched" something, i.e., gave themselves away or made a commitment or a promise of some sort which bound that individual into the future, he or she would be in effect losing their "wealth" or spending it by making choices and commitments. By such a standard, religious martyrs and saints, including Christ, are the poorest and least enviable of all human beings because they choose to give away literally everything they have, to completely spend themselves in the name of others. In turn, the most admirable and reverenced person in a truly secularized society becomes the one able to make virtually no lasting commitments that may, in the end, decrease their autonomy.

Now while it is impossible to live such a theoretical life in any practical way, the existence of the fully autonomous, least committed as possible human being as exemplar will have critical social and political implications if taken to heart. The isolation and solitude that Tocqueville so anxiously worried about becomes but the tip of the proverbial iceberg if this becomes the dominant cultural form. Taken to its logical conclusion in the realm of pure reason, beings such as our new autonomy-hoarding Midases become beings who are alive but do not live. They are as personally, emotionally, socially, and even physically paralyzed as the original King Midas's daughter herself was. Sadly, such beings may as well be dead, i.e., they appear to already be so. In the most profound of all the seeming paradoxes of the Christian faith, true life can only be found in the act of dying to the self, in giving one's self over as fully as possible to Others without regard to self-interest as it is currently understood. In other words, the only certain way to preserve the dignity of the individual is for certain individuals to make it their personal and collective mission to ignore the claims of the self, to refrain from spending one's autonomy, and to spend it all on others in the form of selfless love. Only when this is done can the sacredness of the self or an individual be made manifest and drawn out from within the apparently secular being. This, as should be obvious to even the most casual observer, is not a position that resonates readily with the typical American citizen, but it may be the only way to preserve the essence of what those same citizens claim to value and cherish.

AMERICA

The African American literary theorist Houston Baker Jr. writes "America" in all capital letters to signify an idea or a trope rather than a place or a nation. While related to the Straussian concept of a regime, Baker's AMERICA is first and foremost a cultural concept with political implications. In his book *Blues, Ideology, and Afro-American Literature: A Vernacular Theory*, Baker asserts that there are certain "governing statements" of American discourse that serve as the contextual and hegemonic parameters for an American cultural-linguistic, and hence political, identity. In his words,

> From the seventeenth century to the twentieth, ministerial and lay professors of the white American academy have been official spokespersons, working as teachers, scholars, critics, editors, and so on. . . . The early Providential aura of their instruction has been secularized through time, but one still receives the impression on reading their works that lay ministers are at work, taking account of and perpetuating literary workers and works of art that manifest adherence to the original errand—securing a New Jerusalem . . . a recaptured Eden in America.[5]

5. Duncan, "*Blues* Voice of Houston Baker, Jr.," 233.

Baker's "governing statements" include "Religious man," "wilderness," "migratory errand," "increase in store," and "New Jerusalem," among others. For his project, these statements are juxtaposed to a separate set of statements which he argues governed a distinctive African American discourse that was very different than that of White America. Here, I am not interested in that project, but in the initial premise of the argument itself. At its simplest, that premise is that AMERICA, and what is often called the American way of life, is in some manner divine—a place, a people, and a regime upon which God had quite literally "shed his grace." A would-be nation where the new chosen people would build the bright and shining city on the hill and subsequently prosper and thrive in direct proportion to their fidelity. The master argument on this score is, of course, Max Weber's argument, but the architectonic exemplar, or living embodiment, of the theory in practice is Abraham Lincoln. No American figure before or since has ever approached Lincoln's ability to effortlessly merge and seamlessly conflate religious and political discourse with the same level of sagacity, sincerity, and utility of the deist from Kentucky. More than the civil religion that Bellah wrote of, Lincoln was being quite literal when he argued for the creation of a "political religion," which is not to be confused with the notion of a religiously grounded or inspired politics, but rather with an attempt to spiritualize and make holy a particular political ideology or regime. In Christian discourse, such a project is an act of idolatry in that what is not God is mistaken or intentionally reverenced as if it was. Finding God's presence in all things is far different from confusing the things themselves with God; to worship the United States would be to worship it and its manifestations, such as the Constitution, as themselves perfect and without the taint of sin.

When Baker claims that what was once viewed as Providential—a gift from the divine—has been "secularized through time," he has said something very important even if he does not dwell on it. Implied in the notion of secularization as used here is the process Marx polemically wrote of in the *Communist Manifesto* whereby the bourgeoisie rendered all that was holy profane, i.e., what was religious was made either non-religious or perhaps even irreligious. Such a process diminishes things and makes them smaller than they truly are. Unfortunately for Lincoln, the lawlessness of 1838 that inspired the Lyceum Address and the American Civil War called for a radically more inspiring vision, and ultimately, in Lincoln's words, a rededication that a profaned AMERICA could not deliver or sustain. However, despite Lincoln's vast rhetorical and oratorical skills and ability to capture the spiritual imagination of much of the country, Lincoln's own lack of a significant faith commitment raises a crucial question as to what he was actually attempting to divinize or render holy. My argument is that Lincoln's ultimate reverence was for the people and the ethic of the American middle class or petit bourgeois:

> Lincoln's partisanship was grounded in a deeper ideological commitment to the liberalism and democratic capitalism of the early Republican Party. Foner's title provides the best shorthand expression of those commitments: *Free Soil, Free Labor, Free Men*. Whatever else Lincoln stood for along the way, bourgeois liberty properly understood was the end. All other issues and questions were subsumed into his political matrix and moral vision based on the degree to which he thought they furthered those ends or thwarted them. Failure to grasp this essential and singular purpose will result in the failure to understand *Lincolnism*.[6]

If this argument stands, it quickly follows that Lincoln's deployment of familiar Christian tropes and images, and his use of the theocentric-idiom in his public addresses can be seen as servicing liberal-political rather than Christian ends. In other words, Lincoln can be said to have learned the hard way that the liberalism he so cherished with its emphasis on "self-interest," "contracts," "markets," "labor," "rights," "property," and even "liberty" and "independence," lacked the power over time to compel as they had in earlier revolutionary epochs. They had to somehow be made bigger than they were. Take for example the most famous of all Lincoln's speeches, the "Gettysburg Address." How different do those words feel when the listener hears "four score and seven years ago our forefathers brought forth upon this continent" as compared to: eighty-seven years ago the nation's founders overthrew King George III and created the United States of America. The former, while not religious in content, sounds *religious* and seems far weightier and more spiritually profound to the average member of an American audience familiar with the Bible than the latter—though they mean the same thing. It sounds as if Moses himself might have said something similar from a cliff on Mount Sinai. While no one should begrudge a leader the rhetorical tools needed to convey the gravity of an event or the ability to move an audience, and certainly not the audience at Gettysburg, there are legitimate questions that can be raised given Lincoln's frequent turns to the familiar idiom regarding his true goals and intentions.

Though he has every right to worship what and, for the most part, how he would like, there are important questions of integrity that matter if people are being willfully misled. More importantly, this matters because a liberalism too thoroughly sanctified becomes a cultural Trojan horse. It

6. Duncan, "Lincoln's Theocentric Turn," 511.

eventually may overwhelm and distort the faith whose linguistic clothes it has donned. This would potentially create moral, social, and political chaos if the argument thus far concerning the real need for practicing Christians is a viable one. In such a case, a transcendent Christian faith is itself secularized by being placed in the service of strictly secular ends. How does this work? An example again from Robert Coles is instructive. Writing of a friend he interviewed by the name of Dr. Williams, Coles recounts a story the doctor told him about a young Catholic grandmother from Italy who had become an AMERICAN and who once told him,

> It used to be I prayed to God, that I would learn what *He* wanted from me, and how *He* wanted me to behave (I wanted His help to be that kind of person, the kind He wanted); but now I pray to God that He help us with this problem, and the next one—to be a Big Pal of ours! It used to be, when I prayed to God, I was talking to Him; now, it's me talking to myself, and I'm only asking Him to help out with things.[7]

Such a view of God as a "big pal" and the sort of theology that comes to grow up around it is part and parcel of what Harold Bloom has called the American Religion.[8] This is the God of the self-help set, the God of "how to win friends and influence people." Bloom argues in his provocative and polemical book that despite the deeply held religious beliefs—most of which draw on Christian images and sources—America is in fact emerging as a "post-Christian nation." Generalizing broadly to be sure, Bloom argues that the American religion is marked by a kind of Gnosticism which prizes personal revelation and rejects, for the most part, traditional notions of original sin in particular, but also sin in a general way as well. To be an American Christian for Bloom is to believe that you are basically a good person who occasionally does bad things because you didn't know better or you miscalculated—not because you are attracted to evil itself. To be an American Christian is to believe that God exists to support you in your worldly endeavors, to watch out for you as you make your way in the world, to care about your individual hopes and dreams, and, typically, not to be too judgmental or demanding because He knows you mean well. A comical and banal example of this approach can be gleaned from an episode of the TV sitcom *The King of Queens*, in which the nominally Christian Doug and Carrie Heffernan discover the power of prayer.

The Heffernans pray for field goals so the Jets can cover the spread and win the football game. They pray for designer shoes to go on sale. They

---

7. Coles, *Secular Mind*, 105.
8. Bloom, *American Religion*.

pray for the last piece of fish at the butcher shop and so on. At the end of the episode, the contentious couple get into a battle of prayer with each other where each prays against the other's prayers for their own benefit and gain. Instead of thanksgiving for their gifts or an attempt to discern what God wants from them, they treat God as a kind of cosmic wishing-well. Though devout people are no doubt supposed to laugh at the irony of the situation, the humor is in all likelihood a result of its exaggerated nature instead. In other words, it is the seeming frivolity of the things prayed for that draws the laughs, but not the actual form that the prayer takes. When football players thank God for their victories on the field or musicians declare that they must give it up to the Lord for their awards, it is basically the same thing. The speaker believes God has taken a personal interest in their hopes, dreams, and success—regardless of how they live their life or even what they believe or practice. What this says to the losing side or the other nominees is often an unasked or answered question, but the implications are at least interesting. While Lincoln's Second Inaugural Address suggests that there was sin on both sides, there is little doubt whom he believed God had sided with in that horrific conflict.

The God of the American religion is worried about your individual rights and liberties, including the right to worship God in your own way. As Bloom puts it: "The vast majority of us [Americans] believe in some version of God, and nearly all of that majority actually do believe that God loves her or him, on a personal and individual basis."[9] It is little wonder that the fastest-growing Christian denomination is the more or less creedless Pentecostalism or that the Southern Baptists, with their emphasis on individual "soul-competency," are so prominent in America. Bloom goes so far as to link his view of the American religion as a modern form of Gnosticism with the notion of an almost deistic individualism, writing,

> But *the* Gnostics, in a narrow sense, were a proto-Christian sect of the second century of the Common Era, whose broad beliefs centered in two absolute convictions: the Creation, of the world and of mankind in its present form, was the same event as the Fall of the world and of man, but humankind has in it a spark or breath of the uncreated, unfallen world, in a solitary act of knowledge.[10]

Now while few Americans would want to argue against the idea of protecting the right of individual conscience in religious matters as a *political* ideal, its conflation with an epistemological position is of a fairly recent

9. Bloom, *American Religion*, 257.
10. Bloom, *American Religion*, 27.

historical vintage. In other words, though there has been pretty widespread agreement on the right to worship God as one saw fit, the typical believer did not traditionally believe that all forms of worship were equally right or that he or she was the ultimate source of spiritual knowledge like Gnostic thinking can lead to. Indeed, many believers used to think that salvation depended on learning and getting the theology and the manner of worship correct from those who have gone before, from our religious traditions and teachers. And, it was thought quite possible to be wrong and go to hell as a result of the error in either fidelity or confession. This is now either no longer true or at least no longer considered a reasonable topic for civil discourse. Anecdotally, think back to actor Mel Gibson's famous pronouncement that his "saintly" wife was going to hell because, as an Episcopalian, she was not a member of the "one true Church" (the Catholic Church, for Gibson). I would imagine that the vast majority of Americans—a vast majority who identify as some sort of Christian—recoiled and chafed significantly at that comment. (Your author certainly did.) What, though, were we actually offended by? Was it simply the blunt matter-of-factness with which he said it? Was it the hubris or unseemly confidence with which he made this judgment that so casually cast a loving spouse into what he surely believes is the fiery pit of hell? Was it that he struck us as a bad husband or callous friend? Was it Gibson's own sense that he was saved despite being in his own words not nearly as good of a person as the one whom he thought damned? The truth is, it was probably all of the above and then some. But, I would argue that it was also something deeper—a belief that Gibson himself was wrong and that "good" people, especially those who "know Jesus" in some manner, do not go to hell regardless of their beliefs or religious practices, assuming we even believe in hell at all. Embedded in our contemporary version of the belief that Jesus loves us is the belief that he would not want us to feel bad or guilty about much of anything. Rather than the more traditional notion that God wants his children to be faithful, the American religion tends to believe that God wants us to be happy or pleased and not made too uncomfortable. And, if Bloom is at all on track, we *know* this because of the divine spark within us which tells us it is so.

Now whether Mel Gibson's retro-Catholicism is true is not the point for now. Nor do I want to take up his argument concerning his wife or other "good" people, one way or the other. Instead, what I would like to contend is that regardless of what we thought might happen to other people as a result of their particular confession or degree of fidelity we used to be harder on ourselves. We used to at least have the courage of our own convictions and believe that if we got it wrong, we would suffer for it, and suffer rightly. Many of us who are believers no longer seem to think that we ourselves are under judgment in any way. Religion has become for many of us another version of modern therapy designed to make sure that we feel pretty good about ourselves and help us be good and decent people for the most part. Oddly, when Marx first claimed that religion was the opiate of the masses, most religious believers were deeply offended and indignant. Now I could figuratively imagine many believers saying, "Thank God for religion, let's keep it safe, legal, and convenient so that I do not need to live in pain." Though a little glib, a few visits to one of the contemporary nondenominational Christian megachurches that have sprung up around the country will not yield a view of this picture as being too far off.

No one has diagnosed the American condition or delineated the social and political implications of this important shift with more verve or insight than the late Christopher Lasch. In his seminal work, *The Culture of Narcissism: American Life in an Age of Diminishing Expectations*, Lasch argues that the therapeutic ethic has displaced both rugged individualism and religion as the central feature of an age and culture focused only on the immediate (the secular). The consequence of this shift—which I argue has thoroughly infiltrated the American religious mind—is of critical importance to those who take the core of the Christian belief system (agapic love) seriously, because in Lasch's words,

> Even when therapists speak of the need for "meaning" and "love," they define love and meaning simply as the fulfillment of the patient's emotional requirements. It hardly occurs to them—nor is there any reason why it should, given the nature of the therapeutic enterprise—to encourage the subject to subordinate his needs and interests to those of others, to someone or some cause or tradition outside of himself. "Love" as self-sacrifice or self-abasement, "meaning" as submission to a higher loyalty—these sublimations strike the therapeutic sensibility as intolerably oppressive, offensive to common sense and injurious to personal well-being. To liberate humanity from such outmoded ideas of love and duty has become the mission of the post-Freudian therapies and particularly of their converts and popularizers, for whom mental health means the immediate gratification of every impulse.[11]

Versions of Christianity, or increasingly notions of "spirituality," which tend to dominate the American social world if not fully ensconced in this sensibility certainly do not confront it head on as they might have in another era as, alas, they exist in a market place as well and the demand for programs offering self-denial and sacrifice is not seen as particularly high. Ironically,

---

11. Lasch, *Culture of Narcissism*, 13.

it may prove to be the case that, having gotten what they wanted, Americans may not want what they have got. In other words, while less arduous forms of "community" with easy exit options and few if any irrevocable demands or commitments may sound good in a culture which believes that independence and autonomy are enhanced and secured by the ability to keep as many of one's options as open as possible, it may be the case that human beings want or need to be challenged in more rigorous and substantive ways than this orientation can provide for. As I have argued elsewhere, it may be "the greatest paradox of all, that what we are often seeking can only be found by relinquishing our right to search any further."[12] What was argued in the previous chapter regarding the benefits of such a proposition at the political and societal level may turn out to be true at the psychological level as well. Lasch more or less makes this argument in the following way:

> The trouble with the consciousness movement is not that it addresses trivial or unreal issues but that it provides self-defeating solutions. Arising out of a pervasive dissatisfaction with the quality of personal relations, it advises people not to make too large an investment in love and friendship, to avoid excessive dependence on others, and to live for the moment—the very conditions that created the crisis of personal relations in the first place.[13]

While there is some evidence in the culture that things are changing and people are seeking out more intractable forms of commitment, it is an uphill battle given the liberal-capitalist context and the increasing demands brought about by globalization. Both tend to dominate contemporary life and are omnipresent in the decision calculus the typical American citizen must use regarding the relative depth of their various commitments to others. This is true whether they are dependent or the one on whom others depend. This calculus builds the demand for tentativeness regarding commitments to others, be they individuals, communities, or institutions, into the equation in such a way as to undermine any real attempt to decenter the utility-minded rational actor upon which bourgeois-liberalism itself is premised. In turn, we are left bereft of the resources needed for genuine happiness and true individualism. On my reading of her work, the political theorist Anne Norton captures this ideal with all its attendant ambiguity in the following passage:

> The selves of liberal practice are not the selves of liberal theory. Convinced, in theory, of our individuality, we find ourselves

---

12. Duncan, "Community and the American Village," 91.
13. Lasch, *Culture of Narcissism*, 27.

in common languages and express ourselves (even rebel) in conformity with existing conventions. Convinced, in theory, of our singularity, we exceed ourselves, supplementing the form we inhabited at birth with an array of literary selves not always in accord with one another. Convinced, in theory, of our unity, we deconstruct ourselves in practice, giving ourselves material expression in collections of diverse commodities. Convinced, in theory, that the unity of the self is necessary to happiness and perhaps to sanity, we experience this deconstructive enterprise not only as a source of anxiety but also as an act of authority and a source of pleasure.[14]

Born into a family of "wes" who suborn possessive individualism in obeisance to an ideology which can neither be practically sustained nor theoretically discarded, American men and women vacillate between joy and despair. This is the result of the semiconscious belief that they are each deities and their subsequent realization of the new "God" is so small and powerless. Lasch might put this point in the following way: "The ideology of personal growth, superficially optimistic, radiates a profound despair and resignation. It is a faith of those without faith."[15] Using her work metaphorically for my purposes, Norton might say it thus:

> The practice of shopping enacts liberal theory's identification of choice with freedom and, in that enactment, suggests a critique. Individuality, the conventions governing property, and the utility of representation as an instrument for the expression of the author's will are all called into question. We realize, as we shop, that choice may be experienced as freedom, and as compulsion. The choices we appear to make have already been made for us. The individuality we prize is realized in purchases that deconstruct it. Property shows itself not only as a means for self-protection, self-expression, and self-discovery but also as a means for subjecting us to the authority of others. The enactment of the ideas of liberalism works simultaneously to confirm and subvert them.[16]

When compared to the evils of American slavery, Lincoln's petit-bourgeois vision of a liberal state driven on by democratic capitalism to relative security, comfort, and prosperity is highly appealing. However, it is a far cry from a "New Jerusalem" or the biblical city on the hill. Neither does it aspire

---

14. Norton, *Republic of Signs*, 3.
15. Lasch, *Culture of Narcissism*, 51.
16. Norton, *Republic of Signs*, 4.

to the status of Athens or even Rome. The America Lincoln described as a nation of "almost chosen people" seems apt much of the time. However, it is never completely clear whether this was intended to be descriptive or aspirational. Sadly, I believe that today it is more or less the latter. That might simply be a sign of realism—the best we can hope for given what we have to work with. Unfortunately, it is also possible that we are fated then to behave historically like all other great nations and that Lincoln's greatest hope—that we not perish from the earth—may be in vain. As a person of faith, and therefore a proponent of destiny rather than fate, along with Glenn Tinder, I believe that this is not preordained. The Sisyphus-like struggle of confirmation and subversion embedded in the liberalism described by Norton does not need to be the end of the story. For that to come to pass, however, requires that liberalism cannot be the only American story. At a minimum, the liberal tale must be properly embedded in a larger narrative. Alternatively, it may mean that the liberal story needs to be supplanted over time. Among the more interesting examples of this sort of thinking is the prolific and enigmatic American thinker and theorist, Orestes Brownson, to whom we finally turn.

AMERICAN RELIGION

In 1940, the emergent cold warrior and early neoconservative Sidney Hook described Catholicism as "the oldest totalitarian movement in history."[17] While he would later soften that view in 1955, as real totalitarian movements in the USSR and elsewhere made such hyperbolic rhetoric seem too far removed from reality to be of much conceptual use, he did not move far from the sentiments and image of the faith that lay at the former statement's foundation. While perhaps more ideologically noble than the notorious immigrant bashing anti-Catholicism of the late nineteenth century in its allegiance to the image of the free-thinking American individualist, Hook's anti-Catholicism was nonetheless part of a larger theoretical narrative and political assault on the denomination as old as the republic itself. Although his own famous critique of American political thought emerged from a very different set of ideological commitments, Hook's contemporary, Louis Hartz, shared his basic view and understanding of Catholicism. Although not even rating an entry in the index of his famous work, *The Liberal Tradition in America*, Hartz's view of Catholicism can be gleaned from his discussion of the Catholic convert Orestes Brownson. In a passage discussing Brownson's turn away from the American "proletary" after the election of 1840, Hartz argues that Brownson fled from "the principle of

17. McGreevy, *Catholicism and American Freedom*, 212.

democracy, embracing Catholicism and conservatism."[18] Hartz then moves on to compare that flight to that by intellectuals after the French Revolution. But Hartz notes an important difference writing: "in Europe the flight was due to an excess of radicalism; in liberal America Brownson's flight was due to the fact that there had not been enough [radicalism]."[19] What Hartz fails to ask, of course, is whether both were fleeing to the *same* Catholicism?

While Brownson had certainly rejected the politics of the "mob" after the 1840s, there was no *ancien régime* in America that could have provided him with an intellectual home in which to flee upon his reaction. Hartz's attempt to lump him in with the "southern feudalists" misses the whole point of Brownson's master work, *The American Republic*, and demonstrates a profoundly ill-informed understanding of the possibilities located both within Christianity itself, and more specifically within the Catholicism that was beginning to percolate in the historical period around Brownson's conversion. Unlike those would-be aristocrats and socialists whom Hartz rightfully accuses of looking to Europe and missing the point of American historical development, Brownson believes that he has discovered an America that was latent and authentic. His work in this regard has much more in common with the sort of project Lincoln undertook in his reading of the American political tradition. Here Hartz, like Hook, falls victim to his own model insofar as neither can see past their own caricature of the faith far enough to allow a thinker like Brownson to raise questions that might rankle their own liberal commitments. Despite the importance and insight of his work, Hartz on some level is an odd example of exactly what he was criticizing. After all is said and done, isn't his accusation against American political thought one that finds it guilty for not being *liberal* enough?

In a letter to Francis Hopkinson circa 1789, Thomas Jefferson claimed,

> I never submitted the whole system of my opinions to the creed of any party of men whatever, in religion, philosophy, in politics, or in anything else, where I was capable of thinking for myself. Such an addiction, is the last degradation of a free moral agent.[20]

Ironically, this could be called the quintessential assertion of the American philosophic creed. We are a people for whom "seeing is believing," and a nation where "everyone is entitled to his or her own opinion." At its best, this tradition of individualism liberates Americans, as Thoreau so eloquently put it, to "live deliberately," and subsequently, to create and re-create themselves

---

18. Hartz, *Liberal Tradition in America*, 139.
19. Hartz, *Liberal Tradition in America*, 139.
20. Jefferson, "Letter to Francis Hopkinson."

such that they might "live with the license of a higher order of beings."[21] On the other side of the political ledger, however, it also, in Tocqueville's words, disposes "each citizen to isolate himself from the mass of his fellows and withdraw into the circle of family and friends"[22] and puts Americans at risk of being "thrown back on [ourselves] alone . . . [where] there is danger that [we] may be shut up in the solitude of [our] own heart[s]."[23] It is in between these poles of political liberation and political solipsism that Americans must attempt to forge their political identity as citizens, always keeping in mind how readily the quest for the former might suddenly be transfigured into the reality of the latter. In such a case, the very liberation we sought becomes its own kind of Weberian "iron cage," and we ironically are trapped by the very ideal that was meant to set us free.

No thinker in nineteenth-century American political thought better represents the nature of this conundrum than Orestes Brownson. At various times he was a Presbyterian, a Universalist, a Unitarian, and ultimately a Roman Catholic. His politics ran the gambit from Chartism to Jacksonian Democracy to the Workingman's Party to an independent political philosopher who rejected much of the emphasis on "rights" and instead attempted to reinvigorate an American public discourse on "duties" and "authority." Through the interplay between his very public religious quest and his political theory, Orestes Brownson's life and thought has the power to force Americans to confront both the possibilities and the boundaries of their "Jeffersonian" heritage such that we may be able to explain why Jefferson's own assertion that "there is not a young man now living in the United States who will not die a Unitarian"[24] failed to materialize in Brownson's case and those who sympathize with the positions of his later life.

In what follows, I explore briefly certain representative theorizations and arguments made by Brownson in the context of a particular reading of American political thought and culture as they relate to religious discourse. My objectives here are twofold: first, I would like to provide a glimpse into the life and mind of Orestes Brownson in an attempt to help rescue what are important and relevant, yet now forgotten or neglected, theoretical contributions made by this eclectic, forceful, and once widely known American political theorist; second, I would like to use that "glimpse" to continue the conversation about contemporary American political culture and the intersection and interrelationship between "theology" and political theory

21. Thoreau, *Selected Writings*, 124.
22. Tocqueville, *Democracy in America*, 506.
23. Tocqueville, *Democracy in America*, 508.
24. Jefferson, "Letter to Benjamin Waterhouse."

therein. It is my argument that Brownson's final theorization is intellectually superior to the prevailing conventional wisdom regarding American political theory, but that, despite this, it has lost the battle and perhaps the war for the majority of American hearts and minds. This raises a further set of theoretical and practical political questions regarding the future of both American political thought and American political life.

Regarding the political thought of Thomas Jefferson, Allen Jayne argues persuasively that "Jefferson saw the concepts of God and man upheld by orthodox theological circles in the colonies as antithetical to the Declaration's theological and political ideals."[25] That theology was antithetical to the political ideology undergirding the Declaration of Independence, according to Jayne, because of its "antiegalitarian [and] antidemocratic implications."[26] Among other important theological variances, Jayne argues that a good deal of Jefferson's heterodoxy stems from his rejection of traditional Christianity's assertion of the doctrine of original sin. Where "orthodox versions of Christianity both Catholic and Protestant" asserted "the inability of men and women to save themselves by their own moral acts" because of "the inherited effects of the original sin of Adam and Eve,"[27] Jefferson "was unable to reconcile the Christian doctrine of atonement with his concept of a just God and therefore rejected this doctrine 'in all its circumstances,' which included the fall."[28]

In place of what he believed was an impoverished and politically apostate conception of human nature, Jefferson embraced a view of human nature that saw human beings as "essentially moral beings (not tainted by original sin) [who were] endowed with reason and rights."[29] For Jefferson, such a view was necessary if one was going to argue on behalf of liberty and democracy. For him, history had demonstrated that traditional Christianity's less optimistic view had led to the anti-democratic and anti-egalitarian politics of the preceding ages and epochs of Western political thought, and if those hierarchical and authoritarian political institutions were to be dismantled, the first theoretical construct that would have to go was the mistaken conception of human nature they rested upon. Extrapolating from this line of argument, the implication is that under Jeffersonian political philosophy, the existence of original sin, with its assertion of a fallen human condition, would necessarily authorize some form of anti-republican

---

25. Jayne, *Jefferson's Declaration of Independence*, 7.
26. Jayne, *Jefferson's Declaration of Independence*, 9.
27. Jayne, *Jefferson's Declaration of Independence*, 16.
28. Jayne, *Jefferson's Declaration of Independence*, 36.
29. Jayne, *Jefferson's Declaration of Independence*, 7.

state. On the other hand, the absence of such a "fall" necessarily legitimates and, indeed, necessitates the existence of the liberal-democratic polity he desired. While such a starkly dichotomous reading of the political/philosophical possibilities ignores a position like that of C. S. Lewis, who claimed he "was a democrat *because* he believed in the fall of man,"[30] it is on its own terms rational and quite logical. Yet, there are at least four questions such a position raises that need to be addressed. First, of course, is the question of whether Jefferson's philosophy/theology is correct, e.g., whether we are fallen creatures. Second, as suggested by Lewis's assertion, was the Jeffersonian dichotomy exhaustive, i.e., is it possible to believe in the "Fall" and still embrace liberal-democracy legitimately? Third, if such an un-Jeffersonian possibility is viable, what would such a theorization look like? Finally, to what extent is/was the Jeffersonian theorization in accord with American political thought and culture broadly understood, i.e., can you be an "American" and still believe in original sin? I will start with the last question first.

Regarding pre-Jeffersonian America, Jayne argues that Jefferson's heterodox theology (i.e., the Unitarian rejection of the Trinity, the assertion of the humanity of Jesus, the denial of original sin, a belief in the fundamental goodness of human nature, and a rejection of the necessity of God's grace for human perfection) ran diametrically counter to the dominant American religious traditions. As Jayne puts it: "[Jefferson] was painfully aware of the disparity between the individual reason-based politics of the new United States and its predominantly faith-based religions."[31] Colonial history and the academic literature on this point tells us without a lot of effort that he was right to be concerned.[32] In the "new" United States of the post-Declaration era, both then and, especially, now, however, the evidence is much less clear. Whatever the status of public opinion is regarding the other aspects of the Unitarian formulation above is, the issue of original sin and the essential nature of man, theologically speaking, is clearly open to dispute. Anecdotally speaking, an old survey by the *New York Times Sunday Magazine* suggested that if Americans believe in general that human beings are fallen creatures, they do not believe that its effects are very pronounced or lasting insofar as 94 percent of all respondents who said they believed in heaven

---

30. Lewis, "Equality," 192.
31. Jayne, *Jefferson's Declaration of Independence*, 165.
32. See Sandoz, *Government of Laws*; Shain, *Myth of American Individualism*. Oddly, however, much of that same history and literature ironically demonstrate a pronounced *lack* of theoretical dissonance over the compatibility of fallen man and democracy. See Miller, *Rise and Fall of Democracy*; Duncan, *Anti-Federalists*, especially ch. 1; Zuckerman, *Peaceable Kingdoms*.

(90 percent of the total respondents to the survey claimed they had such a belief) thought that they had a "fair-to-excellent chance of going" there.[33]

While that same *New York Times* article did not ask those same people what they thought their fellow citizen's chances for making to heaven were, it did claim that there were over sixteen hundred different religions and denominations in the United States today (over eight hundred founded since 1965 alone), suggesting at a minimum that there is no one right way (or at least no consensus on what the right way is) to get there. While Jefferson's prediction that "there is not a young man now living in the United States who will not die a Unitarian" (and by implication, that America will become a "Unitarian nation"),[34] has not come to pass officially, the exponential multiplication of denominations does imply the predominance of a societal *ethos* of theological individualism and the ironic preponderance, if not enshrinement, of "creedlessness" as *the* American religious dogma.[35] Over the last forty years, a proportion of all the US traditional Christian denominations (Episcopal, Methodist, Lutheran, and Catholic) are either experiencing large declines in membership or barely staying constant. Furthermore, the most individualistic and least dogmatic denominations are experiencing vast growth (from the Southern Baptists at about +8 percent to the Mormons at +96 percent to the Church of God in Christ at +863 percent). Couple all of this with the fact that even within those denominations, theological individualism (as denoted by phrases like "cafeteria-Catholic") is rampant, irrefutable evidence emerges that post-Jeffersonian America is at its philosophic and theological core Jeffersonian in spirit at least.

Such a state of affairs clearly points to a people who, like Jefferson, are not willing to submit "the whole system of [their] opinions to the creed of any party of men whatever, in religion, philosophy, in politics, or in anything else, where [they are] capable of thinking for [themselves]." Although at this point it is only an observation and not an argument, for now, I would suggest that if the typical American was overtly and strongly concerned with the extent and possible social, political, and spiritual ramifications of original sin, he or she would be significantly more likely to move toward a position of theological convergence and away from what is a historically and politically unprecedented degree of religious toleration and diversity. Toleration, on the vast scale that Americans practice it in an area of such seemingly vital and historically treacherous terrain, only makes sense if a people believes that religious choices are trivial, or if they trust in the ultimate goodness of their

33. "God Decentralized," 61.
34. Quoted in Jayne, *Jefferson's Declaration of Independence*, 166.
35. See Bloom, *American Religion*.

fellow citizens. Since 96 percent of Americans claim that we believe in God, I will reject the former possibility outright for now, thereby leaving the latter proposition as controlling with regard to at least contemporary American political culture and "theology." Hence, on at least one reading of the "data," it would seem that those who take the notion of original sin seriously are, at least today, substantially outside of the American cultural landscape.

The foregoing is not meant to disparage those traditional beliefs or believers, but rather to suggest simply that the historical sweep in such matters is not in their direction in America. Yet, while we know for now how the story ends, the remaining question concerns how we got there and what the larger political implications are for such a people. Since the vast majority of Americans, both in Jefferson's day and now, lacked Jefferson's intellect and learning, we must assume that there were larger cultural/political forces at work that created the fertile soil for our theological individualism and its mostly optimistic outlook. While Tocqueville's observations and arguments in the first few chapters of the second volume to *Democracy in America* are significantly more potent as explication and explanation than they are as prognostication, he does make a strong case that the American penchant for *equality* is among the more important cultural and political forces driving both the multiplication and variation of denominations as well as the lack of reticence about human possibilities they seem to share at least at the level of *praxis*. Furthermore, it is Tocqueville's concerns that I argue serve as the intellectual foundation for Orestes Brownson's mature political theorizations.

In his chapter on the philosophic approach of Americans, Tocqueville argues,

> When it comes to the influence of one man's mind over another's, that is necessarily very restricted in a country where the citizens have all become more or less similar, they see each other at very close quarters, and since they do not recognize any signs of incontestable greatness or superiority in any of their fellows, are continually brought back to their own judgment as the most apparent and accessible test of truth. So it is not only confidence in any particular man which is destroyed. There is a general distaste for accepting any man's word as proof of anything. So each man is narrowly shut up in himself, and from that basis makes the pretension to judge the world. This American way of relying on themselves alone to control their judgment leads to other mental habits. Seeing that they are successful in resolving unaided all the little difficulties they encounter in practical affairs, they are easily led to the conclusion that everything in the world can be explained and that nothing passes beyond the limits of intelligence.

> Thus they are ready to deny anything which they cannot understand. Hence they have little faith in anything extraordinary and an almost invincible distaste for the supernatural.[36]

By the supernatural, Tocqueville is not necessarily referring to an ability on the part of Americans to believe in unseen things like God, but rather to an unwillingness to believe in something that is either inaccessible to our reason or that is deemed outside of our control. Thus, it is not unusual to hear an American argue from the logic of the "city of man" about the workings of the "city of God," as in the following representative syllogism: a just God would not do X; our God is a just God; therefore, our God would not do X. For most Americans, this logic is a familiar method of theological speculation. Taken alongside the notion of the priesthood of the believer and an increasingly conciliar and democratic church structure, this method brings God down from heaven and makes him sensible and discernible such that we can talk about having a friend in Jesus who we walk with and talk with, and ask ourselves what he would do if he was in our shoes? It is no wonder then that Americans would feel unencumbered by the weight of original sin because a just God would not hold anyone accountable for a "crime" that they did not directly commit.

As it was for Jefferson, so it is for many Americans, God increasingly loses the element of mystery and becomes something of a chief moral legislator who provides us with rules and a system of rewards and punishments. The rewards for following the "rules" range from material success in this life to beatification in the next. The punishments are of course the inverse of the rewards. It is in this light that I would argue the book of Job is virtually incomprehensible to most Americans. As a consequence of this discernible and accessible God who thinks a lot like us, it becomes easier and easier to think of ourselves as being a lot like him. Hence, a few pages after his claims about the American philosophic habits, Tocqueville expands his argument thus:

> Equality puts many ideas into the human mind which would not have come there without it, and it changes all the ideas that were there before. I take the concept of human perfectibility as an example, for that is one of the chief ideas which the mind alone can conceive and which by itself constitutes a great philosophical theory. . . . Every man sees changes continually taking place. Some make things worse, and he understands only too well that no people and no individual, however enlightened he be, is ever

---

36. Tocqueville, *Democracy in America*, 430.

infallible. Others improve his lot, and he concludes that man in general is endowed with an indefinite capacity for improvement.[37]

When taken with the earlier assertion that "everything in the world can be explained and that nothing passes beyond the limits of intelligence," this belief in perfectibility certainly echoes if not countenances a form of Pelagianism and perhaps even a modified form of Gnosticism.[38] In other words, it becomes possible for human beings who believe in such a way to come to the conclusion—often unspoken and unacknowledged but still present by implication—that they are capable of saving themselves. Indeed, taken to its logical conclusion, it becomes apparent that they *must* save themselves. For such people freedom, independence, and complete moral autonomy become essential to their happiness in both this life and the next. Freedom of conscience comes to imply the freedom to will which, in turn, comes to imply, for many, the freedom to act on their consciences and wills. So it is that Americans embrace ever-expanding definitions of "speech, press, and religion" under the First Amendment. Though Luther himself was quick to recognize the potential for such things almost five hundred years ago and sought to blunt them with his doctrine of the "inner and the outer-man," it is a distinction of little value to the average American who believes that ideas are only valuable to the degree to which they are useful and you act on them. Indeed, for many of us, the failure to act on one's beliefs becomes a sign that we are insincere or hypocritical. Such charges in a world where insincerity or hypocrisy might cost someone his or her salvation cannot be endured and so the path to action must remain as open as possible.

Leaving aside the theological questions all of this raises, the political problems raised by such a view are without a doubt manifest and numerous. Tocqueville knew this, which is why he argued that

> general ideas respecting God and human nature are therefore the ideas above all others which ought to be withdrawn from the habitual action of private judgment and in which there is most to gain and least to lose by recognizing authority.[39]

---

37. Tocqueville, *Democracy in America*, 452–53.

38. Pelagianism holds that man has free will and that divine grace simply helps a Christian to achieve salvation, but that it is not necessary in order to be saved. Human beings possess the power to in effect save themselves with or without God's help. Although Gnosticism is a complicated subject, I am using the term here simply to refer to the idea that knowledge is the key to salvation as opposed to God's grace. Once again, the point being that human beings can in effect control their own salvation.

39. Tocqueville, *Democracy in America*, 443–44.

He goes on, warning especially of the danger such constant speculation creates in a free country, arguing,

> When there is no authority in religion or in politics, men are soon frightened by the limitless independence with which they are faced. They are worried and worn out by the constant restlessness of everything. With everything on the move in the realm of the mind, they want the material order at least to be firm and stable, and as they cannot accept their ancient beliefs again, they hand themselves over to a master.[40]

Tocqueville's point here should not be seen as a plea for uniformity or religious intolerance. Instead, it is an assertion that if religion is an integral part of determining a person's behavior in relationship to others and society, which he holds it is,[41] and the society and individuals in question are considered both equal and free, then it is imperative that they hold similar and at least semi-compatible views regarding it. It is akin to suggesting that society has a better chance of functioning well if people speak a common language of some sort. Harkening back to the quote above, it would be his argument that without this agreement on theological basics, that we will seek order elsewhere, namely the state—be it a monarchy or a democracy—because as human beings we are only capable of living with so much chaos, ambiguity, and diversity. Bereft of an agreement on an ecclesiastical authority or method for solving wider theological disputes, the United States has historically vindicated Tocqueville's position and turned to the state to provide such resolutions when public opinion or the elected or appointed representatives of the state believe the unspoken boundaries of theological legitimacy are being violated. Examples of this are abundant if infrequent, ranging from the pre-Tocquevillean expulsions of Anne Hutchinson or Roger Williams from Massachusetts Bay Colony, to the persecution of the Mormons and the death of Joseph Smith, to mandatory school attendance, the banning of school prayer, the restriction of "drug churches," to the events at Waco. Without taking a position on any of these particular issues or events, the common point of departure is clear; namely, the intimate involvement

---

40. Tocqueville, *Democracy in America*, 444. It is important to keep in mind here that Tocqueville does not simply mean by "master" some sort of dictator or authoritarian, but rather any one or group, including democratic majorities, who would wield absolute power over individual thought. He was as afraid of the tyranny of the majority as of the one. In his own words, "For myself, if I feel the hand of power heavy on my brow, I am little concerned to know who it is that oppresses me; I am no better inclined to pass my head under the yoke because a million men hold it for me." Tocqueville, *Democracy in America*, 436.

41. Tocqueville, *Democracy in America*, 442–43.

of the state—even in a liberal nation—in what are, at their core, religious questions. Without even taking an explicit side, the choice that Tocqueville leaves us with remains ominous and important when he claims, "For my part, I doubt whether man can support complete religious independence and entire political liberty at the same time. I am led to think that if he has no faith he must obey, and if he is free he must believe."[42]

For Americans imbued with a Jeffersonian outlook, Tocqueville's choice represents at least a paradox if not an oxymoronic assertion. How could anyone hold that the *necessity* of belief and liberty was compatible with the other and hope to be taken seriously? And yet, this is exactly the intellectual route one must travel in order to understand not just the compatibility between liberal democracy and a belief in original sin, but, indeed, the logical necessity of such a belief as well as other aspects of Christian orthodoxy if liberal democracy is to survive close philosophical scrutiny. Of course, such a claim is quite controversial—especially if what was said above concerning American theology and political culture is valid—and likewise, it is also far from self-evident. Fortunately, we have an exemplar who took it upon himself to work through these issues and problems in a most public and straightforward manner. Orestes Brownson is important for this sort of discussion for a number of reasons. First, he was highly visible, well known, and prolific. Second, he was at each very distinctive stage of his public life what we would call a true believer. In other words, Brownson was no mere intellectual skeptic or speculator playing devil's advocate—he more or less "channeled" each newly arrived-at position with a thunderous verve that renounced his old views out loud and proclaimed his new views without apology or hesitancy.

There are a number of solid biographies of Brownson available and a few book-length treatments of his political thought, as well as a very thorough introduction to his mature political theory by Peter Lawler, not to mention the three semi-autobiographies that Brownson himself wrote, for those who are unacquainted with his life and the scope of his work.[43] Fur-

---

42. Tocqueville, *Democracy in America*, 444.

43. See Lapati, *Orestes A. Brownson*; Maynard, *Orestes Brownson*; Ryan, *Orestes Brownson*; Schlesinger, *Orestes A. Brownson*; Sveino, *Orestes A. Brownson's Road to Catholicism*. For the book-length treatments of Brownson's political thought, see Butler, *In Search of the American Spirit*, and Herrera, *Orestes Brownson*. Peter Lawler offers a very tight and focused introduction to Brownson's mature political theory in his introduction to Brownson's master work, *American Republic*. For Brownson's own autobiographical work, see *Convert*; *Charles Elwood*; and *Spirit-Rapper*, all of which can be found in his work as collected and arranged by his son Harry F. Brownson, *Works of Orestes Brownson*. Those works are located in 5:1–331; 4:173–316; and 9:1–235, respectively.

thermore, his collected writings are available thanks to his son Harry who collected them thematically in about twenty volumes. Hence, what follows is not, nor could it be, comprehensive in any way. Instead, what I want to show here is how Brownson's work at the intersection of theology and political theory originally exemplifies and subsequently transcends and radically departs from the "Jeffersonian" thrust in that same area while mirroring and providing theoretical solutions to the issues and problems suggested in Tocqueville's analysis. To do this, I focus my attention on just two works. The first is from his early period and is titled *New Views of Christianity, Society, and the Church* (1836), and the second is from his later period and is titled *The American Republic: Its Constitution, Tendencies and Destiny* (1865).

In *New Views of Christianity*, Brownson lays out what is in essence a theology of liberation for nineteenth-century America. After introductory work, where he claims that Christianity has hitherto been characterized by two extreme and therefore incomplete positions. The first he labels "spiritualism," which he associates with the Catholic Church. The second he calls "materialism," which he associates with Protestantism. The task of his new church, he claims, is the goal of balance and synthesis. According to Brownson,

> Spiritualism regards purity or holiness as predicable of spirit alone, and matter as essentially impure, possessing and capable of receiving nothing of the holy, —the prison house of the soul, its only hindrance to a union with God, or absorption into his essence, the cause of all uncleanliness, sin, and evil, consequently to be condemned, degraded, and as far as possible annihilated. Materialism takes the other extreme, does not recognize the claims of the spirit, disregards the soul, counts the body everything, earth all, heaven nothing, and condenses itself into the advice, "Eat and drink, for-to-morrow we die."[44]

The role of the new church will be to demonstrate how each extreme position itself is insufficient both logically and theologically, and then to provide both the theoretical and the practical basis for the reconstitution of society itself. His most fundamental criticism of the Catholic Church is directed against its doctrine of original sin, which he claims undermines the ability of human beings to accomplish anything worthwhile. As Brownson writes: "From man's original and inherent depravity it results that he has no power to work out his own salvation. Hence the doctrine of human inability."[45] From this starting point, he eventually derives a view of the Church and the

---

44. Brownson, *New Views of Christianity*, 8.
45. Brownson, *New Views of Christianity*, 11–12.

Pope as requiring absolute authority and power in both the civil and the spiritual realm. Furthermore, he argues that the social by-product of this order is a rejection of any emphasis on the well-being of men and women on earth.[46]

For Brownson, Protestantism represents the antithesis to this position. Where Catholicism degraded the material world, Protestantism represents "a revolution in favor of the material order."[47] This "revolution," in turn, brought with it a whole series of things hitherto ignored or suppressed by the Church like civil liberty, human reason, philosophy, industry, and temporal interests.[48] Included in its correctives to the Catholic position was the Protestant assertion of the individual right to read and interpret Scripture. But, here Brownson claims that Protestantism itself did not go far enough because it should have pressed for "the right of private judgment . . . on all propositions to be believed."[49] However, the state intervened and asserted limits on such a right. This, however, for Brownson, still represented an improvement since the state still represented the "material" order and because the tendency since then "has been steadily toward unlimited freedom of thought and conscience."[50]

The weakness of the Protestant view itself, however, is that, "properly speaking, Protestantism has no religious character. As Protestants, people are not religious."[51] When this is taken with Brownson's claim earlier in the book that "religion is natural to man and he ceases to be man the moment he ceases to be religious,"[52] the weakness of a purely Protestant approach begins to emerge. According to Brownson, in the eighteenth century, as a result of the materialist pressures of Protestantism,

> social progress and the perfection of government became the religious creed of the day; the weal of man on earth, the spring and aim of all hopes and labors. A new paradise was imagined forth for man, inaccessible to the serpent, more delightful than that which Adam lost, and more attractive than that which the pious Christian hopes to gain.[53]

---

46. Brownson, *New Views of Christianity*, 45.
47. Brownson, *New Views of Christianity*, 17.
48. Brownson, *New Views of Christianity*, 17.
49. Brownson, *New Views of Christianity*, 20.
50. Brownson, *New Views of Christianity*, 20.
51. Brownson, *New Views of Christianity*, 22.
52. Brownson, *New Views of Christianity*, 3.
53. Brownson, *New Views of Christianity*, 25.

This "paradise" was lost, however, with the military despotism of Napoleon. His assent marked a turning point at which time the pendulum swung back toward spiritualism and

> from that moment enthusiasm died, hope in social melioration ceased to be indulged, and those who had been the most sanguine in their anticipations, hung down their heads and said nothing; the warmest friends of humanity apologized for their dreams of liberty and equality; democracy became an accusation, and faith in the perfectibility of mankind a proof of disordered intellect.[54]

The mission Brownson subsequently undertakes, is to build a new church that is "free from the imperfections of those which have been."[55] While the rise of Napoleon was certainly problematic for the materialist vision, Brownson suggests that it was only a manifestation of a larger problem at the root of the material conception. That problem he sums up as follows: "As soon as men find themselves well off in a worldly point of view, they discover that they have wants the world does not and cannot satisfy."[56] Hence, he argues that the mission must be to "reconcile spirit and matter."[57] On Brownson's new reading of Christianity, this was exactly the reason for Christ's coming in the first place—"the union of spirit and matter."[58] The key now is to complete the work of the Gospel which calls for "the workman to come forth with joy, and bid the Temple rise."[59] To do this the new church will depart drastically from the old by "molding its dogmas to human nature" rather than attempting to "mold human nature to its dogmas."[60]

Hence for Brownson, the notion of a human nature that is wounded or degraded by sin is simply wrong and can form no part of this new construction. In its place, the new church will be guided by the following sort of ideology:

> Human nature is well made, its laws are just and holy, its elements are true and divine. And this is the hidden symbol of the God-Man. That symbol teaches all who comprehend it, to find divinity in humanity, and humanity in divinity. By presenting

54. Brownson, *New Views of Christianity*, 26.
55. Brownson, *New Views of Christianity*, 28.
56. Brownson, *New Views of Christianity*, 30.
57. Brownson, *New Views of Christianity*, 32.
58. Brownson, *New Views of Christianity*, 32.
59. Brownson, *New Views of Christianity*, 33.
60. Brownson, *New Views of Christianity*, 33.

us god and man united in one person, it shows us that both are holy.⁶¹

In turn, for Brownson, human nature becomes the measure of truth and all religious belief will be judged against the degree to which it conforms to it. The "institutional" foundation that strikes him as most closely paralleling his vision comes in the form of the Unitarian Church which he claims "are everyday breaking away more and more from tradition, and everyday making new progress in the creation of a philosophy which explains humanity, determines its wants and the means of supplying them."⁶²

America is the perfect location for the advent of this new church for a number of reasons. First, we are a nation of joiners,⁶³ second, "in this country more than any other is the man of thought united in the same person with the man of action,"⁶⁴ and third, "here every idea may be at once put to a practical test."⁶⁵ In other words, according to Brownson, "we have the liberty, the disposition, and the faith to work with ideas."⁶⁶ In this new world, the "church and state will become one. The state will be holy, and the church will be holy."⁶⁷ The ultimate aim of both associations will be the same and is summed up by Brownson:

> The church will be on the side of progress, and spiritualism and materialism will combine to make man's earthly condition as near like the lost Eden of the eastern poets, as is compatible with the growth and perfection of his nature.⁶⁸

While Brownson's political aims are not Jeffersonian, the conception of human nature and its possibilities certainly are. Since nowhere in Brownson's treatise does he talk about the potential for resistance or the need to organize beyond having a better idea and a formidable philosophy it seems safe to assume that he was placing his faith in the power of reason and democracy. While this precludes a critique of him as a violent revolutionary, it certainly calls forth questions concerning his proposed means and/or *praxis*. The Enlightenment zeal of the proposal speaks for itself and it would be difficult to imagine a description that itself could do justice to the

---

61. Brownson, *New Views of Christianity*, 34.
62. Brownson, *New Views of Christianity*, 39.
63. Brownson, *New Views of Christianity*, 43.
64. Brownson, *New Views of Christianity*, 45.
65. Brownson, *New Views of Christianity*, 45.
66. Brownson, *New Views of Christianity*, 45.
67. Brownson, *New Views of Christianity*, 50.
68. Brownson, *New Views of Christianity*, 49.

ORESTES BROWNSON AND THE HARTZ THESIS   163

hyperbolic rhetoric of Brownson himself. I have purposefully avoided any attempt at analysis because I believe that the piece as parsed speaks clearly for itself and serves the purpose of representing the sorts of tendencies that Tocqueville warned of and that the rejection of "original sin" countenances. Furthermore, the history of the last two hundred years aptly demonstrates the risks of such thought in more powerful, systematic, and less docile hands. Though I do not believe that Brownson's values change dramatically throughout his life, his premises did and as such he moves to a very different place in terms of both his theory and his *praxis*.

A CATHOLIC AMERICA?

Almost twenty years after the publication of his *New Views*, we find Orestes Brownson explaining in the preface to his work *The American Republic: Its Constitution, Tendencies and Destiny*:

> I have not felt myself bound to adhere to my own past thoughts or expressions any further than they coincide with my present convictions, and I have written as freely and as independently as if I had never written or published anything before. I have never been a slave of my own past, and truth has always been dearer to me than my own opinions. This work is not only my latest, but will be my last on politics or government, and must be taken as the authentic statement of my political views and convictions, and whatever in any of my previous writings conflicts with the principles defended in its pages, must be regarded as retracted and rejected.[69]

While such a disclosure is hardly necessary for anyone who takes the time to read his early work, it does save the casual reader the angst he or she might have felt in trying to square the political thrust of his early work with the arguments of his later efforts. Among the factors that drove Brownson's theoretical transformation was, of course, his conversion to Catholicism in 1844. While much of his political work remained ideologically liberal or progressive, his new religious and theological orientation gradually asserted itself on the pages of his political works. *The American Republic* represents the culmination of that movement and stands as one of the most intriguing and, yet, still organically American counter-hegemonic theorizations of American political development and theory I have yet to come across. Space does not permit me to explore all of the important lines of argument

---

69. Brownson, *American Republic*, 1–2.

Brownson lays out, and so I will focus selectively on his theory of American political origins as it relates to both his notion of American constitutionalism, democracy, and the relationship between those newly theorized constructs and his former stance regarding the conception of American political-theology as laid out above. In doing so, I hope to provide answers to the remaining two questions from the start of the section above, namely whether a significantly less Jeffersonian conception of human nature is still compatible with a liberal-democratic political order, and, furthermore, what a theorization of such an order might look like.[70]

Jefferson's oft-cited youthful preference for revolutions every twenty years, coupled with his theoretical prohibition against letting the constitutional arrangements of the dead bind the political hands of the living, stands as rhetorical markers for a decidedly modern and clearly anti-conservative political ideology that implies at least a preference for widespread democracy and an early version of social constructivism. In turn, the theoretical companion to such a vision regarding the origins and legitimacy of the state and its powers is the notion of the *social contract* found in various forms and toward divergent ends in the work of people like Hobbes, Locke, Rousseau, and, in the modern era, Rawls.[71] At its most general, the notion of the state as a contractual entity suggests its conventional character as compared to Aristotle's argument that it exists by nature and is prior to the individual.[72] Furthermore, such a view implies that the form of a given state is only limited by the imagination, creative power, and the ability of the given contractors to achieve consensus or agreement among those affected parties entering into the political bargain.[73] Clearly Brownson's depiction of the coming church and state in his earlier work rests upon this general intellectual and ideological foundation as well. As such, when taken along with his depiction of an untainted and therefore perfectible human nature, the path to a political-theological utilitarian utopia is more or less cleared and made possible, awaiting only the new "word" to be spread and the changes to be implemented by the newly enlightened and empowered. In his rejection of those former views, Brownson is forced to confront both his earlier assumptions about the perfectibility of man through knowledge and enlightenment and the assertion of the contractual nature of state. While he still ends with a brand of liberal democracy, the path for getting there is very

70. For an early treatment of this work, see Cook and Leavelle, "Orestes A. Brownson's *The American Republic*," 173–93.

71. See Hobbes, *Leviathan*; Locke, *Second Treatise of Government*; Rousseau, *Social Contract*; Rawls, *Theory of Justice*.

72. Aristotle, *Politics*, bk. 1.

73. See Kendall, *John Locke and the Doctrine of Majority-Rule*.

different and, in turn, the available "degrees of freedom" within that society are significantly altered.

In place of the *ex nihilo* state of the social contract theorists—one that springs forth from the contractual act of creation itself—Orestes Brownson gives us the "providential nation." In his words: "Every living nation has an idea given it by Providence to realize, and whose realization is its special work, mission, or destiny. Every nation is, in some sense, a chosen people of God."[74] Hence, for the later Brownson, we can say that with regard to nations, *essence* now is claimed to precede *existence*. Such a shift is highly significant insofar as we can now talk about what nations ought to be as compared to simply what they are or what we would like them to be. In one quick move he has asserted the existence and importance of a transcendent standard against which the political development of a given nation can be measured and judged. Yet, he has done so without falling into the Platonic trap of uniformity, the Aristotelian snare of nature, or the Marxist web of history insofar as different nations might have different missions. God remains free and his creations keep their free will sans the Nietzschean assertion of the power to move beyond good and evil. America's "idea" is liberty rightly understood, according to Brownson:

> Yet its mission is not so much the realization of liberty as the realization of the true idea of the state, which secures at once the authority of the public and the freedom of the individual—the sovereignty of the people without social despotism, and individual freedom without anarchy. In other words, its mission is to bring out in its life the dialectic union of authority and liberty, of the natural rights of man and those of society.... The American republic has been instituted by Providence to realize the freedom of each with advantage to the other.[75]

To accomplish America's providential mission—a new and unique mission when compared to the missions of all other nations that have gone before us—a new constitution was needed. Yet the written constitution produced by the framers could only aid our political development to the degree that it properly represented the living or organic constitution of the people themselves which, for Brownson, predated the written constitution and therefore represents the "essence" that the written constitution must give material form to in order to be considered properly constituted. As he puts it much later in his work concerning the US Constitution,

---

74. Brownson, *American Republic*, 7–8.
75. Brownson, *American Republic*, 8.

> The system is no invention of man, is no creation of the convention, but is given us by Providence in the living constitution of the American people. The merit of the statesmen of 1787 is that they did not destroy or deface the work of Providence, but accepted it, and organized the government in harmony with the real order, the real elements given them. They suffered themselves in all their positive substantial work to be governed by reality, not by theories or speculations.[76]

In other words, for Brownson, we would talk about the "spiritual" existence of an American nation before what we might call the "material" existence of the United States of America. In the same way that we might say that the boy contains the man to be, so too does the "nation" contain the state or the government. Analogically speaking, the written constitution is like a set of clothes that we have bought for the boy to wear as a man. If we have done our job well, the clothes will fit him when he was grown and we can say that the choice was appropriate. If we misjudge the man he will grow to be, or if we buy clothes simply for the man we wish him to be, the clothes will not fit and, hence, the choice will be inappropriate and the clothes ill-fitting. Likewise, if the written constitution does not "fit" the people as they will be, the government will fail. For Brownson, the genius of the American state's written constitution is that it "fits" the pre-existing body politic of the American nation well. According to Brownson, "The written constitution is simply a law ordained by the nation or people instituting and organizing the government; the unwritten constitution is the real or actual constitution of the people.... It is providential, not made by the nation, but born with it."[77]

However, there was a degree of luck involved insofar as the US Constitution "fit" the constitution of the American nation because, for Brownson, the theoretical justifications of framers like Madison were deeply flawed. Brownson argues that

> the statesmen of the eighteenth century believed that the state is derived from the people individually, and held that sovereignty is created by the people in convention. The rights and powers of the state, they held, were made up of the rights held by individuals under the law of nature, and which the individual had surrendered to civil society on its formation.[78]

---

76. Brownson, *American Republic*, 139–40.
77. Brownson, *American Republic*, 113.
78. Brownson, *American Republic*, 124.

This standard contractarian view implicitly denies the notion of the "providential nation." Logically speaking, it has no limits beyond those of nature itself and could just as conceivably and rightfully (if convention is the only guide) end in the elected despotism of Napoleon or the democratic anarchy of Plato's democracy in Book VIII of the *Republic*. Fortunately, however, "the general doctrine which he [Madison] had adopted, in common with nearly all his contemporaries, of the origin of the state in compact . . . may be eliminated from his view of what the constitution actually is, without effecting that view itself."[79] After all, according to Brownson, "what binds is the thing done, not the theory on which it was done, or on which the actors explained their work either to themselves or to others."[80]

Were we to take Madison and company's explanation seriously, we might be inclined to take Jefferson's revolutionary extrapolation to heart as well and thereby fail to accomplish the mission Brownson contends that Providence has for us. Certainly Brownson's own earlier work was steeped in exactly the sort of social and political elasticity that logically inheres in the doctrine of compact and convention. So it is that Brownson undertakes a correction of the framer's theoretical justification but not the constitutional product itself. Where Lincoln sought to contain those men of genius who "disdain the beaten path" through the creation of a political religion, Brownson attempts to contain their ambition through the generation of a religious politics. In place of the social contract, he offers us a theory of political origin based on *communion*.

The depth of Brownson's repudiation of his earlier theoretical position is evident in the following assertion:

> But as, under the law of nature, all men are equal, or have equal rights as men, one man can have in himself no right to govern another; and as man is never absolutely his own, but always and everywhere belongs to his Creator, *it is clear that no government originating in humanity alone can be a legitimate government. Every such government is founded on the assumption that man is God, which is a great mistake*—is, in fact the fundamental sophism which underlies every error and every sin.[81]

The contention that man is "never absolutely his own" allows Brownson to make his crucial theoretical move; namely, to argue, counter-distinct to strong versions of the liberal self-ownership argument, that "man is a

---

79. Brownson, *American Republic*, 119.
80. Brownson, *American Republic*, 125–26.
81. Brownson, *American Republic*, 62. Emphasis mine.

dependent being, and neither does, nor can suffice for himself."[82] Fleshing out this argument later, Brownson continues on, writing: "Man is not God, independent, self-existing, and self-sufficing. He is dependent, and dependent not only on his maker, but on his fellow-men, on society, and even on nature, or the material world."[83] He is dependent on these things because they represent for Brownson the mechanisms through which men exist, develop, and fulfill their existence.[84] The end of that process for each of us is "communion with God" and participation in "the divine being and life."[85] The not-so-subtle implication here is the rejection of whatever Pelagianism there was in his earlier position in *New Views*. Salvation here is now outside of the individual's grasp as an individual. He or she needs God's grace, and the mediation of the social and natural world to accomplish his or her final end. For Brownson, this threefold communion is described in following way:

> He communes with God through the divine creative act and the incarnation of the Word, through his kind, and through the material world. Communion with God through creation and incarnation is religion, distinctively taken, which binds man to God as his first cause; communion through the material world is expressed by the word property; and communion with God through humanity is society. Religion, society, property, are the three terms that embrace the whole of man's life, and express the essential means and conditions of his existence, his development, and his perfection, or the fulfillment of his existence, the attainment of the end for which he was created.[86]

He goes on later to argue that this threefold communion generates three institutions; namely, "the church, society or the state, and property"[87] that are separate from each other and yet interdependent. They are interdependent because they are all necessary to achieve the end of communion with God, but they are all separate insofar as each is limited with respect to the other and complete unto itself. Like a lock that needs three distinct keys to open it, each method of communion is necessary but not sufficient. Because we lack the ability to "open" the lock on our own, our dependency creates duties and obligations to those very things we need. In Brownson's

---

82. Brownson, *American Republic*, 13.
83. Brownson, *American Republic*, 34.
84. Brownson, *American Republic*, 13.
85. Brownson, *American Republic*, 13.
86. Brownson, *American Republic*, 13.
87. Brownson, *American Republic*, 46.

words, "The right of that on which man depends, and by communion with which he lives, limits his own right over himself."[88]

Echoing Aristotle, Brownson contends of man that "he is born and lives in society, and can be born and live nowhere else. It is one of the necessities of his nature."[89] Because we are dependent we are obligated. Echoing the Socrates of the *Crito*, via the teachings of the Catholic Church fathers, Brownson goes on to claim,

> The compact itself they held was not voluntarily formed by the people themselves, either individually or collectively, but was imposed by God, either immediately, or mediately, through the law of nature ... [they] maintained that everyone born into society contracts by that fact certain obligations to society, and society certain obligations to him; for under the natural law, everyone has rights, as life, liberty, and the pursuit of happiness, and owes certain duties to society for the protection and assistance it affords him.[90]

However, these obligations and, hence, limits, are not categorically embraced by human beings. As Brownson puts it, "Nothing is more painful to the proud spirit than to receive a favor that lays him under an obligation to another."[91] Unfortunately, following the theological position to its logical conclusion, any rejection of these obligations impairs or undermines the possibility of full communion and as such precludes both the individual reaching his or her final end and, by implication, if the rejection is widespread, the society itself will not be able to realize its own providential mission. This very attempt to reject those limits and accept the responsibilities entailed in the process of communion, I would argue, is in essence sinful. And the outcome of such a willful turning away from God is to leave man painfully alone and adrift with neither purpose, nor meaning, nor hope. We are empowered at the expense of becoming what we were meant to be, and in the process, we learn what true alienation is as we are reduced to mere contractors in a deal without a purpose—free to do what we want, but without any good reason to do it.

Clearly in recognizing human weakness and dependency, the position Brownson argues for later in his life points toward a significantly more limited scope for human action in both the material and the moral spheres. Yet, ironically perhaps, it is precisely the recognition of those limits and

88. Brownson, *American Republic*, 34.
89. Brownson, *American Republic*, 14.
90. Brownson, *American Republic*, 27–28.
91. Brownson, *American Republic*, 34.

adherence to their dictates that will allow the fullest flourishing of the American political community to take place. In the same way that C. S. Lewis gets to democracy through the recognition of human weakness and the commonality of sin, Brownson allows us to get to a liberal democracy that avoids crushing political centralization, majoritarian tyranny, and atomistic individualism. Liberty and authority, individual and community, power and right are balanced and made complimentary in his theorization in a way that they cannot logically be once man is the measure of everything. As Brownson himself puts it,

> The people, holding their authority from God, hold it not as an inherent right, but as a trust from him, and are accountable to him for it. It is not their own. If it were their own they might do with it as they pleased, and no one would have any right to call them to account; but holding it as a trust from God, they are under his law, and bound to exercise it as that law prescribes. Civil rulers, holding their authority from God through the people, are accountable for it both to him and them. If they abuse it they are justiciable by the people and punishable by God himself.[92]

Since Brownson believed that the actual political system devised by the framers was appropriate and sound, his work must be seen as a corrective to mistaken theoretical justifications and understandings of the origin and continuing rationale for that system. Such a project is very important because of the many theoretical and practical dangers that might develop based on an inappropriate understanding of the foundational logic. For example, as Brownson demonstrates quite thoroughly in the book, the whole argument on behalf of succession can be traced to the contractual orientation of many of the theorists. Under Brownson's theorization, much of the convoluted constitutionalism and political theory that took place during the Civil War era to justify the actions of both sides can be done away with—intellectually speaking—if Brownson's model were to be applied. Furthermore, it also has the potential—once again intellectually speaking—to address a wide array of other turbulent issues and radical assertions that have emerged in post–Civil War America in a profoundly disarming manner, if properly utilized. At each juncture, however, such an application would require a degree of submission and humility that seem all but absent from our political culture today, not to mention a good deal of consensus regarding what, for many, is a highly problematic theological approach.

---

92. Brownson, *American Republic*, 68.

CONCLUSION

In the movie *Rudy*, the young protagonist is having a heart-to-heart with a priest about his future and his deepening frustration and sadness at his life, expecting him to offer some great pearl of spiritual wisdom that might set everything right. Instead, the priest offers the following to young Rudy: "Son, I have been a priest for thirty years, and there are only two things after all that time that I know for certain: there is a God and I am not Him." As simple a formulation as that is, it contains the seeds of a worldview that makes it possible to defend a version of liberal democracy in a way that rejecting either element puts at great risk. While Dostoevsky's well-known maxim can still be invoked—without God all is permitted—and can cause us great concern as the specter of a nation of Nietzschean overmen who are beyond good and evil quickly forms in our imagination, the truth is in all likelihood much less dramatic and yet still quite disturbing. In the attempt to preserve ourselves, we become Hobbesian or Lockean contractors seeking safety and security to pursue our individual happiness. While certainly not the worst outcome imaginable by a long shot, it does leave the big question looming for us, namely: Is that all there is?

To build cathedrals—both real and metaphoric—rather than merely pushing bricks up a hill means coming to know the secular world as only part of the equation. To understand the self as existing not only with but also for others becomes the path to self-realization and a purposeful life in a way that isolation from others and a life of endless self-indulgence will ultimately deny to a human being. On the political side of the equation, this means coming to see the regime as something more than a contractual entity for the collective security for individuals and instead as a communal enterprise for the purpose of human flourishing and the realization of individual vocations and not mere survival. In other words, we must come to see both the nation and ourselves as providentially constituted and, subsequently, to begin thinking in terms of our collective and individual destinies within that context. We must see ourselves and political order as part of a larger story or tradition rather than as a series of episodic moments of exchange and barter. Among the services provided by a thinker like Orestes Brownson was exactly such an endeavor: an attempt to provide a Catholic story or tradition for a particular people that was made possible in large measure by his own Catholic sensibilities and approach to the world. It is to that tradition and its contours and political import that we now turn.

5

The Catholic Social Tradition and AMERICA

When the Son of Man comes in his glory, and all the angels with him, he will sit on his throne in heavenly glory. All the nations will be gathered before him, and he will separate the people one from another as a shepherd separates the sheep from the goats. He will put the sheep on his right and the goats on his left. Then the King will say to those on his right, "Come, you who are blessed by my Father; take your inheritance, the kingdom prepared for you since the creation of the world. For I was hungry and you gave me something to eat, I was thirsty and you gave me something to drink, I was a stranger and you invited me in, I needed clothes and you clothed me, I was sick and you looked after me, I was in prison and you came to visit me." Then the righteous will answer him, "Lord, when did we see you hungry and feed you, or thirsty and give you something to drink? When did we see you a stranger and invite you in, or needing clothes and clothe you? When did we see you sick or in prison and go to visit you?" The King will reply, "I tell you the truth, whatever you did for one of the least of these brothers of mine, you did for me." Then he will say to those on his left, "Depart from me, you who are cursed, into the eternal fire prepared for the devil and his angels. For I was hungry and you gave me nothing to eat, I was thirsty and you gave me nothing to drink, I was a stranger and you did not invite me in, I needed clothes and you did not clothe me, I was sick and in prison and you did not look after me." They also will answer, "Lord, when did we see you hungry or thirsty or a stranger or needing clothes or sick or in prison, and did not help you?" He will reply, "I tell you the truth, whatever you did not do for one of the least of these, you did not do for me." Then they will go away to eternal punishment, but the righteous to eternal life.

—Matthew 25:31–46

The desire for God is written in the human heart, because man is created by God and for God; and God never ceases to draw man to himself. Only in God will he find the truth and happiness he never stops searching for.

—Catechism of the Catholic Church

"A CATHOLIC MODERNITY?"

Given the relative indifference to Brownson's work overall and the almost complete triumph of liberalism in the post–Civil War period, it would no doubt strike most readers as strange to re-read Tocqueville's prognostication concerning the eventual progress of Catholicism in the United States in *Democracy in America*, where he claims,

> Our contemporaries are naturally little disposed to belief, but once they accept religion at all, there is a hidden instinct within them which unconsciously urges them toward Catholicism. Many of the doctrines and customs of the Roman Church astonish them, but they feel secret admiration for its discipline, and its extraordinary unity attracts them.[1]

And his concluding sentiments of that chapter where he asserts that "our grandchildren will tend more and more to be divided clearly between those who have completely abandoned Christianity and those who have returned to the Church of Rome," sound perhaps even more far-fetched on the basis of experience.[2] Not only is the American liberal tradition as represented by Jefferson, Madison, and Lincoln antagonistic to Catholicism on a number

---

1. Tocqueville, *Democracy in America*, 450.
2. Tocqueville, *Democracy in America*, 451.

of scores, but mid-nineteenth-century Catholicism was itself explicitly opposed to this kind of American liberalism. Furthermore, as Catholic thought did seriously begin to confront the modern industrial world from a position of immanence rather than strict opposition, its emergent positions and viewpoint seemed to be at great variance from the dominant *ethos* of the American ruling class. How, then, can the historical, theoretical, and political incommensurability of the two traditions be bridged such that the larger argument of this book can be made tenable?

Before answering that question, it is important to try to sketch the contours of the Catholic social tradition as it emerged and developed in the last years of the nineteenth century and the first third of the twentieth century and its relationship to American liberalism. This will help make a preliminary case for the possibility and desirability of building such a bridge between the two traditions at all. Before embarking on that work, however, I need to open up some theoretical space by making an argument that hopefully will compliment and, to a degree, enhance some of the claims made in chapters three and four regarding the relative roles of Christians and Christianity in the liberal story. Briefly, the argument I want to make is for the positive import of liberalism and the modern liberal state in pushing the Catholic Church to more fully realize its own vocational call. Despite the antagonism that has developed between liberalism in its contemporary form and strong religious claims and commitments in the public square, there is an important way that the forces which created that tension actually pushed the Catholic Church to a fuller realization of its own mission in important, even though unintentional, ways.

This argument relies heavily on Charles Taylor's essay "A Catholic Modernity?," where he sums up his general argument as follows:

> The view I'd like to defend, if I can put it in a nutshell, is that in modern, secularist culture there are mingled together both authentic developments of the gospel, of an incarnational mode of life, and also a closing off to God that negates the gospel. The notion is that modern culture, in breaking with the structures and beliefs of Christendom, also carried certain facets of Christian life further than ever were taken or could have been taken within Christendom. In relation to earlier forms of Christian culture, we have to face the humbling realization that the breakout was a necessary condition of the development.[3]

Taylor's provocative and important claim is that any society that attempts to constitute itself as an explicitly "Christian nation" is by that very project

---

3. Taylor, "Catholic Modernity?," 16.

undermining the gospel itself and, hence, being unfaithful to the Christian message.[4] Although there is a wide and varied literature on this basic theme, the name often given to such a project in contemporary parlance is "Constantinianism." Among the more provocative and powerful explicators of this argument are the theologians John Howard Yoder and Stanley Hauerwas.[5] While, I do not share the conclusions that this school of thought comes to regarding the relative role of the larger Christian church in political life and do not believe that Taylor does either, the forcefulness of the critique for people of faith cannot be ignored. The most straightforward way to make this basic case is to look simply at the issue of coercion and violence. Political regimes and states—regardless of their particular forms or ideological orientations—are tied inextricably by their very logic to the use of coercion, power, and, at least occasionally, violence, to carry out their functions and fulfill their roles. While differentiating between so-called legitimate uses of coercion and illegitimate uses is both meaningful and important in the realm of political ethics, it is entirely possible that such a distinction carries no weight in the realm of Christian ethics.

If Taylor is correct when he claims that "the gospel was always meant to stand out, unencumbered by arms,"[6] then any attempt to firmly ensconce or encase the teachings of the gospel into a given political order is fraught with both moral and theological danger. This is not to say that a thoroughgoing pacifism is the only acceptable position for a Christian *qua* Christian—though such thinking must be given serious consideration—but instead it is meant to suggest that it is inappropriate to reduce the fullness of the gospel message to any particular state or political regime. Using what might best be thought of as a modified "two kingdoms" argument,[7] we can

---

4. See Duncan, "Christian Right's Postmodern Turn," 5–31.

5. This is a constant theme in Hauerwasian political theology and theological ethics. Numerous essays are undergirded by this theme in Hauerwas, *Hauerwas Reader*. His earlier book, *Community of Character*, is perhaps the best introduction to this line of argument. See also Yoder, *Politics of Jesus*, for a very provocative argument about the role of Christians in political society especially as their participation relates to participation in or complicity with the state's apparatus of violence.

6. Taylor, "Catholic Modernity?," 18.

7. Without going into this at great length, the basic modification is to take the primary contention of Augustine in *City of God* concerning the stark distinction and juxtaposition between the heavenly city and the earthly city as an important point of departure and add to it a strong dose of Aquinas's positive teachings on the political world and the social nature of human beings derived in part from Aristotle. This leaves the *political* still properly subservient to the *eternal* as an important but "disordered" or "incomplete" good such that Augustine's harsher assertions comparing all kingdoms to merely aggrandized criminal gangs is no longer in order. In such a world, human beings become much less "depraved" and fallen (and therefore in need of authoritarian states

see the political order as a good—perhaps even a necessary good in a fallen world—but still a "disordered" or "incomplete" good since it is made necessary, in its coercive role at least, by human sin rather than God's will or design. As such, it may be part of the natural order but it has no necessary standing in the supernatural order, i.e., it is contingent and not necessary, and, therefore, it is always subordinate and subservient to the divine order. Its ends therefore are extremely limited and, as argued in chapter 3, must always be directed at clearing out the space and making the Christian project of "self-gift" possible. As its work is of a practical or prudential nature, it may take on a number of different forms both in time and over time.

Sometimes such work entails coercion, e.g., peacekeepers stopping one ethnic group from slaughtering another in an act of ethnic cleansing or genocide by using guns and violence in the name of human rights and the protection of innocent life. However, the coercion or violence does not, and cannot, itself generate or create the agapic love it seeks to make possible. The logic here, I would hope, is obvious. "Love one another or be killed" seems to be a concept that does not need an extended argument to demonstrate its fallaciousness. This is why Glenn Tinder is exactly right when he claims: "The aim of social transformation, for Christians, is community. But we cannot create community. All we can do is remove—or attack—obstacles to community, such as poverty, illiteracy, sharp class distinctions, and secretive and unaccountable governments. That is, we can only set people free for community."[8]

When Tinder concludes with the assertion that "social reform seeks liberation," the reader should hear a twofold argument concerning the role of society and the state or political regime. First, that its basic job is to engage in actions both positive and defensive which preserve the possibility of self-gift or agapic love and make it more likely. Second, that any attempt to compel such a "gift" through the use of force or violence is itself inconsistent with the goal of liberation. Christians, we might say, can only be *called*, they cannot be compelled. And this is the point where we can return to Taylor's argument.

When Taylor contends that modern culture *carried certain facets of Christian life further than ever were taken or could have been taken within Christendom*, he is making what may appear like a developmental claim, but in reality is a theological presupposition. Taylor is not arguing against the

---

to check the propensity to sin), and instead views men and women as "deprived" and quite capable of doing good while still remaining weak and liable to sin in the process. At its simplest this opens up the possibility for liberal democracy in ways that the more austere reading of Augustine would seem to reject out of hand.

8. Tinder, *Political Meaning of Christianity*, 150.

idea of Christendom from the perspective of a liberal progressivism such a perspective would posit (with no humility or reticence) its moral and political superiority to the medieval world because in its coming individuals were liberated from archaic and dogmatic fictions. He is, instead, arguing that within Christendom as it worked, human beings could not be fully Christian. In simplified form, the liberation begotten by modern culture, on Taylor's account, was not *from* Christianity, but rather a liberation *for* Christianity. For Taylor, the entanglement of church and state rendered the church inextricably part of the natural or secular order. This diminished it and made the realization of its true calling and function problematic, if not impossible. Metaphorically, imagine if Jesus had decided to remain a carpenter or become the governor of Judaea instead of accepting his call as the Christ. While he may have done good or even great work in either capacity, he would not have done what was specifically his divine and transcendent work. For the church to be the *church* it had to get out of its own way. Unwilling, historically speaking, to do this on its own—partly as a result of the sins and imperfections of the human beings charged with its care and partly because the logic of uniformity embedded in the ideal of Christendom as a concept—modern culture and the politics thereof did the church and the faith an odd, mostly unintentional, and often wrenching service by displacing it.

With its Constantinian dreams and ambitions thoroughly checked in the West by the political orientation and power of the modern world, as well as the development of Protestantism, the church universal could once again be the church. Though remaining critical of many aspects of modern culture and acknowledging that this was often painful for the faith and the faithful, Taylor argues that the "rights culture" begotten by political modernity and liberalism "made possible what we now recognize as a great advance in the practical penetration of the gospel in human life."[9] It did this by displacing any centralized religious authority that needed to be sustained by an inappropriate resort to coercion and violence. Such a resort would have rendered said authority base, unsuitably common, and unable to inspire. It would do so because it would render the Cross just another secular standard or flag to march under. Liberated from what he calls "that continual and often bloody forcing of conscience which was the sin and blight of all those 'Christian' centuries," Taylor argues that Christians could now "live the gospel in a purer way."[10] Taylor sums it up this way:

> This freedom, which is prized by so many different people for different reasons, also has its Christian meaning. It is, for

9. Taylor, "Catholic Modernity?," 18.
10. Taylor, "Catholic Modernity?," 18.

instance, the freedom to come to one's God on one's own or, otherwise put, moved only by the Holy Spirit, whose barely audible voice will often be heard better when the loudspeakers of armed authority are silent.[11]

If the *Catechism of the Catholic Church* is correct in its assertion that the desire for God is written on the human heart, and the universal church in the modern world has been liberated to be the church universal, then Tocqueville might be right after all, though not, strictly speaking, in the way he might have thought. It is entirely possible that the nation may become more Catholic in its orientation and not necessarily more Catholic in terms of individual professions. In other words, there is no reason to expect anytime soon, if at all, that the United States will see a large increase in the number of practicing Catholics, but it may be the case that Catholic social and political thought will be able to penetrate deeper into the American psyche and political culture. Why? Because despite the continuing grip of Lockean liberalism on the American mind and its hegemonic status in our political and social discourse, it has failed to meet our deepest human needs and desires, to solve the increasing number of anomalies and problems it confronts, or to provide an integrated and compelling account of our actual existence. Simply put, just as the Catholic Church and the faith could not fulfill its larger purpose while it was trying to be all encompassing, neither can liberalism accomplish its central purpose of creating the conditions for a flourishing individualism if it comes to believe that it can stand alone. Only by understanding itself as part of a larger tradition can its noble and deserving characteristics and contributions ultimately be sustained and flourish fully. Having done its work to further the Church's mission, liberalism must now accept the favor in return.

WHOSE TRADITION IS IT ANYWAY?

As Charles Taylor's work *A Secular Age* demonstrates in vast detail, the outcome he depicted so succinctly in his essay was achieved with immense tumult and great pain and suffering over the last five centuries. Nothing was yielded freely and no quarter was given by any of the parties involved. The part of this story that played out in the United States was, like many political stories in the US, unique because there was no feudalism, national church, or even a real Catholic history to contend with. Here, instead, the story was about the Church fighting for a place in the existing order rather

---

11. Taylor, "Catholic Modernity?," 19.

than defending itself against the revolutionary forces of modernity. That story is told in any number of fine books, but I have relied on one classic text, *The Catholic Spirit in America* (1927) by George Schuster, and two contemporary histories, *Catholicism and American Freedom* (2003) by John T. McGreevy and *In Search of an American Catholicism* (2002) by Jay P. Dolan, to construct my own brief contextual account of the confrontation between Catholicism and America in the post–Civil War years of the late nineteenth and early twentieth centuries.

While it is impossible to do true justice to Schuster's deeply insightful, eloquent, and cogent book in a few short pages, it is critical for my own argument to try. While certainly an artifact of its times, many of the arguments Schuster makes remain profoundly relevant and even urgent over one hundred years later. Writing well in advance of Louis Hartz, Schuster grasps the overarching petit-bourgeois *ethos* of the non-Catholic American mind with great skill. He notes that the Church has benefited greatly from the American principle of religious liberty. It has staked out beliefs and practices which are on many levels at odds with the dominate mindset of the nation.[12] Schuster, however, also notes the existence of "civic firmness" that has produced "grim moments when it seemed America would betray itself."[13] In his chapter on the American mind, Schuster characterizes early New Englanders by suggesting that, while they claimed that their home was their castle, "it tended more and more to become a bank, a factory or a shipping warehouse."[14] He is no more gentle in the area of religion, where he claims,

> It had plenty of formidable fanatics, who wrote unctuous treatises, burned witches and made God mostly the keeper of the gates of hell. I have never been able to sympathize with any of them, least of all those who, like Cotton Mather, possessed a certain learning; but it is impossible not to admire the granite of their souls, upon which the lure of life could not scratch a phrase. They had character and to some extent they knew why. Their fatal weakness lay in the fact that they had nothing else.[15]

Going on a few pages later, Schuster continues his explication by arguing that "from the start we have been a nation of money getters—a people faithful, in a measure, to the Bible, but dedicated especially to the Book of Proverbs."[16] While noting that the religious fire of the Puritans burned out

---

12. Schuster, *Catholic Spirit in America*, 31.
13. Schuster, *Catholic Spirit in America*, 34.
14. Schuster, *Catholic Spirit in America*, 41.
15. Schuster, *Catholic Spirit in America*, 41.
16. Schuster, *Catholic Spirit in America*, 44.

rather early, the zeal with which they set out to "improve" the world carried on. Christianity in the hands of their descendants became closely linked to their economic enterprises as

> slowly and steadily the circumstances of the marriage-feast at Cana were ignored, and total abstinence became a first principle of Christian morals. Far more important, however, is the fact that the business man's code of rules was identified by many with the maxims of the Savior. Even people who had a thousand reasons to know better accepted the comparison without a qualm.... This mild and unintentional blasphemy may serve to indicate how completely the final tragic sermon of Jesus—"My kingdom is not of this world"—came to be ignored by a prosperous citizenry. And, indeed, of what earthly use is such a sermon, from a business point of view?[17]

Everything not "barnacled to this instinct," was ultimately seen as of little value. Prefiguring Hartz's dictum that in America "law had flourished on the corpse of philosophy," Schuster claims a little later that "philosophy perished so completely that one might well have wondered if it had been forbidden by statute."[18]

To the extent that America was not to succumb to a transcendence denying secularism and the aimlessness of material pursuit to the neglect of her spiritual origins and providential underpinnings, Schuster boldly argues that the nation would need to "take the treasure of the Catholic tradition into [its] purview."[19] This, he claims, we have done throughout our history: "American experience of the nobler sort has been a constant process of getting better acquainted with the work of the Church, though naturally in a humanistic rather than in a theological sense."[20] Understanding that this is novel and perhaps unbelievable, he attempts to make this case in the following chapter. Ironically, what Schuster could not have known when this book was published was that just two years later the nation would be thrown into the Great Depression and that this event would eventually give us the New Deal and Franklin Roosevelt. As I have argued elsewhere, the sociopolitics of this era brought a decidedly Catholic orientation to American national politics and public policy that lasted on some level until the 1980s.[21]

---

17. Schuster, *Catholic Spirit in America*, 48.
18. Schuster, *Catholic Spirit in America*, 68.
19. Schuster, *Catholic Spirit in America*, 77.
20. Schuster, *Catholic Spirit in America*, 77.
21. See Duncan and Moore, "Catholic and Protestant Social Discourse," 57–83.

As bold as Schuster's last claim was, it is his highly provocative argument a little later that must certainly have given his reader's great pause. It is one that at the cultural level I am very sympathetic to and which in many ways is consistent with the larger argument of this book. While admitting throughout the work that he has no intention of converting anyone to the Catholic faith, Schuster does speak in robustly positive terms about noted American converts like Brownson, Isaac Hecker, and Elizabeth Seton. In Schuster's words,

> The men and women who in New England (and to considerable extent elsewhere) voluntarily entered the Catholic society may have been hopelessly misguided, so far as I am concerned. All I claim is this: their conversion, far from weakening the Americanism to which they had clear title by reason of birth, breeding and spiritual heritage, strengthened their desire to serve the nation, to defend and develop the principles to which it had been officially pledged, and to give of themselves that others might live more abundantly. *In a word, they did not attain to the full stature of their Americanism until they joined the Church.*[22]

The unpacking of that last assertion is a weighty task, to say the least. Before doing so, it is important to note Schuster's own contextualization of that position. While recognizing that there were certain converts drawn to Catholicism for aesthetic reasons, Schuster is not much concerned with them. His converts are those like Hecker and Seton, of whom he writes:

> They were logical, truth-seeking, workaday, dogmatic people . . . the men and women who went the whole and often tragic distance were earnest folk intent on accepting truth when they believed it had been offered to them and devoted likewise to the nobler purposes of their country.[23]

The key, then, to the unpacking becomes gaining some understanding of what Schuster believes the "nobler purposes" of the country were. And here, I am going to do some synthesis that leaves important pieces of his argument behind. At its simplest, we can note what it is that Schuster finds of real value in the Catholic tradition and offering to America, politically speaking, in his claim that

> the greatest civic service it has rendered, however, is the moral influence it has exerted over families and individuals. Although the "Thou shalt nots" it has thundered have done much, its most

---

22. Schuster, *Catholic Spirit in America*, 90. Emphasis mine.
23. Schuster, *Catholic Spirit in America*, 93.

genuine achievement has been the promotion of positive good. Dealing with fallible, imperfect men, convinced that man is imperfect and fallible, it has proposed, day in and day out, nothing less than the Eight Beatitudes. One does not know where the nation could look for better or more exalted rules of conduct.[24]

While acknowledging human weakness and error are abundant, as the founders like James Madison certainly knew, the Church understood that human beings were called to something much richer than the pursuit of material goods, personal security, and discipline. Human beings were called quite literally to "put on Christ" and to serve the world by making of themselves a sacramental offering to others. What for Winthrop and the Puritans had been mostly a utilitarian call to brotherhood, i.e., making each other's burdens our own and knitting together as one to avoid a "shipwreck," becomes an end in and of itself for Catholics. If this country was founded simply to give freer rein to possessive individuals to ply their trades and pursue pleasure as compared to happiness rightly understood,[25] rather than to seek the good, the beautiful, and the just, how could one defend it as anything special? Indeed, if we were simply liberated from one tyrant so that we could all become petty tyrants ourselves it may be that we are worse off for our liberation. Knowing that the thoughtful person will always ask what ends are to be pursued with an individual's freedom before risking him or her congratulations, the Church's orientation to liberty is always directional. Subsequently, by having a destination in mind, it can provide a list of skills, practices, and virtues that will aid and make more likely the successful completion of one's mission or quest.

Liberalism in its thinnest and most libertarian guise is purposefully directionless. In such a culture—if in fact such a thing can be called a culture at all—any narrative understanding of the self becomes mostly incoherent and meaning difficult, if not impossible, to come by. Writing of this sort of Lockean liberalism, Schuster claims that while his philosophy ostensibly advocated democracy and liberalism, its primary tendency was to make it appear "unwise to have any views."[26] Here we find an ironic foreshadowing of the liberalism to come in the mid- and late twentieth century as what can be read as a call for a liberalism without "comprehensive doctrines"[27] is seen

---

24. Schuster, *Catholic Spirit in America*, 114. (For the list of the eight, see Matthew 5:3–10.)

25. Happiness "properly understood" refers to the idea of "public happiness" discussed earlier in this book. Again, see Arendt, *Human Condition*; Duncan, *Anti-Federalists*, ch. 2.

26. Schuster, *Catholic Spirit in America*, 127.

27. See Rawls, *Political Liberalism*.

as the essence of the ideology at its inception. Schuster's keen eye sees this for what it is as he sardonically writes: "small wonder that such a point of view could well afford to be liberal!"[28] In other words, it is easy to be tolerant when there is no real substance or threat tied to what one is tolerating. Seen like this, even liberalism's chief mark of courage and virtue becomes nothing special. Only when human beings are both liberated *and* challenged to choose, live by, and defend a set of beliefs, practices, and principles can we talk about a true and morally defensible individualism. To do that is to live with integrity.

Now while it is certainly possible to live that way and not be a Christian, it is impossible to be a Christian and not live that way and remain a Christian. Using the work of Richard Weaver, the historian Eugene Genovese differentiates between what Weaver referred to as "social-bond individualism" and what he called "Christian individualism from bourgeois individualism." The former of which he claims "asserts the inviolability of the human person against the state but that, with Aristotle, assumes the individual personality can only mature within a community to which one owes allegiance and accepts duties and responsibilities."[29] I would expand on Genovese's definition a little and talk not just about a discreet community, but about a living tradition. In any case, it is this sort of distinction that provides Schuster with his argument's sustenance in terms of the case for an America that is more authentically herself as she more genuinely embraces Catholic-Christian ideals and orientations.

While the bourgeois version of an unencumbered and fully liberated individualism has been ascendant and enshrined in the American mind and mythology for much of our history, it has never managed to fully eclipse those "second languages" in American political discourse. In large measure, as I argued in the two previous chapters, it has not been able to do so because, at the end of the day, that version of human anthropology is both ontologically and theologically specious. Despite that fact, the ideal itself still rests on a fundamental truth, namely that each human being, though significantly encumbered and social, is still a separate, unique, and irreducible person in his or her own right. Echoing arguments made earlier in this book, Schuster lays it out plainly: "Individualism is a concept of man which Christianity itself introduced into the world and fostered."[30] He goes on to note the implications of Christian individualism: "As soon as one postulates personal immortality and belief in a personal God, one is forced to conclude

28. Schuster, *Catholic Spirit in America*, 127.
29. Genovese, *Southern Front*, 124.
30. Schuster, *Catholic Spirit in America*, 245.

that each and every human being has not only a separate identity but also his or her own characteristics, bent of mind and destiny."[31]

In turn, the existence of sacred or exalted individuals has social and political implications. But to say that is to say something much more ambiguous than many have often thought. For the historical and prudential reasons noted in the first section of this chapter, as well as for good theological reasons, the relationship between means and ends as they relate to faith-based claims and the authoritative actions of the state are very complex and rarely linear. While it is possible to discern "the normal Christian attitude towards problems created by the existence of society"[32] because of Christianity's primary philosophic commitment to individualism rightly understood, it does not necessarily follow that such "attitudes" or commitments can simply be enshrined and enforced in the form of law and public policy. The practical reasons are obvious since we do not have a confessional state. The theological issues are the more interesting and subtle ones to manage as implied earlier.

Why? Because if states as states are all ultimately forced to rely on coercion and violence—no matter how legitimate its use might be—to enforce its law and policy, and the gospel can never use violence and coercion to compel behavior in its name, then a justifiable Christian *political praxis* is rendered extremely problematic. On the other hand, if the "faithful" citizen cannot perform the requirements of citizenship and remain faithful or the "faithful" citizen's actions cannot be distinguished in any meaningful way from the actions of any other citizens, then the whole notion of "faithful citizenship" is made nonsensical. In the first instance, this is the case because citizenship is ultimately about action—"ruling and be ruled in turn"—such that to not be able to take authoritative action is to not be a citizen at all. In the second instance, it is meaningless because if the actions of the "faithful citizen" are the same as the non-faithful citizens, it is a distinction without a difference, i.e., mere semantics. The traditional Catholic question here is, then, whether there is a both/and solution to what appears as an either/or proposition. Despite Schuster's cogent re-appropriation of the language of individualism on behalf of the Christian worldview, the entrée back to the world of practical politics is still not clear. Yes, *pace* Taylor, the Christian is now freer to live out the gospel as an individual *because* they are no longer compelled to do so by the state. And, as such, can now choose their confession freely. It is also important that they are now allowed to openly tolerate

---

31. Schuster, *Catholic Spirit in America*, 245–46.
32. Schuster, *Catholic Spirit in America*, 246.

the errors of others as a matter of principle. However, this still does not solve the riddle of state action and coercion. Hence, the bridge is still incomplete.

This, though, is a theoretical question. While critically important from a theological perspective, it has not been one that has given the vast majority of the laity much pause. On an implicit level, it seems safe to say that most Christian citizens act on the assumption that an appropriate end wills the necessary means for its accomplishment—like any other citizen. As such, I will focus instead on the actual social and political positions that have been developed in accord with the general case made above and leave the *praxis* question begging until the next chapter. To tell that story and lay out the Church's social teachings means that we detour at least briefly to Europe.

THE RISE OF CATHOLIC SOCIAL TEACHING

While I believe that the orientation delineated above is proper to Christianity itself correctly understood, it is the case that it is more readily discernible in the Catholic-Christianity of the time than the Protestant in America. Simultaneous to Brownson's own conversion was the movement in the Catholic Church toward a radical confrontation with modernity and the social structure and culture of the extant and emergent industrial societies of the day. The intellectual and political story of this period in the Catholic Church's history is documented at length in Jay Corrin's book *Catholic Intellectuals and the Challenge of Democracy*, on which I rely for my own account. In his work, Corrin situates the onset of modern Catholic social thought in the context of the revolutionary Europe of the nineteenth century. There, the victories of the bourgeoisie and the ascendancy of materialism and the market as preeminent values to the detriment and even derision of the sacred and the spiritual were being enforced by the increasing power and prominence of the modern nation-state system the bourgeoisie increasingly controlled. While the bourgeoisie was still fighting a few rearguard actions against certain aristocratic holdouts, the real class struggle of the day was between the liberal capitalists and labor. Having sided for the most part with the losing side in the battles between the nobility and the emerging bourgeoisie, the Catholic Church again faced a crucial historical choice in the newer struggle.

This "choice" divided the Church deeply in large measure because of the multiple levels at which the conversation was simultaneously required to be carried on. Included among those "levels" were conversations about theology, ecclesiology, philosophy, morality, justice, political theory, political activism, economics, sociology, psychology, anthropology, history, the "hard" sciences, and so on. Additionally, like it or not, there were also very real pragmatic questions having to do with institutional survival, power, and, yes, popularity. Because of the comprehensive nature of its mission, the Church did not have the luxury that many others had of focusing on very narrow criteria like efficiency, interests, minimum winning coalitions, and so on in its decision-making. Taking the side of humanity as a whole and attempting to give truthful representation to the transcendent in all its complexity in a world of individuals and groups who almost always seemed to be unyielding in their respective demands for particularistic and intentionally parochial forms of allegiance and loyalty is difficult, to say the least. Recognizing that, in principle, there are things that ought to be rendered to "Caesar" and things that ought to be rendered to "God" is, of course, critical, but the real work begins in deciding who gets what, when, where, and how, so to speak. In other words, if the Church was to play an important role in the world, it would ultimately have to take real sides in very specific social and political debates and questions, like: Are unions morally justifiable forms of human association? Should there be minimum wage/ maximum hour legislation? Should women be given the right to vote? And so on. However, answering the myriad of "theoretical" questions was only the first step as the question of *praxis*, i.e., what should the Church and its followers ultimately *do*, never ceased to loom. For now, I would like to think of the former questions as the "social" questions and the second set as the "political" for the sake of some categorical clarity.

The internal struggle over how to answer both the social questions and the political questions generated by industrial capitalism and liberalism remain vigorously contested till this day. However, there is a coherent and authoritative set of Church teachings on the former that emerged from a particular wing of the Church in the second half of the nineteenth century, which culminated in the publication of the encyclical *Rerum Novarum* (On the Condition of the Working Classes) under the pontificate of Pope Leo XIII in 1891. Taking their inspiration from the concept of a "social deaconry," progressive Catholic intellectuals and clergy confronted the plight of working men and women or "labor" head on. Leading the way was the French Catholic scholar Frederic Ozanam, who studied the work of Saint-Simone and subsequent to the worker's riots in Lyon in 1831 founded the Society of St. Vincent de Paul with the goal of providing for the welfare of the working class.[33] The Society, according to Corrin, "became the training ground for Catholicism's next generation of social activists."[34] Joined in his

---

33. Corrin, *Catholic Intellectuals*, 12.
34. Corrin, *Catholic Intellectuals*, 14.

efforts by people like Bishop Wilhelm Emmanuel von Kettler of Germany, the so called "labor-Catholics" took aim simultaneously at liberal-capitalism and Marxism, which they thought "was simply reaping the harvest of the transgressions of liberalism."[35] Writing a decade before Marx and Engel's *Manifesto* (1848), Ozanam asserted that

> the question which agitates the world today is not a question of *political forms*, but a *social* question; if it be the struggle of those who have nothing with those who have too much, if it be the violent shock of opulence and poverty which is making the ground tremble under our feet, our duty, as Christians, is to throw ourselves between these irreconcilable enemies, and to induce one side to give in order to fulfill the law.[36]

The method of *inducement* was not a call upon the workers to unite in violent revolution, but rather to those who had to voluntarily change their ways in accord with the teachings of the Gospels in an effort "to make charity accomplish what justice and law alone can never do."[37] After Ozanam's premature death at the age of forty in 1853, his cause was taken up and furthered with great vigor by his compatriot Bishop Ketteler, who published the widely distributed and read book *The Labor Question and Christianity* in 1864. In that work, Ketteler argued, based on the teachings of Aquinas, that

> the liberal concept of property as an exclusive right was a perversion of the Christian tradition of proprietorship, a crime against nature, since property and the creatures of the earth ultimately belonged to God alone. Man's use of property could never be unrestricted ... because man has an obligation to God to utilize ownership responsibly ... for the sustenance of the entire community.[38]

This criticism, however, did not then lapse into an apology for the emerging socialism of the day. Ketteler saw the latter in its atheism as simply another entity driving toward absolutism, state power, and uniformity—"liberalism and socialism were simply opposite sides of the same coin" seeking "the power of the state not to advance the commonweal but to promote the interests of their particular constituents."[39] Instead, he attempted to forge a communitarian alternative that simultaneously recognized the rights of

35. Corrin, *Catholic Intellectuals*, 14.
36. Quoted in Corrin, *Catholic Intellectuals*, 16.
37. Quoted in Corrin, *Catholic Intellectuals*, 16.
38. Corrin, *Catholic Intellectuals*, 21–22.
39. Corrin, *Catholic Intellectuals*, 22.

property as well as its responsibilities. Wielding enormous influence among German Catholics, Ketteler's position ultimately was formally accepted as the basis for Catholic social action in his country. His work was carried even further by his student, Fr. Franz Hitze, who helped found the interconfessional Christian Social Workmen's Association in 1882. Similar work was progressing in France as well under the guidance of people like Count Albert de Mun and the Marquis Rene de La Tour du Pin, who branched out from their association with the Society of St. Vincent de Paul and helped form a Committee for the Foundation of Catholic Workingmen's Clubs in the aftermath of the Paris uprisings of 1871.[40] Like the work of Ketteler, these organizations were meant to simultaneously confront the excesses of liberal-capitalism and blunt the appeal of socialism. Although Corrin is correct to point out that there were important differences in terms of analysis and action steps within what might be called the social action wing of the Church, what is crucial to note is the larger critical consensus of the *status quo* that was continuing to gel.

It was in the reemerging Catholic Church in England that social criticism and activism congealed and came to historical life under the broad sway of the convert John Henry Newman and the particular efforts of the younger convert Henry Edward Manning. It would be Manning's life's work to show "British Catholics how their religion could be a tool for social change."[41] Early in his life, Manning took up the cause of labor in the form of the arguments for a living wage and later he became the first high-ranking Roman Catholic prelate in Britain to commit himself "openly to the cause of labor" as a result of his avowed support of the Agricultural Union.[42] In the words of Corrin: "Manning waged relentless warfare from the pulpit and in newspapers against what he called the 'Plutocracy,' a money-hungry clique of power brokers who had shown no compassion or justice for labor."[43] In 1874, Manning published a collection of his lectures under the title of *The Rights and Dignity of Labor*. While Manning certainly believed that there was a role for the interventionist state in rectifying the inequities of the economic order and protecting the rights of labor to organize, he was not in favor of political centralization or the abolition of private property. In other words, he was not a communist. Although Cardinal Manning was already well known in British political circles as a result of his outspoken defense of labor, it was his intervention and negotiated settlement of the London dock

---

40. Corrin, *Catholic Intellectuals*, 37.
41. Corrin, *Catholic Intellectuals*, 43.
42. Corrin, *Catholic Intellectuals*, 49.
43. Corrin, *Catholic Intellectuals*, 50.

strike in 1890 that brought him "popular adulation and international fame" such that he exercised "considerable influence on the labor movement" for the duration of his life.[44]

With the likes of Manning and Ketteler being so visible and vocal it was inevitable that the social face of Catholicism would appear in a new light. Both men not only carried on extensive correspondence with each other and other like-minded clergymen, they also found the ear of Pope Leo XIII who would, in turn, ask Manning to play a key role in the drafting of *Rerum Novarum*. Manning's influence also spread dramatically across the sea through the person of Cardinal Gibbons in America. In his efforts to carry Manning's work forward, Gibbons embraced the American trade union movement and, in particular, the Knights of Labor. After the massive immigration of working-class Catholics to America in the late 1800s, the membership in the Knights swelled and counted among its ranks some five hundred thousand Catholic workers (this represented about two-thirds of the total membership). After some initial consternation in Rome concerning the political nature of the group, Manning and Gibbons interceded and helped deliver official sanction to the group and to trade unionism itself. While ultimately this sanction flowed out of a theological tradition and sensibility, the social and political implications were profound. It is of course with the publication and dissemination of the labor encyclical itself that this official sanction moved from toleration and support for the labor movement to the enshrinement of its ideological orientation as official Church teaching.

Rerum Novarum is a complex and multifaceted document whose foundation rests on Aquinas's teachings and intellectual methods. Situating itself between the radical liberal-individualism of the day and the collectivism of European socialism, Pope Leo XIII rejected both the Jacobin-Rousseau as well as Hegel and Marx. Instead reasserting the idea of an organic society and the natural law proposition that legitimate political authority comes from God and must be exercised in accord with Christian precepts to maintain its legitimacy. Duties and responsibilities devolve to individuals and classes as well in relationship to their respective places in the social order. Rejecting the Marxian notion of class struggle, Leo asserted:

> It is a capital evil with respect to the question we are discussing to take for granted that one class of society is of itself hostile to the other, as if nature had set rich and poor against each other to fight fiercely in implacable war. This is so abhorrent to reason and truth that the exact opposite is true.[45]

44. Corrin, *Catholic Intellectuals*, 53.
45. Leo XIII, *Rerum Novarum*, 5.

In place of class struggle, Leo argues that both workers and owners have reciprocal obligations to each other and the social order itself. The workers are to refrain from violence and associating with "vicious" and crafty men, and the employers are to avoid treating workers as slaves. As Leo puts it: "Justice demands that the dignity of human personality be respected in them, ennobled as it has been through what we call the Christian character."[46] To accomplish this he asserts that "among the most important duties of employers the principal one is to give every worker what is justly due him. . . . The rich and employers must remember that no laws, either human or divine, permit them for their own profit to oppress the needy and the wretched or to seek gain from another's want."[47] This negative injunction, however, does not automatically lead Leo to the redistributive or interventionist state as others might quickly suppose. In his words, "no human devices can ever be found to supplant Christian charity."[48] In place of such a state he suggests the following ideal:

> Therefore those governing the State ought primarily to devote themselves to the service of individual groups and of the whole commonwealth, and through the entire scheme of laws and institutions to cause both public and individual well-being to develop spontaneously out of the very structure and administration of the State.[49]

The above denotes a concern with fairness and process rather than with specific substantive outcomes. Yet unlike the "neutral" or libertarian state, the "Christian" state does not merely enforce contracts and adjudicate disputes under the assumption that the "good" will result purely from the unfettered interactions and competition between self-interested individuals and parties; it takes an active position to generate conditions that will produce just outcomes within a given historical and political context. Hence, the degree and nature of intervention on the part of the state will be proportional to the needs of the common good. In the words of the encyclical itself,

> And since the power of governing comes from God and is a participation, as it were, in His supreme sovereignty, it ought to be administered according to the example of the divine power, which looks with paternal care to the welfare of individual creatures as well as to that of all creation. If, therefore, any injury

---

46. Leo XIII, *Rerum Novarum*, 5.
47. Leo XIII, *Rerum Novarum*, 6.
48. Leo XIII, *Rerum Novarum*, 8.
49. Leo XIII, *Rerum Novarum*, 9.

has been done to or threatens either the common good or the interests of individual groups, which injury cannot in any other way be repaired or prevented, it is necessary for public authority to intervene.[50]

Hence, unlike the image of the state as a referee or a judge that liberalism in the first instance and communism in the second could be viewed as, the emerging Catholic view is better seen as picturing the state as a conductor or director who wants to produce the best possible performance or play with the given individual musicians or actors. Thus, in an era in which the balance between those who labored and those who owned was so distorted, the Church had little recourse but to countenance state intercession and protection for workers and their associations in the name of the common good, not class politics. Given the overwhelming power wielded by the owners and the wealthy, the *least* intrusive method for achieving the balance necessitated by the common good was through the proliferation and legal safeguarding of worker's associations and unions. As Leo puts it,

> We see the road being closed to Catholic associations, which are law-abiding and in every respect useful, at the very time when it is being decreed that most assuredly men are permitted by law to form associations, and at the very time when this freedom is being lavishly granted in actual fact to men urging courses of conduct pernicious at once to religion and to the State.... Under these circumstances, workers who are Christians must choose one of two things; either to join associations in which it is greatly feared that there is a danger to religion or to form their own associations and unite their forces in such a way that they may be able manfully to free themselves from such unjust and intolerable opposition.[51]
>
> In summary, let this be laid down as a general and constant law: Workers' associations ought to be so constituted and so governed as to furnish the most suitable and most convenient means to attain the object proposed, which consists in this, that individual members of the association secure, so far as possible, an increase in the goods of body, of soul, and of prosperity.[52]

While numerous other tracts would follow that developed and expanded contemporary Catholic social teaching, it is ostensibly the case that, in the words of Pope Pius XI in the 1931 *Quadragesimo Anno*, "Leo's Encyclical

---

50. Leo XIII, *Rerum Novarum*, 10.
51. Leo XIII, *Rerum Novarum*, 14.
52. Leo XIII, *Rerum Novarum*, 15.

has proved itself the Magna Charta upon which all Christian activity in the social field ought to be based."[53] That having been said, however, it is still an open question regarding how successful the Church's "third way" was in changing the nature of American political discourse and politics proper. The important truth that must be reasserted here is that the Church came to choose a "side" in this period only because it had come to the conclusion that such a choice would further the larger end of creating a just and humane (and therefore Christian) social order.

CATHOLIC TEACHING AND THE SOCIAL QUESTION IN AMERICA

While there are any number of issues and questions that could be used to underscore and exemplify the tension and even hostility which existed between the American political tradition and the thrust of early Catholic social teaching, clearly the understanding of property, property rights, and the questions of wealth and poverty that flow naturally from those understandings are among the most central and contentious ones imaginable since they go in many ways to the very heart of the liberal enterprise. In 1840, Orestes Brownson claimed that "we believe property should be held subordinate to man, and not man to property."[54] Embedded in that deceptively simple assertion and its possible contrary is a vast set of social, economic, moral, political, and, in the United States, constitutional arguments and debates. While space does not permit a comprehensive rendering of those issues, it is important to paint at least a brief picture to make clear the dominant context with which Catholic social teaching in America had to contend. While a more complicated story of this era has emerged than was once considered the conventional wisdom, that wisdom remains critically important in and of itself. The standard constitutional and political tale of the post–Civil War industrial period is marked by terms like "liberty of contract," "substantive due process," "social Darwinism," and, of course, "laissez-faire."

But, that story itself stands on top of a much earlier one in American jurisprudence which can itself be marked by the term "corporate personhood." Early in the nation's history, the question of the legal status of newly forming American corporations emerged as a critical point of both practical and ideological importance. As the question made its way to the Marshall Court, the basic issue hinged on whether "a corporation derived its legal nature from the individuals who had joined in the enterprise or from the

---

53. Pius XI, *Quadragesimo Anno*, 7.
54. Quoted in Abbott, *Political Thought in America*, 130.

legislature that had granted the charter."[55] If a corporation was essentially an "individual," private property rights would protect it from extensive public control. However, if corporations were essentially the creatures of the governments which chartered them, they could be harnessed to public purposes and regulated in accord with the extant political will. Either path, generally speaking, portended serious consequences for the way in which political economy in American would unfold and develop over time.

Historically speaking, the matter was complicated by the changing nature of the economic landscape itself. In the simplest terms, early corporations were more or less public/private partnerships, which had been chartered by governments for doing what was essentially public work such as colonization, building roads, bridges, canals, and so on. As the nation shifted from a mercantile economy to one based on the increasing production of goods and services, the nature of the corporation looked more and more like what we would subsequently think of as "private" enterprise. Not surprisingly, American legal thinking changed as well in order to apply the Constitution to the changing times.

Led by Chief Justice John Marshall and Justice Joseph Story, the Supreme Court's initial decisions regarding the question of corporate personhood in cases like *Head and Amory v. Providence Insurance Company* (1804) treated corporations as if they were public entities. However, Justice Story's two opinions in separate 1815 cases, *Terrett v. Taylor* and *Town of Pawlett v. Clark*, set the stage for a dramatic change. In the former case, Story argued for the existence of two types of corporations, public and private. This, the constitutional historian Melvin Urofsky claims, was "a distinction hitherto unrecognized in American law."[56] Under his new formulation, Story claimed that "private corporations enjoyed the protection of both natural and constitutional law, and therefore, once chartered, their property and their rights extended beyond the legislative reach."[57] In the latter case, Story expanded his argument and contended that such reasoning was required by "natural justice" itself. These cases served as the precursor for the most important early case in this area of law, namely *Trustees of Dartmouth College v. Woodward* (1819).

In the *Dartmouth College* case, Chief Justice John Marshall begot what can only be called a paradigmatic transformation of Contract Clause jurisprudence. He fundamentally reoriented the relationship between the public (government) and private sectors (business) in American society in

55. Urofsky, *Documents* 1.234.
56. Urofsky, *Documents* 1.235.
57. Urofsky, *Documents* 1.235.

a manner that would render the ideal of an integrated, cooperative social order—like that pictured in the early social encyclicals of the Church—problematic at best and overtly hostile and antagonistic at worst. Radically extending the public/private distinction in Story's earlier opinions, such that charters granted by the states to corporations were now, under Marshall's dramatic new conceptualization, viewed as falling under the purview of Article I, Section 10 of the Constitution. This made it unconstitutional for states to "impair the obligation of contracts." In other words, if publicly granted charters were in fact contracts, strictly construed, then, once granted, the corporation was shielded from any further government intervention. This opinion cleared the way for a number of crucial changes in the course of American political development, not the least of which was setting the nation on a path at great variance with what was taking place in Europe in general and in Catholic social thinking in particular.

By way of assertion rather than systematic argument for now, I want to suggest that the ideological and theoretical trajectory embedded in the Marshall/Story line of reasoning helped firmly secure and embed the Hamiltonian vision of a commercial republic in the American constitutional scheme. While in the aftermath of *Dartmouth* states began issuing charters with clauses reserving their rights to revisit them over time, corporations soon managed to use their political clout to blunt and temper regulation that did not serve their *interests*.[58] It is this idea of *interests* that I contend is the critical wedge that places increasing distance between American social thought and Catholic social thought in the late nineteenth and early twentieth centuries. Although it is commonplace today to think negatively about the notion of interests in general and private or vested interests in particular, such was not always the case. As Albert O. Hirschman argues: "The idea of interest as it had been developed by the political literature since Machiavelli—the idea, that is, of a disciplined understanding of what it takes to advance one's power, influence, and wealth—came into common use early in the seventeenth century."[59]

Though born coincident to modern political thought itself, its normative legitimacy would take a couple of centuries to establish. That legitimacy was purchased at the price of "glory" and "heroism" and, most importantly, the traditional Christian virtues of faith, hope, and charity. Machiavellian realism and Hobbesian social science rejected the virtue ethics of Aquinas and Aristotle and, instead, placed the pleasure seeking, pain avoiding,

---

58. The italicization of the term interests is not meant at this point to be pejorative, but it will soon become clear that I find it very problematic.

59. Hirschman, *Passions and The Interests*, 38.

self-interested "rational actor" at the center of the human drama. Its improved normative status developed in the following manner as "interest" became the new paradigm:

> Once passion was deemed destructive and reason ineffectual, the view that human action could be exhaustively described by attribution to either one or the other meant an exceedingly somber outlook for humanity. A message of hope was therefore conveyed by the wedging of interest in between the two traditional categories of human motivation. Interest was seen to partake in effect of the better nature of each, as the passion of self-love upgraded and contained by reason, and as reason given direction and force by that passion. The resulting hybrid form of human action was considered exempt from both the destructiveness of passion and the ineffectuality of reason. *No wonder that the doctrine of interest was received at the time as a veritable message of salvation!*[60]

Under this new paradigm of *interests*, the pursuit of wealth and upward mobility became sources of social stability and aided in the effort to predict, understand, and effectively direct human behavior rather than the dangerous passions that threatened social upheaval. In Madisonian language, ambition would counteract ambition, and the discipline required for material success would force the pursuers of happiness to restrain themselves to a large extent. Here reason would serve the passions and the passions would become more purposeful and directed. The resultant economic growth would improve society and the lives of increasing numbers of individuals without significant need for political intervention or direction. Adam Smith's "invisible hand" would work its magic and the "rising tide would lift all ships" so long as individuals properly understood and acted appropriately in their individual self-interest. The state's role, hence, becomes minimal and the image of political society provided in the introduction by Macpherson becomes controlling, i.e., *political society is a contrivance for the protection of the individual's property in his person and goods, and for the maintenance of orderly relations of exchange between individuals regarded as proprietors of themselves.*[61]

As a collection of individuals, corporations then too, according to the logic, become rational actors with interests to pursue. Indeed, they are even more rational and, hence, more socially beneficial and powerful because their capacity, energy and collective "wisdom" enable them to act on

---

60. Hirschman, *Passions and Interests*, 43–44. Emphasis mine.
61. Macpherson, *Political Theory of Possessive Individualism*, 264.

a massive scale relative to individuals and small groups. Their pursuit of their *individual* interests, then, supposedly serves the public good despite any specific intention to necessarily do so. While the simplicity of the theory belies what is obviously a complicated and anomalous filled historical reality, such a conception allows us to view the actions of the commercial republicans with a presumption of good faith regarding their commitment to the common good even if we might disagree with how it is conceptualized or find ourselves deeply skeptical of the assumptions the theory entails. It is entirely plausible that this attempt to wrench virtue from what was previously considered vice and to turn the countervailing energy created by the disciplined pursuit of self-interest was well-conceived to achieve the desired ends of increased material prosperity, political order, and security through a devotion to property rights and liberty understood as freedom from political interference. Indeed, there is a solid historical case to be made that at the broadest level the theory actually worked. The United States developed quickly, vast wealth was created, and overall the levels of disorder and violence (post–Civil War) were kept to a minimum. Constitutionally speaking, those achievements were buttressed by the social, political, and legal constructs noted at the front of this section. Those were the natural offshoots of the concretizing of *interest* in the American constitutional scheme as begotten by *Dartmouth College*.

While the ideological lines are hardly straight or overly consistent, the general trajectory was plain. Corporations operating under the same sort of protections from government interference as individuals would be left to pursue what were now seen as private interests with minimal governmental interference. This does not mean that there would be no regulation whatsoever, but rather that the burden of proof, so to speak, regarding political intervention in the marketplace would be shifted dramatically. In other words, corporations conceived of as public concerns could expect routine political interference in their affairs because they were in essence public entities or creations. Conceived of as private entities with rights claims against political interference, the onus was now on the state to demonstrate or prove sufficient reason or cause to interfere with the business conducted by corporations and even the marketplace in general. At the ideological level, laissez-faire economic theory held that the optimal outcome would be achieved through rigorous and relentless competition between parties pursuing their own self-interest. Socially speaking, the same basic theory was thought to hold. This free market approach to the social sphere was loosely called social-Darwinism and was derived in large part from the work of Herbert Spencer in his *Social Statics* (1851). Essentially, the theory claimed that minimal governmental interference in the social sphere through the provision of public goods or support for those who were weak or unable to take care of themselves represented an ill-conceived attempt to thwart nature and only perpetuated undesirable traits and characteristics to the detriment of the overall society.

Fused into one overarching libertarian theory, these interrelated approaches rested on a romantic and anthropologically misbegotten image of the rugged individual—a being who apparently had no parents and raised or nurtured himself like some Zarathustra-like overman in a distant cave before descending to the world of human beings. However, the theory did have a certain power, especially when combined with the notion of "interest" discussed above. Since "passion" had been deemed dangerous, "reason" unreliable, and "virtue" unrealistic, it also appeared to be the only real game in town for those willing to see the world as it was. Such is the deductive logic of possessive individualism—starting from Hobbesian premises, it ends up with neo-Hobbesian conclusions. Yet for all its realism, such a position cannot in fact be realistic because it rests not on a faulty theory of human nature (whatever that is) but on a faulty understanding of what it means to be human. This is obviously not the place to take up that highly involved conversation, though previous chapters have certainly given plenty of clues as to how I would proceed with it. At a minimum, to be human is to be part of a social tradition which both forms and is formed in turn by its members. While this neo-Hobbesian worldview was being presented as sound deductive reasoning with near universal validity, it was, in reality, the logical by-product of a relatively young social and political tradition.

As much normative as it was empirical, the liberal tradition (paradigm) as it came to be constructed in America's industrial period found its chief intellectual spokesperson in the form of William Graham Sumner and its chief popularizer in Horatio Alger. While asserting that it was merely a reflection of the world as it was, the tradition itself was in competition with others for the allegiance of American men and women. Despite a well-prepared intellectual and ideological field dating back to the time of Locke, the hegemonic status of the emergent tradition soon found itself in need of more formidable weapons to sustain and accomplish what was being presented as simply "natural." Ironically, the legal and constitutional arsenal in this regard was stocked as a direct, though largely unforeseen, consequence of the successful effort to *end* the existence of a certain set of property rights; namely, those property rights in other human beings known as slaves.

In the aftermath of emancipation and the Northern victory in the Civil War, the Thirteenth, Fourteenth, and Fifteenth Amendments were passed to consolidate and, in effect, *constitutionalize* what had first been won at great price on the battlefield. While bringing states to heel on the question of slavery was certainly the most important justification for the Amendments, the Fourteenth's broad language in the areas of due process, equal protection, and privileges and immunities afforded the citizens of the various states new rights and constitutional protections still to be imagined and litigated. Among the "citizens" who found themselves with a new cache of still-to-be-defined rights were of course "corporate persons." When taken with the transfiguration of the idea of *property* itself from merely physical entities like land and possessions to something more intangible, pervasive, and even metaphysical in a certain way, the die was cast for a confrontation between state police powers and the newly empowered and emboldened corporate America.

Despite a certain mythos about an autochthonous America that was wholly unregulated and filled with shrewd pupa-like pioneers waiting to let their libertarian inner capitalists emerge, the fact was that states exhaustively regulated all forms of human relations and interactions in the name of the health, safety, and moral well-being of their citizens and immediate society.[62] The advent of the Fourteenth Amendment, however, created a window of opportunity to dramatically modify the tradition as it existed, along with the constitutional practices which had developed around it. The opening salvo came in the form of the *Slaughterhouse Cases* of 1873. There the Court rejected the claims of the Louisiana butchers that they had been denied due process under the Fourteenth Amendment when the state created a monopoly for the landing and slaughter of livestock in New Orleans. Louisiana had done so in the name of public health. However, the narrow majority and the bold dissents by Justices Field and Bradley foreshadowed a much different regulatory world to come.

Without walking through the ensuing cases which followed in the wake of those dissents, the ultimate result was the rise of substantive due process and its cousin, liberty of contract. Both of these developments would help to foster a fairly extreme anti-regulatory *ethos* in American capitalism and give rise to a relatively unbridled marketplace across all economic sectors, but particularly in the area of labor relations. The term substantive due process itself gained the assent of the Court in the 1897 case *Allgeyer v. Louisiana*. Urofsky distinguishes the term from its simpler precursor in the following manner:

> From the beginning, due process has meant a bundle of procedural rights, some of which are spelled out in constitutions, statutes, and regulations, and some of which are of common law derivation. The right to trial by jury is a substantive right, but how jurors are chosen, how evidence may be presented, how witnesses may be procured, and how the trial is conducted in a

---

62. See Lutz, *Popular Consent and Popular Control*.

fair and impartial manner are all procedural in nature. Procedural due process, it has been said, regulates the courts and constitutes the rules of the game; substantive due process regulates the legislature and *is* the game.[63]

In the most basic sense, then, substantive due process ultimately entails strong rights claims against legislative interference of any kind. The things that cannot be legislated away, but instead would have to be amended away constitutionally speaking. Obviously, the questions of which rights are substantive ones like freedom of speech and press or equality under the law, etc., are highly contentious and go to the very heart of a nation's political identity, but once enshrined in the fundamental law they are, despite the ongoing need for interpretation by the courts, considered settled. In other words, while we may argue about whether certain speech is protected or not, we do not argue whether free speech is a bedrock principle or not anymore; it is taken as a political given. However, both the Ninth and Tenth Amendments clearly imply that there are substantive rights that are not enumerated and yet still exist. In some cases these are rights which it would almost seem silly to list given the enumerated rights themselves. Take what in another context I know would be a highly contentious claim (but which here can be used I think rather easily)—namely, that the Constitution implies that human beings have a right to life. There is no amendment to the Constitution which says: "Congress shall make no law abridging the right to life." The same thing is true of freedom of conscience. Yet both of these "rights" must be implied if the other rights like petitioning for a redress of grievances are to make any sense whatsoever. In other cases, though, the inference is much less commonsensical and seems to call out for political adjudication rather than legal adjudication. The case at hand is of course concerned with the right of property and, in turn, the right of contract as it relates to property broadly understood.

If property properly earned through "labor" is taken in Lockean fashion to be a virtual appendage of the person, then it may be regulated in accord with the consent granted to a legitimate government but it cannot be on some level fully alienated such that the person in question could no longer enjoy its fruits or advantages in any manner. Like the inalienable right to liberty cannot be fully alienated such that a person can become the slave of another without in effect becoming something other than a rights bearing human being, so too, the argument goes, property rightfully assigned to a person for his or her use must remain in their possession to an extent sufficient to assure their ability to use it in the pursuit of happiness. The following excerpts from Bradley's dissent in an earlier case and both his and

---

63. Urofsky, *March of Liberty*, 497.

Justice Field's dissents in the *Slaughterhouse Cases* provide a strong taste of this sort of reasoning constitutionally speaking:

> There is no more sacred right of citizenship ... than the right to pursue unmolested a lawful employment in a lawful manner. It is nothing more than the sacred right of labor....
>
> [Every American had the right to follow such pursuits] as he may see fit, without unreasonable regulations or molestation, and without being restrained by any of those unjust, oppressive, and odious monopolies or exclusive privileges which have been condemned by all free governments; it is also his privilege to be protected in the possession and enjoyment of his property....
>
> [There are] valuable rights ... which the legislature of a State cannot invade....
>
> [There are] the fundamental rights, privileges and immunities which belong to [a person] as a free man and free citizen....
>
> [There are] rights that do not derive their existence from [state] legislation, and cannot be destroyed by its power.[64]

Bradley went so far as to "invoke, by name, 'substantive due process' as a protection against the legislature."[65] Taken together, the position derived from this paradigmatic shift makes property and the rights of property owners, whether individuals or corporations, less and less subject to the political process itself. As such, while men and women might not necessarily be subordinated to property explicitly, the vast majority of Americans were increasingly subordinated to those who possessed property and over whom they had little control or political recourse. Legally viewed as equals, corporations and individual workers "negotiated" with one another in a context that was increasingly insulated both ideologically and constitutionally from legislative interference and guided by the edicts of efficiency and profit. Hence, property was certainly not subordinated to men or the public good in the manner suggested by Brownson's formulation or the natural law reasoning of *Rerum Novarum*. Indeed, as unions were broken and even the most minimal social legislation was struck down in cases like *In Re Debs* and *Lochner v. New York*, it can safely be said that the American approach to the "social questions" was almost diametrically opposite of the Catholic approach which had emerged by the early days of the twentieth century.

While the standard historical narrative often views the jurisprudence of the so-called American Gilded Age through the lens of class warfare (i.e., the Court siding with the wealthy and the powerful to promote their

---

64. All quotations are taken from Urofsky, *March of Liberty*, 498.
65. Urofsky, *March of Liberty*, 498.

collective interests to the economic detriment and misery of the working class and the poor), there is another school of thought led by people like Howard Gillman who rejects such simple reductionism and its blatant assumptions of judicial realism. In its place, Gillman argues for a certain kind of continuity that sees cases like *Lochner* not as precedent breaking aberrations, but as part of a larger constitutional vision that rejected class-based or partial social legislation rather than social legislation *per se*.[66] The tradition of neutrality Gillman argues for is perfectly in keeping with the image from above that views the American state as an umpire rather than a conductor and provides real constitutional support for an adversarial political model.[67] Underlying that image is a worldview which enshrines competition and rejects both cooperation and what the Church will come to call solidarity as counterproductive and inimical to progress—material and intellectual.

On my reading of this argument, the Court's position in this period can be viewed as akin to, let's say, a rejection of gerrymandering in the electoral process. Suppose, for the sake of argument, that agonistic competition between political parties was viewed as the best mechanism to ensure social and political "progress." The use of political power once achieved to make elections less competitive by stacking the deck through the drawing of electoral lines would, when done well, greatly diminish competition and, hence, progress so understood, despite, perhaps, being perfectly consistent with the logic of rational choice and procedural democracy. In this analogy, gerrymandering is a form of "class" or "partial" legislation that undermines the chief engine of progress by thwarting the prime driver, namely competition. In this way, were our fictional court to intervene, it would be doing so to preserve the substantive nature of the system so understood. Democracy, then, is not in and of itself a good, or even a good way to make decisions, but rather the best political system to ensure that competition remains constant and, on the most sympathetic reading, make sure that consensus is achieved in an odd sort of dialectical way. It is, in effect, an economic version of Federalist Paper 10 incarnate. In this manner, what might appear to be inconsistency can become consistent under a large enough view. If I can indulge in one more image to make the point, imagine watching someone drive a car through a series of snapshots rather than a video. In one picture, the driver steers to the right while in the next she steers to the left. Looking at a series of such pictures, the viewer might say that the driver is inconsistent and cannot decide whether she wants to go left or right. However, the video or big picture would let us see that her real goal was, of course, to go straight and allow

---

66. Howard Gillman, *Constitution Besieged*.
67. See Mansbridge, *Beyond Adversary Democracy*.

us to conclude that the left/right adjustments were means to that end rather than ends in and of themselves (thesis, antithesis, synthesis, so to speak).

To return to the Court, then, if the question is not what is fair (process) or what is just (outcomes), but rather what maintains systematic equilibrium (driving straight) and dynamism or progress (moving forward at a good rate of speed), i.e., material and scientific advancement, then the Court's uneven intervention suddenly makes sense and becomes in essence pragmatism (i.e., what works). Understood in this way, democracy subsequently becomes less about picking between two or more competing visions of the good society and more about picking those representatives most able to deliver the good society. The issues, then, were practical and instrumental not political (understood as the authoritative allocation of values and resources) or moral. Here again, Hartz's observation that in America "law had flourished on the copse of philosophy" seems apt. However, even if Gillman is correct and my reading of his argument on target, the ultimate reality is still much the same. "Neutrality" benefits the strong as does the presumption of equality among unequals. Gillman acknowledges this as he writes near the close of his book,

> Contrary to neorealist explanations of the period, the story of the *Lochner* era is not about how reactionary justices in the late nineteenth became more daring in their willingness to exploit legal materials in order to protect or promote their personal class or policy biases. Rather, the *Lochner* era is the story of how a changing social structure exposed the conservatism and class bias inherent in the dominant ideological structures first formulated and institutionalized by the framers of the U.S. Constitution; it is the story of how an ideology that was fairly (albeit not completely) inclusive around the time of the founding became more and more exclusive as the century progressed and capitalist forms of production matured; and it is the story of how the Court, loyal to a historically defined conception of political legitimacy, struggles to maintain the coherence of this authoritative ideology in an era that witnessed an unprecedented intensification of class conflict.[68]

CONCLUSION

There is, of course, more than a little irony to be found above for those familiar with the traditional American caricature of Catholic thinking as hostile to free inquiry, dogmatically inflexible, and politically authoritarian. While

---

68. Gillman, *Constitution Besieged*, 199.

the Church was certainly open to such charges on a number of questions and issues, its approach to the social question was profoundly more creative and flexible than the entrenched and anachronistic thinking being done by leading American intellectuals and jurists. Furthermore, it was grounded in a moral vision that retained its traditional integrity while responding with energy to the signs of the times and emergent historical circumstances. Though some might be inclined to use a term like "progressive" to describe the approach found in the Church's early social teachings, the better term is "fullness." While modernity had rendered the Church's Constantinian pretensions mostly unthinkable, it simultaneously opened up new theoretical space for the creation of what Schuster would call a more "genuinely Christian time" by allowing the Church to be the Church rather than the state and the Church at the same time. Freed from its need to protect and defend particular political forms, institutions and people, the Church was at liberty to construct a significantly more robust and universal political and moral vision—a more Christian vision.

That vision held that the natural order was ultimately an important but insufficient good whose components like the state, society, property, and so on, were all, when properly functioning, ordered to ends authored by God. The penultimate combined end was the common good—which was not to be confused with the good of any particular state or any particular part of the natural order as an end in and of itself. The ultimate end, which the common good itself was to serve, is, for the Christian, a supernatural one, i.e., to know and love God. This is accomplished in this life by loving others as God has loved us; which, in turn, means living in solidarity and friendship with all other human beings in a community dedicated to the fullest possible flourishing in mind, body, and spirit of each of its members. This, in turn, means rejecting all ideologies that affirm the priority of matter over spirit, that transform human beings into means or treat them instrumentally, or which embrace modes of behavior that ignore the real differences between unique and individually valued human beings. In other words, the Christian faith is never "neutral," it always chooses (or should always try to choose) the good, the beautiful, and the just. Christians must do this and order their actions and institutions toward them, not with a reckless disregard or disrespect for the consequences of their actions, but with a willingness to suffer and sacrifice convenient and even venerable ideas and ways of life when necessary.

At his most poetic, George Schuster offers a vision of what the world could look like for an individual and society which is properly ordered toward the correct supernatural ends, writing,

> Though the world in which the Church finds itself today were a thousand times more perverse and chaotic than it is, it would not yet be nearly so infamous as the civilization into which Christ came with His redemptive will. We have only to share that will in our paltry but creative way in order to leap once again over the impasses which keep us from numberless realizations of beatitude. Ruskin's idea that the modern artisan needs a purposive freedom of which he was deprived by a mechanistic concept of labor is great and true for better reasons even than those he named. Times in which the shoemaker has confidence that every peg he drives is a song in celestial ears, because it incarnates the humble creative activity in which his natural, personal gift is placed at the service of—is sacrificed for—men, would also be a genuinely Christian time.[69]

The American liberal tradition as it came to be both theorized and embodied in the antebellum period was not one that was capable of fostering anything remotely like a *genuinely Christian time* because, frankly speaking, it had no desire to do so. It was by that time, if not at its inception, centered around austere conceptions of private property, possessive self-interested individualism, and fierce and merciless competition meant to produce material abundance and growth within the context of a very limited conception of governing and political obligation. The emerging Catholic social tradition rejected all of this and proposed a very different conception of human beings, political economy, and governance, not to mention a very different definition of the common good. If America was going to become a place that deserved the support of the Christian in general and Catholics in particular, something was going to have to change. Many non-Catholic Americans thought that it should be the Church and Catholics who ought to change. The Church and many of her members, of course, felt otherwise. Both sides were then forced to confront not only theory then, but also to confront politics and power. In the next chapter, we finally turn to the question of *praxis* and the development of the Catholic social tradition in American political life. Though the Church itself will certainly grow and change, it does not cease to call upon the people of the world and the citizens of the United States to repent and convert.

---

69. Schuster, *Catholic Spirit in America*, 186–87.

6

Inventing a Catholic American Political Tradition

As it was in Noah's day, so will it be when the Son of Man comes. For in those days before the Flood people were eating, drinking, taking wives, taking husbands, right up to the day Noah went into the ark, and they suspected nothing till the Flood came and swept all away. It will be like this when the Son of Man comes. Then of two men in the fields one is taken, one left; of two women at the millstone grinding, one is taken, one left.

So stay awake, because you do not know the day when your master is coming. You may be quite sure of this that if the householder had known what time of the night the burglar would come, he would have stayed awake and would not have allowed anyone to break through the wall of his house. Therefore, you must stand ready because the Son of Man is coming at an hour you do not expect.

—Matthew 24:37–44

All authority in heaven and on earth has been given to me. Go, therefore, make disciples of all the nations; baptize them in the name of the Father and of the Son and of the Holy Spirit, and teach them to observe all the commands I gave you. And know that I am with you always; yes, to the end of time.

—Matthew 28:19–20

INTRODUCTION

At the writing of this chapter, five of the sitting Supreme Court Justices of the United States of America identify themselves as Catholics. Another was raised Catholic and now identifies as Episcopalian. The remaining three are Jewish. Given the country's Protestant origins, and subsequent history regarding both Jews and Catholics, this fact itself is highly noteworthy. Because of the idiosyncratic nature of such appointments, it would be difficult to make any meaningful or valid generalizations about this state of affairs without undertaking a serious and lengthy multivariate analysis, beyond the following one: times change. To sharpen that rather amorphous edge just a little, it seems that we can say that whatever else may be true about this phenomenon, the larger American political culture no longer has a significant "Catholic question" on its mind. Certainly, the nation as a whole has grown much less suspicious and much more tolerant of many religious differences. Furthermore, the fact that Catholics are the largest single denomination in the country today, numbering roughly 25 percent of the populous, clearly has helped to reinforce the aforementioned shifts in the most basic numerical ways. And finally, we know for a fact that Catholics themselves as a group are now far less susceptible to differentiation on the basis of their confession than ever. In other words, it is simply the case that the majority of Catholics are best seen as Americans who happen to be Catholic rather than as a more determinative subculture that could be represented by an identity term like Catholic-American.

Yes, there are many Catholics who carry their religious beliefs with them into the voting booth and other areas of public life, especially on some hot-button issues like abortion. But, we know that simply identifying as Catholic does not correlate significantly with overall political behavior. In general, Catholic political behavior needs to be explained by variables other than just religious affiliation. Or, put another way, there is really no such thing as a Catholic citizen in general. There are Democratic Catholics, Republican Catholics, liberal Catholics, conservative Catholics, pro-choice Catholics, pro-life Catholics, Catholics for Obama, and Catholics for McCain, Catholics for Clinton, and Catholics for Trump, and so on. While it was widely held that for the longest time the Supreme Court had a "Catholic seat" (and a "Jewish seat" as well), those days are now past. I do not believe that the Catholics on the Court were selected by their respective presidents *because* they were Catholic. Obviously, their Catholicism was not held against them either. Whether they hold the judicial philosophy or have the constitutional understandings that they do *because* of their religious identities is for them or other scholars to say. What matters for me here and now is that by and large the branch charged with safeguarding the nation's political Talmud and interpreting its provisions is in the hands of at least six men and women who a century ago might have been depicted by even a number of respectable politicians and citizens as members of the "foreign horde of papists."

Indeed, of the current Catholic members of the Court, not one was asked during their confirmation hearings anything approaching the sort of questions John F. Kennedy famously felt he had to answer during his bid for the presidency. In conservative circles, it was almost the opposite; namely, people, clearly with a very particular view of the faith's political dimensions, wanted to make sure that the nominees were Catholic enough! My point, by way of inference, is a simple one. There is no such thing as an easily discernible or monolithic Catholic political tradition in the American political scheme today. There is a Catholic history, of course. There are Catholic citizens, of course. But, there is not a Catholic political tradition in the United States that is separable in any meaningful way from the existing American political tradition itself as currently constituted. And that, I have been trying to argue, is a mistake. Simply put, Catholics *should* be different.

Part of Catholic-American political folklore is the story often told in Catholic circles concerning the presidential candidacy of Al Smith in 1928 when he was confronted with the "loyalty" question by an open letter in the *Atlantic Monthly* from a New York lawyer named Charles Marshall. The letter called on Smith to account for the various lines of argument in nineteenth-century papal encyclicals that many thought were "un-American" in their conceptions of liberalism and especially religious freedom. Smith's famous response was said to have been on one version, "Will someone please tell me what the hell an encyclical is?" On another version, the quote went, "I never heard of these bulls and encyclicals and books."[1] Whatever the actual utterance, the point itself was a simple one: namely, Smith could not be viewed as some sort of Roman-Manchurian candidate if he was unaware of even the most visible presentations of Church teaching.

Not content, however, to trust mere inference, Smith responded in a widely distributed and extended letter that was reprinted in full by many major newspapers as well as in the magazine itself. Roundly applauded by the liberal intelligentsia of the day, including the *New Republic*, Smith made the case that Catholics were loyal Americans as evidenced by their service in the First World War and elsewhere, and more or less dismissed any tension between public policy and religion as irrelevant to him as a candidate.[2]

1. McGreevy, *Catholicism and American Freedom*, 149.
2. McGreevy, *Catholicism and American Freedom*, 149.

Whatever good Smith's pronouncement of political independence might have done him in earning new friends from the then-wings of American progressivism, it did not suffice in his bid against the Republican, Herbert Hoover. Certainly, anti-Catholic forces played a role in his defeat as a number of traditionally Democratic states went Republican, but for our purposes here, that is not what matters. What matters is the way in which this event symbolizes in microcosmic form what I will call the dominant Catholic American political tradition. With admitted irony, that dominant "tradition" is best called *assimilation*.

There are a number of places where this story is told well, but I have relied on the work of Philip Gleason. While his books make a more substantial contribution,[3] his brief 2000 article in *Logos* does a nice job in making the basic argument that the Catholic story in the twentieth century is one of an ever deepening "identity crisis" brought about by greater and greater assimilation of both individual Catholics and, more importantly, Catholic institutions. In Gleason's words,

> While I do not anticipate extinction, it seems to me quite clear that the problem has gotten a lot bigger. In the era of World War I, Catholics experienced a striking degree of assimilation, but they also forged a new ideological and institutional basis for Catholic identity. That balance was not maintained at mid-century, when accelerating assimilation found no matching deployment of new internal resources. In the sixties, the old ideological and institutional structures collapsed, and nothing comparable was at hand to replace them. That gave rise to a Catholic identity crisis, which has since modulated into a continuing identity problem.[4]

Of course, it is only a problem if we believe that there is something important about "Catholic identity" such that it should be preserved and extended over time. Gleason's own position in the brief essay certainly suggests this, but it does so there under the mantel of "diversity" and "pluralism," which renders his argument a little too aesthetic for my tastes. In other words, it is all well and good if the existence and persistence of Catholic identity creates a richer and more vibrant cultural landscape in the United States, but that contribution alone would not be enough to warrant a sustained *political* defense. Oddly enough, it would not really provide a good *Catholic* rationale for enhancing and sharpening Catholic identity since that identity is predicated in significant ways on its belief that such an "identity" is, existentially

---

3. See Gleason, *Speaking of Diversity*; Gleason, *Keeping the Faith*.
4. Gleason, "Catholic Church in American," 97.

speaking, the right one to have. The problem, however, with giving strong reasons for maintaining a distinctive Catholic identity or tradition that is not totally absorbed or assimilated beyond recognition into the larger American political culture is that the unassimilated or differentiated tradition itself is not altogether coherent or clear. To mimic a contemporary philosopher, we must ask the following kind of question before moving on much further; namely, *whose Catholic identity, which Catholicism?*

The truth was that Al Smith's Catholicism may have led him to the Democratic Party and its particular ideological orientation, at least in its northeastern variety, but it was a fairly inconsequential element of his political *praxis*. For his liberal supporters, such a failing was all to the good and required for their assent. Broadly stated, they lent their approval to his candidacy *despite* his Catholicism. One must imagine that for such "progressives" it became conceptually ascriptive, like race or gender or ethnic identity—something he was born to rather than a faith or set of ideals that defined him or constituted his being, or something that was purely a personal matter and, hence, of no serious political consequence. Essentially, this was what John F. Kennedy was asked to stipulate to in 1960, and one can easily imagine that such assumptions were made by many American citizens and the majority of the US Senate regarding the confirmation of the Catholic Justices. But, such an approach contradicts the entire argument of this book so far. At its simplest, Al Smith's Catholicism should have mattered, Kennedy's and Cuomo's, and Roberts's, Thomas's, Alito's, Kavanaugh's, and Sotomayor's (and perhaps Gorsuch's) should too, for substantive reasons *not* ascriptive ones. Even more importantly, though, it should matter to Catholic citizens and voters in ways that make it irrelevant what the particular confession of an elected representative is so long as he or she is willing to obey the properly ordered will of the people on matters concerning public policy and the common good. But, for that to happen, believers must not only be faithful, they must be knowledgeable too. In other words, faithful citizens are not born, they are made.

TRADITION AND POLITICAL PRACTICES

There is a large literature on the question of "tradition" that in and of itself could take a chapter or more to unpack. But that would not help move this argument along. Instead, I hope to wade in to the conversation at both a well-respected point on one hand, and what I believe to be a very sound and useful place on the other. In general, I take my philosophic lead from Alasdair MacIntyre and his work, most notably, in *After Virtue*. More importantly, however, for the theological grounding for this section I follow the succinct and insightful work of Terrence W. Tilley in his book *Inventing Catholic Tradition*.[5] While Tilley's and MacIntyre's works share a number of important dimensions and concepts, especially the notion of "practices," Tilley is interested in explicating the idea of "tradition" in a concrete and particular manner, rather than conceptually and philosophically. While epistemological questions are certainly present in Tilley's work, his true goal is a practical one. In the sections following this one, I will try to take that practical work a step or two further in an attempt to move from the particular to the specific. What Tilley names, I will try to call by name and give a proper face to.

To get to Tilley's argument we have to begin with the work of Wittgenstein and those who followed in his rather large wake. Chief among his forerunners is Alasdair MacIntyre. MacIntyre's critical contribution to contemporary philosophy has been his extensive elaboration on the basic idea that all philosophic discourse originates in, and is bounded by, a particular historical context which must, by its very logic, accept certain unargued for or quasi-foundational assumptions in order to proceed in any meaningful way. While a figure like Nietzsche used this sort of insight in his assault on all systems of meaning and moral philosophy, such that every such system became just some version of the "will to power," MacIntyre deftly understands that Nietzsche's own critique was in reality only valid in terms of the Enlightenment's own fallacy. At its simplest, that fallacy was that there was a so-called view or vantage point from "nowhere" that rigorous and careful thinkers could somehow ironically inhabit for the purpose of rendering neutral or unbiased judgments. Because no such place exists, Nietzsche and his later interpreters and students themselves came to the conclusion that the whole enterprise itself was irredeemable. Which, on its own terms, now seems to be the case. What MacIntyre and others asserted, however, was that there was at least one other enterprise that did not begin from the flawed premises that gave the critique its deconstructive power.

"What if we talked less about what some thing *was* and more about what it *did* and was supposed to *do*?" they asked. In other words, rather than asking abstract questions about good and evil, right and wrong, etc., in general to try to determine some *a priori* essence or universal position, what if we started with something more particular and concrete, like questions about what should I do in this particular situation, how should I do it and why should I do it? Certainly, for any individual the answer in any particular situation can simply be because "it feels good," or because "I wanted to," but

---

5. Tilley, *Inventing Catholic Tradition*.

as I argued at length in chapter 3, such claims are ultimately self-defeating if they are to be of any significance or be taken seriously, since to be significant or taken seriously implies that there is someone other than myself that must be persuaded in one way or another—someone to do the "taking," if you will. There is an adage that goes: we are entitled to our own opinions, but not to our own facts. As Taylor so ably demonstrated, questions of significance are the preconstructed horizons or standards against which the quality or value of my actions and arguments are measured against.[6] While they are not static or unchanging over time, they are also not overly elastic or malleable. Simply put, the individual alone does not get to decide what matters or counts as significant. Enter tradition.

MacIntyre's well-known understanding of "tradition"[7] rests on his fundamental and carefully defined notion of "practices." A set of well-defined and substantively related practices extended over time and embodied in an ongoing story or narrative is necessary to constitute a tradition. MacIntyre himself explains the concept in the following manner:

> By a "practice" I am going to mean any coherent and complex form of socially established cooperative human activity through which goods internal to that form of activity are realized in the course of trying to achieve those standards of excellence which are appropriate to, and partially definitive of, that form of activity, with the result that human powers to achieve excellence, and human conceptions of the ends and goods involved are systematically extended.[8]

While his meaning is perhaps plain enough as it is, there are a few items that deserve a little amplification. Among them are the phrases *socially established cooperative human activity* and *systematically extended*. While it is certainly the case that individuals can have routines and even rituals that are self-contained and very demanding, or even highly regulative in terms of their personal behavior, they cannot rise to the level of a "practice" in isolation from other human beings. Furthermore, simply performing certain

---

6. See Taylor, *Ethics of Authenticity*.

7. MacIntyre defines a tradition in the following way: "A living tradition then is an historically extended, socially embodied argument, and an argument precisely in part about the goods which constitute that tradition. Within a tradition the pursuit of the goods extends through generations, sometimes through many generations. Hence the individual's search for his or her good is generally and characteristically conducted within a context defined by those traditions of which the individual's life is a part, and this is true both of the goods which are internal to practices and the goods of a single life." MacIntyre, *After Virtue*, 93.

8. See MacIntyre, *After Virtue*, 83.

acts in the midst of other people performing similar acts on a regular basis does not constitute a "practice" either. For example, a group of men and women may all show up at the gym at 6 a.m. every day and perform the same basic routine of exercises alongside each other year after year. They may even come to know one another and become acquaintances or even friends beyond the gym, but unless they cooperatively establish norms among themselves regarding shared goals, measures of excellence, and a shared history or narrative concerning past achievements, present conditions, and future possibilities regarding their shared activity, it cannot be a practice and, hence, cannot become the basis for a tradition. While the activity may matter very much to the men and women engaging in it and may have wonderful benefits which accrue to the various participants (and maybe even society itself), it can have no greater significance, meaning or durability. Without delineating it here, the analogy I would use would be the distinction Robert Bellah and his colleagues drew between the idea of "community" and a "lifestyle-enclave."[9]

Now the fact that MacIntyre understands practices and, hence, traditions as "socially established" will always be problematic from an epistemological perspective for those who continue to demand, either in good faith or bad faith, a strong foundationalism for their assent to the normative claims and warrants of any particular tradition. However, it is not entirely clear what satisfying that desire would actually mean in any case. Satan believes in God, he is a strong "foundationalist," and yet he rejects God and whatever normative claims such a foundationalism suggest. Even if we could demonstrate to the satisfaction of even the strongest skeptic, the non-emotive validity of any particular normative claim, there is no reason to expect that he or she would be compelled or even able to change a single thing about their behavior. That having been said, the parameters, constraints, obligations, and standards of a particular tradition are logically valid among people who at least share a common vocabulary, set of definitions, and at least some form of "grammar." To the extent that a person explicitly or tacitly agrees to participate in a particular tradition, he or she also surrenders their autonomy to decide independently from others—living, dead, and yet to be born—what practices constitute the tradition and how they are to be judged. MacIntyre puts it this way:

> A Practice involves standards of excellence and obedience to rules as well as the achievement of goods. To enter into a practice is to accept the authority of those standards and the inadequacy of my own performance as judged by them. It is to

---

9. See Bellah et al., *Habits of the Heart*.

subject my own attitudes, choices, preferences and tastes to the standards which currently and partially define the practice ... the standards are not themselves immune from criticism, but nonetheless we cannot be initiated into a practice without accepting the authority of the best standards realized so far.[10]

Whatever reasons one might give for participation in a given tradition and set of practices, and however subjective or emotive those reasons might be in the eyes of others, once one has made some level of commitment to the tradition, he or she loses the ability to independently define the goods and standards that define the practices therein. Sean Connery put it bluntly in the movie *The Untouchables*, when he warned an adversary, "Never bring a knife to a gunfight."

Making our way back from this explication of tradition in general to the idea of a *political* tradition, we rely one more time on MacIntyre who contends that "in the ancient and medieval worlds the creation and sustaining of human communities—of households, cities, nations—is generally taken to be a practice in the sense in which I have defined it."[11] This observation, for anyone who has read Aristotle and Aquinas, seems to be readily apparent and true. What is far less apparent is whether this remains the case in the modern political age. So far, we have neglected any discussion of what is perhaps MacIntyre's most salient contribution to contemporary moral philosophy: the revival, reintroduction, and reiteration of virtue ethics as part of the larger conversations about ethical theory.

At its simplest, the virtues are the habits that must be cultivated and adhered to by participants in traditions if they are to successfully achieve the ends and excellences of the practices, which, in turn, comprise and extend over time the traditions themselves. Since the concern here is with the idea of a political tradition, what will matter for our purposes is a web of "virtues" that taken in combination can be called *civic virtue*. The practice which civic virtue seeks to enact and perfect is, of course, the practice of citizenship. The tradition that the practice of citizenship is meant to extend and sustain is a given political tradition, and, hence, often a particular geographically distinctive political community. Because of the plurality of such traditions, it only stands to reason that the practice of civic virtue itself will vary in terms of content from regime to regime. Hence, the ideal citizen will vary from regime to regime as well. Finally, it is also the case, as Aristotle pointed out so ably, that there will be significant differences between the

---

10. Tilley, *Inventing Catholic Tradition*, 85.

11. Tilley, *Inventing Catholic Tradition*, 83. For an excellent and succinct account of MacIntyre's approach to the idea of tradition, see Kallenberg, "Master Argument."

virtues of the "good man" and the "good citizen," with the notable exception of the "best regime," in which they will be one and the same.[12] Regardless of the particular political tradition or regime type, they all have certain essential elements in common that stem from their existence or pretensions to being traditions; namely, that the role or part of a citizen is one that is learned and must be practiced in order to achieve the goods it offers. Like other practices, the standards for excellence are external to the individual participant. The American political tradition and regime are not exceptional in this regard.

The closing argument of the previous chapter, however, depicted the practice of citizenship in the United States in the antebellum period as exceptional in its minimalism, contending that the political tradition *by that time, if not at its inception, centered around austere conceptions of private property, possessive self-interested individualism, and fierce and merciless competition meant to produce material abundance and growth within the context of a very limited conception of governing and political obligation.* Compared and contrasted to almost any previous political tradition, the practice of citizenship implied here would have been viewed as a degenerate one. What virtually all other historical regimes, regardless of their particular goals, natures, or forms, would have asked their respective citizens to reject as antithetical to the common good of the particular regime, became in essence the American ideal. Now certainly almost all historical regimes failed in one way or another to avoid the corruption of the ideal as evidenced by the perpetual cycle of decay and decline, but none that I know of thought it wise to reject explicitly the ideal. Even the infamous advice Machiavelli gave to his *Prince* was predicated by the notion of the prince "learning how not to be good" rather than simply rejecting the notion of the good prince altogether. Furthermore, one could never imagine the republican Machiavelli giving that same advice to the citizenry itself. Yet, this is somehow by intent or default where the logic of the American political tradition had led.

For Sheldon Wolin, and for myself as well, this can be broadly understood as the by-product of the revolution of 1787.[13] Though there is certainly a pejorative and even incendiary subtext to this characterization, I do not want to rehash the more detailed argument behind the implied claim here since I have done that in a number of other places.[14] Instead, I would like to lay out the coincident narrative that accompanies the characterization as

---

12. Aristotle, *Politics*, bk. 7.

13. See Wolin, *Presence of the Past*; Duncan, *Anti-Federalists*.

14. See Duncan, *Anti-Federalists*, as well as Duncan, "Southern Agrarians, Progress, and the Tragic Voice," 3–46; Duncan, "Lincoln's Theocentric Turn," 508–39.

plainly as possible while stipulating at the start to the contested nature of the premise that the adoption of the Constitution represented a revolution. Now, indeed, this was a bloodless revolution, at least until 1861, but it was a *revolution* nonetheless insofar as it saw the displacement and virtual destruction of one political tradition and its attendant practices and virtues and its replacement with another. Broadly speaking, I have argued that pre-1787 America was hermeneutically "communitarian" and "civic republican" in its order and orientation and that in the post-Constitution scheme the hermeneutic was better described as "liberal-individualist." The former was marked by decentralization, diversity, and a very robust, even though inegalitarian, participatory-democratic ethos. The latter more by centralization, uniformity, and hierarchy. The former sprang from the history, circumstances, and corresponding political culture. The latter was a function of ideology, artifice, and invention. The terminology Wolin adopts for these phenomena is "tending" and "intending." His claim is that these "refer broadly to two persistent modes of thinking about and practicing politics which first confronted each other during the ratification of the Constitution."[15]

He goes on to argue that "ratification might be thought of as a contest in which the intending conception triumphed, while the tending conception was so deeply wounded by the encounter that its viability remained in doubt for most of the two centuries that followed."[16] Rich and powerful, Wolin's argument in simplified form is that the Founders displaced numerous organically developed state and local political cultures and traditions in the name of what he calls the "master idea" of a consolidated union.[17] Since there was no tradition to sustain this idea, and, hence, no practices associated with it that would mark the standards of excellence for would be citizens, they had to be generated *de novo* and without precedent. In turn, this generative work fell to those who created the new construct and came in the form of *The Federalist Papers*. Those now well-known essays, however, were not *descriptive*, but rather *prescriptive*. They represented an attempt to constitute reality rather than explain it. Since there was no one who had actually experienced or lived that theoretical reality, their task of legitimation was a highly complicated one. In simplified form, the newly established "people" of "we the people" had to be persuaded that the new constitutionalism was the logical historical climax of the events set in motion in 1630 and culminating in the document of 1776, despite all appearances to the contrary. In Wolin's words,

15. Wolin, *Presence of the Past*, 82.
16. Wolin, *Presence of the Past*, 82.
17. Wolin, *Presence of the Past*, 84.

> *The Federalist* furnished an exegesis of it, these were not solutions to a political vacuum but the superimposition of a new form of politics, national politics, on top of political life forms that, at the time, did not represent local politics because there was virtually no national politics to which they could be compared. Ratification of the new constitution necessarily signified the subjugation of other forms of politics. The myth of The Founding belongs not to the archetype of Athena springing full-blown from the brow of Zeus but instead a muted version of the fratricidal story of Romulus.[18]

While perhaps the even "muted" image might be a little overdrawn when compared to the mass fratricide that would come during the terror following the Revolution of 1789, the metaphoric import is apt on a number of levels, broadly speaking. While the Second American Founding was not literally predicated on a murder, it did depend on destruction of the Schumpeterian variety in terms of the eradication of a way of life and political identity.[19] In addition, it did so indirectly in the name of an empire building scheme that was not only foreign to the American political tradition until that time, but indeed represented for many of those who brought the revolution of '76 to its eventual conclusion the very antithesis of their original intention in undertaking the struggle in the first place. While subterfuge is better than outright repression in terms of the physical carnage and loss the latter would have meant, the outcome still represented its own kind of violent departure from the extant political consensus of the day. Furthermore, though I cannot argue the point here, I do believe the case can be made that the paradigm shift set in motion by the radical displacement of the Articles of Confederation begot the constitutional contradictions and theoretical fissures which became the fault lines leading to the Civil War just a political generation later. Bracketing for now the importance of the Thirteenth and Fifteenth Amendments, the real engine of federal power and consolidation was of course the Fourteenth Amendment, which represented the beginning of the final stage of victory for the nascent Whig vision for American political development set in motion, but only imagined, by Hamilton and Madison and foreshadowed by Lincoln as early as 1838 in his Lyceum Address. Why am I belaboring this point here?

Because it is critical to understand that the *neutral* constitutionalism which gave rise to "liberty of contract" and "substantive due process" as described by Gillman in the previous chapter was in fact part of the whole

---

18. Wolin, *Presence of the Past*, 87.
19. See Schumpeter, *Capitalism, Socialism, Democracy*.

cloth of the "intending" vision of Alexander Hamilton and his compatriots (keeping in mind that neutrality always benefits the strong rather than the weak when all is said and done). To bring the novel ideal (in an affirmative way) of a *commercial republic* into existence from its highly disreputable place in the long history of republican theories concerning the relationship between luxury and civic corruption was no mean feat of either imagination or will. It required the creation of a brand-new language and set of descriptions whose linguistic agility and rapid-fire adoption (in historical terms) would be enough even to make Richard Rorty blush. Under the seemingly progressive banner of a "new science of politics," Hamilton and his fellow travelers sought to create "new opportunities for [the exercise of] wealth, power, and intellect"[20] that were checked by existing political structures and mores to the detriment of national glory. Wolin's description of the two approaches to politics represented by his categories of "tending" and "intending" are important to this conversation, and so I quote him at length to help frame further the argument for a rupture in the American political tradition:

> Tending inclines toward a democratic conception of political life, intending toward an authoritarian conception as the nineteenth century understood the term: one who loves the principle of authority, that is the right to command and enforce obedience.

I begin with a simple dictionary definition of tending: to apply oneself to looking after another, as when we tend a garden or tend to the sick. It implies active care of things close at hand, not mere solicitude. Active care is not, however, a synonym for expert knowledge. Expert knowledge is typically predicated upon attitudes of detachment, upon disavowing personal involvement and disregarding historical associations. Perhaps skill would be a better prerequisite, but the crucial point is that tendance is tempered by a feeling of concern for objects whose nature requires that they be treated as historical and biographical beings. The beings are such as to need regular attention from someone who is concerned about their well-being and is sensitive to historical needs. Going one step further, we might say that proper tendance requires attentiveness to differences between beings within the same general class:

> What does it mean practically? The idea of intending is one that centers politics around practices, that is around habits of

---

20. Wolin, *Presence of the Past*, 91.

competence or skill that are routinely required if things are to be taken care of.[21]

Those who embraced the politics of *intending* generated a new vocabulary that seemed on its face to be apolitical, according to Wolin, and included the following kinds of terms found repeatedly in *The Federalist Papers*: "'systematical,' 'efficient,' 'well-administered,' and 'energy.'"[22] All of these were designed to project an image of disinterested rationalism. However, the substantive import of this "new science" was the radical undermining of the existing political tradition and culture and the replacement by it of a new order and a revolutionary vision that saw diversity and to a great extent the decentralized democratic states as the barriers to national greatness and power. Again from Wolin:

> Weakness was thus associated with difference—the different governments of the separate states, different policies on commerce, taxation, money, militias, and debtors. Difference presented a problem because it did not comport with the Founders' conception of power. Difference signified exception, anomaly, local peculiarities, and a thousand other departures from the uniformity that a certain kind of power prefers. Difference rejects the notion of a single narrative history and a unifying single purpose. It favors a pluralistic conception of history, or histories, rather than history. Difference is not about a unified collective self but about the biography of a place in which different beings are trying to live together.[23]

And so it is that we are in some ways back where this book began, only now with a firmer sense of the *politics* of the American liberal tradition as compared to its *philosophic* development. That the power and energy so absorbed and established would eventually be used to produce the so-called neutral state was not simply the natural outcome of the logic of Locke, but instead an active choice on the part of powerful men with a particular vision for American political development. Their *intentionality* required the creation of a new "tradition" with a new language, grammar, narrative, symbolism, and so on. Eventually this "tradition" would produce what are now familiar tropes in American politics, constitutionalism, law, culture, and so forth that have been hinted at in the arguments made in previous chapters but that need a different book to unpack fully. Among the most important

---

21. Wolin, *Presence of the Past*, 87–89.
22. Wolin, *Presence of the Past*, 94.
23. Wolin, *Presence of the Past*, 96–97.

changes the new political "science" had to foster was the creation of a new type of citizen; Wolin describes this in the following way:

> *The Federalist* had to invent a new and abstract conception of the citizen, a citizen who would be national in character, an unmediated subject designed for a politics of intendment. . . . But first such a citizen had to be extricated from the political culture of intendment and to be the object of a new form of power emanating from the center. . . . The new power would regulate him, tax him, and legislate for him without passing through the intermediary authority of the states; it would institute its own agencies, courts, and officials for that purpose. At the same time the political nature of the new citizen would be diminished. His political nature would be confined to periodic elections once every two, four, or six years.[24]

To say all of this is not to say that what has developed was somehow inevitable or preordained despite the continuing appeal of a peculiar kind of Whig-Hegelian *ethos* that seems to hold sway over the general American mind till this day. There were critical points, historically speaking, when things might have gone a different way, for better or for worse. But they didn't. The North won the Civil War, the US was victorious in the two world wars, we survived the Great Depression and the Cold War without a revolution and managed to weather the upheavals of the 1960s with the basic structures of the new regime intact and extended in each instance. The events of September 11, 2001, and the political aftermath have only served to consolidate the tradition's victory and embolden both political parties to further extend the reach and power of the central government, albeit in different spheres occasionally. The upshot of all of this has been that neoliberal hegemony in the United States appears to be alive, well, and, by and large, unchallenged in any serious way. To cast this in a religious idiom, there is but one sword here now. However, if all that has been argued so far in this book has any validity, then the risks to such a regime grow in direct proportion to its increased confidence and increasing inability to articulate a rationale for its continued existence. As I turn to the next section of this chapter, I believe that the words of John Courtney Murray, SJ, should serve as a warning to those of us who still believe in much of the promise of the first new nation. In Murray's words,

> In any case, it is true to say that a nation cannot survive the tests of terrestrial life without a public philosophy, least of all in this our day when the very bases even of terrestrial life are being

---

24. Wolin, *Presence of the Past*, 98.

called into question. *And what is not true will somehow fail to work. Hence one does well in America today to raise the issue of survival.*[25]

TRADITION, INVENTION, AND A RETURN TO TENDING

While the tone above certainly betrays a certain sort of judgment concerning those who practiced the politics of *intending*, it does not follow that I believe that their motives were nefarious or lacking in public spiritedness. In a much earlier essay, I explored a reading of the founding by the students of the highly influential political philosopher, Leo Strauss, that argued as much.[26] Through their readings of the second founding, I argued that the framers deployed language intended to persuade their revolutionary counterparts of the democratic nature of their constitutionalism while at the same time creating a system that would ultimately empower and perpetuate elite rule. Unlike Beard or others who wanted to see in this move a class conspiracy of the Marxist variety,[27] I believe that the line from the movie *Crimson Tide* is apt. Delivered by the commander played by Gene Hackman to his number two, played by Denzel Washington, Hackman explains that the Navy exists to "defend democracy, not to practice it." In other words, it is entirely possible and, historically speaking, highly probable that the founders had serious reservations about both the practical truth of the Declaration of Independence's assertion of human equality as well as the democratic political implications that seemed to flow so readily from it.[28] In turn, a generous case might be made that given their doubts about democratic-equality and assuming a deep love of country, that they indeed saw themselves as centralizing power and accruing authority to in effect save us from ourselves.

Whether, *pace* Woodrow Wilson, freemen need guardians[29] or not was certainly an open question in the eighteenth century, and for many may remain so today. While in the context of their day the second founders may have been the political radicals that Wolin and I claim they were, they were not even close to being such in the larger scheme of human political history.

25. Murray, *We Hold These Truths*, 100. Emphasis mine.
26. Duncan, "Democratic Posturing and Peculiar Liberalism," 281–311.
27. See Beard, *Economic Interpretation*.
28. See Wood, *Radicalism of the American Revolution*.
29. See then-president-elect Woodrow Wilson's essay, "Freemen Need No Guardians," first published in *Fortnightly Review* in 1913 and reprinted in Levy, *Political Thought in America*, 350–55.

Reasons of State, if you will, are almost always invoked under the guise of an extreme emergency or existential threat (real or perceived) for the use of extra-constitutional, extra-legal, and even extra-moral actions. This, I will argue later, is the general problem or dilemma caused by contemporary forms of idolatry or, in secular terms, the *fetishism of the state*. But, given the fact that the American political tradition that the second founders gave life to is now not "new" but normal, creating an alternative tradition and narrative is problematic, to say the least. Even if the reader is willing to accept Fr. Murray's claim that "what is not true will somehow fail to work." And even if the claims throughout this book suggesting that America's general account of itself is, at the end of the day, untrue, it is still the case that we have managed to get many of the answers to important questions "right." It remains the case that you cannot beat something with nothing.

Despite the conversions of some well-known Americans like Orestes Brownson, it is simply the case that there was little to no such thing as an American Catholic tradition for the first hundred years of the republic because of both the relatively small numbers of Catholics prior to the mass immigrations of the mid-nineteenth century and because those who were here, for the most part, were viewed as historical anachronisms. The reigning American religious narrative viewed the Reformation as the start of the modern world, intellectually speaking, and Catholicism as a remnant of some dark authoritarian period that would soon become extinct. Indeed, most Catholics had nothing good to say about America and its liberal philosophy and were constantly warned by the Church hierarchy to remain suspicious and on guard against the creeping modernism in their midst. Industrialization and the emergence of full-blown American capitalism only served to heighten religious and social tensions and to transform them into political ones. It is no wonder that the immigrant-church and its transplanted members engaged in what can best be characterized as "defensive" political initiatives rather than proactive ones. By both virtue and necessity, the Church and its religious created institutions and organizations like schools, social service providers, charities, and workingmen's associations or unions to both meet the unmet needs of their mostly poor and at risk members as well as to insulate the faithful from the more pernicious assimilative measures being pushed by the dominant culture and power structures of the day. Over time, both the need and the opportunity to compete for actual political power would be realized, but as noted with politicians like Al Smith and then later on John F. Kennedy, the price for success would be the rejection of any hint of religious sectarianism or particularism.

This tension between insularity and cultural preservation on the one hand and integration and assimilation on the other, is among the chief impediments to the creation of a distinctively Catholic American political tradition because it represents what strikes us as an illogical paradox: the desire to be different but the same, if you will. However, for Catholic thinkers who enter many conversations with a both/and rather than an either/or mindset, it is far easier to make sense of this desire. But for those monistic patriots who coined the motto "from many, one," such anti-reductionism could not be tolerated—both figuratively and literally. For them, practices and ideas that could not be suppressed or co-opted would be privatized. Long before John Rawls gave it academic credibility, "public reason" was the operating construct of political debate in America insofar as religious arguments *qua* religious arguments, especially those associated with Catholicism, concerning public policy were rejected as inadmissible in the public sphere. Unlike Rawls, though, his philosophical and political predecessors were not nearly so polite when it came to the question of "comprehensive doctrines," especially those of the Thomist variety.

John McGreevy's fine book *Catholicism and American Freedom* does an excellent job in chapters 4–6 at laying bare the widespread and surprisingly fashionable anti-Catholic nature of American society in the first half of the twentieth century, and I urge any readers who may be less familiar with this period in American history to review it through his eyes. Many, if not most, of the leading intellectuals of the day expressed again and again with varying degrees of vitriol, disdain, and condescension the thought that Catholicism was philosophically, ecclesiastically, theologically, and ultimately politically incompatible with Americanism. And, by extension, so too were any citizens who took their Catholicism seriously. Such notables as John Dewey, Horace Kallan, Reinhold Niebuhr, Albert Einstein, Bertrand Russell, George Boas, and Sidney Hook, to name a few, chimed in and accepted in whole or in part the arguments made by writers like Paul Blanshard (originally writing in the *Nation*) in his widely read, anti-Catholic texts: *American Freedom and Catholic Power* (1949) and *Communism, Democracy, and Catholic Power* (1951). In McGreevy's words,

> Blanshard claimed that "the Catholic problem is still with us." His solution was the formation of a "resistance movement" to counter the "antidemocratic social policies of the hierarchy and . . . every intolerant or separatist or un-American feature of those policies." Blanshard's second treatment of the matter, *Communism, Democracy, and Catholic Power*, defined Catholicism and Soviet communism as parallel threats to American democracy.[30]

---

30. McGreevy, *Catholicism and American Freedom*, 166.

Now it is important to note (as McGreevy does)[31] that the word "democracy" does not appear in either of the foundational documents of the Catholic social tradition, *Rerum Novarum* or *Quadragesimo Anno*. It was also the case that the institutional Church and some of its representatives had, through their own doctrinaire lack of humility, dogmatic assertions, and uncharitable criticism within the American context, created conditions ripe for backlash. However, by the time of Blanshard's publication, it was also true that tens of thousands of American Catholics had fought, suffered, and died for their country in two world wars, had joined political parties, voted, run for office, and were actively working hard, paying taxes, and raising their families as full-blooded American citizens, including one young former PT boat commander who was serving his third term in Congress and would soon become President of the United States. While some of them were no doubt participating loyally in their society *despite* their religious confession, many were doing so *because* of it. In most cases, it is safe to assume that there was little to no dissonance for the typical Catholic citizen and that whatever incompatibility the American intelligentsia saw between their Catholicism and their devotion to country was surprisingly imaginary or metaphysical for such self-proclaimed pragmatists. What was also clear, however, was that to get from 1950 to the elections of 1960, some important intellectual work was going to need to be done to combat the perception that the Catholicism of American Catholics was not foreign or out of place—let alone antithetical to—the American political tradition rightly understood. This effort would require an inventive and creative *re-description* of both AMERICA[32] and Catholicism, as well as what I will argue was at least a partial return to the politics of *tending*. The task was undertaken by a number of thinkers and activists, but two deserve special mention for their work on this front: the European philosopher Jacques Maritain (whom I will deal with in the next chapter), and John Courtney Murray, SJ, himself.

Before proceeding, however, there is a small, but important theoretical detour that needs to be made regarding the idea of *tradition* itself. In his book *God, Philosophy and Universities*, Alasdair MacIntyre tells us that

---

31. McGreevy, *Catholicism and American Freedom*, 197.

32. The African American literary theorist Houston Baker Jr. writes "America" in all capital letters in his *Blues, Ideology, and Afro-American Literature*, asserting, "Writing AMERICA in capitals enables one to distinguish between an *idea* and what Edmundo O'Gorman describes in one of the epigraphs to this chapter as a 'lump of cosmic matter.' As an idea, AMERICA represents a kind of 'designated' entity. . . . From an Ellisonian perspective, the sign AMERICA is a willful act which always substitutes for a state description. The substitution imposes problematical unity and stasis on an ever-changing American scene." Baker, *Blues*, 66. For a deeper dive into Baker Jr.'s work, see Duncan, "*Blues* Voice of Houston Baker, Jr.," 281–311.

> traditions are defined retrospectively. It is only on looking back that the unity of a project to which over considerable stretches of time there have been many different contributors, each with their own goals and concerns, becomes apparent. When it does, it is sometimes because of some challenge to a tradition from outside it, a challenge that awakens in those whose lives and work are informed by that tradition a new awareness, both of their shared inheritance and of the issues and problems that they now have to address, if they are to sustain their tradition in the future.[33]

Hence, we can say that a "tradition" is at once a conscious matter and a subconscious matter, socially constructed and true, embodied and theorized, created and evolving, a solution and a problem, all at the same time potentially—unless it is "dead." In the binary world of American pragmatism, such a thing is almost incoherent insofar as for each "and" above they would substitute an "or." Rooted in an ideology of progress where the question is simply whether something either works or it doesn't, the binary mind understands "history" as an account of what was done, but has little truck with "tradition," which is about being, or, more precisely, *how* to be in the world as compared to simply *what* we should do. The primary descriptors for tradition rightly understood are fullness, faithfulness, growth, or coherency. It is, as I will explain more fully later, dialogical, not dialectical. As such, I will suggest that any important or meaningful tradition will be one associated with what we called *tending* rather than *intending* above. To get there, though, it is important to deal with what is an important possible objection to this line of reasoning; namely, the question of *invention*.

There are different ways to ask this question but they each tend to revolve around a sort of existential puzzle that is begged in MacIntyre's first sentence above with the word "retrospectively." Having spent much of this book arguing that despite serious inconsistencies in its theoretical and practical composition, the austere liberalism captured by Hartz and Macpherson has maintained and solidified its domination of the American political imagination, any attempt to "find," "reclaim," or "invent" some possibly radical alternative "tradition" could be seen as intellectual sophistry. There too is an ethical dimension to this question that Philip Abbott alludes to in his book on social invention and the idea of community in America, which he puts like this: "Critics are correct to condemn orientations in which the existing structure of society is treated with disdain and in which inventors

---

33. MacIntyre, *God, Philosophy, Universities*, 165.

of new forms are given moral license."[34] Taken together, these two issues can be restated in the following manner: Is it really possible to generate a new tradition given the entrenched historical, sociological, and psychological nature of the extant tradition, and, even if it is possible, would such a thing be both justifiable and desirable? Obviously, by this point in the book it is clear that I think the answer to all these questions is yes. As a theorist, my degree of confidence about the latter questions is certainly higher than it is about the first one (and given the number of previous failures and the relative weakness of most contemporary efforts to overturn the current hegemonic consensus, rightfully so), but it is also the case that I am something of a weak determinist regarding the possibility of change. Simply put, I do not believe that the current American "public philosophy" (to use Murray's term) can sustain the normative or political ends which it is supposed to serve indefinitely. Unfortunately, I am far less sanguine about what may follow in its wake, but fear that V. F. Calverton's work in the middle of the twentieth century might be instructive to revisit (especially in the age of Donald Trump).[35]

Although he was ostensibly speaking about the history of science, Thomas Kuhn's still important book argues about "revolutionary" change in the following way:

> In these and other ways besides, normal science repeatedly goes astray. And when it does—when, that is, the profession can no longer evade anomalies that subvert the existing tradition of scientific practice—then begin the extraordinary investigations that lead the profession at last to a new set of commitments, a new basis for the practice of science. The extraordinary episodes in which that shift of professional commitments occurs are the ones known in this essay as scientific revolutions. They are the tradition-shattering complements to the tradition-bound activity of normal science.[36]

He goes on to note important examples of this and concludes about the process that "each of them necessitated the community's rejection of one time-honored scientific theory in favor of another incompatible with it.

34. Abbott, *Seeking Many Inventions*, 3.

35. V. F. Calverton was the longtime editor of the *Modern Quarterly* who argued that the American lower-middle-class mindset was too imbued with the "pioneer spirit" and too easily manipulated by bankers and industrialists to make collective action possible. As such, this rendered them much more pliable and open to "collectivization" from the top, i.e., "fascism." For an excellent full-length account of Calverton's thought see Abbott, *Leftward Ho!*

36. Kuhn, *Structure of Scientific Revolutions*, 6.

... And each transformed the scientific imagination."[37] In this way Kuhn is able to create space in his understanding of paradigms for what we might call disruptive as well as developmental change. While this approach was certainly difficult to adjust to in the natural and physical sciences due to the emphasis on incrementalism, it is even more problematic in the political world and more so once again in the theological world because such thinking goes to the very identity of a people and even to individuals. Whatever the consequences have been for authoring or ushering in a new paradigm or holding steadfast to the old in the wake of the new for scientists, they pale in comparison for those who have done so in the political or religious realms. Terms like "schism," "insurrection," "heretic," and "traitor" are often deployed in the discourse surrounding radical change in those realms—Copernicus and Galileo notwithstanding—and such terms often lead to suppression, repression, exile, excommunication, imprisonment, torture, and even death. Benjamin Barber once said at a political science conference that "since 1789 democracy had everywhere been born in a river of blood and midwifed by death."[38] Dramatic? Yes. True? Mostly, yes.

Certainly, this is due in large measure to the very real assault on the material interests of a particular elite or, dare we say it, ruling class that radical political and social change often entails. However, it is also the case that there is great risk at the psychological level for the average person who may find him or herself being told that they have on some level been living a "lie." Whatever the usefulness of concepts like "false consciousness" or "bad faith" have at the level of political theory or philosophy for helping draw the subjects of those accusations toward a new rationality, they contain within them the very real possibility of psychological and spiritual damage. As such, we should not be surprised when they resist radical innovation or social/political/religious invention in the name of their nonmaterial interests. This is perhaps why changes in these areas are often cast in the language of systemic, developmental, or perhaps dialectical modification or adjustment rather than sharper more radical terms. Simply put, there are great benefits to continuity regardless of its (often relative) truth-value. Discontinuity creates anxiety and insecurity and can become paralyzing and even depressing. Think here about the choice that Morpheus gives Neo (Neil) in the movie *The Matrix*: "You take the blue pill, the story ends. You wake up in your bed and believe whatever you want to believe. You take the red pill, you stay in wonderland and I show you how deep the rabbit hole goes." While

---

37. Kuhn, *Structure of Scientific Revolutions*, 6.
38. Barber, "Rousseau's Bloody Hand," 1.

Enlightenment thinkers would like us to believe that most men and women would take the "red pill," the fact is the "blue" one has a lot of appeal.

Now in the case at hand, this sort of disruptive work is doubly difficult because there are two well-entrenched paradigms or long traditions, Americanism and Catholicism, that must each be changed significantly while not provoking the insurmountable backlash that overt radical discontinuity might evoke. While Brownson provides us with one model, it is not wholly useful because of his seeming comfort with what we might call a discontinuous self. The real master of this, as I will try to show in a few minutes, is Murray himself. However, before turning to his important project, it is necessary to briefly explore this approach in relationship to the idea of tradition in the realm of religion itself rather than in science or politics. This is because while we are relatively used to the idea of revolutionary "discoveries" in science that fundamentally change the way we look at the world, e.g., heliocentric vs. geocentric, or with political revolutions and international conflict as ushering in new modes of order and thinking, religion remains perhaps the most resistant to the appearance of change, if not to change itself. Hegelianism (and Francis Fukuyama)[39] aside, the sheer degree of "vertical" pluralism (historical differences) between regime types and political forms and "horizontal" pluralism (the diversity among existing states and political regime types) makes it very difficult for all but the most myopic and intransigent thinker to believe that any sort of large-scale political monism and uniformity are really possible. In other words, there will always be competing and probably incommensurable narratives at the international level, politically speaking. But, the idea of diversity and perhaps even of incommensurability existing *within* a particular and long-standing world religion like Catholicism strikes many believers (as well as critics) as a very real threat to the integrity and viability of the faith itself (though obviously for different reasons). Intradenominational conflict about what are often cast as timeless things is almost always thought to lead to schism, reformation, and even outright holy wars, not revision. Explaining both why this is the case and how it can be countered is the task that Tilley set for himself in an important little book titled: *Inventing Catholic Tradition*.

In Tilley's opening chapter, he sets the stage by asking the simple question of whether traditions are made or given. His answer is that they are "neither made nor found, yet both constructed and given."[40] He is quick, however, to point out that among the faithful, this position is highly problematic because "the position that traditions are 'found' is practically

---

39. See Fukuyama, *End of History and the Last Man*.
40. Tilley, *Inventing Catholic Tradition*, 15.

ubiquitous among people who dwell in strong traditions."[41] It is in that very image of "finding" that many modern and postmodern thinkers anchor their pejorative and/or condescending critiques (regardless of political affiliation) of religion and faith as an ossified, uncritical drug (Marx) or crutch for weak and fearful creatures (Freud) who are afraid to embrace either the power of reason (Kant or Mill) or their own will to power (Nietzsche or Rorty) because it suggests that we are inclined to subservience and slavishness rather than authentic and rational individualism and moral agency. Tilley puts it more politely when he writes that the goals of many scholars post Enlightenment "are to understand traditions, often in order to undermine them, rather than dwell in them."[42] While the ability to take apart or deconstruct a given tradition or belief system in a critical manner is of course a time-honored and important skill for theorists, philosophers, and social critics to have in the name of knowledge and understanding, the epistemological ground on which many of them have stood has shifted beneath their feet in ways they have only begun to acknowledge, especially in regard to religion.[43] As Leo Strauss taught us quite a while ago, even if we agreed with the statement "everything was historically relative," the assertion itself could not escape its own grasp.[44] In Tilley's words, "while one might participate in one tradition rather than another, to take a position beyond all traditions is incoherent."[45] As such, intellectual honesty and personal integrity now demands that critics at least explain what ground they are occupying and hopefully even why they have selected that territory rather than somewhere else before we should take them seriously. This, I have argued elsewhere, was what I took to be liberalism's original impetus.[46] In any case, the simple point here is that both the "true believers" and the self-styled men and women of reason need to rethink their positions if they truly want to understand rather than merely judge.

---

41. Tilley, *Inventing Catholic Tradition*, 15.

42. Tilley, *Inventing Catholic Tradition*, 18.

43. For an excellent analysis of this phenomenon, see Cahoy, "Sense of Place." In that essay, Cahoy argues for a four-point thesis that he explains in the following way: "1. The modern university is rooted in a distinctly modern, specifically Enlightenment epistemology that makes the role of place irrelevant. 2. This epistemology makes the idea of a church-related college a virtual oxymoron. 3. The postmodern critique calls into question this modern epistemology, arguing that knowing, sense-making, is always related to one's location, i.e. place. 4. This opens up the possibility of rethinking the idea and rationale of the church-related college." Cahoy, "Sense of Place," 75.

44. See Strauss, *Natural Right and History*.

45. Tilley, *Inventing Catholic Tradition*, 19.

46. See Duncan, "Liberalism and the Challenge of *Fight Club*," 119–44.

Speaking once again to the traditionalists rather than the mere critics, it is simply the case that "if that which is passed on as tradition has to be passed on 'unchanged and uncorrupted' over long periods of time, then there will be no concrete traditions that will pass the test."[47] While the critic of tradition might be tempted to say good riddance, she should be careful of what she asks for since if such a thing was literally possible, what we would have is not the Age of Reason, but the time of Babel. Even the tradition that believes it stands opposed to tradition has rules and practices, ironically enough. To be faithful to a tradition, Tilley tells us, "may require extensive reworking of the tradition if the tradition is to be received in a new context.... Whether intentionally or not, traditions, to endure, seem to require reconstruction, revisions, and reinvention as circumstances change."[48] Such an enterprise, however, raises important questions about both authenticity and credibility for obvious reasons. And, there is no easy formula for getting it right, nor is there any way to avoid unleashing unintended and potentially disturbing consequences as a result of the changes. An ironic but telling example might be the *political* consequences of Luther's theological and ecclesiastical "revisions" to the Catholic tradition; not in terms of the Reformation, which was itself probably unintended, but in terms of the post-Wittenberg demands for new forms of political equality which Luther himself explicitly condemned as not being in accord with his intentions. That having been said, it is simply the case that a viable living tradition will have to change and adapt to project itself into the future and the *how* of its doing so will make a real difference in the eventual success or failure of the tradition to flourish and thrive in its new context. Push too hard and you get schism; push too little and you court irrelevancy.

The Jesuits have a term that Tilley does not deploy directly, but implies repeatedly called "creative fidelity." Because, as Tilley notes, "there cannot be a theological discourse free from contemporary signifying practices" because it is always "enculturated";[49] it is simply true that the tradition will be enacted differently at different times and places and that this will foster mutations and modifications in the practices of believers and the institutions who share in it. Imagination, he argues, is among the most important traits that those who seek to keep a given tradition relevant and pertinent in varied historical, cultural, and political contexts. Rather than seeing such changes as diminutions or betrayals of the tradition, we need to see them as modes of translation and extension across both space and time. The

---

47. Tilley, *Inventing Catholic Tradition*, 27.
48. Tilley, *Inventing Catholic Tradition*, 29.
49. Tilley, *Inventing Catholic Tradition*, 42.

exemplar here is the missionary not the monastic. The name Tilley gives to those who move such changes in the tradition is the "transgressor." Those who do it well he says have "to know how to violate boundaries in ways that others can understand and incorporate into their practices."[50] Echoing Wolin above though, Tilley is quick to point out that: "Save for manipulation, overbearing authority, and other similar circumstances, that enable one person or a small group to have extraordinary power to shape a culture, traditions cannot be *intentionally* made."[51]

This, it seems, pushes Tilley squarely in the direction of "tending" and a little later we know he is there when he asserts that "engaging in specific practices learned in local communities is the way in which even universal claims are learned. The universal necessarily is enculturated and learned through the particular."[52] This point will become critical in the next chapter through the transgressive ideal of *universal particularism*. There I will use this idea to reorient and reinvent American liberalism while remaining faithful to the philosophy's most worthy and defensible contribution to the good society. However, before undertaking that argument, serious attention has to be paid to the thinker and original "transgressor" who cleared the space and made such a move even possible by helping make sure that Catholicism was indeed safe for what I would call the authentic practice of American liberalism rightly understood.

THE MYSTICAL BODY, SELF-EVIDENT TRUTHS, AND A PUBLIC CHURCH

Now to be fair, the institutional Roman Catholic Church of the first half of the twentieth century and many of its apologists were rightfully suspected of harboring anti-democratic prejudices and, in the European setting at least, of supporting authoritarian and even protofascist regimes and ideologies. Despite the fact that almost a century and a half had passed since the events of 1789 and its aftermath, the bitter taste of Jacobin-style democratic "reform" was still fully present on tongues of the Church leadership. Combine this with the elite-driven anti-Catholicism of leading American liberal intellectuals and the rise in the east of a truly Godless communism and the reactionary option and flight into the arms of dictators offering state support, protection of the faith, and privileged status for the faithful is not difficult to understand. While it is the case that I, along with Charles Taylor,

---

50. Tilley, *Inventing Catholic Tradition*, 47.
51. Tilley, *Inventing Catholic Tradition*, 50. Emphasis mine.
52. Tilley, *Inventing Catholic Tradition*, 59.

suggested previously that the challenges of modernity helped the Church become a better church, it is also the case that this is a view that is far easier to hold once the very real existential threat has been successfully navigated and survived than it is when the actual crisis is upon it. The old dictum that whatever doesn't kill you makes you stronger can obviously only be appreciated by those who have not been killed. That having been said, at least two things were true both theologically and practically on my reading of the times as the world approached mid-century. First, if the "Good News" of the gospel stood in need of dictators and thugs to sustain its place in the world, the Church and its people had bigger problems than modernity to contend with. Second, as the United States moved into a position of prominence on the world stage with a Catholic population approaching 25 percent, the Church courted irrelevancy and indifference if it pursued a strategy simply of antagonism and alienation with regard to it. For better or worse, the fifty years between 1899's *Testem benevolentiae nostrae* and the launch of the Bumper V-2 from Cape Canaveral (not to mention the start of the Korean Conflict) rendered the question of "Americanism" one that could not be resolved simply by a Papal decree.

Jay Dolan provides a quick overview of the Church's basic position regarding matters of church and state at the turn of the last century as still clinging to the medieval ideal of a Christian society, led by a Christian ruler, who understood the subservient position of the political to the spiritual realms and acted accordingly. History, of course, was vastly more complicated all of the time, but the implications derived from the ideal gave rise to a number of derivative propositions that would never pass muster in the American context even in its most theocratic iterations during the early colonial period in Massachusetts. Among those would be the notion that there was but one "true religion" (Catholicism); that error had no rights and therefore the state acting on Christian principles could repress false doctrine and even belief if needed; and that toleration was not a moral principle but a matter of political expediency, i.e., "tolerance whenever necessary and intolerance whenever possible."[53] All of this taken together was, in fact, thoroughly illiberal and, hence, un-American. Now while that alone does not serve as an argument against the Church's position on either theological or philosophical grounds, it certainly counts as a devastating *political* argument against its viability, even for American Catholics.

The extended argument above regarding the inventive imperative for living traditions might cause some to fear that said revision might contribute to a decline in authority and a loss of confidence rendering even the

---

53. Dolan, *In Search of an American Catholicism*, 158–59.

work of even faithful "transgressors" problematic and even heretical. For a church that had a stake in the idea of "infallibility" and for whom "dogma" was not a pejorative term, these are not, on their face, unreasonable worries. But, as Butch said to Sundance when the latter explained that his fear about jumping from the cliff into the river below to get away was that he did not know how to swim and might drown, "Don't worry about drowning—why, the fall will probably kill you!" Simply put, the Church, at least in the United States, was more or less up against the wall by the middle of the century as it faced the prospect of modernity's final victory (which comes in the form of indifference, *not* repression or reinvention). As with all such important moments in time, there were forces on both sides of the issue (though the conservatives would not like my framing of them here). For those who favored reinvention, however, the big question that loomed large was, in John Courtney Murray's words, whether "the Catholic Church can adapt herself vitally, on principle, and not merely on grounds of expediency, to what is valid in American political development."[54] He and his fellow travelers believed it authentically could, but, it was complicated, as they say.

According to Dolan, Murray's starting point for his American project began in a series of lectures given at Loyola University in Baltimore in 1940 that opened with the statement: "American culture, as it exists, is actually the quintessence of all that is decadent in the culture of the Western Christian world." This was due to the denial in America of "the primacy of the spiritual over the material and the social over the individual, as well as the reality of the metaphysical."[55] While hardly out of line within the Catholic intellectual circles of the day, such a position obviously makes it difficult at first blush to see how concord between the two traditions, let alone integration, was going to be possible. However, it is also the case that by 1940, the price the Church was paying for its material and political support in Europe was itself an increasing source of spiritual anguish and self-loathing, and, where it wasn't, it should have been. McGreevy writes of a group of Catholic exiles who had fled Europe as fascism ascended for teaching positions at Catholic universities in the United States who were chagrined and deeply critical of the ease with which many Catholics, both lay and vowed, were making their peace with dictators and tyrants who happened to take communion on Sunday morning. Among this group of exiles was Waldemar Gurian, who founded the important journal of political philosophy, *Review of Politics*, at Notre Dame. It is Gurian who lays out in blunt terms the prophetic challenge to the European clergy, especially those in Germany, who

---

54. Quoted in McGreevy, *Catholicism and American Freedom*, 192.
55. Dolan, *In Search of an American Catholicism*, 156.

were seeing, hearing, and speaking no evil as the Third Reich's position and power solidified and morphed into the world's first truly totalitarian state. Gurian put it this way: "The church is not an association which adapts itself to the particular power relationships of the time, but it is the guardian and protector of the moral order for all human beings and all peoples."[56] So it is that not only would the eventual vanquishers of fascism in Europe be launched from the shores of the land of Washington, Jefferson, Madison, and Hamilton, but so too would some of the critical resources for reforming the Church itself in the name of human rights and non-Jacobin democracy.

John Courtney Murray, SJ, was born in New York City in 1904 and joined the Jesuits after graduating from high school. He spent the bulk of his academic career teaching at Woodstock College and Seminary and edited the journal *Theological Studies* for twenty-five years. He died in 1967. To this day, he is still considered one of the most important Catholic thinkers in American history. While he wrote thousands of pages on numerous subjects, it is his work on the American question that is our focus here. Even this slice of his work is too much to treat comprehensively in this book, but I will try to lay out his most salient contributions. Much of what he argued for remains both relevant and controversial, and, like any good Catholic thinker who enters the political fray, there is plenty to agitate liberals and conservatives alike—both politically and theologically speaking. While Murray worked from a neo-Thomist, natural law framework, there are important elements of his approach which extend that tradition in ways that allow those who may not be willing to embrace the whole scholastic structure entrée to his arguments and enable them more readily to accept his conclusions. Without parsing that "innovation" here in too much detail, the door he opens to non-Thomists rests on what McGreevy calls Cardinal Newman's (1859) "once scandalous claim that the *experience* of the faithful might prove decisive in the formulation of doctrine."[57] This claim led one American Jesuit in 1952 to "applaud Newman's skepticism regarding 'universals' [due to his worry] that contemporary Catholic apologetics tended 'to become one with the cause of minor logic: save the syllogism and you save all.'"[58] A title of one of Murray's essays published in 1949, itself, points us in a similar a-scholastic direction: "Contemporary Orientations of Catholic Thought on Church and State in the *Light of History*."[59]

56. Quoted in McGreevy, *Catholicism and American Freedom*, 198.
57. McGreevy, *Catholicism and American Freedom*, 196. Emphasis mine.
58. McGreevy, *Catholicism and American Freedom*, 196.
59. See Murray, "Contemporary Orientations of Catholic Thought," 177–234; Murray, "Freedom of Religion," 229–87. Emphasis mine.

This willingness to entertain *experience* and *history* in the formulation and "reinvention" of doctrine and Church teaching was both essential to the success of Murray's project and fraught with danger both methodologically speaking as well as politically. While the Church's hierarchy and intellectuals had practiced an almost Machiavellian prudence as necessary when it came to church/state relations, it tenaciously resisted the idea that its ultimate position regarding the proper ordering of society could be culturally or historically contingent for reasons outlined in the previous sections, as well as ones that were far less intellectual. As such, any theoretical fruit yielded from such mistaken philosophical soil was surely tainted and deeply suspect. This was doubly true in the case at hand since the soil being proposed was tied to the "decadent" and previously denounced land known as *America*. Murray would, of course, find out firsthand just how far the Church leadership and his ideological opponents among the Catholic intelligentsia of the day would go to defend both dogma and prerogative when he was literally banned by the Vatican from writing any more on church/state issues (a ban that he faithfully, if grudgingly, accepted). Although anti-Catholic American intellectuals lacked the "ecclesiastical" tools to make the same demands, one must imagine their own quasi-priestly chagrin from the perspective of American liberalism at what Murray had the nerve to argue as well. So what did he actually say?

Murray's most audacious claim regarding the American political tradition vis-à-vis his liberal antagonists begins with the notion that the American founders "built better than they knew." This phrase comes from a statement made in 1884 by the Third Plenary Council of Baltimore (a national meeting of Catholic Bishops) in which they claimed: "We consider the establishment of our country's independence, the shaping of its liberties and laws, as a work of special Providence, its framers 'building better than they knew,' the Almighty's hand guiding them."[60] In essence, the bishops, and later Murray via his appropriation of this idea, are reframing the classic motif of America as the "city on the hill" through a distinctively Catholic lens. In effect, they are both attempting to disarm the vast array of anti-American clerics and Catholic intellectuals by reassuring them that the country is not only a place that is at its core safe for the faithful, but in fact is one that is at least "catholic," if not Catholic. Murray's argument on this score is that because "the American political community was organized in an era when the tradition of natural law and natural rights was still vigorous,"[61] those who made the Revolution and later organized the American regime were

---

60. Quoted in Murray, *We Hold These Truths*, 46.
61. Murray, *We Hold These Truths*, 46.

intrinsically carriers and translators of the universal law, such that their work can be reasonably viewed as consistent with the overall *substance* of Catholic political theology even though the *form* was itself brand new. They were, if you will, at least accidental "Catholics." In this way, then, for Murray, the American experiment can be favorably compared to the experience in France which was viewed, correctly I believe, as explicitly and overtly un-Catholic as well as anti-Catholic by both design and intention. As such, Murray can be seen as asking those who would see in every liberalism the lurking presence of a Robespierre to look beyond superficial similarities and a shared vocabulary to the actual historical lineage and radical ethical commitments of the particular versions of the larger tradition.

For Murray and his modern sympathizers,[62] the French experiment owed its existence to the work of theorists like Hobbes and, of course, Rousseau, who, despite their differences, were both part of the modern decentering and displacement of God and natural law as sovereign in the name of what we would now call secular authority and, perhaps, "the people."[63] The American experiment though, for Murray, could, with careful attention, trace its lineage all the way back to St. Thomas Aquinas, whom he calls "the first Whig."[64] This bold claim rests on Murray's reading of medieval constitutionalism and the limits of political sovereignty. Those restrictions included an understanding of political rule or government as severely circumscribed in both scope and authority and bounded by the law, both positive and natural, as well as by the consent of the governed themselves (yes, even in monarchies). The latter restriction was the by-product of the American recognition of a strong line of demarcation between *state* and *society* (in Murray's classical usage, *studium* and *imperium*).[65] This line prevented the state from interfering in the field of ideas or opinions and the non-governmental associations that men and women formed as a result of them starting with the family and working out to the universal church. This, existentially speaking, means that human beings are, in their original condition, social beings absolutely, but not citizens. While "states" may have "natural" status they are not, *pace* Augustine, part of the supernatural order and therefore possess what I would call only derivative dignity or value, i.e., how useful are they for maintaining the conditions needed for men and women to achieve their supernatural ends? Continental liberalism, as practiced in

---

62. For a strong statement and important perspective see Peter Lawler's introductory essay in Murray, *We Hold These Truths*.
63. See Elshtain, *Sovereignty*, which I will discuss in detail in the next chapter.
64. Murray, *We Hold These Truths*, 47.
65. Murray, *We Hold These Truths*, 50.

the late eighteenth and early nineteenth centuries, had, for Murray, rejected this distinction as both a matter of theory, policy, and fact. In his words:

> They believed that a state could be simply a work of art, a sort of absolute beginning, an artifact of which human reason could be the sole artisan. Moreover, their exaggerated individualism had shut them off from a view of the organic nature of the human community; their social atomism would permit no institutions or associations intermediate between the individual and the state.[66]

This path was avoided by the American revolutionaries because, for Murray, theirs was better seen as a restoration rather than a revolution. The distinction allows him to point to the Declaration of Independence and later on the Bill of Rights as fundamentally natural law documents rooted in the idea of pre-political, God-given rights. In turn, this allows him to make another exceptionally bold claim that further transplants the thinking of the revolutionary generation to a more ancient time and differentiates them from their European counterparts dramatically:

> The American Bill of Rights is not a piece of eighteenth-century rationalist theory; it is far more the product of Christian history. Behind it one can see, not the philosophy of the Enlightenment but the older philosophy that had been the matrix of the common law. The "man" whose rights are guaranteed in the face of law and government is *whether he knows it or not*, the Christian man, who had learned to know his own personal dignity in the school of Christian faith.[67]

While I believe that this stunning claim, whose historical rationale and basis I will flesh out a little more in the next chapter, can withstand a certain amount of what I am sure was (and still would be) a high degree of incredulity from the American intellectual class, the seemingly unintentional quality of this happenstance, begs the question of what they actually believed they were doing? In other words, while I can appreciate Murray's position that this brand of constitutionalism was in effect placing old wine in new bottles, and therefore a reasonable reimagining of the tradition under new historical and cultural circumstances, I am not convinced that the grace he extends to the founding generation writ large is properly nuanced nor that such an ascription would be for many even welcomed. Isn't it at least plausible to ask whether they, in whole or in part, had other intentions that

---

66. Murray, *We Hold These Truths*, 52.
67. Murray, *We Hold These Truths*, 53. Emphasis mine.

were only able to be realized and made visible over time such that their constitutionalism was in fact something of a Trojan horse for the faithful? Keep in mind the earlier caveat that while appearing to take the position that it has no position, "neutrality" always benefits the strong, the powerful, and the general at the expense of the weak, the powerless, and, the particular and that it ironically gets to do so in the name of "fairness." In his inclusive and consensus minded historiography, Murray overlooks the radical diversity present at the founding as argued for earlier. While the line from the Magna Carta to colonial constitutionalism to the Declaration of Independence seems straightforward enough, and the line from the Declaration to the Bill of Rights makes good sense, I remain unconvinced about that lineage extending to the second US Constitution. So as not to belabor what I have already labored at length again here, the fact that those who fought constitutional ratification and held it off until the Bill of Rights was included in the amended document (the Anti-Federalists) believed strongly that the Constitution, as written, was an utter betrayal of the spirit of the Revolution will have to suffice for an argument here.[68]

That caveat noted, I agree with Murray's larger and more important claim that the American founding owes a far larger debt to Christian thought than can be found in the meager instrumental theology of John Locke and the unamended Constitution he inspired. This, in turn, allows me to move on to a mutual and provocative set of questions and claims. It is Murray's widely shared contention that "political freedom is endangered at its foundations as soon as the universal moral values, upon whose shared possession the self-discipline of a free society depends, are no longer vigorous enough to retrain the passions and shatter the inertia of men,"[69] leads him to ask whether what he calls the "American consensus still endures"?[70] To which he answers, perhaps, but notes that it is not in very good shape. In his words, the "seeds of dissolution were already present in the ancient heritage as it reached the shores of American,"[71] and he worried, now over

---

68. In my previous work *Anti-Federalists*, I made the argument that the Anti-Federalist's opposition came out of a communitarianism embedded in the civic republican tradition that stood in stark contrast to the new Lockean liberalism of the Federalists and the US Constitution. At that writing my, own engagement with the Christian tradition was limited and I had not read Murray and many others who have since pushed me to reconsider certain arguments. While I stand by the book's larger narrative and argument in general, I would, now twenty years later, need to rethink and deepen parts of it.

69. Murray, *We Hold These Truths*, 51.
70. Murray, *We Hold These Truths*, 53.
71. Murray, *We Hold These Truths*, 55.

half a century ago, that said dissolution "may one day be consummated" and lamented:

> Perhaps one day the noble many-storied mansion of democracy will be dismantled, leveled to the dimensions of flat majoritarianism, which is no mansion but a barn, perhaps even a tool shed in which the weapons of tyranny may be forged.[72]

This leads him, in turn, to assert without any apparent irony whatsoever that were this philosophical or sociological catastrophe to occur:

> The guardianship of the original American consensus, based on the Western heritage, would have passed to the Catholic community, within which the heritage was elaborated long before America was. And it would be for others, not Catholics, to ask themselves whether they still shared the consensus which first fashioned the American people into a body politic and determined the structure of its fundamental law.[73]

Suffice it to say that Murray's arguments for both an *a priori* as well as the possibility of an *a posteriori* American catholicity certainly turn the conventional wisdom concerning the Catholic mind and tradition vis-à-vis America on its head from both the perspective of the American intellectual class and the Catholic Church. However, Murray is properly Augustinian in his argument insofar as the embrace of the American regime is conditional on it remaining attached to its natural law consensus regarding both the limits of the state, the practice of a certain social ethos, and the protection of certain fundamental Christian values or human rights. While this set of conditions is itself a perpetually open question and calls for constant vigilance on the part of the faithful citizen (as well, by implication, of the constant practice of citizenship), it will also force the Church to hold up a mirror to its own *praxis* regarding "democracy," "rights," "individualism," and "liberty," in what will at first be extremely discomforting ways. In other words, having brought America to the Church (at least in theory), the Church would also have to see America in its own reflection despite the very public historical denials of any familial relationship.

To avoid both the "expediency" he himself decried and charges from the Catholic establishment that amounted to his defining "decadence" up, Murray attempted to find the much-needed link between the two sides through the explication of the central *political* insight of both Christianity and the American regime. Harkening back to my discussion in chapter 3

---

72. Murray, *We Hold These Truths*, 56.
73. Murray, *We Hold These Truths*, 56.

and the assertions of thinkers like Tinder and Habermas on what the former called the "exalted individual," Murray joins with Lincoln in seeing the true essence of the American genius in the proposition to which we were all supposed to have been dedicated, namely, the sacred equality of all human beings under God. Now while the *political* insight of Christianity is not *its* central or primary teaching to the world, it is the one that provides legitimation for the American polity for the would-be Christian citizen. Murray makes the initial point below in the following manner, which I quote at length:

> Finally, an incarnational humanism appeals to history and sees in history a manner of law. The fact that Christianity did give rise to a culture, to an enormous explosion of human effort that altered the face even of this earth. This was not its primal mission, of course. But, as Leo XIII loved to repeat, Christianity could not have operated more beneficial effects upon the whole process and order of human living-together, if it had been instituted precisely for this purpose. Christianity freed man from nature by teaching him that he has an immortal soul, which is related to matter but not immersed in it or enslaved to its laws. Christianity released man from a Greek bondage to history and its eternal cyclic returns. *It taught him his own uniqueness, his own individual worth, the dignity of his own person, the equality of all men, the unity of the human race.*
>
> On the impulse of these lessons he set about building himself a world in which he might live as a man and a Christian, in the enjoyment of his birthright of freedom and in the discharge of the responsibility this birthright imposed upon him.[74]

Murray describes the American consensus in a manifestly parallel way earlier in his text, writing, "The argument here should be made to include the notion that the whole consensus has its ultimate root in the idea of the sacredness of man, *res sacra homo*. Man has a sacredness of personal dignity which commands the respect of society and all its laws and institutions. His sacredness guarantees him certain immunities and it also endows him with certain empowerments."[75] Contra Locke, but especially Hobbes, and, then later in his own right, John Rawls, the equality of human persons is at its core metaphysical and supernatural, not merely natural or political.[76] To the extent it loses that character in the minds of the citizenry, it loses its

---

74. Murray, *We Hold These Truths*, 178. Emphasis mine.
75. Murray, *We Hold These Truths*, 89.
76. See Coons and Brennan, *By Nature Equal*.

moral force. Subsequently, the restrictions of human conscience will undoubtedly give way to some brand of the war of all against all be it literally or figuratively as we are methodically returned to the "history" the faith had allowed us to possibly transcend. Peter Lawler sums it up this way in his critical introduction to Murray's book when he claims that "all governments that protect rights depend on the assumption that man is not God, and all despotism originates in the 'sophism,' 'error,' or 'sin' that in some sense he is."[77] In such a world, to steal a line from Thucydides, "the strong do what they will and the weak accept what they must," either overtly or covertly. None of this, of course, should be taken to imply the possibility of perfection or the establishment of heaven here on earth. Even at its best, the church, let alone the state, remains a place where sin and sinners abound. The hope is that those self-same Christians-citizens are of the repentant rather than the unrepentant variety!

Having cleared the theoretical space for at least the possibility of a Catholic America, Murray's next great task was to clear the *theological* space needed for an Americanized Catholicism. This would prove to be the more treacherous of the two tasks insofar as Murray would have to convince the hierarchy that "error" did indeed have rights. While the notion that individuals in America had the "right to be wrong" was practically an article of faith for most of her citizens (Catholics included), Murray's position and natural law framework belied him the easygoing tolerance that many just took for granted. This was especially true in the case of grave and historically encumbered matters like the relationship between church and state and the relative claims to loyalty and prerogative each made with regard to the lives and consciences of the individual citizen/congregant. In his 1946 article on "the ethical problem" in the question of freedom of religion, Murray notes that the Church's position had been reduced to two poorly conceived "formulas": "dogmatic intolerance" and "personal tolerance."[78] In other words, the Church's position that it remained the "one true Church" was still considered unassailable at the institutional, philosophical, and theological levels, but that the norms, mores, constitutional construction, and the sheer facticity of pluralism in the United States required Catholic citizens to act respectfully toward those of different confessions out of their devotion to peace and civility. This prudential tolerance, coupled with the overarching thesis of superiority was, of course, a losing proposition in Tocqueville's America, where it was said the citizenry would prefer slavery and barbarism to aristocracy, and Murray knew it. On the other hand, there was a logic

---

77. See Lawler, critical introduction to *We Hold These Truths*, 1–22.
78. Murray, "Freedom of Religion," 230.

to the Church's less pejoratively stated position that the theologian-theorist could not simply dismiss as a serious thinker.

A Catholic God seemed by reason to require a Catholic church and a charitable reading of the Church's position would see in it a desire to not let the souls of the of those outside its embrace remain in a state of mortal and even eternal peril. Murray denotes the larger tension in the Church's position in the following way:

> We love God in the truth that He has given us, and we love man in that which is most divine in him, his conscience. We love God and His truth with a loyalty that forbids compromise of the truth, even at the promptings of what might seem to be a love of man; were it otherwise, our love of both God and man would be a *caritas ficta*. And we love man and his conscience with a loyalty that forbids injury to his conscience, even at the promptings of what might seem to be a love of truth; were it otherwise, love both of God and man would again be a *caritas ficta*. In either case, what we abhor is any *feigning*.[79]

In this construction, Murray has captured what may well be the single most important *practical* question faced by an evangelical faith that is rooted in love and the inviolability of the human person and therefore opposed to coercion and violence in the name of the faith. This is why he shifts the conversation quickly to one of strategy and tactics as quickly as possible through his subsequent division of the "problem of religious liberty" to the three distinct planes that he names "the ethical, the theological, and the political."[80] On my own simplified reading of this move, I think it might be helpful to think about the three planes as three questions. First, what is the good (the theological plane); second, what is the right action to take to promote and secure the good (the ethical plane); and, finally, what action in light of both the good and the securing of it is possible under the prevailing circumstances of the world (the political plane). As to the "good," the simplest formulation of the goal is to ensure and direct "the freedom of the human person to reach God, and eternal beatitude in God, along the way in which God wills to be reached."[81] From a theological perspective and, hence, the Church's perspective, all other activities and actions must be in service to this end to the greatest degree possible under the extant circumstances of the world at a particular historical moment.

---

79. Murray, "Freedom of Religion," 232.
80. Murray, "Freedom of Religion," 233–34.
81. Murray, "Freedom of Religion," 236.

Time and space do not permit me to unpack all of this as Murray so ably does, so instead I will just state the outcome of his work as it relates to my purpose here. If we can understand the "free church" tradition in America broadly conceived as *the* dominate "ecclesiological" tradition with a corresponding political and constitutional apparatus designed to defend and support the derivative religious voluntarism such an ecclesiology demands, then the question Murray must answer is how Catholic ecclesiology is not either an existential or a political threat to that tradition. But, of course, he must try to do so without simultaneously undermining or negating his own tradition at the same time, which, to be honest, was doctrinally and theologically opposed to the existence of exactly those alternative churches and which had historically and in parts of the contemporary world of the day used political power to suppress them. Again, no easy task. After a lengthy set of arguments concerning the proper understanding of the idea of conscience (which Murray describes as the "voice of God"), the freedom thereof for individual men and women, and its relationship to both natural and positive law, Murray proposes to his American believers of all denominations that they collectively condemn and reject the following two propositions in the name of the common good and their shared faith in one God.

1. Human reason, without any regard whatsoever to God, is the sole arbiter of truth and falsity, right and wrong; it is a law unto itself, and is able by its own powers to secure the welfare of men and nations.
2. The State, as the origin and source of all rights, possess a juridical competence that is circumscribed by no limits.[82]

The implications of these dual condemnations are the rejection of the notion of religious privatization in the first place because God must be part of the *political* conversation and, second, the idea that there are any states or other forms of political order that are unaccountable to the natural law and therefore all are limited in the scope of both their competency and their authority. Chief among those limits in competency would be the ability to define both the ultimate ends for human beings and the ecclesiastical order that would provide the method for doing so as well as the methodology for enactment. In other words, the political order cannot assume the role or responsibilities rightly left for the churches. And, by reading his first condemnation back into the second, those churches, their congregant-citizens, and their political leaders must, in turn, be left free to, indeed are required to, use the fruits of their religious and theological reflections to inform, promote, and circumscribe the various actions of the state and its representatives. In

---

82. Murray, "Freedom of Religion," 284–85.

sum, the congregant-citizen, reflecting on his or her religiously formed and informed conscience, provides direction to the highly limited religiously/theologically/reasonably constrained political order for carrying out its particular role in delivering a constitutional and legal system which properly reflects and provides the subsequent political and social space for the ongoing refinement and enactment of the common good grounded in the natural law.

In this way, Murray simultaneously does a couple of important things that allow him to make common cause with not only Protestants, but also potentially with other Abrahamic religions, while not betraying his Catholic faith, nor asking other faithful citizens to convert. First, he asserts and maintains both the primacy of God and the publicness of faith. Second, he asserts and maintains both the inviolability of human conscience and the role of the churches in the ongoing formation and refinement of those consciences. And, finally, he asserts and maintains the proper ordering of the supernatural and the natural orders by reaffirming the state's instrumental and secular purposes and ends. Each of these being something that virtually all American Christians operating in good faith would find both acceptable and at least constitutionally permissible, if not intended, by the First Amendment. This, however, still left Murray with his own extant and historical "Catholic problem" in the form of state-churches and the specter of theocracy to deal with if he was going to further allay clearly justified fears of Catholic disingenuousness regarding religious freedom and its possible counterpart, political authoritarianism.

Here, two essays by Murray become critical and return us full circle to the discussion of tradition earlier in this chapter. One of them I have already mentioned, "Contemporary Orientations of Catholic Thought on Church and State in The Light of History," and the second is simply titled: "The Problem of State Religion." In these two articles, Murray addressed two audiences with at least two broad purposes. The audiences are those suspicious Americans who see Alexander VI lurking just behind the curtain of Catholic political involvement, and his own Church, whose reaction to the political events associated with the European Enlightenment had prevented them from remembering what they really stood for. Hence, for the first audience the purpose was to demonstrate that while they may disagree about strategy and tactics, they shared the same civic goals of protecting the properly grounded civil rights and liberties of American citizens and achieving the common good of a reimagined "city on the hill." For the second, the purpose was to provide the needed education and reaffirmation and renewal of first principles in light of changed and evolving historical circumstances and events.

In the first essay, Murray's subject, broadly speaking, is the proper interpretation of the traditional doctrine of the "two swords" first suggested by Gelasius I early in Church history and then later developed more explicitly by Pope Gregory VII (1073–85) and later still, and more infamously, by Pope Boniface VIII (1294–1303) and its appropriate application to the modern world. Again, this is a rich and complicated essay that I will need to oversimplify for my purposes here. By way of historical analogy drawn from the era of Boniface VIII and his papal bull *Unam Sanctam*, Murray states the problem he is attempting to "solve" as such: "a political development has created a situation of social fact and of political right which must be reckoned with in solving the ancient problem of the relation between the spiritual and temporal orders."[83] That political development is, of course, the rise of the democratic state. Recognizing that at least the American constitutional scheme of civil liberties (*libertas civilis*) required both freedom of religious association and expression without exception (beyond the demands of order and peace), Murray wants to make the affirmative case that this is not merely a pragmatic compromise in the absence of the ability to realize a Catholic ideal, but rather an intrinsic requirement of the common good rightly understood. This, I would contend, represents *both* a radical departure from prevailing (circa 1940s) Catholic political thought as well as a radical return to a more authentic theological position regarding the relationship between church and state. To get there, Murray claims that his effort will be one that attempts "to construct a doctrinal synthesis of Church-state relations which will be at once true to permanently valid traditional principle and also universally valid within the horizons of today's factual and legitimate political development."[84] Such an attempt represents the ultimate both/and as, non-pejoratively speaking, it is an attempt to find what some might call a relative-universal principle that is both consistent and distinctive, traditionally speaking, at the same time.

Without meaning to state the obvious, what makes this move possible and necessary is the simple fact that other traditions have their own existential existence and autonomy while also frequently occupying the same historical and geographic space. In other words, the existence of multiple, competing and, in many cases, incommensurable traditions will mean, as Murray understands, that they will often find their own trajectories to be changed and skewed in reaction to one another. Hence, to use a physical analogy, if an object intends and is proceeding in a westerly direction and is hit by another object and, in effect, spun around and now faces east, it

---

83. Murray, "Contemporary Orientations of Catholic Thought," 181.
84. Murray, "Contemporary Orientations of Catholic Thought," 184.

will need to adjust its route to return to its intended course. This deviation does not imply that the original direction has somehow changed nor that the choice of a direction was itself an unreasoned or unprincipled one, but rather it is a simple recognition that the world lacks uniformity and unity such that action and reaction are constant even when the route seems certain. In simplified form, I believe that Murray's argument is that the "permanent traditional principle" at stake is the primacy of the spiritual realm to the physical, or the primacy of the religious order to the political order. This does not change insofar as the "supernatural" is always lexically prioritized over the "natural." However, since the way in which this lexical ordering is enacted rests in the hands of human beings who, by definition, must operate from a position within the natural world, how this is managed at the level of human institutions like the Church and the state remains a contextual question, i.e., what is possible and what is probable under the prevailing circumstances. Thus, the question of practical wisdom or prudence; not to the neglect or rejection of principle, but in the name of protecting it and extending it into the future. To see this on a grand scale, from a literary perspective, the reader should visit or revisit the classic Catholic science-fiction novel by Walter Miller, *A Canticle for Leibowitz* (1960).

In oversimplified form, Murray's argument can be summed up along the following lines: the struggle over primacy between the Church and the state in the secular order based on the lexical ordering of the spiritual and the political in the created world is the result of both intellectual confusion and the very human tendency to reductionist thinking. When confronted with two swords, the logician's spirit rises up in those who inhabit the city of man and leads them to ask in some manner "Yes, there are two, but which of the two is the final and superior authority?" So powerful is the distaste for ambiguity and paradox (not to mention that there appear to be real practical issues related to this dualism), as well as the prevalence of good old-fashioned sin and its child arrogance, that most human beings are willing to seek uniformity even at the price of radical distortion and outright falsification or bad faith. But, of course, to order the two swords hierarchically in the secular world is to ultimately reduce the two to one first in practice and then in fact. And, indeed, this becomes the root cause of the story that takes place from the Middle Ages through the Reformation and on to the modern world concerning the struggle between the Church and the various iterations of states and those who led and ruled both of them. Unwilling to accept that dynamic-tension rather than resolution *was* the point, the two swords struggled for domination and control and in turn lost sight of the virtues and strengths of *complementarity*.

Now while the Church had at least a universal reach (though obviously not grasp) going for it, the particularism that states and nations offered, when coupled with their ready and growing access to the tools of violence and coercion, meant that the Church as a *church* was ill-equipped to compete in the long run in the battle for supremacy even if it wanted to or could have. Though excommunication, or the threat thereof, had some "success," its power would of course fade with the rise of national churches. Having already discussed earlier the theological and moral pitfalls associated with the Church's attempt to commandeer the apparatus of the state, I will simply say that the practical difficulties associated with a unified Christendom were even more ominous and inhospitable over the long-run than the former "theoretical" problems would ever be. That having been said, however, Murray's argument later in the essay prefigures Charles Taylor's as discussed in chapter 5, when he writes,

> My point here is that history and experience have brought the Church to ever more perfect respect for the autonomy of the state (as a form of respect for an essential element in the "whole of man") and consequently to evermore purely spiritual assertions of her power in the temporal order. . . . With seeming paradox, the withdrawal of the Church from a certain identification with the *state* in the medieval *respublica* and (in a different way) with the confessional state has not meant a withdrawal from *society*, but rather a more profound immanence, so to speak, in society, as the spiritual principle of its direction to both the temporal and the eternal ends of the human person.[85]

States as *states* tend by nature to monism unless, as argued earlier, checked constitutionally or through the common law by statesmen, citizens, or subjects with at least a transcendent natural law sensibility or philosophical framework, i.e., some standard external to the state itself to measure and judge its actions against. And it was/is this tendency toward absolutism regardless of the political form, i.e., monarchy, aristocracy, or democracy, that Murray had to contend with as he pushed the Church to reconsider its hostile stance toward the liberal-democratic state in general (as a direct consequence of the French experience) and the United States in particular. The Church as *church* suffers and is diminished proportionally by its involvement in the political order either through the direct wielding of power and the mechanisms of coercion or, more often, by its machinations behind the scenes and collusion with the powerful. Even with the best of intentions, i.e., the protection and safeguarding of the Church and its mission, the

---

85. Murray, "Contemporary Orientations of Catholic Thought," 214.

Church undermines its own special status in the world by becoming commonplace at best and just another faction vying for temporal goods at worst. In other words, Murray's argument ultimately comes to this: the Church must actively resist the temptations to secular power and assert the necessity and distinctiveness of *both* swords as *the* proper order of the world. The name he gives to this approach is *dyarchy*. His general description of this new version of the old theory is as follows:

> In these perspectives, which are set by the full development, through theological reflection and political experience, of the Gelasian doctrine, the whole system pivots on the principle of freedom. There is first the free obedience of the Christian conscience to the magisterial and jurisdictional authority of the Church; there is secondly the free participation of the citizen, as a Christian, in the institutions whereby all the processes of temporal power to their proper ends.
> This, I take it, is the Catholic thesis in its application to democratic society.[86]

While cautioning against the "political canonization of the American state, which, like any political realization, labors under ambiguities and defects," Murray forcefully suggests that at least the United States, in its formative understanding of itself, realizes that this is the proper formulation of the problem.[87] In this rejection of the confessional state and what is best thought of as the "unity" thesis, Murray repositions the Church as a moral authority that respects the equal dignity and rights of conscience for all citizens while simultaneously contending that the Church is the preeminent conscience forming institution. Hence, to simplify, the Church must be left free to form through its teaching and liturgical functions, the dispositions and consciences of individual men and women who are then, in a properly functioning democratic state, left free as citizens to construct binding social and public policies that allow them to "live in civil society according to the precepts of reason and conscience."[88] In this way, men and women can be whole human beings practicing dual obedience to both God and country without any inherent conflict.

---

86. Murray, "Contemporary Orientations of Catholic Thought," 224.
87. Murray, "Contemporary Orientations of Catholic Thought," 226.
88. Murray, "Contemporary Orientations of Catholic Thought," 234.

A CATHOLIC-LIBERAL SOCIETY

Now while those of a Rawlsian bent will still want to argue against this formulation based on the way in which it carries ideas and arguments derived from "comprehensive doctrines" into the public sphere, I will not rehash the arguments made throughout this book concerning inadequacy of a privatized Christianity whose believers must somehow try to check their faith at the door of city hall to be good citizens. Instead, I want to focus in the conclusion to this rather long chapter on one final essay of Murray's directed primarily at his religious critics who believe that he yields too much theoretical space to the proponents of the modern liberal-democratic state. In simplified form, we can hear those critics saying roughly this: If indeed the Church is the preeminent former of consciences and the opportunity arises to literally establish the Catholic Church within the boundaries of prudence and morality, then those democratic citizens should do so in the name of the common good. To get a taste of this line of argument a passage from the previous essay from a 1948 conference in Spain will suffice:

> We Catholic Spaniards will avoid criticizing our brethren, who are in a minority in other states and nations, because they shelter themselves under the banner of liberty. However, that will never lead us to grant, as a thesis, the same rights to error as truth. And let Catholics of all countries, if they truly be Catholics, if they wish to be faithful to papal teachings—let them be on their guard against ridiculing, as intransigent and backward, the Catholics of Spain or of any other country which has the great fortune of preserving Catholic unity, because of their defense of this Catholic unity.[89]

It is Murray's argument that the notion of an established church was never a question of principle nor dogma, but instead a particular and prudential solution to a specific historical situation.[90] Under threat of eradication and suppression, it was only reasonable for the Church in its temporal manifestation to seek its own preservation safety in the arms of a sympathetic protector. However, this defensive posture lent itself to both an excessive degree of entanglement with a given state which, in turn, severely detracted from the Church's true mission and, subsequently, led to a gravely distorted view of its real intentions by friends and possible allies alike. While it would not have been possible for the Church to come to terms with the continental liberalism of the nineteenth century, it was entirely possible for it to

---

89. Murray, "Contemporary Orientations of Catholic Thought," 228.
90. See Murray, "Problem of State Religion," 161, 170–71.

INVENTING A CATHOLIC AMERICAN POLITICAL TRADITION   249

adapt itself to the twentieth-century version as at least portended in the US Constitution.[91] Indeed, Murray goes further still by arguing that Continental Liberalism was "a deformation of the liberal tradition; it was in effect simply another form of absolutist state-monism, to which the liberal tradition stands in opposition" and then audaciously makes the following set of claims which I quote at length:

> Democracy today presents itself with all the force of an idea whose time has come. And there are two reasons why the present task of Catholics is to work toward the purification of the liberal tradition (which is their own real tradition) and of the democratic form of state in which it finds expression, by restoring both the idea and the institutions of democracy to their proper Christian foundations. First, this form of state is presently man's best, and possibly last, hope of human freedom. Secondly, this form of state presently offers to the Church as a spiritual power as good a hope of freedom as she has ever had; it offers to the Church as the Christian people a means, through its free political institutions, of achieving harmony between law and social organization and the demands of their Christian conscience; finally, by reason of its aspirations towards an order of personal and associational freedom, political equality, civic friendship, social justice, and cultural advancement, it offers to the Church the kind of cooperation which she presently needs, and it merits in turn her cooperation in the realization of its own aspirations.[92]

If the liberal tradition properly understood is in fact the true Catholic tradition, and the democratic form at this historical moment, if not forever, is the best available political structure for its ongoing development and realization, then it follows that a state-church is not a permissible alternative so long as the present historical conditions of freedom and toleration remain intact. However, and of critical importance, the ideal of a "Catholic society" not only is permissible, but, in point of fact, becomes the normative ideal. Such an assertion will of course cause many contemporary liberals to shudder and recoil as it no doubt did in 1951. That is because what they hear and what is actually being said are two very different things. What they hear is that they will all live in a Catholic state and that they will be subjected to an established church. This set of fears is, of course, exactly what the entire argument of this chapter was meant to not only allay, but also to demonstrate

---

91. Murray, "Problem of State Religion," 165.
92. Murray, "Problem of State Religion," 163.

would itself be both un-Catholic and un-Christian were it true. If, as Murray puts it,

> properly "society" designates a structured order of human relationships (familial, civic, economic, religious, etc.) which is constituted in view of an end. A society is not constituted by a mass of individuals but by a patterned ensemble of purposive human associations—in a word, by institutions. It is a structured social entity (or perhaps better, a social action, a *conspiration*) whose structure is determined by institutions. In this sense a "Catholic" society would be one whose institutional structures were shaped by the dictates of nature and reason, derived from consideration of the social aspects of human personality, which the Church teaches as the rational principles governing the social order: the principles of justice (in its three forms), social charity, the "subsidiarity function," personal and associational freedom. A "Catholic society" would further be one in which the ethical-theological principles of the freedom of the Church, *Concordia*, and cooperation were properly observed.[93]

Then, the notion of a Catholic society would be one that, yes, does indeed prioritize the right over the good *politically* speaking, while continuing to prize the good over the right *spiritually* speaking. While it is doubtful, given the natural condition of human beings post-Fall, that the right will produce the good for any length of time or with any optimism that tragedy will be overcome as part of the human condition, it remains a position that continues to recognize that there is a God and we are not that being.

In the final substantive chapter, I will try to flesh out what such a society would look like in very general terms as that picture emerges in the philosophic, political, and social teachings of the Church as a result of the Second Vatican Council and the pivotal document *Gaudium et Spes*.

---

93. Murray, "Problem of State Religion," 175.

7

Tending to Catholicism *and* America in the Modern World

Everyone who comes to me and listens to my words and acts on them—
I will show you what he is like. He is like a man who when he built his
house dug, and dug deep, and laid the foundations on rock; when the
river was in flood it bore down on that house but could not shake it, it
was so well built. But the one who listens and does nothing is like the
man who built his house on soil, with no foundations: as soon as the
river bore down on it, it collapsed; and what a ruin that house became.

—LUKE 6:47–49

Do not be afraid of those who kill the body but cannot kill the soul;
fear him rather who can destroy both body and soul in hell. Can you
not buy two sparrows for a penny? And yet not one falls to the ground
without your Father knowing. Why every hair on your head has been
counted. So there is no need to be afraid; you are worth more than a
hundred sparrows.

—MATTHEW 10:28–31

"LOVE IN THE RUINS"

Jacques Maritain was a contemporary of John Courtney Murray's and is widely considered one of the most important Catholic philosophers of the twentieth century. While the fascist and totalitarian movements, and the world war they begot, served as the backdrop for much of Murray's political theory, for Maritain that context was both central and personal to his political philosophy and his politics proper. Born in Paris in 1882 and raised there, Maritain, along with his wife Raïssa, converted and joined the Catholic Church in 1906 after encountering the religious thinker Léon Bloy. As the author of fifty books on widely ranging subjects, Maritain's corpus of work does not yield to easy summary. For my purposes, this chapter relies exclusively on his books *Man and the State* and *The Person and the Common Good*. The former was published in 1951 and based on a series of lectures he gave at the University of Chicago in 1949 just after the Universal Declaration of the Rights of Man (whose construction Maritain participated in) was issued. It was path-breaking in its import because of Maritain's deft conjunction of the natural law tradition and the idea of natural rights. While Murray's support for the democratic political form was significantly conditional, Maritain's is almost unequivocal. Part of the reason for this difference, to be sure, can be explained by the differing rules of engagement that Murray as a vowed-religious and Maritain as a relatively unconstrained philosopher had to play by. Part of it can also be explained by the fact that Maritain's experience of those European totalizing movements was far less distant and philosophically detached. In other words, democracy's authoritarian challengers no longer existed for Maritain as live options, even at the level of theory. While democracy may not have been the last word for Maritain, anything that might follow would have to build upon and respect its particular modern sensibility rather than attempt to retard or degrade it in the name of either some retrograde premodern sentiment or some fully modern brand of authoritarian collectivism.

As McGreevy asserts, quoting Maritain in part,

> By the early 1940s, however, Maritain defended democracy as a system of government morally superior to any alternative. At one time, perhaps, a poorly educated population could accept authoritarian rule, but the "democratic impulse" must now be understood as an "inspiration of the Gospel." "It is necessary to show," he told Yves Simon in 1941, "that Thomism is what is strongest against false democracy. . . . St. Thomas was

a democrat, in this sense ... the Gospel works in history in a democratic direction.¹

It is important to note, however, that this "democratic direction" was neither a synonym for liberal-individualism of a Lockean variety or capitalism as many contemporary readers might be tempted to assume. Hence the phrase "false democracy." For Maritain, false democracy is rooted in a confusion sketched indirectly in the previous chapter by John Courtney Murray between the concepts of Nation and State. While accustomed in the modern world to conflating the two ideas into one, i.e., the nation-state, this represents for Maritain a category error of the highest variety. To get there, he begins by making an important distinction between *community* and *society* whereby the former is said to be "a work of nature" and the latter is "more a work of reason."² They are differentiated by Maritain insofar as a community or social life "brings men together by reason of a common *object* . . . but in a *society* the object is a *task* to be done or an *end* to be aimed at, which depends on determinations of human intelligence and will."³ To oversimplify, a community is a pre- or a-rational grouping of human beings who are drawn together by a force or set of circumstances that they did not intentionally choose, such as where they were born or falling in love. Societies, however, are the product of rational and indeed voluntary associational choices in the name of some goal like a labor union or a business corporation. The important move that Maritain then makes is to claim that "the *Nation* is a community, not a society. The Nation is one of the most important, perhaps the most complex complete community engendered by civilized life."⁴ Again, to oversimplify, think here about being Greek or German; wherever I might live or make my life I cannot escape from that pre-rational ethnic or national group that gave "birth" to me. At its most basic, it provided me with the first and most ingrained language through which I came to know myself and the objects of the world. On the other hand, if I join the order Sons of Italy in America with the intent of preserving and enhancing the lives and culture of Italians in America, I have formed a society. Counter-distinct, then, to a community, the State is a society. Hence, a Nation can give rise to a State or a political society, but that entity should never be confused with the former object. So it is that the German nation (or people) produced two wholly antithetical forms of political society that included both the Third Reich in the first half of the twentieth century and the German Republic in

1. McGreevy, *Catholicism and American Freedom*, 200.
2. Maritain, *Man and the State*, 2.
3. Maritain, *Man and the State*, 3.
4. Maritain, *Man and the State*, 4–5.

the second half. Assuming I have not done too much damage to Maritain's work, why do these distinctions matter so much?

The answer is contained implicitly in Maritain's pithy and Brownsonian formulation: "But man is by no means for the State. The State is for man."[5] Oversimplifying again, the State should always be viewed as an instrument of the Nation (or the people) and never the other way around, i.e., the people or the Nation used instrumentally by the State. This, as Maritain would say, is a "perversion."[6] If I might be allowed a small analogical digression to clarify the danger of this, I would point the reader to the *Terminator* movies for a minute. For those who do not remember, the basic story line is that the United States (for our purpose now, the Nation) created something called Skynet (for our purpose now, the State), an artificial intelligence charged with the digital command and control of the defense capabilities of the country in an effort to increase response time and reduce human error in national defense, especially in the area of nuclear weapons. As the story goes, Skynet learned at an exponential rate and soon had infiltrated every aspect of the digital world, and, eventually, it achieved "consciousness." Recognizing the threat of a now "independent" Skynet/superpower, the creators attempted to shut it down. Skynet came to "see" this as an existential threat. At the root of that threat to its very existence was in fact the people who created it and everyone else like them, i.e., human beings. So, Skynet unleashed the machines and the weaponry of death upon the human race killing off most of the planet with the exception of some whom they retained as slaves to service the machines and a small band of resistors who were actively fighting back. Returning to Maritain now, he writes of the phenomenon I am trying to explain:

> The consciousness of the political society is raised to a more completely individualized idea of itself in the idea of a State. In the absolutist notion of the State, that symbol has been made a reality, has been hypostasized. According to this notion the State is a metaphysical monad, a person; it is whole unto itself, *the* very political whole in its supreme degree of unity and individuality. So it absorbs in itself the body politic from which it emanates.... And it enjoys absolute sovereignty as an essential property and right.[7]

This is the essence of "false democracy." This is the nation-state in action at its worst and most perverse. This is the democracy which understands its

---

5. Maritain, *Man and the State*, 13.
6. Maritain, *Man and the State*, 13.
7. Maritain, *Man and the State*, 17.

role as "forcing its citizens to be free," if you will. The truly democratic state does not have an independent existence or good that is in any way detachable or independent from the people. In other words, it is never supposed to be an end in and of itself, but rather always a means. Hence, a concept that is often taken for granted in contemporary political discourse, "reasons of state," is both a subversive and analytically dangerous malapropism which reifies what is theoretically and theologically impermissible; namely, the idea that there could be a state interest that was separable or potentially distinct from the interests of the nation. It is this sort of road that allows some statesman to utter the phrase "mutually assured destruction" with a straight face. Here I quote Maritain at length:

> For democracies today the most urgent endeavor is to develop social justice and improve world economic management, and to defend themselves against totalitarian threats from the outside and totalitarian expansion in the world; but the pursuit of these objectives will inevitably involve the risk of having too many functions of social life controlled by the State from above, and we shall inevitably be bound to accept this risk, as long as our notion of the State has not been restated on true and genuine democratic foundations, and as long as the body politic has not renewed its own structures and consciousness, so that the people become more effectively equipped for the exercise of freedom, and the State may be made an actual instrument for the common good of all. Then only will that very topmost agency, which is made by modern civilization more and more necessary to the human person in his political, social, moral, even intellectual and scientific progress, cease to be at the same time a threat to the freedoms of the human person as well as of intelligence and science. Then only will the highest functions of the State—to ensure the law and facilitate the free development of the body politic—be restored, and the sense of the State be regained by the citizens. Then only will the State achieve its true dignity, which comes not from power and prestige, but from the exercise of justice.[8]

It is exactly that sort of philosophical restoration and the theoretical projection of a properly oriented democratic regime that the remainder of Maritain's treatise is ultimately directed toward. While resolutely maintaining the oppositional stance regarding liberal-democratic states theorized and enacted alike in the early modernity of the leading contract theorists, he, unlike other Catholic defenders of democracy of his day, is unabashedly a

8. Maritain, *Man and the State*, 18–19.

democratic partisan. More importantly though, for my argument, Maritain's commitment to the democratic state is grounded and defended theologically and in the name of the gospel. As such, the contemporary theological-political project for him would involve at least three major components. First would be the theological work necessary to reconstruct or reimagine a faith tradition that, at its birth and throughout most of its history, would have had little to actually say about democracy, for obvious reasons. Second, there would need to be a working out and hermeneutic unpacking and thick description of the true nature of the *democratic* as a phenomenon. Finally, he would need to engage in at least some metapolitical activity, if not actual political *praxis* or strategizing, to further and enhance the approximation of the real to the ideal. The last item would entail both an "offensive" posture in the form of positive law, constitutionalism, public policy, and education or formation, as well as a "defensive" posture to help ward off decay and corruption resulting from both ideological and institutional mistakes, as well as both social and individual sin. None of this would be easy since his historical point of departure was so far removed from any proverbial "garden," if you will.

To build what a contemporary thinker has called "the Order of Love"[9] from the intellectual, physical, spiritual, and political "ruins" of the first half of the twentieth century has proven to be no simple task, to say the least. That we appear to be significantly further away in the first half of the twenty-first century from such a thing could be cause for despair if we were not people of hope. Hope, as noted earlier, is not to be confused with some mushy idea of optimism, but instead is grounded in the notion that God is good and the created order is, therefore, also good. That order, however, is currently in disarray because of what an Augustinian might call our disordered loves. For Augustine, contra Cicero, a "people" was not a multitude united by their common interests and agreements about what was right, but rather a multitude united by "a common agreement as to what it loves."[10] Further, Augustine himself says in a famous section of *The City of God* that "the better objects of this agreement, the better the people; and the worse the objects, the worse the people."[11] In this vein, Gregory tells us that "taking up Augustine's invitation to view a 'people' in terms of their objects of love, Augustinian liberals have engaged in immanent criticism of a variety of social practices and institutions that jeopardize the dignity of the human

---

9. See Gregory, *Politics and the Order of Love*.
10. Gregory, *Politics and the Order of Love*, 50–51.
11. Quoted in Gregory, *Politics and the Order of Love*, 51.

person and goals of justice and peace."[12] One of the chief impediments to properly ordered loves in contemporary political thought is a fundamental misunderstanding of what should be the primary object of affection which produces a corresponding error concerning the simple question of who is in charge.

DEMOCRATIC SOVEREIGNTY RECONSTRUCTED

To understand the historical process that has led to this disordered state of affairs and the need to "restate" the true grounds of the democratic state, I turn to the historical-political-theological story told by Jean Bethke Elshtain in her sweeping 2008 book *Sovereignty: God, State, and Self*. While some may find Elshtain's work here a little overly ambitious (she starts with Augustine and works all the way to Camus and even Pope Benedict XVI), the general picture she paints strikes me as entirely accurate. That picture is one that takes us from debates concerning the nature of God and God's sovereignty to the contemporary notion of the "sovereign self." Her self-described task is to recover a "moral concept of sovereignty"[13] as compared to a territorial one. Although she does not say it directly, her larger target is the delineation and deconstruction of Dostoevsky's nightmarish world where all things might in fact become permitted. Because, as she writes near the very end of the book, "we are persons, not individuals; we must refrain from doing everything of which we are capable."[14] Her distinction between "person" and "individual" is far more dense than it may appear to the casual reader and in many ways carries the book's argument in crystalloid form. To get there, we start about as far away, conceptually speaking, as possible, at least at first glance. Elshtain begins her argument with nothing less than the question of God's own nature as represented by the distinction between God as *logos* (reason) and God as *will*. This is also characterized in the text as the distinction between God as bound or God as unbound. Simplistically put, the issue is whether the Christian God can be both all-powerful and limited at the same time. In succinct form, Elshtain begs the question like this: "If God's power is absolute and immutable, is God in anyway bound; or is, instead, God free to undo what he has already done, overturn the laws of nature perhaps, or even bring creation to an end?"[15]

---

12. Gregory, *Politics and the Order of Love*, 51.
13. Elshtain, *Sovereignty*, 2.
14. Elshtain, *Sovereignty*, 230.
15. Elshtain, *Sovereignty*, 2.

While a philosophic answer to this theological question ultimately resides in the domain of logic of the variety concerning whether God can make a stone so heavy that even God cannot lift it, Elshtain's concern is not with theology proper but rather with the political implications potentially entailed in holding one position or the other. She sides theologically with those who understand God as *logos*, including Pope Benedict XVI, whom she quotes as saying "the God who is logos guarantees the intelligibility of the world, the intelligibility of our existence, the aptitude of reason to know God . . . and the reasonableness of God."[16] In other words, God is in fact "limited" by God's own power in the context of an event horizon that is beyond human capacity to see or know such that even when it might appear that God is breaking one of God's own rules, God is not actually doing so in what we might literally call the grand scheme of things. As such, there are things that God will simply never do, not because God *could* not do them, but because God's own nature will not let God do them. By way of a very under-nuanced and poorly drawn analogy, picture a human being who knows that left unshackled he might do something that he would regret, i.e., something that the very existence of remorse implies that it is not representative of who he truly is. Imagine then that to avoid even the chance that he might do that thing, chains himself to the wall and throws the key out of reach. By so doing, he has in effect willed himself to be bound and therefore limited. This is how to at least begin to make sense of the notion of a bound but all-powerful God. When history has presented us with a seeming contradiction to the ideal of a bound or "reasonable" God, it is because of human finiteness and our restricted scope or vantage point rather than God's arbitrariness. We simply do not know or see all that God knows or sees. The incarnation and God's self-revelation in human form was of course the single most important attempt to mitigate the vastness of human distance from the Creator. As Elshtain puts it, "This God comes down to us through the Son so that we might rise to meet him."[17]

Hence, the "bound" God would in effect never even try to lift the stone that he had made so heavy in the first place and we would have to be satisfied with knowing first, that no human being can possibly lift it and, second, that it never moves. In this way, we know that we are not God and that God is intelligible and all-powerful at the same time. It is this unartfully constructed theological-philosophical view of what Elshtain calls "moral sovereignty" that gets undone in the earliest days of modernity by the philosophic and theological nominalists and monists who enshrine an image of God as Will

---

16. Elshtain, *Sovereignty*, 3.
17. Elshtain, *Sovereignty*, 6.

to the detriment of the notion of limits and the benefit of political absolutism. Foreshadowing her very complicated historical argument, Elshtain provides her tentative thesis with a question and the claim: "If God acts outside his laws, can an earthly sovereign act outside the established laws of a polity? Yes, say the nominalists, rulers may suspend the laws if the need arises."[18] This will later allow her to claim that "absolutism was a 'modern' not medieval theory of rule"[19] and that "the articulation and enactment of divine right monarchy, mistakenly associated in the popular mind with medieval authoritarianism is, in fact, an early modern invention."[20] After a relatively quick trek through the work of Hobbes, Locke, Rousseau, and Hegel, we end up with the unbound God begetting the unbound state. While it still matters mightily whether that unbound sovereign state is liberal or authoritarian from a practical and humane perspective, the theoretical implications remain the same: modern states are in essence all *modern* states.

While this in and of itself is deeply problematic for Elshtain, it is ultimately not her real target. Building out from her earlier work on Augustine,[21] Elshtain's larger critique is reserved for the derivative rise of the "sovereign self" whom she argues, contra the sovereign state, has emerged and is today virtually unchallenged in the West. In her words:

> So, despite the fact that, theologically, a voluntarist will-centered God was ongoingly challenged by an emphasis on a triune God of reason and love, the voluntarist strand triumphed in a strong state sovereigntist projects and, as we shall see, in the emergence and solidification of sovereign selves.[22]

Since I have already covered much of this ground in early parts of the book in my own way, I will not do a thorough recounting of Elshtain's historical argument here except to note that her move from the Augustinian "person" to the modern "individual" will help us return to Maritain's Christian-democratic apology more forcefully than ever in a moment. Arguing from what she calls "Augustine's dynamic trinitarianism,"[23] Elshtain sets out to dethrone the liberal/modern self who is essentially solitary and alone[24] with his or her ability to "engage in certain highly abstract men-

---

18. Elshtain, *Sovereignty*, 38.
19. Elshtain, *Sovereignty*, 66.
20. Elshtain, *Sovereignty*, 95.
21. Elshtain, *Augustine and the Limits of Politics*.
22. Elshtain, *Sovereignty*, 160.
23. Elshtain, *Sovereignty*, 162.
24. Elshtain, *Sovereignty*, 184.

tal operations"[25] and replace such a creature with a human person whose "ability to love" is their defining characteristic or essence.[26] Building from this position leads her to the claim that "above all, we are created to love and to be loved."[27] This, in turn, matters immensely because it launches us down a theoretical path that denies the naturalness of the "war of all against all" and the sort of instrumental reason that leads to the rationalization of so many forms of modern oppression and repression as well as the legitimation of violence, killing, and even genocide in the wrong hands. The path love takes us to is one where all persons have value and dignity by virtue of their humanity alone. The gospel requires its believers to extend that respect to the alien, the stranger, and even the enemy, thereby rendering the Other a concrete human being to be loved rather than an abstraction to be feared, controlled, vanquished, or destroyed. This belies the image of singular self-directed and self-interested monads bumping into one another from time to time and eventually forming a pact not to enslave or kill each other out of either an innate, but not necessarily rational, desire to survive at worst or a categorical imperative derived from pure reason at best.

The Christian rejects such a view in favor of one derived from "the God who humbles himself, God as the 'man-for-others' in theologian Dietrich Bonhoeffer's locution . . . who serves to highlight responsibility and limits," according to Elshtain.[28] The by-product of that view is such that: "Human life is always lived in concrete communities—not in nowhere. Even as God is dialogic and related and gives of himself, so are we called—in Christianity—to be likewise."[29]

The modern individual, however, is "unique" and revels in his or her "separate-ness" or "apartness" from other individuals, whereas the Christian "person" is a particular version or a kind of instantiation of all persons and, thus, revels in his or her "togetherness" or "with-ness" regarding others who are the same and yet distinct. Indeed, Sam Wells has eloquently argued that the latter understanding is actually the cure for the first, which is discussed as a pathology rather than an achievement.[30] Which brings us back, finally, to Maritain's project. Unlike the idea of rights found in the social contract theory of liberals, Maritain's "personalistic" philosophy (like Elshtain's) are not what Murray might call "articles of peace," but rather prescriptive or

---

25. Elshtain, *Sovereignty*, 167.
26. Elshtain, *Sovereignty*, 167.
27. Elshtain, *Sovereignty*, 230.
28. Elshtain, *Sovereignty*, 229.
29. Elshtain, *Sovereignty*, 230.
30. Wells, "Rethinking Service," 6–14.

enabling devices designed to allow for the full realization of each human being within a context that, by definition, is both social and subsequently political. So it is that Maritain asks and answers his own question below and in doing so provides us with an understanding of the democratic state as one designed not for the preservation or expansion of sovereign selves (let alone human hierarchies), but rather the growth and flourishing of each and every *person*. In his words,

> What is the final aim and most essential task of the body politic or political society? It is not to ensure the material convenience of scattered individuals, each absorbed in his own well-being and enriching himself. Nor is it to bring about either industrial mastery over nature, or political mastery over other men. It is rather to better the conditions of human life itself, or to procure the common good of the multitude, in such a positive manner that each *concrete person*, not only in a privileged class but throughout the whole mass, may truly reach that measure of independence which is proper to civilized life and which is ensured alike by the economic guarantees of work, property, political rights, civil virtues, and the cultivation of the mind.[31]

What this view does in essence is shift the analogical ground under the feet of American democracy from the hyper-competitive and seemingly limitless conception of equality as "opportunity" to one of equality as human "development." In turn, the common good here does not simply imply the sum total of all individual goods, nor is it—*pace* the earlier argument about the dangers of the notion of an *independent* nation-state—simply what is in the best interest of the whole or the *general*. Instead, it is something far more complicated and demanding that is being suggested. In this scheme, I would argue, the idea of the common good is ultimately geared toward the notion of perfection. The opening language of the Lord's Prayer points us in this direction, though most of us praying probably give it little real thought anymore. But, look carefully at the words:

> Our Father, who art in heaven.
> Hallowed be thy name.
> Thy kingdom come. Thy will be done.
> On earth as it is in heaven.

On earth as it is in heaven. At its most pristine, of course, God's will is that we love one another as he has loved us. And how is such agapic love made (with at least a nod toward irony) practical? By dying to the self. And

---

31. Maritain, *Man and the State*, 54.

what does this in effect mean? It means, at its most basic, that we are each called upon to sacrifice for (love) the Other up to and including the Cross, if necessary, so that the Other might become the person he or she was called to be. However, it is also the case that each and every Other person is supposed to do the same for me. The Christian God is a very demanding god, to say the least, but our God is not an exploitative one. Such a way of thinking gets bastardized in Rousseau's most famous work and we end up with a democratic state that one writer proclaimed was "born in a river of blood and midwifed by death"[32] as one set of immoral class-based shackles was cast off and newer more comfortable and egalitarian ones were fastened on. This least common denominator approach to the social order was in most regards an improvement at the material and political level, but it wants desperately for aspiration. Furthermore, it, as we all know too well, must continue to rely on the often unstated and *unbounded* prerogative to utilize violence to achieve its ends when necessary.[33]

To get a sense of the aspirational gravitas of Maritain's vision and the raw distance between his work and that of the premier democratic contract theorist, Rousseau, compare two similar rhetorical constructions of the relations between citizens as an experiment. In *The Social Contract*, Rousseau writes,

> Finally, since each man gives himself to all, he gives himself to no one; and since there is no associate over whom he does not gain the same rights as others gain over him, each man recovers the equivalent of everything he loses, and in the bargain he acquires more power to preserve what he has.
> If, then, we eliminate from the social pact everything that is not essential to it, we find it comes down to this; 'Each one of us puts into the community his person and all his powers under the supreme direction of the general will; and as a body, we incorporate every member as an indivisible part of the whole.[34]

This is a socially constructed community designed to protect the individual elements with collective force of all by generating mutually enforceable reciprocal obligations onto each part to serve the whole as insurance that one will be so served if needed by the collective. By contrast, Maritain gives us a picture of a community of social beings who serve without the *quid pro quo*, writing in his 1946 text, *The Person and the Common Good*,

---

32. Barber, "Rousseau's Bloody Hand?," 2.
33. See Abbott, *Shotgun behind the Door*.
34. Rousseau, *Social Contract*, 61.

> For insofar as it advances, this movement tends to realize gradually, in social life, man's aspiration to be treated as a whole and not as a part. To us this is a very abstract but exact expression of the ideal to which, from their inception, modern democracies have been aspiring, but which their philosophy of life has vitiated. This ideal, the complete realization of which cannot be expected here below, is an upper limit drawing to itself the ascending part of history. It calls for an heroic philosophy of life fastened to absolute spiritual values. It can be gradually realized only by the development of law, of a kind of a sacred sense of justice and honor, and by the development of civic amity. For justice and right, by imposing their law upon man as upon a moral agent and by appealing to reason and free will, concern as such, personality; they transform into a relation between two wholes—the whole of the individual person and the social whole—that which otherwise would be no more than the pure subordination of the part to the whole. And love, by assuming voluntarily that which would otherwise be servitude, transfigures it into liberty and a free gift.[35]

This latter construction rejects out of hand the ability to move to an assertion like the one that claims that the refusal of a citizen to acquiesce to the general will would result in their being "forced to be free." Among the things the Christian knows better than most is that no one can take from you by either force or negotiation that which you are willing to give away freely. For example, take a brief passage from Luke where Jesus says, "Give to everyone who asks you, and do not ask for your property back from the man who robs you" (6:30) as an indicator of how this works. The thief becomes the receiver of a gift and not a criminal and the victim becomes the giver of a gift thereby transforming the power relationship by an act of intentional acquiescence or purposeful passivity. Odd as it may sound to our own contemporary sense of justice, such an act of sacred justice actually has the power to create the very civic amity Maritain prizes above as an important part of democratic aspiration. Such a sensibility is evident in John Winthrop's city on the hill sermon in 1630 Boston as he invokes the prophet Micah (as discussed previously in this book). Why, one might ask, do the grounds of the argument matter so much as long as the outcome is more or less the same? Maritain's response would be along the following lines:

> The advocates of a liberal-individualistic, a communistic, or a personalist type of society will lay down on paper similar, perhaps identical, lists of the rights of man. They will not, however,

---

35. Maritain, *Person and the Common Good*, 78–79.

> play that instrument in the same way. Everything depends on the supreme value in accordance with which all these rights will be ordered and will mutually limit each other. It is by virtue of the hierarchy of values to which we subscribe that we determine the way in which the rights of man, economic, social, as well as individual, should, in our eyes, pass into the realm of existence.
> ... The advocates of a personalistic type of society see the mark of human dignity first and foremost in the power to make these same goods of nature serve the common conquest of intrinsically human moral, and spiritual goods and of man's freedom and autonomy.[36]

In other words, the sociopolitical order does not exist to serve the ends of the *unbounded* or "sovereign-self" any more than it does to create the conditions for the unbounded state. Instead, it exists to foster an increasingly fuller realization of the dignity of each human person by both the subject his or her self and by others. Although much bandied about, the term "dignity" is seldom unpacked in any specific way. In standard usage, the term means something like "worthiness." In other words, to treat someone with dignity is to treat him or her as something that possesses value or worth. But, of course, human beings are not just anything of value, we are a very particular kind of valuable thing. This is why the word "dignity" is almost always reserved for human beings and not used to describe other objects of worth or value. We do not say that a house or a painting or a car or even other animals have dignity, nor do any of these objects have the capacity to feel indignant (the belief that one has not been properly honored or treated as something of value) or undignified (to be in some sort of state or condition where one might appear to have less value or worthiness than one should). Dignity, in the Christian tradition, is a term that means that human beings are special in their value or worthiness insofar as they have this quality in and of themselves and not in relation to anything else. That is to say, the value of any woman or man is always absolute rather than relative or instrumental. In turn, this immediately places questions that might be appropriate for other objects of value or worth, like, "What can I do with it?" "What can I use it for?" or "What can I get for it?" off limits. However, these are primarily negative injunctions and therefore fall far short of the Christian-personalist ideal. The positive duties demanded by the existence of human dignity are summed up by the philosopher Karol Wojtyla (Pope John Paul II) in his 1960 book *Love and Responsibility* in the following way:

---

36. Maritain, *Man and the State*, 106–7.

> This norm [the personalistic norm], in its negative aspect, states that the person is the kind of good which does not admit of use and cannot be treated as an object of use as such as a means to an end. In its positive form the personalistic norm confirms this: the person is a good towards which the only proper and adequate attitude is love. This positive content of the personalistic norm is precisely what the commandment to love teaches.[37]

In this scheme, the individual—an artificial construct first introduced into the world in the early nineteenth century for very specific sociopolitical reasons[38]—is decentered in favor of the person—a social creature embedded in a thick web of relationships who is at once both a part of a series of wholes (the human race, their nation, their families, etc.) and a whole unto himself or herself. This is the famous Catholic both/and at its most profound. Each person, as well as each society he or she belongs to, has an integrity and good of its own that is both immanent and intrinsic to it, and which is not interchangeable or exchangeable at an essentialist level with other independent persons or societies despite their clear inter-relationships. In simplified form, it is the case that a child is obviously dependent upon, and closely related to, his or her parents and that as a family they share a common good. However, the child (and the parents as well) are also independent beings with their own personal goods or vocations to live out and up to. While the family-as-society has claims on each of its family members *qua* family members, it cannot legitimately make a claim that requires the member simply become a use-value to the familial society such that they can no longer view themselves and their value as separate and distinct from the unit at the same time. This is obviously easier to see in theory than it might be to in practice as each member at least *appears* from time to time to sacrifice the self to the collective, but this is again an example of love transforming through the process of gift what might appear to be servitude into an act of liberty and autonomy. In Wojtyla's words, "Man's capacity for love depends on his willingness consciously to seek a good together with others, and to subordinate himself to that good. *Love is exclusively the portion of human persons.*"[39]

While human beings are capable of having great affection for many things that are not persons from pets to art to a sports franchise, it is sinful for the Christian to place anything, no matter how adored or cherished it might be, ahead of a single other human being created in the image and

---

37. Wojtyla, *Love and Responsibility*, 41.
38. See Bird, *Myth of Liberal Individualism*.
39. Wojtyla, *Love and Responsibility*, 29.

likeness of God. To do so is to engage in idolatry (however unintentional such an act may be). Yes, it is the case that our dogs and cats often seem more loving and tender to us than a good number—even most—human beings we encounter. There is nothing wrong with the joy the relationship with a non-human being brings and it is something to truly be thankful for. However, the existence or lack of reciprocity from other human beings cannot be controlling for the Christian, as outlined earlier. Our response to the Others in our midst, at the deepest level, must always be to love them above all other creatures and things in the world because in doing so we obey the commandment to "love one another as I have loved you." So, when Wojtyla joins the ultimate political goal (justice) to his Christian phenomenology, we get a formulation that says, "For to be just always means giving others what is rightly due them. A person's rightful due is to be treated as an object of love"[40] and, I would hasten to add, not merely as a holder of rights, let alone an object of use. A restructured democratic sovereignty places the sacred human person at the center of its order and attempts to build out a regime of values, norms, policies, and laws that is at once faithful to this project in a manner that is providential, prophetic, and prudential at the same time.

PERSONALISM AND THE LOVE REGIME

So it is that the proper object of a proper democratic people's love is persons, not wealth, or material goods, or health, or war, or even liberty, or equality, or individualism (in its typical American possessive form). That is a steep hill to climb in the contemporary world, and I am under no illusions about the practicality of such an assertion. However, I am completely convinced of its veracity and would challenge those of all ideological stripes who might choose some other item from this list, or something else entirely, as the prime object to demonstrate how over time the degenerative consequences of such an attachment will not necessarily undermine the democratic rationale itself by eventually treating the human person instrumentally as an object of use (or as an object to whose ends we are indifferent) rather than an end. Assuming for just a moment that I could demonstrate this process with more space and time, the result of such a degeneration would eventually be to subject democracy itself to a utilitarian test and render it too into just another means rather than an end itself. This position of "what works" rather than "what's right" contains the seeds of every movement that has come to deny a set of human beings their respective dignity since carried to its

---

40. Wojtyla, *Love and Responsibility*, 42.

logical conclusion it sees all limits in relative rather than absolute terms. The easiest example of this might be the contemporary conversations around torture we have seen since 9/11 and the Iraq War and more recently with the rise of ISIS. Instead of saying that there are simply some things we will never do because they undermine fundamentally who we are as a people, we now often hear from our public leaders that it is only the weak, the unfaithful, or the sympathizer who would refuse the toughest measures *needed* (ironically I would claim) to preserve our way of life. As then-presidential candidate Trump once put it with a strong note of condemnation and scorn: "They cut off heads and put people in cages and drown them and we will not even allow waterboarding!" He would go on to say that if in power he would push for far more intrusive forms of "enhanced interrogation" than even this method. How far behind, if at all, can it be before we hear about the need to sacrifice democracy in order to save it?

While I will not delve too deeply into the possible relationship between the practical and the prophetic here, I would urge the reader to see Kristin Heyer's fine book *Prophetic and Public: The Social Witness of U.S. Catholicism* as a starting point for this conversation. Instead, I want to flesh out the personalist position a little more fully. The subject at the core of the personalist position is a self that is radically different from the self that is reflected through the prism of modern American individualism described so well by Tocqueville. That "self" looked inward and slowly withdrew into the solitude of his or her own heart. The self of the Personalist is one that spends significant time looking outward at the other selves with whom he or she shares the world. The self of the Personalist knows that a solitary heart is one in decay. Think of the phrase we often hear about an individual who is self-absorbed. If we were to take this idea literally, the image we would get is one akin to a dried-out sponge. It is a self that has collapsed in on itself and leaves no part of itself overflowing available to the world. In seeking both to love and to be loved, the Personalist-self is always expanding both his or her reach and grasp of the Other.

Harkening back to Elshtain's earlier work, the Personalist-self is the same kind of self found in Augustine's *Confessions* in many ways. That self, Elshtain tell us, bears little resemblance to contemporary selves exposing themselves in today's "confessional" culture. She writes that

> one is struck by the harshness, the meanness, and the utter predictability of many of these displays, as well as the aggressive ways in which confession and scandal have become weapons of

war and instruments of assault against family and friends and that obscure enemy, Society, the world at large.[41]

Writing as she was in the age of *Jerry Springer* and other such shows, this image is apt. Extrapolating out for the last twenty years and factoring in the growth of social media with its ceaseless call for self-exposure and its faux intimacy with neither actual contact or context whereby we are "friends" with dozens, hundreds, even thousands of virtual strangers whom we "follow" episodically and who do the same for us, Elshtain's observation that "one is saddened by the thinness of the selves put on display" with neither "density" nor "texture" is even more telling.[42] The result for Elshtain is the opposite of the Personalist-self above. In her words,

> When one loves only one's self, the self grows thin and flattens out; it reduces to a defensive point of order or oozes indiscriminately into a general sociological morass. If every external point of reference is lost, we lose our very selves. But we do not want to hear this. For the most part, I doubt that we believe it.
> We don't believe it because we have turned the loss of a confessing self who is drawn *out* of the self in order to be for others into an all-consuming self, an expressivist exhibition.[43]

While still obviously a person under our rubric, such selves are antithetical to the democratic regime properly understood, and instead create the conditions for what might best be called a neoliberal or even objectivist regime. This is the regime of the contracting individual whose portended lack of sociality renders the subject unfit for even Rousseau's brand of republican citizenship, let alone that of the Christian-democratic regime. When Elshtain borrows the phrase from the philosopher Jan Patočka, "the solidarity of the shattered," we get the picture of a sad and even tragic optimism that the modern liberal world is reduced to. The "last best hope" is transformed into the best worst hope, if you will—better than the war of all against all, but still pretty thin gruel to nourish a self on at the end of the day. Although a bit over the top, I want to say (all apologies to Patočka) that we might find such a "community" in the pages or film version of Chuck Palahniuk's *Fight Club*. Those denatured young men bonding over a violence that allows them to feel alive compared to their humdrum existences are excoriated by the film's anti-hero in one scene when he exclaims: "You are not special. You are not a beautiful or unique snowflake. You are the same decaying

---

41. Elshtain, *Augustine and the Limits of Politics*, 5.
42. Elshtain, *Augustine and the Limits of Politics*, 5.
43. Elshtain, *Augustine and the Limits of Politics*, 14.

organic matter as everything else." The individualists of the neoliberal world would neither accept nor reject this leveling assertion because despite its pall, it is not the cry of the indifferent that the "whatever, it's not for me to judge" crowd would embrace. Indeed, it is the pained cry of those who feel forsaken and near the edge of despair dressed up as so-called realism that we are really hearing. The Christian-Personalist knows this and asserts the defiant truth of the gospel for all the cynics and homogenizers to hear, that indeed each of us is special, beautiful, and unique, and we are each loved in all our particularity.

Explaining, *pace* Aquinas, that human beings are the only things in the universe "willed for their own sake,"[44] Maritain, in his book *The Person and the Common Good*, notes with approval the "Angelic Doctor's" argument that "the good of grace of one person is worth more than the whole universe of nature."[45] He goes on in breathtaking fashion to explain,

> The beatific vision is therefore the supremely personal act by which the soul, transcending every sort of created common good, enters into the very bliss of God and draws life from the uncreated Good, the divine essence itself, the uncreated, common Good of the three Divine Persons.[46]

It is this image of the Trinity that Maritain turns to later in the text which becomes an important prelude to his conception of "wholes" and the common good discussed earlier in this chapter. Each part of the Trinity is complete unto itself, and yet the Whole is itself both complete and greater than the sum of its "parts." The communion of persons in society works in a similar fashion such that it is not possible for the individuals of the social contractors whose "society" is *at best* the sum of its parts. Thus, they are forced in their own ways to spend so much time and energy legitimizing the use of force and the need for control in the form of a strong absolute monarch (Hobbes), a strong occasionally unbound chief executive with the rights of prerogative (Locke), or the general will of Rousseau. The Christian-democratic order is tied to metaphors of releasing, liberating, overflowing, and so on, not on containing, quelling, or circumventing. By way of a simpler metaphor, think of the union between a man and a woman that produces a child. Assuming here that the union is the consummation of the deep love that both have for the other, the child so produced is, in essence, the epitome of that which is quite literally out of control. Their love has unleashed in the

---

44. Maritain, *Person and the Common Good*, 17.
45. Maritain, *Person and the Common Good*, 20.
46. Maritain, *Person and the Common Good*, 21.

world something (someone) that despite some initial dependency and their seeming ability to "contain" the young being through physicality is, when all is said and done, an unpredictable, unimaginable, uncontrollable life-force. By its very presence in the world, that child will change it, its materiality, its historical trajectory, and even, in its own way, the past.[47] Countless (literally countless) things in the world change with each and every human birth. Often, these changes will be imperceptible and often they will not be, strictly speaking, attributable to any single person, but it is also true that without him or her being present, they cannot be the same as they were with the person present. A politics that celebrates this disruptive force rather than fearing it is a truly democratic politics.

This vision of the sacred person is what provides the foundation for the entire architecture of Catholic "constitutionalism" as I understand it. Here I want to quote Maritain at length because, as I read him, this argument makes it virtually impossible to defend non-democratic forms of political rule while at the same time making any democratic politics *not* grounded in a similar manner seem unreasoned. Maritain writes,

> Man is constituted a person, made for God and life eternal, before he is constituted a part of the city; and he is constituted a part of the family society before he is constituted a part of the political society. This is the origin of those primordial rights which political society must respect and which it may not injure when it requires the services of its members.

We have stated that, on the one hand, it is the person itself which enters into society and, on the other, that it is ultimately by reason of its material individuality that it is in society as a part whose good is inferior to the good of the whole. If that is the case, it is understandable that society cannot live without the perpetual gifts of persons, each one of whom is *irreplaceable* and incommunicable; and that, nevertheless, the very thing of persons which in social usage is retained is transmuted into something communicable and *replaceable*, always individualized but depersonalized.

> The common good, by its very essence, directs itself to the persons as persons and directs the persons as individuals to itself.

---

47. I know this sounds odd, but what I have in mind here is that numerous previously understood events that happened in the past will suddenly take on new meaning and significance. Think here of the *Back to the Future* movies and the significance of a single kiss. Had love not bloomed for the McFly family as the result of the kiss, that kiss would have just been a passing and perhaps forgotten moment between two people. But, the arrival of Marty a few years later imbued that past moment with far more importance than anyone might have imagined at the time.

> It directs itself to persons in a two-fold way: first, in so far as the persons are engaged in the social order, the common good by its essence must flow back over or redistribute itself to them; second, in so far as persons transcend the social order and are directly ordained to the transcendent Whole, the common good by its essence must favor their progress toward the absolute goods which transcend political society.[48]

With this, we have returned now to Maritain's call for a *heroic philosophy of life* and the notion of transformation of coercion by way of self-gift. The sociopolitical order can make no claims upon the human person that she or he is not in essence the author of and neither can the person as an *individual-citizen* authorize legitimately any claim that attempts to thwart or negate the transcendent ends of persons. Or, put another way in keeping with the earlier sections of this chapter, the common good properly understood cannot countenance actions which treat human beings as objects rather than ends who possess the right to be loved and the duty to love others.

This is all highly theoretical and no doubt will strike even sympathetic readers as hopelessly academic and unrealistic (and for others who take it seriously, it may be even seen as dangerous).[49] However, that line of criticism tends to presume implicitly that somehow, where we currently are was the result of a well-thought out and intentional plan, i.e., something *intended*, and, even more importantly, that it is sustainable in the long run. It is the whole argument of this book that neither proposition is true *and* that something of real value hangs in the balance if it proves unsustainable as a result of our not *tending* to it properly.[50] Maritain's natural law closing to his text some sixty years ago was no doubt inspired in large measure by the historical events he had witnessed just "moments" before, but it strikes me at this historical moment as eerily prescient as well. I close this section in his words as they seem both timely and timeless and necessary for us to hear:

> In this light, the tendency towards the materialism and atheism inherent in *the city of the individual* appears as one of the absurdities by which it destroys itself. In the political order, the internal dialectic of this tendency, by similar absurdity, drags it towards dictatorship which is its proper negation.
>
> These reflections lead us to believe that the drama of modern democracies has consisted in the unwitting quest of something good, the city of persons, masked by the error of the city of

---

48. Maritain, *Person and the Common Good*, 75–76.
49. See Gregory, *Politics and the Order of Love*, ch. 4.
50. See Wolin, *Presence of the Past*, ch. 4.

the individual, which, by nature, leads to dreadful liquidations. It is not for the philosophers to forecast whether they can reorient themselves decisively in the direction of the truth which they seek by disengaging the parasitical errors from their quest. Such a reorientation would presuppose a radical transformation and vast return towards the spirit.[51]

THE PASTORAL IS THE POLITICAL

Common historical lore tells us that the events and documents of Vatican II mark the moment in time of the Church's "democratic turn" and its entry into the so-called modern world. For "progressives," this was good news indeed. For "traditionalists," it was the moment of capitulation and acquiescence. I will leave much of this qualitative debate to the theologians and the historians to hash out, though it is clear that the Church's position and tone vis-à-vis democracy certainly shifted in critically important ways as a result of the Council's work. What the *political* implications of this shift were/are, however, remains highly contestable. How can that be, someone might reasonably ask? If the Church turned to a positive and even Maritainian position regarding *democracy*, then wouldn't that indicate or imply democratic partisanship by definition? The answer is yes and no, depending on at least two factors. The first is how the term *politics* is understood; and the second is what are the Church's reasons were for its shift. In other words, regarding the latter question, we must assume that the Church's political loyalties, purely understood, are always conditional and prudential since they are by definition, non-pejoratively speaking, secular or worldly in nature. The value of a particular political order is a function of its utility in achieving or facilitating (or at least not thwarting) the realization of sacred ends. Were the Church's attachment to a particular order be otherwise, it would risk fetishism and even idolatry because the Church is in the people-loving business, not the state-loving business.

This, in turn, leads us back to the first question; namely, how the term *politics* is used. To embrace, à la Maritain's argument, the democratic political *form* as the only currently defensible one according to natural law does not mean that such an embrace need be an eternal or "infallible" position. Conditions may change in unforeseen ways and new political inventions or circumstances on the ground (literally) may necessitate rethinking in light of the sacred goals being serviced someday. Because of the necessary conditionality of the Church's democratic allegiance (again, an *unreliable ally*),

51. Maritain, *Person and the Common Good*, 104–5.

both confidence and humility are called for. Humility, by its nature, in this case, means a rejection of any form of hard partisanship precisely because worldly loyalty for the Church and its members must always be tentative. Practically speaking, this means that while the Church can come to look favorably, even adoringly, upon the democratic form it cannot sacrifice its larger values in the name of its achievement by allowing the ends to justify the means as strong forms of partisanship typically end up doing. In simplified form, the following construction will have to suffice to clarify what I am trying to say: The Church can (and should) by its own logic embrace democracy as defined previously in this chapter and elsewhere, but it cannot, by that same logic, embrace the kind of partisanship that would call for a violent revolution in order to secure democracy in the first place. To harken back to a previous argument in this book, it is not permissible to shoot it out with the Roman guards to save Christ from the Cross. While some may want to argue that this is hypocritical—to enjoy the fruits of democracy and yet question to the point of judgment the manner in which it was achieved—I prefer the term paradox. Such is the nature of those called pilgrims in this world.

It is against this rather awkwardly constructed argument that I want to turn to an important text to help move this part of the narrative along. Written in 2011 by Emile Perreau-Saussine, *Catholicism and Democracy* is a provocative and compellingly argued political-theological history of the developmental relationship between the First and Second Vatican Councils. Although situated in the European context, the insights of the text are applied without too much difficulty to the argument at hand and its American frame. One of the central contributions of the text is its ability to delve beneath the surface of the two Councils deep enough to find an important political-philosophical convergence between what are often depicted as divergent and even oppositional episodes in Church history. In vastly simplified form, the first Council is often viewed through a conservative and even reactionary lens, while the second Council is often portrayed as liberal and reformist, with the superficial conclusion being that this terminology is not somehow time-bound or in need of appropriate contextualization. If the two councils are conflated and viewed through the lens of a sports team that must play both offense and defense to "win the game," then suddenly what might appear to be two very different courses of action or modes of behavior in the course of the "game" suddenly make perfect sense. At its core, the question that unites the two councils is how to maintain the integrity of the Church as Church in the context of changing political and cultural orders while continuing to deliver on its primary mission to serve God though worship and evangelization. Particular strategies and tactics designed to create the necessary political and social space to make enactment of those ends viable are, in due course, malleable and situational. In other words, the Church's own politics are by their nature prudential even while the ultimate values the Church seeks to secure are fixed and permanent.

The threat that the Church faced in the mid- to late nineteenth century was a brand of Gallicanism ("the bone marrow of [which] . . . was the identification of Catholics with the life of the nation"[52]), whereby the increasingly secularist state not only separated itself from the authority and moral tutelage of the Church, but was also interfering in Church matters and doctrine so as to reduce the Church to another bureaucratic appendage of the same. This process produced a reaction that Perreau-Saussine describes thusly: "The humiliation of the church, reduced to a mere instrument of state, provoked a reaction among Catholics, who started to look to Rome as a symbol of independence."[53] In turn, the larger critique of the faithful is succinctly put as follows:

> Thus, ironically, the reactionaries condemned liberalism in the name of liberty of the church. For them, the "liberals" aimed not at setting believers free but at confining them to the private sphere, in such a way as to dominate and marginalize the church. This privatization of belief was in their view a way of securing the hegemony of godless state power.[54]

So it is that the only way to safeguard the Church and its larger *public* mission was to consolidate and defend its sphere of existence and prerogative through vehicles like infallibility and dogmatism and to wean itself from the all-too-compromising reliance on particular states and their princes, broadly understood. In jettisoning the status and favors conferred by the confessional states, the Church no longer needed to retain a semblance of deference that persistently would undermine or cause it to silence its prophetic voice in the face of injustice and immorality. For Perreau-Saussine, it becomes the state's combination of political overreach and underspecified sense of morality that begets what is too often mischaracterized as a conservative or anti-modern reaction by the Church and its hierarchy. In simplified form, as the modern state's gravitational pull increased and sought to absorb and repurpose the Church for its own needs and interests, the Church's defiance and resistance in the name of independence and service to its own ends may appear retrograde to the casual observer or the partisan when in fact it is merely an act of institutional authenticity and self-preservation.

52. Perreau-Saussine, *Catholicism and Democracy*, 20.
53. Perreau-Saussine, *Catholicism and Democracy*, 43.
54. Perreau-Saussine, *Catholicism and Democracy*, 46.

In essence, the Church's attempt to consolidate was not directed at the faithful, but at the increasing "faithless" politics of the day. Whatever the theological or ecclesiastic arguments or justifications might be, the *politics* of the First Council were about the preservation of the Church's independence and assertion of its overarching value as an integral and authoritative social institution. In Perreau-Saussine's words: "The freedom of the church is not a gracious concession on the part of the state: it is part of God's order, enshrined in canon law. The church claims to govern itself by its own laws and conceives of itself as existing by inherent right."[55]

All of this, however, is not meant to say that the Church at this time was firmly on the path toward a full-throated embrace or defense of liberal-democracy as has already been noted earlier in the book. This is because the Church still had what I would call a "Hartz problem," metaphorically speaking. What I mean by this is that the phenomenon Hartz described as the liberal tradition in America is in its own way the liberal tradition period. While the lack of a feudal order might have made America's historical journey unique, it does not mean that the same hegemonic tendencies were not present elsewhere. It is just that in the European context there were countervailing forces that did not exist in the land where people were "born equal." So it is that the Church, while asserting claims to free association and self-determination that are often associated with liberalism itself, was doing so in the name of a hierarchical and undemocratic institution that was desperately trying to preserve itself in the face of the homogenizing liberal juggernaut that would render it just another partisan institutional appendage. Here the Church becomes, analogically speaking, like those frustrated aristocrats Hartz talked about as trying to "break out of the confines of middle-class life." Unlike the characters in the Hartzian drama, the Church succeeds in gaining its independence. However, in having had to fight for its right to not be annexed by the liberal-democratic state, it retained an appropriate wariness of what they would argue were the totalizing tendencies of liberalism and the states it begot. Sadly for the world, the rise of real totalitarianism just a few decades later would make the stakes involved in the debate about liberal-democracy seem quite academic and even trite. To ironically steal a phrase from another debate, the rise of Hitler and Stalin, would ensure that the contradictions of the day were heightened to the point of no return. Enter Maritain and the Second Vatican Council.

While the anti-liberals and some ultramontane thinkers persisted (and do in certain forms till this day), their influence and appeal grew increasingly muted as fascism in its various guises drove the human body count

---

55. Perreau-Saussine, *Catholicism and Democracy*, 94.

into the tens of millions. It soon became clear on the practical level that if there were going to be states (and there were) and those states were not going to be confessional states (they were not) and even if they were that it would ultimately be bad for the Church as *Church* (it would), then the only real alternative was liberal-democracy. Shifting into the second part of his book, Perreau-Saussine puts this point in the following way:

> Yet at Vatican II the Catholic Church officially recognized religious freedom and came to terms with some of the key features of liberal democracy. How come? It was in fact the totalitarian movement that proved decisive. Totalitarianism was the dead-end destination of all French anti-liberalisms, from that of Maistre to the Christian Marxists.[56]

Though such grudging acceptance does not make for a ringing endorsement, this critical step, which Perreau-Saussine calls the most significant change in the Church's political history,[57] soon thereafter begets a veritable explosion of documents that dramatically increase the scale and the scope of the corpus of the Church's social teaching that continues till this day. In the documents that comprise what we can now call the tradition, the Magisterium of the Church weighs-in both broadly and deeply about the most important political and social questions facing the world and its people. Just a truncated list of the sorts of topics the Church's Popes and Bishops have spoken to would include issues of life and death, war and peace, wealth and poverty, crime and punishment, human rights, civil rights, immigration, human sexuality, education, and environmental ethics and climate change. Freed from the shackles of deference stemming from confessional or quasi-confessional states and its own aversion to democratic politics, the Church found and exponentially amplified its prophetic voice and developed an emergent sociopolitical *praxis*. After years of playing mostly defense, the Church was now making affirmative arguments and taking positions that challenged and confronted believers, nonbelievers, and, especially, the powerful and the well-positioned in the spirit of the Gospels, with strong bias in favor of social justice and a preference for the least among us. Needless to say this has not always endeared the Church to either the powerful or its own flock, let alone its more persistent detractors. Yet the Church remains undeterred, and, indeed, with Pope Francis at the helm, all signs point to even more robust political and social engagement. While the backdrop of totalitarianism serves as a reasonable explanation for

---

56. Perreau-Saussine, *Catholicism and Democracy*, 116.
57. Perreau-Saussine, *Catholicism and Democracy*, 127.

the Church's turn to liberal-democracy itself, it does not explain the participatory energy unleashed by the Second Council. So what does?

Oddly enough, the answer to that question is a kind of classical liberal economic one of the Adam Smith variety. In simplified form, Smith's argument for free markets in his famous text, *The Wealth of Nations*, was that the breaking down of the protectionist walls of the mercantilist system would unleash the pent-up energy and dynamic creativity of the newly liberated classes and radically increase the production and supply of goods and services in the world's economy driven by competition and enlightened self-interest. Which, of course, happened. The rising tide he spoke of may not have lifted all the ships, but it lifted a lot of them. Analogically speaking, what the shift to religious freedom did for the Church was to liberate it from the burdens of confessional protectionism as alluded to above and allow it to experience the positive release that true and authentic liberty enables. Confident in its own truth and the power and inevitability of *truth* itself, the Church embraced, at the institutional level, the "liberal perfectionism" addressed previously. Religious freedom was the freedom to seek fullness both of the Word and the communion of the body of Christ here on earth. Perreau-Saussine puts it the following way:

> In short, the Catholic Church aligned itself with liberal democracy because it offered its own interpretation of what liberal democracy ought to be. The separation of church and state was accepted because it imposed an unprecedented limitation on the power of the state, which could no longer intervene in the highest matters or substitute itself for individual conscience.[58]
>
> ... In recognizing freedom of religion, the church certainly did not stop hoping that society might become as Christian as possible. It rallied to the cause of liberty all the more readily because it saw in liberty an opportunity to evangelize more effectively.[59]

In its embrace of liberalism on its own terms and for its own ends, the Church was establishing a counter-narrative to what we would now call neoliberalism[60] that was at its core Christian, thereby setting up the tension that undergirds this book. For Perreau-Saussine, "The liberalism that it [the Church] endorsed was a liberalism that allows people to find truth by the light of Christ's teaching."[61] It was not the neutral state of the possessive

---

58. Perreau-Saussine, *Catholicism and Democracy*, 130.
59. Perreau-Saussine, *Catholicism and Democracy*, 131.
60. See Plant, *Neo-liberal State*.
61. Perreau-Saussine, *Catholicism and Democracy*, 137.

individuals that by and large sought to engulf and align all the institutions of civil society and even those associations in the private sphere to its regulated and gentler version of the "war of all against all" that marks the libertarian worldview that the Church sought to ensure and grow, but in many ways its opposite. The state in such a world remains increasingly modest in its aims and sphere, but only because it is being restrained from embarking on the Borg-like project of conformism that would reduce the created world of *persons* to mere states of *individuals*. To give one final word to Perreau-Saussine on this score, he concludes his book in the following way, claiming about the Pope as the Church's representative figure in this alternative political story:

> He manifests the Christian refusal to be entirely swallowed up in the democratic order. That is the church's service to society: to resist the docile conformism to which egalitarianism can lead.... They [believers] form a breakwater against the tide of conformity. They are, par excellence, a sign of contradiction.[62]

While there are any number of ways to proceed with the argument from this point, I want to do so by using the *Pastoral Constitution on the Church in the Modern World: Gaudium et Spes* (1965) as my authoritative text and lens through which to view the Church's strong "democratic" turn. Such a move is made slightly problematic since a word search of the document produces exactly zero hits for either the word *democracy* or *democratic*. The theological, historical, as well as the prudential reasons for this are well developed throughout this work and the politics of it are easily inferred by simply noting the array of nations and national cultures represented at the Council. Indeed, among the most prominent and, for some, surprising themes found in the text is a warm embrace of what we would now call *multiculturalism*. However, I contend that the ubiquity of those positive references to diversity and the stated tolerance for a wide variety of cultural orders and individual conscience itself are *because* of the Church's embrace of a properly understood liberal-social-democratic *ethos* and not evidence of partisan indifference. As a thought experiment, imagine if the only text someone had to read was *Gaudium et Spes* and from it they had to discern, *Canticle for Leibowitz* style, the constitutional form of political regime implied by its teachings. What they would conclude, quite readily, was that it would look a lot like a variant of various liberal and social democratic states found in nineteenth- and twentieth-century North America, Western Europe, and Scandinavia. The *substance* or *content* of said regimes, however, is another matter entirely. Hence the need for the continuing prophetic

---

62. Perreau-Saussine, *Catholicism and Democracy*, 152.

witness and persistent contradiction in the name of social justice and what John Paul II called "authentic democracy."

In *Centesimus Annus* (1991), John Paul II taught that "authentic democracy is possible only in a state ruled by law, and on the basis of a correct conception of the human person." While not phrased precisely this way in *Gaudium et Spes*, the ideal is clearly present in only a slightly encoded form. And while the formulation is seemingly simple on its face, the reality is that the phrase carries with it demands and meanings that are both wide and deep. Take just the simple expression "rule of law." On the surface this is a basic idea for any constitutionally bound regime that is typically contrasted to the notion of the "rule of men." And certainly, John Paul II meant at least this. However, the following passage from *Gaudium et Spes* complicates this simple statement profoundly:

> In the depths of his conscience, man detects a law which he does not impose upon himself, but which holds him to obedience. Always summoning him to love good and avoid evil, the voice of conscience when necessary speaks to his heart: do this shun that. For man has in his heart a law written by God; to obey it is the very dignity of man; according to it he will be judged. Conscience is the most secret core and sanctuary of a man. There he is alone with God, Whose voice echoes in his depths. In a wonderful manner conscience reveals that law which is fulfilled by love of God and neighbor.[63]

Suddenly, a state "ruled by law" must be a state where the law is in accord with the law of God to the extent possible. In other words, there is a substantive component to the law which belies a simple procedural approach characteristic of the legal positivism that prominently marks much of contemporary liberal political thought and constitutionalism. Complicating this immeasurably is the notion at the core of the passage above whereby what the "law" ultimately requires is actions that demonstrate the love of God and neighbor. Now I realize that the reader might quickly claim that I am confusing categories and that the law pertaining to conscience and the laws of the legal system are conceptually distinct, but I respectfully reject that claim. I do so because this is precisely the sort of privatizing move that I have rejected throughout this work on both theological as well as practical grounds. The Christian enters the public sphere as a *Christian*, period. And so it is that John Paul II's second clause sees laws as legitimate only to the extent that they are grounded in the correct conception of human persons. That conception is laid out early in the first chapter of *Gaudium et Spes*,

---

63. Vatican Council, *Gaudium et Spes*, 15–16.

which is titled "The Dignity of the Human Person." In that chapter, we find a conception of the human person such that we are created by God in his image as dialogic and social creatures with both bodies and souls who are both free and wounded by sin and therefore in need of God's grace, and who are capable of a wisdom that "attracts the mind of man to a quest and a love for what is true and good."[64] We realize our full call as human persons and achieve our rightful dignity in the words of Paul VI as follows:

> Man achieves such dignity when, emancipating himself from all captivity to passion, he pursues his goal in a spontaneous choice of what is good, and procures for himself through effective and skillful action, apt helps to that end. Since man's freedom has been damaged by sin, only by the aid of God's grace can he bring such a relationship with God into full flower. Before the judgment seat of God each man must render an account of his own life, whether he has done good or evil.[65]

While noting that communion with God and life with him eternally is the ultimate goal of the believer, the Council is quick to assert the importance of what they call "intervening duties" or the activities in this life. In their words, "This faith needs to prove its fruitfulness by penetrating the believer's entire life, including its worldly dimensions, and by activating him toward justice and love, especially regarding the needy."[66]

That penetrating fruitfulness need not necessarily entail political activism. However, the political community is noted along with the family as being "among those social ties which man needs for his development . . . [because it] . . . relate[s] with greater immediacy to [our] innermost nature."[67] The nature of that community must be one designed to enhance and make fuller the possibilities for human flourishing at the personal or individual level and it will need to include the following intensely progressive substantive understandings and elements:

> At the same time, however, there is a growing awareness of the exalted dignity proper to the human person, since he stands above all things, and his rights and duties are universal and inviolable. Therefore, there must be made available to all men everything necessary for leading a life truly human, such as food, clothing, and shelter; the right to choose a state of life freely and to found a family, the right to education, to employment, to a

---

64. Vatican Council, *Gaudium et Spes*, 15.
65. Vatican Council, *Gaudium et Spes*, 16.
66. Vatican Council, *Gaudium et Spes*, 20.
67. Vatican Council, *Gaudium et Spes*, 24.

good reputation, to respect, to appropriate information, to activity in accord with the upright norm of one's own conscience, to protection of privacy and rightful freedom, even in religious matters....

This social order requires constant improvement. It must be founded on truth, built on justice, and animated by love; in freedom it should grow every day toward a more humane balance. An improvement in attitudes and abundant changes in society will have to take place if these objectives are to be gained.[68]

Such an undertaking simply cannot be done in the modern world outside of the work of politics and public policy. This becomes, *pace* Aquinas, the idea that the appropriate ends will appropriate means and, hence, such large-scale undertakings and the enforcement of the long list of negative rights that follow the list of positive ones listed in the text[69] can ultimately only be managed by something approximating the contemporary state and its political subsidiaries. This is true no matter how robust the civic culture and the institutions of civil society and the non-governmental sphere might be.

Now while it remains true that the Church's own role remains what is called its "saving" and "eschatological" purposes, and, furthermore, that "Christ gave His Church no proper mission in the political, economic or social order" binding it "to no particular form of human culture, nor to any political, economic, or social system," such that it is able to retain its universal character, it is also true that certain modes of political and social organization are vastly more likely to achieve the stated ends and less are liable to corruption.[70] In other words, while the Church's mission is both transhistorical and transcultural, it is always situated, as is any other temporal institution, in a particular time and place. By 1965, conditions throughout much of the world dictated the superiority of the liberal-democratic form for accomplishing the proper sociopolitical ends of sustaining and enhancing human dignity and establishing justice and seeking the common good. Furthermore, it is nearly impossible to read the calls throughout *Gaudium et Spes* for robust participation in the civic sphere and the admonishments against those who would neglect their social and civic duties without simultaneously drawing a strong democratic inference. The following passages are exemplars of the Church's position in this area:

This council exhorts Christians, as citizens of two cities, to strive to discharge their earthly duties conscientiously and in response

---

68. Vatican Council, *Gaudium et Spes*, 26.
69. Vatican Council, *Gaudium et Spes*, 27.
70. See Vatican Council, *Gaudium et Spes*, 38–42.

> to the Gospel spirit. They are mistaken who, knowing that we have no abiding city but seek one which is to come, think that they may therefore shirk their earthly responsibilities. For they are forgetting that by faith itself they are more obliged than ever to measure up to these duties, each according to his proper vocation.[71]
>
> The split between the faith and their daily lives deserves to be counted among the more serious errors of our age. Long since, the Prophets of the Old Testament fought vehemently against this scandal and even more so Jesus Christ Himself in the New Testament threaten it with grave punishments. Therefore, let there be no false opposition between professional and social activities on the one part, and religious life on the other. The Christian who neglects his temporal duties, neglects his duties toward neighbor and even God, and jeopardizes his eternal salvation.[72]

Although not exactly a full-fledged and explicit assertion of the priority of a democratic regime, such calls to public witness and the fulfillment of temporal duties can and, I would argue, must be read as *de facto* calls to citizenship and to a *political* life broadly understood. Such a life is one that is shared and common with other men and women and directed to questions of how we ought to live with one another and united à la Augustine by the objects of our shared love. This argument is reinforced as the text progresses through a discussion of what Pope Paul VI labels "The Proper Development of Culture." In that chapter, by simple inference, we glimpse a subdued, but still present, Hegelianism of a sort as the sense of progressive historical development regarding human society and culture unfolds:

> The word "culture" in its general sense indicates everything whereby man develops and perfects his many bodily and spiritual qualities; he strives by his knowledge and his labor, to bring the world itself under his control. He renders social life *more human* both in the family and the civic community, through the improvement of customs and institutions. Throughout the course of time he expresses, communicates and conserves his works, great spiritual experiences and desires, that they might be *of advantage to the progress of many, even of the whole human family*.[73]

---

71. Vatican Council, *Gaudium et Spes*, 42.
72. Vatican Council, *Gaudium et Spes*, 43.
73. Vatican Council, *Gaudium et Spes*, 57–58. Emphasis mine.

While not exactly an "end of history" argument *per se*, it is clear that development properly understood is directional and that while there is room for pluralism and diversity, it is also the case that there is no room for any sort of hard cultural relativism at the moral or political levels. Indeed, the closing sentences of the introductory section of chapter 2 point explicitly to a universal destination whereby "there is formed a historical milieu which enfolds the man of every nation and age and from which he draws values which permit him to promote civilization."[74] The difficult issue that emerges in this process that sees "a mounting increase in the sense of autonomy as well as responsibility" such that the "spiritual and moral maturity of the human race" might grow and expand to a unified world where the duty is imposed on us to "build a better world based upon truth and justice" growing from a "new humanism" in which we are "defined first of all by this responsibility to his brothers and sisters and to history" is how to prevent secularism and its twin hubris from displacing the true story of human ascent. In the words of *Gaudium et Spes*, "How is the dynamism and expansion of new culture to be fostered without losing a living fidelity to the heritage of tradition?"[75]

A significant part of maintaining fidelity to the tradition involves avoiding the slide into a mode of humanism that is a-religious or anti-religious and places instead what the text calls a cultural autonomy that is "merely terrestrial" at the center of its worldview. Such a move would result in the worst sort of secularization, whereby the world would not only have the sacred and transcendent shorn from its nature and its existential lexicon, but would also marginalize any hopes of transnational or transcultural norms associated with ideas like universal human rights from being successfully propagated and enculturated across distinct peoples and places. In other words, such a humanism would foster and enshrine, at best, an international order based on a hard realism that would elevate the dictum "reasons of state" to the status of a categorical imperative and, at worst, produce a universe of purely unbounded, uncontainable, and unaccountable materialism and consumption. Such a world would be in effect a globalized version of Hobbes's state of nature, only with multi-national corporations possessing advanced technology, weaponry, and private armies to aid them in the postmodern version of the war of all against all. In such a world, the very language of justice—social or otherwise—becomes either quaint or irrational and the notion of sin—personal or social—is no longer relevant and neither is the Church *qua* Church. What I mean by this last clause is that in

---

74. Vatican Council, *Gaudium et Spes*, 58.

75. Vatican Council, *Gaudium et Spes*, 59. All quoted excerpts are from paragraphs 55–56.

such a world "order," the Church and religion would be either reduced to a part of the superstructure or, worse yet, to just another large-scale interest group competing for territory, resources, and power. Once sheered of its supernatural elements and character, the Church would be subordinated to culture—either local, national, or transnational—and subsequently either vanquished, enslaved, or so fully compromised that the Christian who remains committed to the faith of the Gospel can no longer consider it home. Hence, the text's assertion that

> the Church recalls to the mind of all that culture is to be subordinated to the integral perfection of the human person, to the good of the community and of the whole society. Therefore it is necessary to develop the human faculties in such a way that there results growth of the faculty of admiration, of intuition, of contemplation, of making personal judgement, of developing a religious, moral and social sense.[76]

In that hierarchical scheme, the Church and its teachings and people constrain and limit the dominion of the political order and do what is possible to restrict it to its proper sphere. Hence the following description from the closing of section 2:

> As for public authority, it is not its function to determine the character of the civilization, but rather to establish the conditions and use the means which are capable of fostering the life of culture among all even within the minorities of a nation. It is necessary to do everything possible to prevent culture from being turned away from its proper end and made to serve as an instrument of political or economic power.[77]

In turn, the Church calls on those in positions of authority to create inclusive and egalitarian systems designed to develop and foster the civic personality of each of its members in what can only be described as a truly democratic spirit when it claims,

> Therefore it is necessary to provide all with a sufficient quantity of cultural benefits, especially those which constitute the so-called fundamental culture lest very many be prevented from cooperating in the promotion of the common good in a truly human manner because of illiteracy and a lack of responsible activity.[78]

---

76. Vatican Council, *Gaudium et Spes*, 63.
77. Vatican Council, *Gaudium et Spes*, 64.
78. Vatican Council, *Gaudium et Spes*, 64.

The Council makes it very clear that they are especially concerned for the least well off among the population having the necessary tools and opportunities to participate in the life of the community. They go out of their way to include women in their argument in a manner that was itself very progressive for its day. In Brownsonian fashion, they reject the reduction of the human person to *homo economicus* and the corresponding anxiety, insecurity, and inevitable inequality and subjugation such a view always leads to in a world marked by scarcity through the contention that "man is the source, the center, and the purpose of all economic and social life."[79] As to the priority of equality that is the hallmark of democratic thinking at its most substantial, they makes no bones about the Church's position, writing,

> While an immense number of people still lack the absolute necessities of life, some, even in less advanced areas, live in luxury or squander wealth. Extravagance and wretchedness exist side by side. While a few enjoy very great power of choice, the majority are deprived of almost all possibility of acting on their own initiative and responsibility, and often subsist in living and working conditions unworthy of the human person.[80]

Rectifying those disparities requires that economic development itself is purposefully designed and regulated to maximize the positive impact on the whole human family. Radical inequality and increased social and economic stratification are to be avoided and the economy itself needs to be subjected to strong democratic intervention in the name of the common good and human flourishing. While markets are to be used in order to increase efficiency and expand capacity, they are not meant to be fetishized or reified such that their strictly instrumental nature becomes distorted based on some a-rational ideological commitment to a laissez-faire economic order. Directionally speaking, the economic organization locally, nationally, and internationally needs to be ordered to the "demands of justice and equity" and what is called in the document "just liberty," and not to the goals of personal wealth maximization or consumption tied to a false and distorted understanding of the created order and of the human person as some isolated a-social creature. While clearly oppositional to the American liberal tradition and the interpretation we have ascribed throughout this book to Locke, the Church's position leaves the idea of private property intact, but conditions it in a manner that acknowledges the distinction between creator and created as implied by the following passages:

79. Vatican Council, *Gaudium et Spes*, 68.
80. Vatican Council, *Gaudium et Spes*, 69.

> Whatever the forms property may be, as adapted to the legitimate institutions of peoples, according to diverse and changeable circumstances, attention must always be paid to this universal destination of earthly goods. In using them, therefore, man should regard the external things that he legitimately possess not only as his own but also as common in the sense that they should be able to benefit not only him but others. On the other hand, the right of having a share of earthly goods sufficient to oneself and one's family belongs to everyone. The Fathers and Doctors of the Church held this opinion, teaching we are obliged to come to the relief of the poor and to do so not merely out of their superfluous goods. If one is in extreme necessity, he has the right to procure for himself what he needs out of the riches of others.[81]

However, it is not merely survival that is at stake in such a view of the world's goods; it is also the independence and autonomy that having one's material needs met begets that matters here. Such goods constitute one of the conditions for civil liberties and, hence, citizenship itself.[82] When the text finally turns officially to "the life of the political community" in chapter 4, the full embrace of the liberal democratic order comes into view as the rights bearing individual, who must be allowed to take an active part in the "life and government" of the state, becomes the standard against which political regimes are to be measured and judged. In that chapter, the political community and public authority are declared part of the natural order designed by God and while there remains a prudential openness to a variety of regime types, there are pointed conversations not only about individual rights and liberties, but also about voting itself that leaves no actual space for any explicitly non-democratic order to pass muster. All dictatorial and totalitarian systems are explicitly rejected as illegitimate and the practice of politics as a profession is declared noble when done with a view toward civic virtue and the common good.[83]

The final portion of the chapter is devoted to a brief but important discussion of the relationship between the authority of the state as endorsed and delineated and the Church. Intoning a version of the "two cities" thesis, the document makes it clear that the Church's responsibility is to safeguard "the transcendent nature of the human person" and work alongside the political community in her own sphere to foster the "personal and social vocation" of every human person.[84] To do this, however, the Church must

---

81. Vatican Council, *Gaudium et Spes*, 75.
82. Vatican Council, *Gaudium et Spes*, 77.
83. Vatican Council, *Gaudium et Spes*, 79–83.
84. Vatican Council, *Gaudium et Spes*, 84.

always be mindful that "those dedicated to the ministry of God's Word must use the ways and means proper to the Gospel which in a great many respects differ[s] from the means proper to the earthly city." Thus, the Church is in the world in a very active and thick way while ultimately being called to avoid being of the world. This is a tricky piece of work and all too often the Church has failed to walk the proper line. However, as the Council so aptly puts it when speaking of the Apostles and their successors, the strength of the gospel "often shows forth . . . on the weakness of its witnesses."[85] The Church's role in the political sphere is the same as its role generally speaking and is summed up in the last line of the chapter:

> While faithfully adhering to the Gospel and fulfilling her mission to the world, the Church, whose duty it is to foster and elevate all that is found to be true, good and beautiful in the human community, strengthens peace among men for the glory of God.[86]

Amen.

CONCLUSION

The title of this chapter calls on us to "tend" in the Wolinian sense to both the faith and the nation in the modern world. Where "intending" in his model can be seen as the absorption of one sphere by another, "tending" implies the care and nurturing of the pluralism and the inherent tension between them, such that the ongoing conversation and dialogue they are engaged in both challenges and enhances each, while retaining the essential integrity of both. For its part, the modern Church both recognizes and affirms both the rightful place of the political community in the natural order—it is no longer just a necessary evil, but a part of the created order and therefore good—and that community's unique and separate nature and vocation. The political community, on the other hand, must recognize and acknowledge both that the Church is not simply one other interest group vying for resources and power—and therefore liable to regulation, domestication, and co-option—and its genuine call to publicness and public witness in the name of the supernatural order at the same time. In other words, a private church is no church at all for the Christian. The Christian is called by his or her living faith to participation in public life and to the work and

---

85. Vatican Council, *Gaudium et Spes*, 84.
86. Vatican Council, *Gaudium et Spes*, 85.

demands of citizenship to participate in the construction and deepening of the civic culture and the common good.

The call of the Christian as citizen originates in the commandments that we love God with all our hearts and that we do this by loving our neighbor as we love ourselves. Such a love is not a general or vague love of humanity (whatever that actually is) or a general feeling of goodwill toward all, but rather a deeply personal love of each human person in all their particularity and diversity. It is a love that must see past the sins of the other, past their brokenness, beyond their descriptors and status as friends or strangers, allies or enemies, and instead see each unique person as a child of God created in his image and likeness. To say this is to say no more and no less that each and every individual man, woman, and child are in and of themselves sacred beings who must be treated as such and who must treat all others as such. This is the profound truth at the often forgotten core of a genuine liberal-democratic spirit and it is a religious truth. At the same time though, the Church itself took a while to "remember" what it always knew well. Namely, that the same sacredness that placed very real boundaries around political regimes in terms of what they could and could not do to human bodies and minds as well as what genuine political obligations to the poor and marginalized look like, applied to it as an institution as well. When it allowed itself to become entangled and complicit with the powerful in the name of its own preservation and status, its prophetic voice too often went mute. That silence did, of course, not cause the political events to unfold in the manner that they often did with oppression, repression, war, violence, and holocausts alike, but neither did it place the Cross at the center of the public square where it belonged and lived out its own sacred call. With *Gaudium et Spes* and other documents from the Second Vatican Council and beyond that comprise modern Catholic social teaching, the Church made it clear where it stood and whom it stood with, as well as what it would not stand for at all. And this, I would argue, is a very good development and a true sign of Christ made visible and his love made manifest and present in the world.

8

Radical Conversion: A Conclusion

You are the salt of the earth. But if salt becomes tasteless, what can make it salty again? It is good for nothing, and can only be thrown out to be trampled underfoot by men. You are the light of the world. A city built on a hilltop cannot be hidden. No one lights a lamp to put it under a tub; they put it on the lampstand where it shines for everyone in the house. In the same way your light must shine in the sight of men, so that, seeing your good works, they may give praise to your father in heaven.

—Matthew 5:13–16

FAITHFUL APOSTATE

Something can be both *necessary* and *impossible*; which is certainly a paradox, but it is not a contradiction. Such situations are the essence of a certain kind of tragedy. In the physical world examples are easy to come by. Take a person who finds himself tossed from a boat in the middle of the ocean who cannot swim. To possibly survive, he must swim and swim well or else he will drown. As such, swimming is necessary if survival is the goal. However, the fact that he cannot swim means that he will almost surely drown. Hence, in the case at hand, swimming is both *necessary* and *impossible*. The argument of this book, in brief, is that the sort of free liberal and democratic society most Americans enjoy and want to continue living in requires what

I am calling *radical conversion*. I use the term "radical" in different senses. The first sense simply being something extreme. The second sense I use the term is more in keeping with the idea of returning to the source or original position of something. The final sense in which I use the term is more substantively political and is meant to evoke the idea of a political actor whose ideological position and program is one which is significantly opposed to and distinct from the existing array of acceptable political positions. That final sense, as developed throughout the text, in the context of American liberalism is one whereby I argue for an orientation to the political world that is significantly to the "right" of the current social and legal regime and significantly to the "left" of the current neoliberal economic consensus. If that is not enough, the text is also positioned in such a way that the undergirding *political theology* will please very few people of faith and certainly none of those who are agnostic, atheistic, or simply irreligious. Given the overall tenor of the book, such a relatively friendless or alien position is probably appropriate. To be clear, this is not my preferred position. In my heart, I truly want to be a "reliable ally." But, I am not. Nor, however, am I a pessimist or a cynic. Indeed, though I am not optimistic, I am immensely hopeful. I believe that at some broad level, I know what is true, right, and necessary to help heal and make healthy a broken and often sickly world. As utopic as much of what I have argued for might seem, I believe that knowing those things makes me the true realist. That much of it seems improbable or impossible even is a reasonable critique of someone who was going to be placing a bet on the project's success or failure. However, it is not a fair or sensible critique of the argument itself. Because the drowning man cannot swim does not count as an argument against swimming. To return to an old joke that I steal from Kirkpatrick Sale: A man approaches another man on the street and asks him for directions to the train station. After thinking for a long moment, the man who was asked the question responds by saying that "if he was going to the train station he would not start from here." While not very helpful, the answer may still be the right one under the circumstances. While I am under no illusions about the possible ascendency of the Catholic social tradition and its component Catholic social teaching to a place of prominence in the American political tradition of the future, or even of the ability of an argument such as this to inspire even those who already believe to embrace it, I do remain fundamentally convinced that it is both necessary and possible. The capacity exists. The tradition is available for appropriation. While the "language" is not a primary one, it is also not so foreign as to be incomprehensible to Americans if used well. It is something that a democratic citizenry has the right to pursue. And, finally, it would be both right and just to do so. What we lack is both courage and will. How can I say all this? Because we have been given a picture of it, only partially realized though it has ever been, in action on a number of occasions in the American experiment. Below I share just one critical example in the form of a man named Michael Harrington.

In 1962, Michael Harrington wrote one of the most important political books of the mid-twentieth century, *The Other America: Poverty in the United States*. There, in a book about the lives and faces of the poor in America and his outrage about it, he quotes the poet W. H. Auden, who wrote,

> Hunger allows no choice
> To the citizen or the police;
> We must love one another or die.[1]

From someone who used to be called a "man of the Left," the last line is surprising to say the least. Such appeals to sentiment were typically viewed with jaundiced eyes and deep suspicion by fellow travelers since they lack a proper orientation to the material circumstances of the world and the hardheaded political orientation associated with class consciousness and political interests. And yet, there it is; front and center. For those familiar with the life and work of Harrington, this should not come as a huge surprise. What is no doubt surprising to those who have stuck with this book till this point is that I am choosing a man who was a self-professed atheist for the final forty years of his life and the author of a provocatively titled book, *The Politics at God's Funeral*, as an exemplar. And yet, here it is. I will be claiming Michael Harrington for the Catholic intellectual as well as the Catholic social traditions, in part to demonstrate that the argument I have been making is at its core still a *political* argument and not a religious or theological one. In other words, it is still a book about the secular world and it is directed to the affairs of the earthly city in general and to an actual "city" called the United States of America in particular.

Before moving this argument forward, it is important to note what Harrington said in his own words that might make my move here problematic. In *The Politics at God's Funeral*, Harrington writes that his first conclusion is "that the basic religious tradition of the West can no longer, as a *religious* tradition, provide the core values of Western society."[2] However, his second proposition renders the first deeply problematic insofar as he claims that "Western society needs transcendentals [sic]."[3] That need, Harrington correctly understood, stems from the rightfulness of his claim that "men and

---

1. Harrington, *Other America*, 2.
2. Harrington, *Politics at God's Funeral*, 199.
3. Harrington, *Politics at God's Funeral*, 199.

women cannot decently live by demythologies alone [sic]" as well as his assertion that "if, then, the coherent profundities of Judaism and Christianity are incapable of providing the integrative consciousness for modern Western society, it is preposterous to think that superficial counter-cultures or fashionable gurus will accomplish this task."[4] As such, the door is open for the tragic possibility alluded to in the chapter's opening, and Harrington freely admitted in 1983 that we might already be too far gone. However, he did have a path forward that he describes in his chapter titled "Prolegomena to Political Morality" that involved an alliance between religious believers and secular humanists around common values and the re-appropriation of shared political symbols and ideals in what he would call eventually the "next Left."[5] That, however, is not what is of interest to me here for a number of reasons, not the least of which is how far away we are now from the future Harrington imagined thirty years ago. What is of interest is the *who, why,* and *how* of Michael Harrington's politics, activism, and positions.

One of Harrington's intellectual heroes, Antonio Gramsci, said that all human beings were philosophers and that all action was, in effect, political action and that, therefore, the philosophy of every person is contained in their political action. Taking that as a truism for now, I want to suggest that Michael Harrington's philosophy was at its core Catholic. I say this because in so many ways, he himself both said it with his words, but also by the political action he took over the course of his life. Though it is true that he was not in the end a practicing Catholic or even a believer, that does not change the existential nature of his commitments and ideas, let alone what I would contend was his essential character. While biography, like biology, is not destiny, it is the case that destiny without biology or biography is simply fantasy. In other words, if we reject the possibility of some Cartesian emptying out of the self or a reified original position where some denatured prototype of a human being might choose from without reference to the people, places, roles, and stories that make us who we are, and instead focus on the sufficient and the particular rather than the necessary or the universal, it is possible to see the person in his or her unreconstructed form or nascent if not natural state of being who he or she is. While it would be an imperfect experiment, it would still be a valid one if we were to take Thomas Groome's guidebook, *What Makes Us Catholic: Eight Gifts for Life*, and map Michael Harrington's biography and autobiographies against it. There, I believe that we would find immense symmetry to a much greater extent than a superficial kind. Perhaps another time.

4. Harrington, *Politics at God's Funeral*, 198.
5. See Harrington, *Next Left*.

For now, what I would like to say is that if one takes the social and political vision Michael Harrington to its logical conclusion, it would look a lot like the world would look if we took *Gaudium et Spes* to its own logical conclusions. While Harrington himself might be quick to say that it was Marx that he was helping follow through, I would claim that he was mistaking the effect for the cause. In other words, Harrington becomes a Marxist and a democratic-socialist *because* of his Catholicism, not in spite of it. In his second autobiography, *The Long-Distance Runner*, Harrington tells us that "though I have been an atheist for years, I am culturally and psychologically a Catholic."[6] A few pages later, he writes,

> Taking religion very seriously while I was growing up was a critical part of the destiny my childhood packed into me. It meant, above all, that I accepted the idea that life was a trust to be used for a good purpose and accounted for when it was over. I have been an atheist for about thirty years, yet in this fundamental conception of the meaning of existence I am as Catholic as the day on which I made my first communion.[7]

Soon thereafter he explains that despite his shortcomings as a person, his ultimate goal was to bring into being a world "built on love."[8] Michael Harrington grew up in Saint Louis, Missouri, and his early life was dominated by his family, the Catholic Church, and Catholic schools. "From the time Michael's parents sent him off to kindergarten to the day he graduated from high school, he received intense schooling, both in the religious doctrines of Catholicism, and more importantly, in habits of thought."[9] At the Jesuit-run Saint Louis University High School he attended, "Michael's classmates were told they were a 'trained, formidable army of youth . . . serried marching ranks in the Mystical Body of Christ,'"[10] while the yearbook of the same school claimed that the education they received "instilled the necessary fortitude and enthusiasm to step forth into battlefield, college or workaday world and strive toward urgent conversion of a perverted, pagan universe."[11] While the American Catholic Church of the 1940s and 1950s was certainly not a hothouse of political radicalism, the moral thought and intellectual tools developed in such schools as well as the overarching sense of responsibility for the world and sense of efficacy would be ingrained and

6. Harrington, *Long-Distance Runner*, 1.
7. Harrington, *Long-Distance Runner*, 4.
8. Harrington, *Long-Distance Runner*, 10.
9. Isserman, *Other American*, 14.
10. Isserman, *Other American*, 17.
11. Isserman, *Other American*, 19.

made manifest throughout Harrington's life. Continuing his education with the Jesuits at the College of the Holy Cross, Harrington became a member of the Sanctuary Society, "whose members rose at dawn every morning of the academic term and donned cassock and surplice to assist college priests in the celebration of mass."[12] As he moved toward graduation, his biographer, Maurice Isserman, contends that Harrington "was moving toward the view that proof of Christ's promise of redemption could be measured best through the practical social consequences of Christian teachings. As he declared in his 1947 Salutatory Address, 'every man was created in the image of God.'"[13]

Soon after college, Michael Harrington's spiritual restlessness and desire to put his faith into action led him to the doors of the Catholic Worker House in New York city and the sainted Catholic radical Dorothy Day.[14] Although Day's own mentor and spiritual guide, Peter Maurin, had passed on a few years before Harrington arrived, his French-Catholic Personalism[15] and soft anarchist tendencies had imprinted themselves on the movement. When asked about his time with the movement, Harrington once said that when people would ask why he was there, the standard Catholic Worker answer was: "Well, I want to be a saint." He went on the say that this response was viewed as both "perfectly rational and legitimate."[16] Devoting himself to the cause and under the tutelage of Day, Harrington became devoted to living a Catholic life as well as thinking in Catholic categories and terms and became a daily communicant.[17]

A WAR OF POSITION

The political theology of the Catholic Worker movement was as much lived as it was theorized, but at its most elemental it called for direct service to

---

12. Isserman, *Other American*, 30.

13. Isserman, *Other American*, 39.

14. For reasons of time and space I will not provide a detailed account of this important and ongoing Catholic movement beyond some cursory remarks. The unfamiliar reader is urged to see *Loaves and Fishes* and *The Long Loneliness* by Dorothy Day herself, and the excellent biography by Coles, *Dorothy Day*.

15. Although this ground was well covered in the previous chapter, the brief description of "personalism" provided by Isserman in the context of Harrington and Day is worth noting. Isserman explains it in the following way: "Personalists insisted on the uniqueness and autonomy of the human self and on the responsibility of individuals to involve themselves in the great moral issues of their times. There was obvious kinship between these personalists and those of the existentialists." Isserman, *Other American*, 73.

16. Isserman, *Other American*, 68.

17. Isserman, *Other American*, 80.

the poor and for nonviolent direct action when confronting injustice by the state. While its economic model was a sort of primitive communism supported by the publishing of a daily newspaper sold on the streets and an organized begging operation,[18] the movement's politics were decidedly anti-statist and therefore were not aligned with the political party system of the United States. As Isserman puts it, "Taken to its logical conclusion, the Catholic Worker stance precluded voting or sympathizing with any political party, however radical its pedigree."[19] The mantra of the movement would have been something like no statist solutions to statist problems. It was that devotion to purity, coupled with Harrington's own intellectualism and aversion to the hands-on work of hospitality (as well as perhaps the voluntary poverty the workers lived in) that pushed Harrington to start questioning the *political* model of the movement. The question he was confronting was as simple as it was profound, namely, "was personal sainthood a selfish indulgence in an imperfect world?"[20] Harrington soon answered the question for himself with a resounding yes. However, rather than becoming a Democrat or a Republican or even an Independent and beginning his work within the system as it existed in the United States, Harrington turned to Marxism and eventually the Socialist Party of America. The best known and most successful politicians coming out of the party were Eugene V. Debs and Norman Thomas, both of whom Harrington admired greatly, especially Thomas, with whom he had a strong personal relationship. While the party experienced some minor electoral successes and mounted an interesting presidential bid from a jail cell in 1920, the general American hostility to anything that smacked of collectivism as well as continuous infighting among the various parts of the American Left, more or less sealed its fate as minor party of the protest variety, especially in the wake of the New Deal reforms that benefited American workers and the labor movement itself.

While this move coincided with Harrington's loss of faith and his departure both physically and ideologically from the Catholic Worker movement, I contend that the shift at the political level was tactical, not ideological in a deep sense. In other words, the adoption of a Marxist analytic framework and the move to political organizing and party building were new means to achieve old ends; namely, social justice, democracy, and human rights. In his study of Harrington's political theory, Robert Gorman argues that "Harrington always measured his behavior by Catholic standards," and quotes

---

18. For a wonderful account and thought-provoking ethical discussion of begging in the Christian tradition with a special emphasis on the teachings of Peter Maurin, see Johnson, *Fear of Beggars*.

19. Isserman, *Other American*, 99.

20. Isserman, *Other American*, 102.

Harrington himself as saying that he remained "very much outside of the Church but within its orbit."[21] Gorman goes on to claim,

> He learned from living and working with Dorothy Day that the Christian God was immanent to this world, not something to be feared in an afterlife. Religion had to inspire actions that realized God's kingdom on earth, such as ending capitalist exploitation and establishing a moral socialist community.[22]

The realization of the kingdom of God on earth as well as God's immanency do not imply a necessary devotion to a stringent materialism, but in many ways the opposite. The distinction between the natural and supernatural order remains intact from such a vantage point and prevents falling into idolatry, heresy, or sacrilege. Whatever Harrington's personal atheism might mean for his salvation or the next life that the devout Christian believes will be a moment of judgment, his politics remained deeply respectful and entrenched in the values and morality of the Sermon on the Mount. Indeed, his Marxism itself is noteworthy on this point insofar as Harrington was staunchly anti-communist and did not allow himself to be compromised by indefensible defenses of the Soviet Union and Joseph Stalin like many American leftists did. On that score, Harrington, correctly or incorrectly, pursued a path of interpretation that moralized and democratized Marx in ways that made him compatible with the democratic socialism that became Harrington's lifelong political cause. As such, the Marxism that Harrington embraced was not incompatible with Catholicism because it was not at its core militantly materialistic or derogatory toward religious beliefs and practices that fulfilled people's spiritual needs (no less than John Courtney Murray, SJ, assured him of this).

Now it is certainly the case that Harrington's own atheism renders much of his reconciliatory language toward religion in general and Christianity in particular tactical and pragmatic, but it is also true that this level of prudence was not shared by the majority of what traditionally had constituted the American Left. While his noted cultural and spiritual Catholicism clearly explains much of this, a significant portion can also be explained by his turn to Gramscian political analysis and his notion of the "integral state" as well. In Gramsci's notion of hegemony, Harrington found a non-reductive and non-deterministic Marxist framework that was both more demanding and complex as well as suitable for his robust commitment to both substantive and procedural democratic values and norms. The notion

---

21. Gorman, *Michael Harrington*, 13.
22. Gorman, *Speaking American*, 14.

of the integral state defined by Gorman as it related to Harrington "embodied coercive or political power to subdue class enemies, and cultural or civil power to subdue dangerous ideas."[23] As such, "socialists had to defeat both the political and the civil components of capitalism."[24] While traditional Marxism reductively positioned religion in the superstructure and made it at best a balm of passivity and at worst a reactionary force on behalf of the ruling class, Catholicism's oppositional stance toward the original liberal states and especially toward the American liberal state positioned it after its "democratic turn" as an important critical force in a way that the traditional Protestantism and certainly Evangelicalism could never be.[25] Additionally, Harrington understood that the vast majority of those working-class men and women he wanted to organize into a powerful progressive-democratic force were themselves religious believers who would not embrace a political movement that was hostile to their faith and beliefs.

Understanding and respecting the role of religion and people of faith was just one part of Harrington's "war of position." The other critical part was his deep-seated Americanism itself. Here, again, Harrington's project mirrors my own (or *vice versa*) insofar as he is not interested in grafting some foreign and ahistorical political program and philosophy onto the American frame so much as he is interested in the fullest possible realization of the liberal (read: Personalist) dream. In his own words, Harrington exclaimed, "I do not want to destroy it [liberalism], I want to sublimate it."[26] The creation of such a movement was not going to get done through the creation of new language or the deployment of foreign symbols and ideals, but rather through the ability to take the central ideals of the American experiment and employ them in new and transgressive ways. In Harrington's words, "If workers knew that exploitation was not only wrong but un-American, then their shame would become anger, their guilt, pride, and their isolation, rebellion."[27] That rebellion, however, would be a democratic one based on a long term strategy of education, organization, mobilization, and, eventually, legislation. However, before any of that could happen, there

23. Gorman, *Speaking American*, 158.
24. Gorman, *Speaking American*, 158.
25. Harrington is quoted on p. 110 in Gorman's *Speaking American* as claiming, "Fundamentalism could not ethically rebuild society because it lived in and for lonely individuals and became fashionable only because people had already lost faith in public life. It may be profound and even holy but it is not an organizing principle of civilization. That is what Judeo-Christianity was for several millennia. That is what is sorely missed now."
26. Quoted in Gorman, *Speaking American*, 71.
27. Gorman, *Speaking American*, 39.

would first have to be a prophetic moment whereby the social and political contradictions were made manifest and the distance between our current state and our ideals was confronted.

VISIONARY GRADUALISM

In his aptly titled autobiography, *The Long-Distance Runner*, Michael Harrington explains his strategy and the argument he made to other progressives, claiming that "American liberalism, for all its flaws, was the mass Left of the society and that radicals had to speak to what was positive in it and what made it possible move liberals to the Left—not simply focus on its inadequacies."[28] His opening gambit in this regard was a move best described as reverse social psychology in that *The Other America*, while certainly a particular kind of prophetic jeremiad designed to wake the nation up to desperate straits of millions of citizens, was more or less a way of saying, "Hey, I know that we are better than this as a country!" That landmark book closes in a way that is at the end of the day particularly American in its import, and I quote it at length:

> What is needed if poverty is to be abolished is a return of political debate, a restructuring of the party system so there can be clear choices, a new mood of idealism.
>
> These, then, are the strangest poor in the history of mankind.
>
> They exist within the most powerful and rich society the world has ever known. Their misery has continued while the majority of the nation talked of itself as being "affluent" and worried about the neuroses in the suburbs. In this way tens of millions of human beings became invisible. They dropped out of sight and out of mind; they were without their own political voice.
>
> Yet this need not be. The means are at hand to fulfill the age-old dream: poverty can now be abolished. How long shall we ignore this underdeveloped nation in our midst? How long shall we look the other way while our fellow human beings suffer? How long?[29]

Harrington's pleas did not fall on deaf ears. Nor, however, has his larger vision been realized in any significant way. Perhaps at the time the most important reader of Harrington's best-selling study of poverty in America was

---

28. Harrington, *Long-Distance Runner*, 58.
29. Harrington, *Other America*, 184.

then-President John F. Kennedy. America's first Catholic President—at least by baptism and practice—had entered the White House in 1960 and immediately made the eradication of poverty a priority. This was pre-Harrington, however. The five-prong approach Kennedy took ranging from an increase in the minimum wage, to urban renewal and improvement in housing, to educational reforms, to healthcare, ultimately created a lot of smoke but no real fire. The reasons for this are documented well by various writers, but probably the most succinct and lucid account is found in Allen Matusow's *Unraveling of America: A History of Liberalism in the 1960s*.[30] Without going into detail here, the simplest explanation for the failures of the original policies were basically poor design, poor political execution, and, perhaps most importantly, a basic misunderstanding of poverty itself. Indeed, on Matusow's reading of the history of the period, most of the policies launched actually had adverse or even perverse effects, and made the plight of the poor worse while funneling significant dollars into the hands of local elites and business interests. This happened for at least two broad reasons (aside from the bad design issues): the programs had no input at all from anyone who was actually poor concerning what they needed and what would be helpful and because there was exactly zero interest in discussions about the redistribution of wealth. It is, of course, more likely than not that if the former had happened the result would have been demands for the latter, but there was a belief that somehow the social and political experiments launched would somehow improve the economic position of the poor while leaving the privilege, power, and wealth of the middle and upper classes fully intact. This, in retrospect at a minimum, was simply not possible and, to the extent that it might have been, the plans woefully misunderstood the lengths to which the entrenched social, political, and economic powers would go to prevent it from happening either through subversion or simple resistance.

Two years into the process, Kennedy had become disillusioned with the progress being made and came upon *The Other America*. The book provided him with the visceral images and consciousness-raising analysis he needed to get fired up about poverty anew. This sense of moral outrage coupled with Kennedy's own "we will go to the moon" mentality got him talking about a "war on poverty." But, as Matusow correctly points out, that would not have led the politically cautious Kennedy to take significant action in and of itself. In his words:

> But the government did not undertake a War on Poverty because Michael Harrington wrote a book. A constituency both aggrieved and vocal had first to demand it. In the spring of 1963

---

30. Matusow, *Unraveling of America*.

the civil rights movement took on mass dimensions, creating that constituency overnight.[31]

Unfortunately, not long after the administration began organizing and mobilizing for the legislative battles around the poverty question, Kennedy was assassinated. To the surprise of many, his presidential successor from Texas took up the cause with fervor. In his first State of the Union Address not two months after Kennedy had fallen, Lyndon Baines Johnson called for an unconditional war on poverty in America. Johnson moved quickly and named Kennedy family brother-in-law and the founder and first director of the Peace Corps, R. Sargent Shriver, to be his "poverty czar." With Johnson's demand for urgency in hand, Shriver began his work in earnest. Catholic to his core, Shriver would later explain his understanding of the War on Poverty during a Congressional hearing in the following and deeply telling way:

> Because for us—for all America—the war on poverty is a moment of conscience—a national act of expiation, of humbling and prostrating ourselves before our Creator. And when all is said and done, what the war on poverty will have achieved—is to have gained for an entire people an appreciation of those words attributed to St. Vincent De Paul: Before you go out and help the poor, you must first beg their pardon. And that is what the war on poverty is all about.[32]

Just a few weeks after being appointed by Johnson, Shriver quietly brought in the socialist Michael Harrington and his friend and fellow radical Paul Jacobs (cofounder of *Mother Jones* magazine) as consultants to the Office of Economic Opportunity he was directing. They would help with drafting the outlines of the legislation that would later become the Equal Opportunity Act—the cornerstone of Johnson's Great Society! All in all, it seems that Harrington was present for about twelve meetings and whatever imprint he left is not well documented. What appears to be the case, however, is that of the five major initiatives in the legislation none, save perhaps the Head Start program, achieved much success, and in many cases created unintended consequences that either made things worse or simply resulted in the transfer of millions of dollars to individuals and organizations who had no real interest in ending poverty at all.[33] That, however, is a story for another time. What matters the most for this argument is that the initiatives happened at all and that poverty on such a scale actually made it to the top

---

31. Matusow, *Unraveling of America*, 119.
32. Quoted in Gettelstein and Mermelstein, *Great Society Reader*, 208–9.
33. See Matusow, *Unraveling of America*, especially chs. 4, 8, and 9.

of the country's political agenda. As this book goes to press, it is difficult to imagine this happening again any time soon. The other reason for mapping this out here in brief is to point to two important features of Michael Harrington's brand of activism that remain salient for the Christian citizen. The first is that he understood that politics required that the perfect not be allowed to become the enemy of the good; and the second was that it was necessary to make common cause with those who were willing to work toward shared goals even if it was for different reasons and occasionally get one's hands "dirty."

While it is true that Harrington gave up on "sainthood," as defined by the radical Catholics he started his adult public life with, it is not true that he gave up any of his convictions or beliefs derived from his original faith and faith-filled education. He was fond of saying throughout his life that you "could take the boy out of the Church but you can't take the Church out of the boy."[34] However, Harrington also recognized from his exposure to the War on Poverty in its earliest stages (as well as the co-option of his discourse around the culture of poverty by democrats and neoconservatives alike later on for their own assaults on the welfare state), that the two parties in America were incapable of the sort of radical thinking that was needed to actually address the true root causes of poverty. Those causes were, of course, the vast disparities in wealth and all of the attendant social and material consequences they produced. A true reformation of the social order would depend on a political organization that was guided by principles of justice, compassion, equality, human dignity, and basic fairness. For Harrington, this was what socialism was all about. In his rejection of violent revolution and embrace of the democratic order, he drew a strong moral line that belied the political worldview where the end justified the means which the New Left came to embrace in the late 1960s and early 1970s as well as the drift toward statism and the authoritarianism of the Old Left. Both these positions would place him at odds with friends and would-be fellow travelers throughout his life.

All told, I feel safe in saying that Harrington was an unreliable ally of both the American Right and the American Left in many of its forms. I believe that this is the case because of his Catholicism—intellectualized and cultural though it may have been. So, when Gorman writes in his fine book after quoting the socialist Max Shachtman calling Harrington a "creative Marxist" that "Harrington can indeed take credit for modernizing and Americanizing socialism by redefining dialectics and re-tooling an outdated

---

34. Quoted in Isserman, *Other American*, 309.

politics,"[35] I would agree, but press the issue a little. In this very brief and incomplete foray into Harrington's life and thought, I would want to add, if not supplant, that, by saying that on my reading Harrington "socialized" Catholicism and supplied it with *a* if not *the* political form it might take. Simply put, he was more creative than the categories allowed by those who viewed him through a strictly secular or a-religious lens. It is that creative Catholicism that I believe opens the door for the kind of faithful politics I have been arguing for in this book.

A CONCLUSION

Does this mean that after hundreds of pages that the final word of this treatise is that Catholics all should become democratic socialists? No. But hopefully the above shows that the gospel has ways of penetrating the hard exteriors as well as the porous ones and often appears in forms and guises that we must work hard to reveal. Near the end of Michael Isserman's biography, he writes of Harrington: "An honorable, even heroic, vision, it was also, as Michael reluctantly conceded in the last years of his life, one for which there remained precious little room in American culture."[36] The same epitaph many in this country want to write about the place of faith in our political life and regime. The language of liberalism and now neoliberalism, not to mention a virulent form of populism, that are now ascendant in American political life on the "right" and the extreme forms of identity politics and so-called anti-fascist anarchists on the "left" seem to leave very little space for what we might call social democratic politics. While at this writing, the language of "democratic socialism" has appeared on the American stage again and has won over many younger men and women in certain parts of the country, it is too soon to tell how the small victories will play out. Despite some increases in the ranks of independents and the gains of some third parties, the reality is that the two-party system remains intact, if battered. As such, the Democratic Party remains the only seeming home for serious progressives. Unfortunately, however, as a party it increasingly seems inhospitable to people of faith and to allowing a fair hearing for religiously based concerns. Beyond that issue, the reality is that despite rhetoric that tends to emphasize differences and attempts to carve out space between the two major parties, the Hartzian "iron cage" remains intact insofar as neither party is even trying to represent the holistic set of issues and agenda called for by a properly understood Christianity and the social teachings of

---

35. Gorman, *Speaking American*, 176.
36. Isserman, *Other American*, 363.

the Catholic Church. The departures around life issues, wealth and poverty, immigration, the environment, labor and capital, healthcare, crime and punishment, family support, education, war and peace, and so on remain for the most part ensconced in a liberal-capitalist-possessive individualistic discourse that is embraced in disparate ways by both political parties and most contemporary politicians. And, outside of certain white nationalists and self-proclaimed anarchists, so does the rhetoric of even the so-called populists and members of the Democratic Left. In other words, the "politics of love" are virtually nowhere to be found.

As such, the politically homeless Christian remains a real thing. Furthermore, the indifference to religious ideas and faithful politics in any but the most reductive senses by the public in general, and the people of faith in particular, is a trend that shows no signs of abating. Indeed, those arguing for the privatization of religion are increasingly religious people themselves enamored by things like the new monasticism and such. I have tried to argue in this volume that these trends are not only theologically wrong, but also practically dangerous.

It has been my argument in the preceding chapters that while there is no essential political ideology to be gleaned in the Christian gospels, there are certainly implied modes of communal and social *praxis* that will eventually take on political forms that are more or less consistent with intelligible readings of those texts and the larger Christian tradition that builds up in the centuries-wide wake that follows. I have contended that the rise of liberalism itself is both consistent with that tradition and provides much of the ontological and normative framework that the liberal state and its emphasis on the rights-bearing citizen who is equal under the law rests upon. Furthermore, I have claimed that forgetting this foundational claim and its import puts the tradition's great advances at risk and leads to both a theoretical and practical incoherence that undermines the tradition's broadest contribution to political thought; namely, the assertion that *all people matter all of the time* at serious risk.

To confront that risk, I proposed confronting the possessive individualism and story of the liberal state reflected in the teachings of theorists like Hobbes and more importantly Locke with an alternative and more truthful Catholic story of human beings who were socially constituted and made to seek fulfillment and achieve their personal calling in an environment directed toward human flourishing and bounded by the desire for the common good. In the American context, I sought to demonstrate that while the tradition was in many ways hostile to such a shift that it did have within it the necessary resources, language, and space to at least be possible, as exemplified by the American thinker Orestes Brownson.

In the chapters that followed, I tried to map out the contextually bound theoretical path by which this alternative approach might travel, beginning first with the Catholic Church's prophetic confrontation with the liberal-capitalist state in the late nineteenth and early twentieth centuries and then moving through the important philosophic and theological work of John Courtney Murray, whereby people of faith could find their way to a safe embrace of a properly reconstituted understanding of the American liberal tradition. In its call for a rejection of "neutrality," the Church and its more prominent American thinkers like Jacques Maritain took the side of the gospel message in the name of equal human dignity and the primacy of the human person as unique and sacred beings who were each created in the image and likeness of God as the core and unalterable ideal of political association and politics rightly understood. This embrace of the democratic form and the values that it rests upon were then indirectly reflected in the documents that marked the beginning of the Church's contemporary social teaching beginning with the Second Vatican Council and documents like *Gaudium et Spes*. It is my argument and belief that the large body of work that has followed in the wake of the Council in the form of papal encyclicals, Bishop's letters, and the work of numerous theologians, scholars, and teachers who are familiar with and sympathetic to the Catholic social tradition has much to offer America and Americans that is essential to the long-term sustainability of the critical project of emancipation, liberation, and commitment to the value and worth of each and every individual human person that was begun in 1776.

To close out this book, I want to return to one of its first themes again, namely that if the Incarnation means anything for the Christian and anyone else who believes it happened, it is that the people and things of this world matter. Yes, we remain people who are pilgrims whose final home is not here on earth. However, this does not mean that what happens here does not have cosmic consequences. We are not a mistake. We are not the children of a lesser God or an indifferent God. We are children of a God who created us from grace—the overflowing all-encompassing love of a being who wants to know us and wants us to know him. The Christian citizen's first job is not to forget this and to take every opportunity to remind all who will listen through word and witness of its truth. His or her second job is to work tirelessly to make sure that the obstacles that interfere with any human being's ability to seek and know God and God's love directly and through other human beings are diminished and removed. This involves both personal and private commitments, to be sure. But the scale and multiplicity of many of the obstacles means that collective action will be required. That means that we will on some level have to engage in political action of one kind or another. It is not optional. That means that understanding the whos, whats, whys, and hows of obstacle removal matters. In other words, because we are Christians, we are also by definition called to be citizens. Acknowledging this, we are at least called upon to remember that the way we will mark our approach as different from those who simply seek power or to secure the interests of some class or faction is that we are called to seek the good of all people all the time. We are called upon to remember that they will know us Christian-citizens by our love.

Bibliography

Abbott, Philip. *Exceptional America: Newness and National Identity*. New York: Lang, 1999.
———. *Leftward Ho! V. F. Calverton and American Radicalism*. New York: Praeger, 1993.
———. *Political Thought in America: Conversation and Debates*. Itasca: Peacock, 1991.
———. *Seeking Many Inventions: The Idea of Community in America*. Chattanooga: University of Tennessee Press, 1987.
———. *The Shotgun behind the Door: Liberalism and the Problem of Political Obligation*. Athens: University of Georgia Press, 1976.
Ackerman, Bruce A. *Social Justice in the Liberal State*. New Haven: Yale University Press, 1980.
Anderson, Benedict. *Imagined Communities: Reflections on the Origin and Spread of Nationalism*. New York: Verso, 1991.
Arendt, Hannah. *The Human Condition*. 1958. Reprint, Chicago: University of Chicago Press, 1977.
———. *On Revolution*. New York: Penguin, 1965.
———. *On Violence*. San Diego: Harcourt Brace Jovanovich, 1970.
———. *Totalitarianism: Part Three of The Origins of Totalitarianism*. San Diego: Harcourt Brace Jovanovich, 1968.
Aristotle. *Ethics*. Translated by J. A. K. Thompson. London: Penguin, 1953.
———. *The Politics*. Translated by Carnes Lord. Chicago: University of Chicago Press, 1984.
Arnett, Ronald C., et al. *Communication Ethics: Literacy and Dialogue*. Thousand Oaks, CA: SAGE, 2009.
Ashcraft, Richard. *Revolutionary Politics and Locke's Two Treatises of Government*. Princeton: Princeton University Press, 1986.
Bailyn, Bernard. *The Ideological Origins of the American Revolution*. Cambridge: Belknap, 1967.
Baker, Houston, Jr. *Blues, Ideology, and Afro-American Literature: A Vernacular Theory*. Chicago: University of Chicago Press, 1984.
Banning, Lance. *The Jeffersonian Persuasion: Evolution of a Party Ideology*. Ithaca: Cornell University Press, 1978.
Barber, Benjamin R. *An Aristocracy of Everyone: The Politics of Education and the Future of America*. New York: Ballantine, 1992.

———. *The Conquest of Politics: Liberal Philosophy in Democratic Times*. Princeton: Princeton University Press, 1988.
———. *The Death of Communal Liberty: A History of Freedom in a Swiss Mountain Canton*. Princeton: Princeton University Press, 1974.
———. "Rousseau's Bloody Hand? Revolutionary Violence and the Politics of Release." Paper presented at the Annual Convention of the American Political Science Association, Atlanta, 1989.
———. *Strong Democracy: Participatory Politics for a New Age*. Berkeley: University of California Press, 1984.
Beard, Charles A. *An Economic Interpretation of the Constitution of the United States*. New York: Free Press, 1986.
Bellah, Robert, et al. *Habits of the Heart: Individualism and Commitment in American Life*. New York: Harper & Row, 1984.
Berger, Peter L. *Pyramids of Sacrifice: Political Ethics and Social Change*. Garden City, NY: Anchor, 1976.
Berger, Peter L., and Thomas Luckmann. *The Social Construction of Reality: A Treatise in the Sociology of Knowledge*. New York: Doubleday, 1966.
Berman, Marshall. *All That Is Solid Melts into Air: The Experience of Modernity*. New York: Penguin, 1988.
Bird, Colin. *The Myth of Liberal Individualism*. Cambridge: Cambridge University Press, 1999.
Bloom, Allan. *The Closing of the American Mind: How Higher Education Has Failed Democracy and Impoverished the Souls of Today's Students*. New York: Simon & Schuster, 1987.
Bloom, Harold. *The American Religion: The Emergence of Post-Christian Nation*. New York: Simon & Schuster, 1992.
Boorstin, Daniel. *The Genius of American Politics*. Chicago: University of Chicago Press, 1953.
———. "Our Unspoken National Faith: Why Americans Need No Ideology." *Commentary* 15 (1953) 327–37.
Bredvold, Louis I., and Ralph G. Ross, eds. *The Philosophy of Edmund Burke: A Selection from His Speeches and Writings*. Ann Arbor: University of Michigan Press, 1960.
Bretherton, Luke. *Christ and the Common Life: Political Theology and the Case for Democracy*. Grand Rapids: Eerdmans, 2019.
Brooks, David. *On Paradise Drive: How We Live Now (and Always Have) in the Future Tense*. New York: Simon & Schuster, 2004.
Brownson, Orestes A. *The American Republic: Its Constitution, Tendencies, and Destiny*. In *The Works of Orestes Brownson*, edited by Harry F. Brownson, 18:1–222. New York: AMS, 1966.
———. *Charles Elwood*. In *The Works of Orestes Brownson*, edited by Harry F. Brownson, 4:173–316. New York: AMS, 1966.
———. *The Convert*. In *The Works of Orestes Brownson*, edited by Harry F. Brownson, 5:1–331. New York: AMS, 1966.
———. *New Views of Christianity, Society, and the Church*. In *The Works of Orestes Brownson*, edited by Harry F. Brownson, 4:4–56. New York: AMS, 1966.
———. *The Spirit-Rapper*. In *The Works of Orestes Brownson*, edited by Harry F. Brownson, 9:1–235. New York: AMS, 1966.

Budziszewski, J. *Written on the Heart: The Case for Natural Law*. Downers Grove: InterVarsity, 1997.

Burgos, Juan Manuel. *An Introduction to Personalism*. Washington, DC: Catholic University of America Press, 2018.

Butler, Gregory S. *In Search of the American Spirit: The Political Thought of Orestes Brownson*. Carbondale: Southern Illinois University Press, 1992.

Cahoy, William J. "A Sense of Place and the Place of Sense." In *Professing in the Postmodern Academy: Faculty and the Future of Church-Related Colleges*, edited by Stephen R. Haynes, 73–111. Waco: Baylor University Press, 2002.

Carter, Stephen L. *The Culture of Disbelief: How American Law and Politics Trivialize Religious Devotion*. New York: Anchor, 1993.

———. "Liberalism's Religion Problem." *First Things* 121 (March 2002) 21–32.

Chaput, Charles J. *Render Unto Caesar: Serving the Nation by Living Our Catholic Beliefs in Political Life*. New York: Image, 2012.

Cochran, Clarke E., and David Carroll Cochran. *Catholics, Politics, and Public Policy: Beyond Left and Right*. Maryknoll: Orbis, 2003.

Coles, Robert. *Dorothy Day: A Radical Devotion*. Cambridge: Perseus, 1987.

———. *The Secular Mind*. Princeton: Princeton University Press, 1999.

Cook, Thomas I., and Arnaud B. Leavelle. "Orestes A. Brownson's *The American Republic*." *Review of Politics* 4 (1942) 173–93.

Coons, John E., and Patrick M. Brennan. *By Nature Equal: The Anatomy of a Western Insight*. Princeton: Princeton University Press, 1999.

Cornell, Saul. *The Other Founders: Anti-Federalism and the Dissenting Tradition in America, 1788-1828*. Chapel Hill: University of North Carolina Press, 1999.

Corrin, Jay P. *Catholic Intellectuals and the Challenge of Democracy*. Notre Dame: University of Notre Dame Press, 2002.

Curtis, George M., and James J. Thompson Jr., eds. *The Southern Essays of Richard M. Weaver*. Indianapolis: Liberty, 1987.

Davis, Derek. "Separation, Integration, and Accommodation: Religion and State in America in a Nutshell." *Journal of Church and State* 43 (2001) 5–17.

Day, Dorothy. *Loaves and Fishes*. Maryknoll: Orbis, 1997.

———. *The Long Loneliness: The Autobiography of Dorothy Day*. New York: Harper & Row, 1952.

Deneen, Patrick J. *Why Liberalism Failed*. New Haven: Yale University Press, 2018.

Descartes, René. *Discourse on Method and the Meditation*. Translated by F. E. Sutcliffe. New York: Penguin, 1968.

Diggins, John Patrick. *The Lost Soul of American Politics: Virtue, Self-Interest, and the Foundations of Liberalism*. Chicago: University of Chicago Press, 1986.

Dolan, Jay P. *In Search of an American Catholicism: A History of Religion and Culture in Tension*. Oxford: Oxford University Press, 2002.

Duncan, Christopher M. *The Anti-Federalists and Early American Political Thought*. DeKalb: Northern Illinois University Press, 1995.

———. "The *Blues* Voice of Houston Baker, Jr. as Political Theory: An(Other) American Paradigm?" *New Political Science* 22 (2000) 231–48.

———. "Catholicism, Poverty and the Pursuit of Happiness." *Journal of Poverty* 12 (2008) 49–76.

———. "The Christian Right's Postmodern Turn: Sometimes Satan Comes as a Man of Peace." *Listening: Journal of Communication Ethics, Religion, and Culture* 47 (2012) 50–76.

———. "Christianity, Secularism, and the American Public Square." *McNesse Review* 40 (2002) 28–39.

———. "Community and the American Village on Paradise Drive." *Public Voices* 9 (2007) 83–91.

———. "Democratic Posturing and Peculiar Liberalism: Leo Strauss, His Students, and America." *Southern Political Review* 23 (1995) 281–311.

———. *Fugitive Theory: Political Theory, the Southern Agrarians, and America.* Lanham, MD: Lexington, 2000.

———. "Liberalism and the Challenge of *Fight Club*: Notes toward an American Theory of the Good Life." *disClosure: A Journal of Social Theory* 12 (2003) 119–44.

———. "Lincoln's Theocentric Turn." *Politics and Policy* 32 (2004) 508–39.

———. "Men of a Different Faith: The Anti-Federalist Ideal in Early American Political Thought." *Polity* 26 (1994) 387–415.

———. "A Question for Richard Rorty." *The Review of Politics* 66 (2004) 385–413.

———. "Southern Agrarians, Progress, and the Tragic Voice." *Politics and Policy* 29 (2001) 3–46.

Duncan, Christopher M., and Diane B. Moore. "Catholic and Protestant Social Discourse and the American Welfare State." *Journal of Poverty: Innovations on Social, Political and Economic Inequalities* 7 (2003) 57–83.

Elazar, Daniel J., and John Kincaid, eds. *The Covenant Connection: From Federal Theology to Modern Federalism.* Lanham, MD: Lexington, 2000.

Elie, Paul. *The Life You Save May Be Your Own: An American Pilgrimage.* New York: Farrar, Straus and Giroux, 2003.

Elliot, T. S. *Christianity and Culture: The Centenary Edition.* Orlando: Harcourt Brace, 1976.

Elshtain, Jean Bethke. *Augustine and the Limits of Politics.* Notre Dame: University of Notre Dame Press, 1995.

———. *Real Politics: At the Center of Everyday Life.* Baltimore: Johns Hopkins University Press, 1997.

———. *Sovereignty: God, State, and Self.* New York: Basic Books, 2008.

Euben, J. Peter. "The Battle of Salamis and the Origins of Political Theory." *Political Theory: An International Journal of Political Philosophy* 14 (1986) 359–90.

Filmer, Robert. *Patriarcha; or, The Natural Power of Kings; By the Learned Sir Robert Filmer Baronet.* London: Chiswell, 1680.

Fish, Stanley. "A Reply to J. Judd Owen." *American Political Science Review* 93 (1999) 925–30.

———. "Stanley Fish Replies to Richard John Neuhaus." *First Things* 60 (February 1996) 35–40.

———. *There Is No Such Thing as Free Speech: And It's a Good Thing, Too.* Oxford: Oxford University Press, 1994.

———. "Why We Can't All Just Get Along." *First Things* 60 (February 1996) 18–26.

Fowler, Robert Booth. *Enduring Liberalism: American Political Thought since the 1960s.* Lawrence: University Press of Kansas, 1999.

Freud, Sigmund. *The Future of an Illusion.* Translated by James Strachey. New York: Norton, 1961.

Fustel de Coulanges, Numa Denis. *The Ancient City: A Study on the Religion, Laws, and Institutions of Greece and Rome.* 1956. Reprint, Baltimore: Johns Hopkins University Press, 1980.

Fukuyama, Francis. *The End of History and the Last Man.* New York: Free Press, 1992.

Galston, William A. "Value Pluralism and Contemporary Political Philosophy." *American Political Science Review* 93 (1999) 769–78.

Genovese, Eugene D. *A Consuming Fire: The Fall of the Confederacy in the Mind of the White Christian South.* Athens: University of Georgia Press, 1998.

———. *The Southern Front: History and Politics in the Cultural War.* Columbia: University of Missouri Press, 1995.

———. *The Southern Tradition: The Achievement and Limitations of an American Conservatism.* Cambridge: Harvard University Press, 1994.

Gettelstein, M. E., and D. Mermelstein, eds. *The Great Society Reader: The Failure of American Liberalism.* New York: Random House, 1967.

Gillman, Howard. *The Constitution Besieged: The Rise and Demise of Lochner Era Police Power Jurisprudence.* Durham: Duke University Press, 1993.

Gleason, Philip. "The Catholic Church in American Public Life in the Twentieth Century." *Logos* 3 (2000) 85–99.

———. *Keeping the Faith: American Catholicism Past and Present.* Notre Dame: University of Notre Dame Press, 1987.

———. *Speaking of Diversity: Language and Ethnicity in Twentieth-Century America.* Baltimore: Johns Hopkins University Press, 1992.

Glendon, Mary Ann. *Rights Talk: The Impoverishment of Political Discourse.* New York: Free Press, 1991.

Glenn, Gary D., and John Stack. "Is American Democracy Safe for Catholicism?" *Review of Politics* 62 (2000) 5–48.

"God Decentralized." *New York Times,* December 7, 1997. https://www.nytimes.com/1997/12/07/magazine/god-decentralized.html.

Gorman, Robert A. *Michael Harrington: Speaking American.* New York: Routledge, 1995.

Gregory, Eric. *Politics and the Order of Love: An Augustinian Ethic of Democratic Citizenship.* Chicago: University of Chicago Press, 2008.

Habermas, Jürgen. "A Conversation about God and the World: Interview with Eduardo Mendieta." In *Religion and Rationality: Essays on Reason, God, and Modernity,* edited by Eduardo Mendieta, 147–68. Cambridge: Polity, 2002.

———. *The Philosophical Discourse of Modernity.* Translated by Frederick G. Lawrence. Cambridge: MIT Press, 1987.

Hamburger, Philip. *Separation of Church and State.* Cambridge: Harvard University Press, 2002.

Harrington, Michael. *The Long-Distance Runner: An Autobiography.* New York: Henry Holt, 1988.

———. *The Next Left: The History of the Future.* New York: Holt, 1986.

———. *The Other America: Poverty in the United States.* New York: Penguin, 1981.

———. *The Politics at God's Funeral: The Spiritual Crisis of Western Civilization.* New York: Penguin, 1983.

Hartz, Louis. *The Liberal Tradition in America: An Interpretation of American Political Thought Since the Revolution.* 1955. Reprint, Orlando: Harvest/HBJ, 1983.

Hauerwas, Stanley. *A Community of Character: Toward a Constructive Christian Social Ethic*. Notre Dame: University of Notre Dame Press, 1981.

———. *The Hauerwas Reader*. Edited by John Berkman and Michael Cartwright. Durham: Duke University Press, 2001.

Heft, James L., ed. *A Catholic Modernity? Charles Taylor's Marianist Award Lecture*. New York: Oxford University Press, 1999.

Hennelly, Alfred T. *Theologies in Conflict: The Challenge of Juan Luis Segundo*. Maryknoll: Orbis, 1979.

Herrera, R. A. *Orestes Brownson: Sign of Contradiction*. Wilmington, DE: ISI, 1999.

Heyer, Kristin E. *Prophetic and Public: The Social Witness of U.S. Catholicism*. Washington, DC: Georgetown University Press, 2006.

Himes, Michael J. "Finding God in All Things: A Sacramental Worldview and Its Effects." In *As Leaven in the World: Catholic Perspectives on Faith, Vocation, and the Intellectual Life*, edited by Thomas Landy, 91–103. Franklin, WI: Sheed & Ward, 2001.

Himes, Michael J., and Kenneth R. Himes. *Fullness of Faith: The Public Significance of Theology*. Mahwah: Paulist, 1993.

Hirschman, Albert O. *Exit, Voice, and Loyalty: Responses to Decline in Firms, Organizations, and States*. Cambridge: Harvard University Press, 1970.

———. *The Passions and the Interests: Political Arguments for Capitalism before Its Triumph*. Princeton: Princeton University Press, 1977.

Hobbes, Thomas. *Leviathan*. Edited by C. B. Macpherson. New York: Penguin, 1968.

Hollenbach, David. "A Communitarian Reconstruction of Human Rights: Contributions from Catholic Tradition." In *Catholicism and Liberalism: Contributions to American Public Philosophy*, edited by R. Bruce Douglass and David Hollenbach, 127–50. Cambridge: Cambridge University Press, 2002.

Holloway, Carson. *The Way of Life: John Paul II and the Challenge of Liberal Modernity*. Waco: Baylor University Press, 2008.

Huston, James H. *The Founders on Religion: A Book of Quotations*. Princeton: Princeton University Press, 2005.

"Is There a Catholic Problem?" *New Republic*, November 16, 1938.

Isserman, Maurice. *The Other American: The Life of Michael Harrington*. New York: Public Affairs, 2000.

Jamieson, Dale. "The Poverty of Postmodernist Theory." *University of Colorado Law Review* 62 (1991) 577–95.

Jayne, Allen. *Jefferson's Declaration of Independence: Origins, Philosophy, and Theology*. Lexington: University Press of Kentucky, 1998.

Jefferson, Thomas. "Jefferson's Wall of Separation Letter." *USConstitution.net*. http://www.usconstitution.net/jeffwall.html.

———. "Letter to Benjamin Waterhouse, 26 June 1822." *Founders Online*, January 2, 1998. https://founders.archives.gov/documents/Jefferson/98-01-02-2905.

———. "Letter to Francis Hopkinson." In *The Portable Thomas Jefferson*, edited by Merrill D. Peterson, 435–37. New York: Penguin, 1977.

Johnson, Kelly. *Fear of Beggars: Stewardship and Poverty in Christian Ethics*. Grand Rapids: Eerdmans, 2007.

Kant, Immanuel. *Groundwork of the Metaphysic of Morals*. Translated by H. J. Paton. New York: Harper & Row, 1964.

Kallenberg, Brad J. "The Master Argument of MacIntyre's *After Virtue*." In *Virtues and Practices in the Christian Tradition: Christian Ethics after MacIntyre*, edited by Nancey Murphy et al., 7–29. Notre Dame: University of Notre Dame Press, 1997.
Kendall, Willmoore. *John Locke and the Doctrine of Majority Rule*. Urbana: University of Illinois Press, 1965.
Kierkegaard, Søren. *The Present Age*. Translated by Alexander Dru. New York: Harper & Row, 1962.
Knight, Kelvin, ed. *The MacIntyre Reader*. Notre Dame: University of Notre Dame Press, 1998.
Kramnick, Isaac. "Republican Revisionism Revisited." *American Historical Review* 87 (1982) 629–64.
Kraynak, Robert P. *Christian Faith and Modern Democracy: God and Politics in the Fallen World*. Notre Dame: University of Notre Dame Press, 2002.
Kraynak, Robert P., and Glenn Tinder, eds. *In Defense of Human Dignity: Essays for Our Time*. Notre Dame: University of Notre Dame Press, 2003.
Kuhn, Thomas S. *The Structure of Scientific Revolutions*. Chicago: University of Chicago Press, 1962.
Kurun, Ismail. *The Theological Origins of Liberalism*. Lanham, MD: Lexington, 2016.
Kymlicka, Will. *Liberalism, Community and Culture*. Oxford: Clarendon, 1989.
Lambert, Frank. *The Founding Fathers and the Place of Religion in America*. Princeton: Princeton University Press, 2003.
Landy, Thomas M., ed. *As Leaven in the World: Catholic Perspectives on Faith, Vocation and the Intellectual Life*. Franklin, WI: Sheed & Ward, 2001.
Lapatia, Americo D. *Orestes A. Brownson*. New York: Twayne, 1965.
Lasch, Christopher. *The Culture of Narcissism: American Life in an Age of Diminishing Expectations*. New York: Norton, 1979.
———. *The True and Only Heaven: Progress and Its Critics*. New York: Norton, 1991.
Lawler, Peter Augustine. *Aliens in American: The Strange Truth about Our Souls*. Wilmington, DE: ISI, 2002.
———. "Conservative Postmodernism, Postmodern Conservatism." *Intercollegiate Review* 38 (2002) 16–25.
———. Critical Introduction to *We Hold These Truths: Catholic Reflections on the American Proposition*, by John Courtney Murray, 1–22. Lanham, MD: Rowman & Littlefield, 1988.
———. Introduction to *The American Republic*, by Orestes Brownson, xiv–cviii. Wilmington, DE: ISI, 2003.
Leo XIII. *Rerum Novarum (On the Condition of the Working Class)*. Encyclical Letter. Vatican website. May 15, 1891. http://www.vatican.va/content/leo-xiii/en/encyclicals/documents/hf_l-xiii_enc_15051891_rerum-novarum.html.
Levy, Michael B. *Political Thought in America: An Anthology*. Prospect Heights: Waveland, 1992.
Lewis, C. S. *The Abolition of Man*. 1947. Reprint, New York: Macmillan, 1965.
———. "Equality." *The Spectator*, August 27, 1943.
———. *Mere Christianity*. New York: Macmillan, 1952.
Lilla, Mark. *The Stillborn God: Religion, Politics, and the Modern West*. New York: Knopf, 2007.
Locke, John. *A Letter concerning Toleration*. Buffalo: Prometheus, 1990.
———. *The Second Treatise of Government*. New York: Bobbs-Merrill, 1952.

Luther, Martin. "Admonition to Peace: A Reply to the Twelve Articles of the Peasants in Swabia (1525)." In Vol. 4, *The Works of Martin Luther with Introductions and Notes*, translated by C. M. Jacobs, 152–57. AGES Digital Library. Albany, OR: AGES Software.

Lutz, Donald S. "Liberty and Equality from a Communitarian Perspective." In *The Covenant Connection: From Federal Theology to Modern Federalism*, edited by Daniel J. Elazar and John Kincaid, 223–44. Lanham, MD: Lexington, 2000.

———. *Popular Consent and Popular Control*. Baton Rouge: Louisiana State University Press, 1980.

———. *A Preface to American Political Theory*. Lawrence: University Press of Kansas, 1992.

Machiavelli. *The Prince*. Translated by George Bull. New York: Penguin, 1961.

MacIntyre, Alasdair. *After Virtue: A Study in Moral Theory*. Notre Dame: University of Notre Dame Press, 1984.

———. *God, Philosophy, Universities: A Selective History of Catholic Philosophical Tradition*. Lanham, MD: Rowman & Littlefield, 2009.

Macpherson, C. B. *The Political Theory of Possessive Individualism: Hobbes to Locke*. Oxford: Oxford University Press, 1962.

Madison, James, et al. *The Federalist Papers*. Edited by Isaac Kramnick. New York: Penguin, 1987.

Main, Jackson Turner. *The Antifederalists: Critics of the Constitution, 1781–1788*. New York: Norton, 1961.

Mansbridge, Jane J. *Beyond Adversary Democracy*. Chicago: University of Chicago Press, 1983.

Marcuse, Herbert. *One-Dimensional Man: Studies in the Ideology of Advanced Industrial Society*. Boston: Beacon, 1964.

Maritain, Jacques. *Man and the State*. Washington, DC: Catholic University of America Press, 1951.

———. *Natural Law: Reflections on Theory and Practice*. South Bend: St. Augustine's, 1952.

———. *The Person and the Common Good*. 1946. Reprint, Notre Dame: University of Notre Dame Press, 2015.

Marty, Martin E. *The Public Church: Mainline-Evangelical-Catholic*. 1981. Reprint, Eugene, OR: Wipf & Stock, 2012.

Marx, Karl, and Frederick Engels. *Manifesto of the Communist Party*. New York: International Publishers, 1948.

Mathewes, Charles T. *A Theology of Public Life*. Cambridge: Cambridge University Press, 2007.

Matusow, Allen J. *The Unraveling of America: A History of Liberalism in the 1960s*. New York: Harper Torchbooks, 1986.

Maynard, Theodore. *Orestes Brownson: Yankee, Radical Catholic*. New York: Hafner, 1971.

McConnell, Michael. "Getting Along." *First Things* 64 (June/July 1996) 1.

McDonald, Forrest. *Novus Ordo Seclorum: The Intellectual Origins of the Constitution*. Lawrence: University Press of Kansas, 1985.

McGreevy, John T. *Catholicism and American Freedom: A History*. New York: Norton, 2003.

Mill, John Stuart. *On Liberty*. New York: Norton, 1975.

Miller, Joshua. *The Rise and Fall of Democracy in Early America, 1630–1789: The Legacy for Contemporary Politics*. University Park: Pennsylvania State University Press, 1991.

Mills, C. Wright. *The Power Elite*. New York: Oxford University Press, 1956.

More, Thomas. *Utopia*. Translated and edited by H. V. S. Ogden. Arlington Heights: AHM, 1949.

Morandé, Pedro. "The Relevance of the Message of *Gaudium et Spes* Today: The Church's Mission in the Midst of Epochal Changes and Challenges." *Communio* 23 (1996) 141–55.

Morgan, Edmund S. *Inventing the People: The Rise of Popular Sovereignty in England and America*. New York: Norton, 1988.

Mounier, Emmanuel. *Personalism*. London: Routledge & Kegan Paul, 1952.

Muncy, Mitchell, and Richard John Neuhaus, eds. *The End of Democracy: The Judicial Usurpation of Politics*. Dallas: Spence, 1997.

Murphy, Andrew R. "Rawls and Liberty of Conscience." *Review of Politics* 60 (1998) 254–57.

Murray, John Courtney. "Contemporary Orientations of Catholic Thought on Church and State in the Light of History." *Theological Studies* 10 (1949) 177–234.

———. "Freedom of Religion I: The Ethical Problem." *Theological Studies* 6 (1946) 229–87.

———. "The Problem of State Religion." *Theological Studies* 12 (1952) 155–78.

———. *We Hold These Truths: Catholic Reflections on the American Proposition*. Lanham, MD: Rowman & Littlefield, 1988.

Neuhaus, Richard John. *The Naked Public Square: Religion and Democracy in America*. Grand Rapids: Eerdmans, 1984.

———. "Why We Can Get Along." *First Things* 60 (1996) 27–34.

Newman, John Henry. *The Idea of a University*. Notre Dame: University of Notre Dame Press, 1986.

Norton, Anne. *Republic of Signs: Liberal Theory and American Pop Culture*. Chicago: University of Chicago Press, 1993.

Novak, Michael. *The Catholic Ethic and the Spirit of Capitalism*. New York: Free Press, 1993.

Nozick, Robert. *Anarchy, State, and Utopia*. New York: Basic Books, 1974.

Nussbaum, Martha C. *The Fragility of Goodness: Luck and Ethics in Greek Tragedy and Philosophy*. Cambridge: Cambridge University Press, 1986.

Owen, J. Judd. "Church and State in Stanley Fish's Antiliberalism." *American Political Science Review* 93 (1999) 911–24.

———. "The Tolerant Leviathan: Hobbes and the Paradox of Liberalism." *Polity* 37 (2005) 130–48.

Pangle, Thomas. *The Spirit of Modern Republicanism*. Chicago: University of Chicago Press, 1988.

Pelikan, Jaroslav. "Christianity as an Enfolding Circle." *U.S. News and World Report*, June 26, 1989.

Perreau-Saussine, Emile. *Catholicism and Democracy*. Translated by Richard Rex. Princeton: Princeton University Press, 2012.

Perry, Michael J. *Under God? Religious Faith and Liberal Democracy*. Cambridge: Cambridge University Press, 2003.

Peterson, Merrill D., ed. *The Portable Thomas Jefferson*. New York: Penguin, 1977.

Pius XI. *Quadragesimo Anno (On Reconstruction of the Social Order)*. Encyclical Letter. Vatican website. May 15, 1931. http://www.vatican.va/content/pius-xi/en/encyclicals/documents/hf_p-xi_enc_19310515_quadragesimo-anno.html.
Plant, Raymond. *The Neo-liberal State*. Oxford: Oxford University Press, 2010.
Plato. *The Republic*. Translated by Allan Bloom. New York: Basic Books, 1968.
———. *The Trial and Death of Socrates: Euthyphro, Apology, Crito, Death Scene from Phaedo*. Translated by G. M. A. Grube. Indianapolis: Hackett, 1975.
Pocock, J. G. A. *The Machiavellian Moment*. Princeton: Princeton University Press, 1975.
———. *Politics, Language and Time: Essays on Political Though and History*. New York: Atheneum, 1973.
Prothero, Stephen. *American Jesus: How the Son of God Became a National Icon*. New York: Farrar, Straus and Giroux, 2003.
Putnam, Robert. "Bowling Alone: America's Declining Social Capital." *Current* 373 (June 1995) 3–9.
Rawls, John. *Political Liberalism*. New York: Columbia University Press, 1993.
———. *A Theory of Justice*. Cambridge: Belknap, 1971.
Roberts, Kathleen Glenister. *The Limits of Cosmopolis: Ethics and Provinciality in the Dialogue of Cultures*. New York: Peter Lang, 2014.
Rorty, Richard. *Achieving Our Country: Leftist Thought in Twentieth-Century America*. Cambridge: Harvard University Press, 1998.
———. *Contingency, Irony, and Solidarity*. Cambridge: Cambridge University Press, 1989.
———. *Philosophy and Social Hope*. New York: Penguin, 1999.
Rousseau, Jean-Jacques. *A Discourse on Inequality*. Translated by Maurice Cranston. New York: Penguin, 1984.
———. *The Social Contract*. Translated by Maurice Cranston. New York: Penguin, 1968.
Ryan, Thomas R. *Orestes Brownson: A Definitive Biography*. Huntington, IN: Our Sunday Visitor, 1976.
Sale, Kirkpatrick. *Human Scale*. New York: Coward, McCann & Geoghegan, 1980.
Salisbury, John of. *Policraticus: The Statesman's Book*. Edited by Murray F. Markland. New York: Frederick Ungar, 1979.
Sandel, Michael J. *Liberalism and the Limits of Justice*. Cambridge: Cambridge University Press, 1982.
Sandoz, Ellis. *A Government of Laws: Political Theory, Religion, and the American Founding*. Baton Rouge: Louisiana State University Press, 1990.
Sartre, Jean-Paul. *Existentialism and Human Emotion*. New York: Philosophical Library, 1957.
Schlesinger, Arthur M., Jr. *Orestes A. Brownson: A Pilgrim's Progress*. New York: Octagon, 1963.
Schumpeter, Joseph A. *Capitalism, Socialism, Democracy*. 1947. Reprint, New York: Harper & Row, 1976.
Schuster, George Nauman. *The Catholic Spirit in America*. New York: Dial, 1927.
Shain, Barry A. *The Myth of American Individualism: The Protestant Origins of American Political Thought*. Princeton: Princeton University Press, 1994.
Shklar, Judith N. *Men and Citizens: A Study of Rousseau's Social Theory*. Cambridge: Cambridge University Press, 1987.

Siedentop, Larry. *Inventing the Individual: The Origins of Western Liberalism*. Cambridge: Harvard University Press, 2014.

Siemers, David J. *Ratifying the Republic: Antifederalists and Federalists in Constitutional Time*. Stanford: Stanford University Press, 2002.

Smith, Rogers. "Beyond Tocqueville, Myrdal and Hartz: The Multiple Traditions in America." *American Political Science Review* 87 (1993) 549–66.

———. *Civic Ideals: Conflicting Visions of Citizenship in U.S. History*. New Haven: Yale University Press, 1997.

Smith, Steven B. "Separation and the 'Secular': Reconstructing the Disestablishment Decision." *Texas Law Review* 67 (1989) 955–1032.

Spaemann, Robert. *Persons: The Difference between "Someone" and "Something."* 1996. Reprint, Oxford: Oxford University Press, 2017.

Stolzenberg, Nomi Maya. "'He Drew a Circle That Shut Me Out': Assimilation, Indoctrination, and the Paradox of a Liberal Education." *Harvard Law Review* 106 (1993) 581–667.

Storing, Herbert J. *What the Antifederalists Were For*. Chicago: University of Chicago Press, 1981.

Strauss, Leo. *Liberalism Ancient and Modern*. Ithaca: Cornell University Press, 1968.

———. *Natural Right and History*. Chicago: University of Chicago Press, 1953.

Sveino, Per. *Orestes A. Brownson's Road to Catholicism*. New York: Humanities, 1970.

Taylor, Charles. "A Catholic Modernity?" In *A Catholic Modernity: Charles Taylor's Marianist Award Lecture*, edited by James L. Heft, 13–37. Oxford: Oxford University Press, 1999.

———. *The Ethics of Authenticity*. Cambridge: Harvard University Press, 1992.

Taylor, Michael. *Community, Anarchy and Liberty*. New York: Cambridge University Press, 1985.

Thoreau, Henry David. *Selected Writings*. Arlington Heights: AHM, 1958.

Tilley, Terrence W. *Inventing Catholic Tradition*. Maryknoll: Orbis, 2000.

Tinder, Glenn. "Against Fate: An Essay on Personal Dignity." In *In Defense of Human Dignity: Essays for Our Times*, edited by Robert P. Kraynak and Glenn Tinder, 11–51. Notre Dame: Notre Dame University Press, 2003.

———. *Community: Reflections on a Tragic Ideal*. Baton Rouge: Louisiana State University Press, 1980.

———. *The Political Meaning of Christianity: An Interpretation*. Baton Rouge: Louisiana State University Press, 1989.

Tocqueville, Alexis de. *Democracy in America*. Translated by George Lawrence. Edited by J. P. Mayer. New York: Harper & Row, 1988.

Torrance, James B. "The Covenant Concept in Scottish Theology and Politics." In *The Covenant Connection: From Federal Theology to Modern Federalism*, edited by Daniel J. Elazar and John Kincaid, 143–62. Lanham, MD: Lexington, 2000.

Tropman, John E. *The Catholic Ethic in American Society: An Exploration of Values*. San Francisco: Jossey-Bass, 1995.

Tushnet, Mark. "Reflections on the Role of Purpose in the Jurisprudence of the Religion Clauses." *William and Mary Law Review* 27 (1986) 1008–9.

The Twelve Articles. In *The Works of Martin Luther with Introductions and Notes*, vol. 4. Translated by C. M. Jacobs. The AGES Digital Library. Albany, OR: AGES Software.

Unger, Roberto Mangabeira. *Knowledge and Politics*. New York: Free Press, 1984.

———. *Social Theory: Its Situation and Its Task*. New York: Cambridge University Press, 1987.

United States Conference of Catholic Bishops. *Forming Consciences for Faithful Citizenship: A Call to Political Responsibility from the Catholic Bishops of the United States*. Washington, DC: USCCB, 2007.

Untener, Ken. "Prophets of a Future Not Our Own." United States Conference of Bishops, 1979. http://www.usccb.org/prayer-and-worship/prayers-and-devotions/prayers/prophets-of-a-future-not-our-own.cfm.

Urofsky, Melvin I., ed. *Documents of American Constitutional and Legal History*. 2 vols. New York: Knopf, 1989.

———. *A March of Liberty: A Constitutional History of the United States*. New York: Knopf, 1988.

Vatican Council. *Gaudium et Spes*. Boston: Pauline, 1965.

Wallis, Jim. *God's Politics: Why the Right Gets It Wrong and the Left Doesn't Get It*. New York: HarperCollins, 2005.

Walsh, David. *Politics of the Person as the Politics of Being*. Notre Dame: University of Notre Dame Press, 2016.

Walzer, Michael. *The Revolution of the Saints: A Study in the Origins of Radical Politics*. New York: Atheneum, 1968.

———. *Spheres of Justice: A Defense of Pluralism and Equality*. New York: Basic Books, 1983.

Wells, H. G. *The Time Machine*. 1895. Reprint, Boston: Squid Ink Classics, 2017.

Wells, Samuel. "Rethinking Service." *The Cresset: A Review of Literature, the Arts and Public Affairs* 86 (2013) 6–14.

Wilson, Woodrow. "Freemen Need No Guardians." In *Political Thought in America: An Anthology*, edited by Michael B. Levy, 350–55. Chicago: Dorsey, 1988.

Wittgenstein, Ludwig. *Tractatus Logico-Philosophicus*. Translated by D. F. Pears and B. F. McGuinness. London: Routledge & Kegan Paul, 1961.

Wojtyla, Karol. *Love and Responsibility*. Translated by H. T. Willetts. New York: Farrar, Straus and Giroux, 1981.

Wolin, Sheldon S. "Political Theory as a Vocation." *American Political Science Review* 63 (1969) 1062–82.

———. *The Presence of the Past: Essays on the State and the Constitution*. Baltimore: Johns Hopkins University Press, 1989.

Wood, Gordon S. *The Creation of the American Republic, 1776–1787*. New York: Norton, 1969.

———. *The Radicalism of the American Revolution*. New York: Knopf, 1992.

Yoder, John Howard. *The Politics of Jesus: Vicit Agnus Noster*. Grand Rapids: Eerdmans, 1994.

Zuckerman, Michael. *Peaceable Kingdoms: New England Towns in the Eighteenth Century*. New York: Knopf, 1970.

Index

A Canticle for Leibowitz, 245, 278
Abbott, Philip, 1, 3, 13, 224
Ackerman, Bruce, 41n34, 72
agape, 14, 71–72, 111
Agricultural Union, 188
Alger, Horatio, 197
alienation, 114, 199, 169, 231
Allegyer v. Louisiana, 198
American exceptionalism, 4, 12–13
Anti-federalists, 13, 237
anti-foundationalism, 81
Aquinas, Thomas, 16, 18, 32–33, 53, 99, 187, 194, 213, 235, 269, 281
Arendt, Hannah, 27, 32, 115
Aristotle, 27–28, 39, 44, 164, 169, 183, 194, 213
Arnett, Ronald, 18–19
Articles of Confederation, 216
Ashcraft, Richard, 10n24
Auden, W. H., 291
Augustine, 31, 127, 175–76n7, 235, 256–257, 259, 282
autonomy, 38, 82–83, 95, 116–17, 138–39, 146, 156, 212, 265, 283, 286

Back to the Future, 270n47
Bailyn, Bernard, 10n25
Baker, Jr., Houston, 139, 223n32
   AMERICA, 139, 140, 223n32
Banning, Lance, 10n25
Barber, Benjamin, 109, 226
Beard, Charles, 11n26, 220

Bellah, Robert, 13, 140, 212
Berger, Peter I., 20n50
biblical language, 13–14, 16
Bill of Rights, 58, 236–237
Black, Hugo, 50, 56n57
Blaine Amendments, 54
Bloom, Harold, 42, 142–44
American Religion, 42n35, 71n8
Boas, George, 222
Bonhoffer, Dietrich, 260
Book of Job, 155
Bradley, Joseph, 198–200
Bretherton, Luke, 30n12
Brooks, David, 83, 93
Brownson, Orestes, 148–50, 158–71, 181, 192, 221, 227, 303
   materialism, 162
   New Views of Christianity, Society, and the Church, 159–62
   Protestantism, 159–60
   providential nation, 165, 167
   spiritualism, 159, 161–62
   The American Republic, 149, 159, 163–70
Burger, Warren, 57
Burgos, Juan Manuel, 20n52
Bush, George W., 6

Cahoy, William, 228n43
Calverton, V.F., 225
capitalism, 17, 186, 198, 221, 253, 297
   democratic, 141, 147
   liberal, 187–88
Carter, Stephen, 78–81, 84, 89, 90

Catholic Church, 13n36, 17, 24, 26, 32, 41, 111, 144, 159, 169, 174, 178, 185, 188, 230, 232, 238, 241, 248, 252, 276–77, 293, 303–4
Catechism of the Catholic Church, 39, 178
Catholic social teaching, 191–92, 288, 290
Catholic social tradition, 20, 174, 204, 223, 290, 304
Catholic Worker, 189, 294–95
Centesimus Annus, 279
Christendom, 246, 174, 176–77
Christian anthropology, 14
Christian Social Workman's Association, 188
Christianity, 20, 31, 34, 40–41, 44, 48, 60–61, 67, 69, 78, 80, 84, 86, 88–89, 91, 93, 103–4, 106, 121, 133, 145, 149, 151, 159, 161, 173–74, 177, 180, 183–85, 238–39, 248, 260, 296, 302
city on the hill, 14, 140, 147, 234, 243, 263
Civil War, 140, 170, 173, 179, 192, 196–97, 216, 219
class legislation, 17
Coles, Robert, 136–37, 142
commercial republic, 194, 196, 217
common good, 18, 22, 40–41, 190–91, 196, 203–4, 209, 214, 242–44, 248, 255, 261, 265, 269–271, 281, 284–86, 288, 303
communion, 22, 27, 111, 167–69, 232, 269, 277, 280, 293
compact, 13, 36–37, 167, 169
confident humility, 101
Connery, Sean, 213
Constantianism, 177, 203
Contract Clause, 193
Corrin, Jay, 185–86, 188
cosmopolitan(ism), 20–21
covenant, 13–15, 36–37
creationism, 100
Crimson Tide, 220
crucifixion, 30, 106

Day, Dorothy, 294, 296
Davis, Derek, 49
Debs, Eugene V., 295
Deneen, Patrick J., 6n16
Declaration of Independence, 22, 151, 220, 236–37
democracy, 4–5, 17, 25, 61, 80, 94, 104, 113, 149, 151–52, 158, 164, 167, 170, 182, 201–2, 220, 223, 226, 238, 249, 252, 255–56, 261, 266–67, 272–73, 275–79
Descartes, 114
    Cartesian, 98, 114–16, 127, 292
DeVito, Danny, 124
Dewey, John, 222
dialogic ethics, 18
dialogical individualism, 16, 118
Diggins, John Patrick, 10n25
Dolan, Jay P., 179, 231–32
Dostoevsky, Fydor, 29, 171, 257
dying to self, 131, 139, 261
Dylan, Bob, 85

Edict of Milan, 31
Edict of Thessalonica, 31
Einstein, Albert, 222
Eliot, T. S., 81, 100, 132–34
    Christian organization of society, 132–34
Elshtain, Jean, 3n7, 247, 257–60, 267–68
emotivism, 94, 122
Enlightenment, 79, 94, 100, 103, 162, 210, 227–28, 236, 243
equality, 5–8, 12, 15, 17, 21–22, 29, 33, 35, 101, 104, 113, 131, 154, 161, 199, 202, 220, 229, 239, 261, 266, 285, 301
Establishment Clause, 43, 47, 49–56, 56n57, 57–58, 60, 86
Euben, J. Peter, 97
Eucharist, 22
Everson v. Board of Education, 50, 56n57

faithful citizenship, 38, 40, 68, 184
Federalist Papers, 201, 215–16, 218–19
Field, Stephen, 198, 200
Fifteenth Amendment, 197, 216

Fight Club, 16n43, 268
Filmer, Robert, 75
First Amendment, 47, 49, 56n57, 57, 61, 74, 156, 243
First Commandment, 31, 71
First Vatican Council, 273, 275
Fish, Stanley, 87–91, 90n48
Foundation of Catholic Workingmen's Clubs, 188
Fourteenth Amendment, 197–98, 216
Fowler, Robert Booth, 12n34
Free Exercise Clause, 49
Freire, Paulo, 19
Fritz, Janie Harden, 18–19
Fukuyama, Francis, 227
fundamentalists, 100

Gallicanism, 224
Gaudium et Spes, 17, 20n51, 250, 278–79, 281–88, 293, 304
Genovese, Eugene, 183
Gibbons, James (Cardinal), 189
Gibson, Mel, 144
Gillman, Howard, 201–2, 216
Gleason, Philip, 208,
Glendon, Mary Ann, 7
Glenn, Gary F., 50–52, 55
Gnosticism, 42n35, 142–143, 156, 156n38
Gorgias, 2
Gorman, Robert, 295–297, 301
Gospels, 13n36, 15, 17, 28–29, 40–41, 161, 174–75, 177, 184, 187, 231, 252–53, 256, 260, 269, 276, 282, 284, 287, 302–4
grace, 14, 22, 71–73, 89–90, 99, 140, 152, 156n38, 168, 280, 304
Gramsci, Antonio, 292, 296
Groome, Thomas, 292
Groundhog Day, 9–11
Gurian, Waldemar, 232–33

Habermas, Jürgen, 103, 239
Hackman, Gene, 220
Hamburger, Philip, 53, 59
Hamer, Fannie Lou, 78–79
Hamilton, Alexander, 194, 216–17, 233
    Federalist Paper #78, 45n38

Harrington, Michael, 18, 291–302, 294n15
Hartz, Louis, 6n16, 8, 10–13, 12n34, 16, 45, 148–49, 179–80, 202, 224, 275, 302
Hauerwas, Stanley, 117, 175, 175n5
Head and Armory v. Providence Insurance Company, 193
Hecker, Isaac, 181
Hegel, W. F., 74, 102, 189, 219, 227, 259, 282
Heidegger, Martin, 71
Heist, 124
Herder, 116
Heyer, Kristin, 267
Himes, Kenneth, 43, 73, 111
Himes, Michael, 39, 43, 70–73, 111
Hirschman, Albert O., 194
Hitze, Franz, 188
Hobbes, Thomas, 40, 76, 102–103, 109, 122, 164, 171, 194, 197, 235, 239, 259, 269, 283, 303
Hollenbach, David, 112n22
Hook, Sydney, 148–149, 222
Hoover, Herbert, 208
Hopkinson, Francis, 149
Huguenots, 37
human dignity, 94, 106, 111, 264, 281, 301, 304
human flourishing, 6n16, 12, 16, 82, 171, 280, 285, 303
human nature, 45n38, 108–109, 114, 127, 151–152, 156, 161–162, 164, 197
human rights, 17, 103, 111, 176, 233, 238, 276, 283, 295
Humphrey, Hubert H., 78–79
Huston, James H., 46n39
Hutchinson, Anne, 157

idolatry, 35, 71, 140, 221, 226, 272, 296
In Re Debs, 200
Incarnation, 20, 20n51, 22, 39, 70, 106, 168, 174, 239, 258, 304
individualism, 5, 7–8, 12, 16, 21, 33, 35, 102, 105, 119, 143, 145–46, 149, 153–54, 170, 178, 183–84, 189, 228, 236, 238, 253, 266–67

inescapable horizons, 118, 131
infallibility, 232, 274
Isserman, Maurice, 294–95, 294n15, 302

Jacobs, Paul, 300
James, William, 46,
Jayne, Allen, 151
Jefferson, Thomas, 27, 49, 53, 55, 56n57, 62, 149–55, 158–59, 162, 164, 167, 173, 233
    wall of separation, 49, 56, 90
Jesus, 22, 28–30, 39, 49, 105n8, 106, 144, 152, 155, 177, 180, 265, 282
Johnson, Lyndon Baines, 78–79, 300
Judaism, 27, 292
justice, 65–67, 75–77, 103, 123–24, 131, 187, 190, 225, 263, 266, 280–81, 283, 285, 301

Kallen, Horace, 222
Kallenberg, Brad, 213n11
Kennedy, John F., 207, 209, 221, 299–300
Kierkegaard, 81
Knights of Labor, 189
Kramnick, Isaac, 10n25
Kraynak, Robert, 94
Kuhn, Thomas, 225–226
Kurun, Ismail, 13n39

La Tour du Pin, Marquis Rene de, 188
Lasch, Christopher, 25n5, 145–47
Lawler, Peter, 158, 158n43, 240
Lemon v. Kurtzman, 56–57, 72
    Lemon test, 57, 69, 87–88
Levinas, Emmanuel, 22
Lewis, C.S., 81, 122–128, 152, 170
liberalism, 6n16, 8, 10–21, 33, 67, 69, 74–107, 113–14, 117, 132, 137, 141, 146–48, 173–74, 177–78, 182–83, 186–87, 191, 207, 224, 228, 230, 234–37, 248–49, 274–77, 290, 297–98, 302–3
liberty(ies), 15, 26, 33–35, 51–52, 65, 75–76, 104, 141, 151, 158, 160, 162, 165, 169–70, 170, 182, 196, 199, 238, 244, 248, 263, 265–66, 277, 286
liberty of conscience, 33
liberty of contract, 17, 192, 198, 216
Lincoln, Abraham, 140–43, 147–49, 167, 173, 216, 239
linguistic contextualism, 1, 45
Lochner v. New York, 200–202
Locke, John, 10–11, 34–37, 47–48, 53, 76, 102–3, 109–10, 112, 122, 164, 171, 178, 182, 197, 199, 218, 237, 239, 253, 259, 269, 285, 303
Luckmann, Thomas, 20n50
Luther, Martin, 29, 33–34, 156, 229
    priesthood of the believer, 33
Lutz, Donald, 34–37

Machiavelli, 32, 40, 102, 132, 194, 214, 234
MacIntyre, Alasdair, 104–5, 209–13, 211n7, 223–24
Macpherson, C. B., 8, 13, 195, 224
Madison, James, 38, 52, 53, 55, 88, 166–67, 173, 182, 195, 216, 233
Federalist Paper 10, 38
Manning, Henry Edward, 188–189
Maritain, Jacques, 17–18, 223, 252–56, 259–63, 269–72, 275, 304
    false democracy, 252–54
Maritain, Raïssa, 252
Marsden, George, 90
Marsh, David, 79
Marshall, John, 193–94
    Marshall Court, 192
Marty, Martin, 39n30
Marx, Karl, 16, 40, 121–22, 140, 145, 187, 189, 228, 293, 296
Marxist, 46, 102, 105, 165, 220, 293, 295–97, 301
Matusow, Allen, 299
Maurin, Peter, 294, 295n18
Mendieta, Eduardo, 103
McConnell, Michael, 80, 90
McGreevy, John T., 179, 223, 232–33, 252
Mill, John Stuart, 52, 228
Miller, Joshua, 152n32

INDEX   323

Miller, Walter, 245
Morandé, Pedro, 20n51
Mormons, 153, 157
Mounier, Emmanuel, 20n52
Mun, Count Albert de, 188
Murray, Bill, 9–10
Murray, John Courtney, 17, 91, 219, 221, 223, 225, 227, 232–53, 260, 296, 304

Napoleon, 161, 167
National Conference of Catholic Bishops, 40
natural law, 17, 32, 34, 37, 44, 122, 126, 169, 189, 200, 233–36, 238, 240, 242–43, 246, 252, 271–72
neoliberalism, 19, 277, 302
Neuhaus, Richard John, 42, 87, 91–92
    Naked Public Square, 42n35, 47, 56
neutral discourse, 41, 78
New Deal, 180, 295
New Left, 301
New Republic, 24, 27, 207
Newman, John Henry, 188
Niebuhr, Reinhold, 222
Nietzsche, 83, 103, 121, 127, 165, 171, 210, 228
Ninth Amendment, 199
Norton, Anne, 146–48

Owen, J. Judd, 90n48
Ozanam, Fredric, 180, 187

Pacem in Terris, 111
Palahniuk, Chuck, 268
Paris uprisings, 188
Patočka, Jan, 268
Paul (apostle), 12n36, 30–31
Pelagianism, 156, 156n38, 168
Pelikan, Jaroslav, 126n44
Pentecostalism, 143
Perreau-Saussine, Emile, 273–78
Perry, Michael, 25, 50, 58
personalism, 20, 20n52, 294, 294n15
Plato, 28, 64–66, 93, 97, 101–2, 121–22, 167
    Apology, 66
    Crito, 93

Euthyphro, 64
Republic, 102, 167
Pocock, J. G. A., 1–2
Polybius, 28
Pope Benedict XVI, 257–58
Pope Boniface VIII, 244
Pope Francis, 276
Pope Gelasius I, 244
Pope Gregory VII, 244
Pope John Paul II, 186, 189. See also Wojtyla
Pope Leo XIII, 186, 189
Pope Paul VI, 282
Pope Pius XI, 191
populism, 302
possessive individualism, 8, 16, 102, 147, 197, 303
postmodern(ism), 16, 74, 93, 98, 100–101, 103, 121, 228, 228n43, 283
privatization (of religion), 38, 53, 55, 61–62, 78, 242, 274, 303
prophetic voice, 275, 276, 288
Protestant(s) 25, 54, 160, 243
public happiness, 27, 182n25
Puritans, 13, 36–37, 51, 179, 182
pursuit of happiness, 7, 169, 199
Putnam, Robert, 7n19

Quadragesimo Anno, 191, 223

Rawls, John, 41n34, 75–77, 101–3, 109, 131, 164, 222, 239, 248
religion
    civic, 65, 66
    civil, 66, 68, 140
    political, 140, 167
republican discourse, 10n25, 13, 37, 120, 215, 217, 237n68, 268
Rerum Novarum, 186, 189, 200, 223
Review of Politics, 232
Roberts, Kathleen Glenister, 20–22
Romero, Oscar, 89
Roosevelt, Franklin D., 180
Rorty, Richard, 2–4, 3n7, 81, 93–94, 101, 217, 278
Rousseau, Jean Jacques, 40, 75, 109–11, 122, 164, 189, 235, 259, 262, 268–69

Rudy, 171
Russell, Bertrand, 222

sacramental principle, 70–72, 136
Saint-Simone, 186
Sale, Kirkpatrick, 9, 98, 290
Sandoz, Ellis, 10n25, 152n32

Schumpeter, Joseph, 216
Schuster, George, 179–84, 203
Second Commandment, 71
Second Vatican Council, 17, 250, 273, 275, 288, 304
secular(ism), 16, 43–44, 47–49, 53, 55, 61, 89, 180, 283
secularization, 43–44, 54–56, 65, 107, 140, 283
self-gift, 111–13, 176, 271
self-ownership, 112, 167
separation of church and state, 41, 53–55, 277
Seton, Elizabeth, 181
Shachtman, Max, 301
Shain, Barry A., 10n25, 152n32
Shriver, R. Sargent, 300
Siedentop, Larry, 12n36, 15n42
sin, 14, 22, 32, 37, 39, 85, 89, 92, 121, 140, 142–43, 151, 161, 170, 176, 176n7, 177, 240, 245, 256, 280, 283
  original, 142, 151–55, 158–59, 163
  structures of, 85
Slaughterhouse Cases, 198, 200
Smith, Adam, 277
Smith, Al, 207, 222
Smith, Joseph, 157
Smith, Rogers, 10n24
Smith Steven D., 46–48, 55
social capital, 7
social contract (theory), 36, 76, 131, 164–65, 167, 260, 269
  state of nature, 37, 76, 109, 122, 283
social Darwinism, 192, 196
social justice, 12, 15, 17, 249, 255, 276, 279, 295
socialism, 187, 188–89, 301
  democratic, 296, 302

Society of St. Vincent de Paul, 186, 188
Socrates, 34, 64–69, 93, 169
solidarity, 22, 103, 106, 201, 203, 268
Southern Agrarians, 13
Southern Baptists, 143, 153
  soul-competency, 143
Spaeman, Robert, 20n52
Spencer, Herbert, 196
Stack, John, 50–52, 55
Stalinism, 105, 275, 296
Story, Joseph, 193–94
Strauss, Leo, 81, 81n33, 101n11, 139, 220, 228
substantive due process, 17, 192, 198–200, 216
Sumner, William Graham, 197

Taylor, Charles, 16, 115–19, 174–78, 184, 211, 230, 246
Tenth Amendment, 199
Terrett v. Taylor, 193
Testem benevolentiae nostrae, 231
the Cross, 22, 28, 101, 117, 177, 262, 273, 288
The King of Queens, 142
The Matrix, 226
The Terminator, 254
The Untouchables, 213
Theological Studies, 233
Thirteenth Amendment, 197, 216
Thomas, Norman, 295
Thoreau, Henry David, 149
Tilley, Terence W., 210, 227–30
Tillich, Paul, 136–37
Tinder, Glenn, 16, 85, 85n44, 102, 106, 121, 129, 132, 148, 176, 239
Tocqueville, Alexis de, 4, 12–13, 157n40, 158, 163
  On American philosophic mind, 154
  on Catholicism, 178
  on equality, 6, 101, 155
  on individualism, 267
  on language in democracies, 5
  on loneliness, 7, 120, 138
  on religious authority, 155–56
tolerance, 22, 27, 53, 75, 92, 101, 157, 231, 240, 278
Town of Pawlett v. Clark, 193

traditionalism, 126, 126n44
Trinity, 111–12, 152, 269
Trump, Donald, 6, 225, 267
Trustees of Dartmouth College v. Woodward, 193
Tushnet, Mark, 67
two-kingdoms thesis, 175

Unam Sanctum, 244
unencumbered-self, 109, 115, 185
Unger, Roberto M., 81, 99
Unitarian, 150–153, 162
Universal Declaration of the Rights of Man, 252
Untener, Kenneth, 90n46
Urofsky, Melvin, 193, 198
U.S. Constitution, 52, 54–55, 57–58, 61–62, 67, 140, 165–66, 193–94, 199, 207, 215, 237, 249
U.S. Supreme Court, 45–47, 51, 53, 55, 68, 73, 87, 93, 193, 206

von Ketteler, Wilhelm Emmanuel, 187

Walsh, David, 20n52
War on Poverty, 299–301
Washington, Denzel, 220
Weaver, Richard, 16
social bond individualism, 183
Weber, Max, 140, 150
Wells, H. G., 134–35
Wells, Sam, 260
Williams, Roger, 157
Wilson, Woodrow, 220
Winthrop, John, 13–14, 51, 182, 263
A Modell of Christian Charity, 13
Wittgenstein, L., 210
Wojtyla, Karol, 264, 266. *See also* Pope John Paul II
Wolin, Sheldon, 214–20, 230, 287

Yoder, John Howard, 175, 175n5

Zeno's paradox, 125
Zorach v. Clauson, 56

www.ingramcontent.com/pod-product-compliance
Lightning Source LLC
Chambersburg PA
CBHW021342300426
44114CB00012B/1048